Building Great Sentences: Exploring the Writer's Craft

Brooks Landon, Ph.D.

THE
GREAT
COURSES

PUBLISHED BY:

THE GREAT COURSES
Corporate Headquarters
4840 Westfields Boulevard, Suite 500
Chantilly, Virginia 20151-2299
Phone: 1-800-832-2412
Fax: 703-378-3819
www.thegreatcourses.com

Brooks Landon, Ph.D.

Professor of English and Collegiate Fellow
Director of the
General Education Literature Program
The University of Iowa

Brooks Landon is a Professor of English and Collegiate Fellow at The University of Iowa and Director of the University of Iowa General Education Literature Program. From 1999 to 2005, Professor Landon served as chair of the Iowa English Department. He received his B.A. in English from Centre College of Kentucky and his M.A. and Ph.D. from The University of Texas at Austin.

Professor Landon has published widely in the fields of science fiction and contemporary American literature. His books include *Science Fiction After 1900: From the Steam Man to the Stars*; *The Aesthetics of Ambivalence: Rethinking Science Fiction in the Age of Electronic (Re)Production*; and *Thomas Berger*. He researched, wrote, hosted, and coproduced *Watch the Sky: The American Science Fiction Movie*, a 13-week series on science fiction film that was produced and broadcast by Iowa Public Television in 1983. He is a member of the Executive Committee of The University of Iowa's Nanoscience and Nanotechnology Institute. He has taught courses in contemporary American fiction, literature and culture of 20th-century America, modern fiction, hypertext fiction and scholarship, science fiction, nonfiction writing, and electronic textuality. Since 1978, he has regularly offered a prose style course focused on the sentence.

He is the recipient of a 2001 Alumnus Election to Phi Beta Kappa at Centre College, the 2001 International Association for the Fantastic in the Arts Distinguished Scholarship Award, and the 1996 University of Iowa M. L. Huit Teaching Award. ■

Table of Contents

Table of Contents

Table of Contents

Building Great Sentences:
Exploring the Writer's Craft

Scope:

Just sentences. This is a course that will run through all the ways that sentences get longer—and shorter. We will touch upon whatever we can learn about how they work, what they do, how we can think and talk about them in ways that will help both our own writing and our understanding of prose style. Part of our concern will be with stretching our sense of options—all the things a sentence can be and/or do—and part with the notion of style itself. In other words, this is a course in which we will dance with language, not a course in which we will trudge toward remedial correctness.

As we work with sentences, we will examine, think about, and write sentences suggested by the following terms, some traditional, some nontraditional, and most of them probably unfamiliar: kernels and masters, predicatives, subordinatives, conjunctives, cumulatives, Suspensives, adjectivals, adversatives, interruptives, Intensives, cohesives, extensives, Balances, Serials, and so on. These *terms* refer more or less to rhetorical phenomena—ways in which sentences do whatever they do. In many cases the terms overlap and should probably be thought of as suggesting qualities demonstrated by sentences rather than as kinds or categories of sentences. Always, our focus will be on understanding a sentence's strategy based on these terms not on the importance of the terminology itself.

Sentences are shaped by specific context and driven by specific purpose, so no rules or mechanical protocols can prepare us for the infinite number of tasks our sentences must accomplish. There are a number of basic strategies or moves we can learn that help make our sentences more effective, no matter what the specific task. This course will concentrate on a broad range of effective moves or strategies, many of them associated with the cumulative sentence, a particularly useful syntax employed by professional writers and best understood in terms first laid out by Francis Christensen. Before we can work with a specific syntax, such as the cumulative or its opposite, the suspensive, we need to understand the basic principles that guide the creation and use of all sentences. Accordingly, this course will look closely and carefully at sentences from a number of different angles, starting with their underlying logic and moving through the reasons why we cannot rigorously separate the form of a sentence from its content, its meaning from its style. We will look at the ways sentences work, whether the most basic and minimal kernel sentences that are nothing more than a subject joined with a verb, to the most elaborate and extended master sentences, some stretching to lengths of more than one hundred words.

Whether short or long, sentences are the most important building blocks of prose, the foundation of written communication, and always the essential units of prose style. "This is what I mean when I call myself a writer," writes novelist Don DeLillo, "I construct sentences." We will look at the ways in which DeLillo and other accomplished writers construct their sentences. Sentences convey information, organizing it into propositions or statements and then combining those propositions through syntactical arrangements that establish the logical relationships between and among them. Thus sentences join ideas, sometimes just putting them side-by-side, sometimes subordinating one to another, sometimes marking temporal or causal relationships. So one of our first goals will be to understand how sentences combine ideas to present information—and how we can use our knowledge of the ways in which sentences combine ideas to present our own ideas more effectively.

But sentences do much more than just convey information: The way in which a sentence unfolds its meaning may be as important as the propositional content—the information—it presents. The sequences of words we identify as sentences are capable of providing pleasure just as surely as they are capable of conveying crucial information. Sometimes, the most important information sentences convey is pleasure, as they unfold their meanings in ways that tease, surprise, test, and satisfy. Sometimes, the way sentences unfold their meaning is the most important meaning they offer. When we talk about sentences *as sentences*, as the essential building blocks of prose that may be as or even more important for the ways in which they organize and present ideas than they are for the information in those ideas, we talk about their style, usually suggesting that a sentence can be understood in

2

two ways—for its content and for its style. However, we now know that the style of a sentence *is* its content. Poet Marvin Bell reminds us that the content of a poem is not the same as a poem's contents, reminding us that when we paraphrase what a poem is about (its contents) we are not talking about the poem itself (its content or meaning), losing sight of what it does to us as we read it. The same is true of sentences. Or, to put this another way, the informational or propositional content of a sentence is not the same as the sentence's meaning, since sentences don't just carry information, like putting objects in a canister, but do things with it and to it, shaping it to particular purposes and effects. In this important sense, sentences work like verbs, doing things, taking action, rather than like nouns that only name.

We will learn how what is generally referred to as a sentence's style results from the strategies it employs for combining its underlying ideas or propositions. Accordingly, our goal will be to learn everything we can about the way sentences combine ideas. Understanding how sentences put ideas together is the first step in understanding how they do things, the ways in which they work, the ways they present information, and the ways they unfold their meanings—and to learn how to make them work for us. We will do this by studying the ways in which sentences combine information by coordinating it, subordinating it, or subsuming it in modification. We will look at the difference between sentences that combine information through loose syntax and those that do so through periodic syntax, focusing on the generative or heuristic power of cumulative sentences. Because our concern will be with how sentences work, the terms we will use will be rhetorical rather than grammatical, terms that help us understand how sentences move, how they take steps, speeding up and slowing down, how they make us feel, rather than terms that label the parts of a sentence much as we would label the parts of a dissected—and quite dead—frog. This means that we will study the sentence as a thing in motion, a thing alive, considering the strategies that give sentences pace and rhythm, particularly the duple rhythms of balance and three-beat rhythms of serial constructions.

In short, this course will reveal some of the syntactical strategies professional writers regularly employ. These are also strategies we can use in our writing to ensure that our sentences will be effective—and possibly even elegant. ∎

A Sequence of Words
Lecture 1

Our goal will be to learn about how sentences work, what they do, how we can think and talk about them in ways that will help both our own writing and our understanding of prose style. Part of our concern will be with stretching our sense of options—all the things a sentence can be or do—and part with the notion of style itself.

This lecture will introduce a number of the assumptions upon which the entire course will rest. Using a sentence from Gertrude Stein, I will demonstrate how our understanding of sentences depends on much more than just knowing and stringing together the individual definitions of key concepts. This lecture will explore including the vertical ladder of abstraction into which each word in a sentence fits and the horizontal syntax of the sentence—the order in which its sequence of words appear. Most importantly, this lecture will introduce the underlying assumptions of this course—that the same words in different order have different meanings, that the way sentences convey information adds to and/or changes the information they convey, and that, consequently, there is no difference between the style of a sentence and its content.

This is a course that will run through all the ways sentences get longer—and shorter—and how control of these ways can improve our writing. Sentences are shaped by specific context and driven by specific purpose, so no rules or mechanical protocols can prepare us for the infinite number of tasks our sentences must accomplish. But there are a number of basic strategies or moves we can learn that can help make our sentences more effective, no matter what the task. This course will look closely and carefully at sentences from a number of different angles, starting with their underlying logic and moving through the reason why we cannot rigorously separate the form of a sentence from its content, its meaning from its style.

This course will also be devoted to understanding some of the secrets of prose style. Even though the nature of prose style has been a subject of heated debate for at least a couple of thousand years, we find ourselves today with no clear definition of what we mean by style, and only the most subjective standards for judging when it is effective, much less elegant. Yet, somehow, we generally agree that there is something called prose style, we generally agree on a number of aspects of writing that seems to have something to do with it, and we generally agree that some writers are better at it than others.

This course looks closely and carefully at sentences, the most important building blocks of prose, the foundation of written communication, and always the essential units of prose style. The sentence is where we must start if we hope to understand why some writing captivates us and other writing leaves us unmoved. To be better writers we must first and foremost write better sentences. Whatever elegant and effective writing may be, the secret to achieving it has largely to do with first learning how to write elegant and effective sentences. This will be a course about how to make sentences longer; longer sentences, when carefully crafted and tightly controlled, are essential keys to elegant and effective writing.

The sentence is where we must start if we hope to understand why some writing captivates us and other writing leaves us unmoved.

Why should a sequence of words be anything but a pleasure? The sequences of words we identify as sentences are capable of providing pleasure just as surely as they are capable of conveying crucial information. Sometimes the way sentences unfold their meaning is the most important meaning they offer. Let's start with that question from Gertrude Stein. What does this seemingly simple sequence of words actually *mean*? How does it actually work? What are some of the ways she could have gotten that meaning across with different sentences?

Sentences are sequences of words, but just adding words together does not create a sentence. A proposition, which is usually expressed in the form of a sentence, is a statement about reality that can be accepted or rejected. The relationship between propositions and sentences is a little hard to pin down, since a sentence will always advance or express one or more propositions and a proposition will always be in the form of a sentence. While many of us have been taught that a sentence is a sequence of words containing a subject and a predicate that expresses an idea, most sentences express or imply a number of ideas. The basic unit of writing is the proposition, not the word or even a sequence of words, and we build sentences by putting propositions together. The style of our sentences is determined by the ways in which we combine not words, but the propositions those words stand for or refer to. One of our first goals will be to understand how sentences combine propositions to present information, and how we can use our knowledge of the ways in which sentences put propositions together to present our own ideas more effectively.

Each sentence we write reflects three main kinds of choices we make: (1) what to write about and what we want to accomplish by writing about it, (2) which words to use, and (3) what order to put them in. There's not much any writing teacher can do in this course to help you choose your subject matter or propositional content, or decide what you want your writing to do. I can address some important things you'll want to keep in mind as you choose the words you use: *Paradigmatic* choices affect the degree of precision in your vocabulary choices; *syntagmatic* choices affect the way you put together the words you choose that is, the syntax.

Now that we've identified the three main factors that determine the style and effectiveness of our writing—propositional content, word choice, and syntax—let's go back to our sentence from Gertrude Stein to see the most important assumption underlying this course—that the same words in different order have different meanings. Or, to put this another way, style is content. Most of us have been taught to think of style and meaning or form and content as two different things. We think of content as the ideas or information our writing conveys. We think of style as the way in which we present those ideas. Many aphorisms and metaphors have been used to describe style, ranging from "Style is the man himself" to "Style is the dress of thought." If we have to use a metaphor to explain style, we might think of an onion, which consists of numerous layers of onion we can peel away until there is nothing left—the onion is its layers, and those layers don't contain a core of onionness but are themselves the onion.

Similarly, the way we choose to order a sentence's propositional content subtly affects that content so that the meaning changes ever so slightly with every vocabulary and syntactical choice we make. The summarizable and paraphrasable information conveyed in our sentences is only a part of what sentences mean since what they do to a reader—the way they direct a reader's thinking and unfold information—may be as important or more important than the information they contain.

Understanding how sentences put propositions together is the first step in understanding how they do things and how to make them work for us. We will study the ways in which sentences combine information, by coordinating it, by subordinating it, or by subsuming it in modification. We will look at the differences between sentences that combine information through *loose* syntax, that put the subject and the verb near the beginning of the sentence, and those that do so through *periodic* syntax, delaying the unfolding of the sentence's most important news until the end of the sentence, creating a sense of suspense that demands the reader's attention, sometimes to the last word. We will pay particular attention to the cumulative sentence, a special kind of loose syntax that can also function suspensively and offers powerful generative or heuristic advantages to the writer who understands its form. We will study the sentence as a thing in motion, considering the strategies writers can use to give sentences pace and rhythm. This course will reveal some of the syntactical strategies professional writers regularly employ, strategies we can use in our own writing to ensure that our sentences will be effective, and possibly even elegant. ■

Question to Consider

1. Find five sentences of varying lengths that definitely give you pleasure. Break each one down into propositions and see how many propositions each one yields.

A Sequence of Words
Lecture 1—Transcript

Just sentences: This is a course that will run through all the ways sentences get longer, and sometimes shorter, and how control of those ways can improve our writing. Our goal will be to learn about how sentences work, what they do, how we can think and talk about them in ways that will help both our own writing and our understanding of prose style. Part of our concern will be with stretching our sense of options—all the things a sentence can be or do—and part with the notion of style itself. In other words, this a course in which we will dance with language, not a course in which we will trudge toward remedial correctness. This is a course designed to help you write better sentences.

Sentences are shaped by specific context and driven by specific purpose, so no rules or mechanical protocols can prepare us for the infinite number of tasks our sentences must accomplish, but there are a number of basic strategies or moves we can learn that help make our sentences more effective, no matter what the specific task. This course will concentrate on a broad range of effective moves or strategies, many of them associated with the cumulative sentence, a particularly useful syntax employed by professional writers and best understood in terms first laid out by composition theorist Francis Christensen back in the 1960s.

Before we can work with a specific syntax, such as the cumulative or its opposite, the suspensive, we need to understand the basic principles that guide the creation and use of all sentences. Accordingly, this course will look closely and carefully at sentences from a number of different angles, starting with their underlying logic and moving through the reasons why we cannot rigorously separate the form of a sentence from its content, its meaning from its style. We will look at the ways sentences work, whether the most basic and minimal kernel sentences that are nothing more than a subject joined with a verb, to the most elaborate and extended master sentences, some stretching to lengths of more than 100 words.

This will be a course devoted to understanding some of the secrets of prose style. It will have as its goal and reason for being the double challenge of understanding elegant and effective writing, and of learning some of the ways in which we can produce it. But I have to start with an acknowledgment, if not an admission: Even though the nature of prose style has been a subject of heated debate for at least a couple of thousand years, we find ourselves today with no clear definition of what we mean by style, and no agreement on any but the most subjective standards for judging when style is effective, much less elegant. Everyone who writes about prose style explicitly or implicitly advances a particular view of it, and each view reflects the personal values and preferences of that particular writer. Yet somehow we generally agree that there is something called prose style. We generally agree on a number of aspects of writing that seem to have something to do with style, and we generally agree that there are some writers, ranging from Shakespeare to Virginia Woolf, Joan Didion to John Updike, Don DeLillo to Marilynne Robinson, who just seem to be better at it than others.

Accordingly, this course can't begin to explain all—or even very many—of the mysteries of prose style. Nor can it offer universally agreed-upon standards for writing that is elegant or effective, that former term always a matter of personal taste, and the latter term always a combination of personal taste with the particular requirements of a specific rhetorical situation. What this course can do is look closely and carefully at sentences, the most important building blocks of prose, the foundation of written communication, and always the essential units of prose style.

"This is what I mean when I call myself a writer," writes novelist Don DeLillo. "I construct sentences." Thomas Berger, the author of *Little Big Man* and a writer, like DeLillo, long celebrated for the vitality of his language, makes much the same point when he terms the sentence "the cell beyond which the life of the book cannot be traced, a novel being a structure of such cells."

> In another sense, [Berger explains] only the sentence exists or at any rate can be proved to exist. Even at the stage of the paragraph, things are becoming theoretical and arbitrary. A "novel" is an utter hallucination: no definition of it, for example, can really distinguish it from a laundry list. But a sentence—there you have something essential, to which nothing can be added and from which nothing can be taken.

I think I know why DeLillo and Berger declare their passionate allegiance to the sentence, and while I don't pretend to understand and certainly can't write sentences as well as either of them, I think I do understand that the sentence is where we must start if we hope to understand why some writing captivates us and other writing leaves us unmoved, uninterested. I think I do understand that to be better writers, we must first and foremost write better sentences. I'm absolutely certain that whatever elegant and effective writing may be, the secret to achieving it has largely to do with learning how to write elegant and effective sentences. As I said before, this will be a course about sentences. Even more bluntly, this will be a course about how to make sentences longer.

Why longer? It's hard to improve on any of the well-known, justly celebrated one- and two-word sentence classics our culture has enshrined. "Jesus wept," the shortest verse in the New Testament, comes to mind, as does "Nuts!" the famous reply offered by General Anthony McAuliffe, acting commander of the 101st Airborne, when the Germans demanded his surrender during the Battle of the Bulge. But no one can really teach how to write one- and two-word sentences, and most of us will go a lifetime without being presented with the opportunity for crafting stunning short sentences.

So, for reasons I hope to make clear as the course proceeds, this is a course about how we make sentences longer, and a course based on my assumption that longer sentences—and this is important—when carefully crafted and tightly controlled, are essential keys to elegant and effective writing. Listen to Joseph Conrad's elegantly balanced and extended sentence describing a native woman in the *Heart of Darkness*, and I love this sentence, "She was savage and superb, wild-eyed and magnificent; there was something ominous and stately in her deliberate progress." I find that sentence more interesting as a sentence than either "Nuts!" or "Jesus wept." And I can show you the writing principles that underlie Conrad's celebrated sentence, while "Nuts!" or "Jesus wept" were both dictated by unique situations quite beyond the study of prose style.

My assumption that longer sentences are the keys to elegant and effective writing crucially and inextricably rests on yet another assumption, one unfortunately best expressed in an old advertising slogan originally made famous by a cigarette manufacturer and quickly appropriated by wags to refer to something other than cigarettes: "It's not how long you make it, but how you make it long." Accordingly, this course will not be about making sentences longer nearly as much as it will be about the ways in which we can do that.

"Why should a sequence of words be anything but a pleasure?" is a saying attributed to Gertrude Stein, and certainly the sequences of words we identify as sentences are capable of providing pleasure, just as surely as they are capable of conveying crucial information. Sometimes the most important information sentences convey is pleasure, as they unfold their meanings in ways that tease, surprise, test, and satisfy. Sometimes the way sentences unfold their meaning is the most important meaning they offer.

Let's start by thinking about what a sentence is and how it works, and let's start with that sentence from Gertrude Stein: "Why should a sequence of words be anything but a pleasure?" We know sentences can function as exclamations, imperatives, declarations, or interrogatives, and this one seems at first glance to be an interrogative. It asks a question. It's a simple question. Or is it? Isn't it really a declaration that a sequence of words should be a pleasure? Or is it? Or is it an invitation to list the numerous occasions when a sequence of words is definitely not a pleasure? "I have a case of stomach flu" comes to mind, or "The Internal Revenue Service has selected your return from last year for an audit." Not much pleasure there! Or is it an argument that language should do nothing but give pleasure? Does it almost have the force of an exclamation—saying, in effect "Words in sequence—always a pleasure!" What, in point of fact, does this seemingly simple sequence of words actually mean? How does it actually work?

Insofar as we think we understand what Stein meant with the above phrase, what are some of the ways she could have gotten that meaning across with different sentences? Just think of a few of the many, many different ways she might have written this sentence:

> Why should a sequence of words not be a pleasure?
> Why should a sequence of words not give pleasure?
> Shouldn't a sequence of words always give pleasure?
> A sequence of words should always be a pleasure.

A sequence of words should always be pleasurable.
Words in sequence should always give pleasure.
We should always find pleasure in a sequence of words.
Why should a sequence of words not always give us pleasure?

And so on and on and on.

Stein's question, of course, is a sentence, itself a sequence of words, but it is a sequence of words that can be understood in a number of different ways, and I want us to think about some of the important things we can learn about sentences just from thinking carefully about Stein's question. Sentences are sequences of words, but just adding words together to make a sequence does not create a sentence. "Teacher yellow September swims hungry" is a sequence of words, but it's not a sentence because it lacks a subject and a predicate, and therefore does not express a proposition. "I am a teacher" is a sequence of words that is a sentence because it contains a subject *I* and a predicate *am a teacher*, and thus it does advance a proposition. The subject is who or what is spoken of or talked about, and the predicate is what is said about the subject. Usually the subject of a sentence will be a noun or noun phrase or pronoun, and the predicate will contain some form of verb.

A proposition, which is usually expressed in the form of a sentence, is a statement about reality that can be accepted or rejected. The relationship between propositions and sentences is a little hard to pin down, since a sentence will always advance or express one or more propositions, and a proposition will always be in the form of a sentence. The key here is to think of a sentence as being a visible piece of writing, and the propositions it advances as assumptions and ideas not necessarily written out. The easiest way of thinking about this relationship is to say that a written sentence usually rests on or contains or combines a number of underlying propositions, most of which the sentence simply assumes, and which would be too basic or simple-sounding to actually write out.

I like to think of the written sentence as the part of the iceberg you see above water, while many of its underlying propositions remain out of sight underwater. To put it another way, propositions are the atoms from which the molecule of the sentence is constructed. Most propositions usually contain several smaller or constituent propositions, as we see in the proposition I mentioned a moment ago, "I am a teacher," which contains within it the proposition that I exist, there is an I, and that there is a thing called teacher, and that I am one of those things.

So, while many of us have been taught that a sentence is a sequence of words containing a subject and a predicate that expresses an idea, it's actually the case that most sentences express or imply a number of ideas. "I like hamburgers" expresses a thought, but what exactly do I mean by *like*? What kind of hamburger am I thinking of, and why do I want someone to know this about my taste habits? As is frequently the case, a number of questions can be asked about this simple declaration, and each question reminds us of unspoken, unwritten propositions that may underlie the surface of this seemingly simple and clear sentence.

We all know that sentences can convey a host of meanings, both intended and unintended, just as the manner of conveying any meaning may differ along a continuum of emotional impacts, described by one stylistic theorist Walker Gibson as ranging from tough style to sweet style to stuffy style. For instance, I might have said "You better believe I like hamburgers," which would be tough style, or "Don't you just think hamburgers are fabulous?" which would be a sweet style, or "My gastronomic preferences include, but are not limited to, that peculiarly American version of the sandwich known as a hamburger"—definitely a stuffy style.

If we return for a moment to Gertrude Stein's sentence, "Why should a sequence of words be anything but a pleasure?" we can see that it actually advances a number of propositions, including there are these things we call words. Words can be put together in a sequence. Words in a sequence can give pleasure. Words in a sequence ought to give pleasure. Words in a sequence should give nothing but pleasure, and are there reasons why words in a sequence should not be a pleasure?

The point here is simply that the basic unit of writing is the proposition, not the word or even a sequence of words, and we build sentences by putting propositions together. The style of our sentences is determined by the ways in which we combine not words, but the propositions those words stand for or refer to. Sentences convey information, organizing it into propositions or statements, and then combining those propositions through syntactical arrangements that establish the logical relationships between and among them. So one of our first goals will be to understand how sentences combine propositions to present information, and how we can use our knowledge of the ways in which sentences put propositions together to present our own ideas more effectively.

Each sentence we write reflects three main kinds of choices we make: What should we write about and what do we want to accomplish in writing about it? Which words should we use? What order should we put those words in? There's not much that I or any other writing teacher can do in this or any writing course to help you choose your subject matter or propositional content, or to help you decide what you want your writing to do. But I can address some important things you'll want to keep in mind as you choose the words you use, particularly the degree of precision in your vocabulary choices, and I can address some even more important concerns in the way you put together the words you choose. We call that order syntax, and the order in which our sentences unfold or hit the reader is entirely within our control. Even better, syntactical choices can actually help us increase the precision of our writing, bringing what we say into sharper focus, even if we don't have command of the most precise vocabulary.

Sometimes we refer to the choice of words we use as paradigmatic choices, and to the choices about the order we put them in as syntagmatic choices. In this sense, we might imagine that each sentence we write results from paradigmatic choices we make along a vertical axis of alternate vocabulary choices we might make for each word in the sentence. Each sentence we write results from syntagmatic choices we make along a horizontal axis we read from left to right, deciding whether to put the verb early or late in the sentence, deciding where to put modifying phrases, deciding whether the information in the sentence will be coordinated, adding phrases like cars to a train, or subordinated, one piece of information made a clarifying helper to a more important piece of information.

The terms paradigmatic and syntagmatic are not in themselves important for us to remember, but they help us understand two of the most important variables in our writing. Add the large factor of subject and purpose which, as I pointed out, may not always be within our control, and the sentences we write combine three kinds of choices: the propositions we want to advance, the vocabulary we choose, and the syntax or order in which we want our readers to experience our propositions. Paying closer attention to the precision and syntax of the sentences we write can dramatically sharpen or improve propositional content.

Going back to Stein's "Why should a sequence of words be anything but a pleasure?" we can see that in place of "sequence of words" she might have said "string or words" or "series of words" or "bunch of words" or "combination of words" or "number of words." Or she might just have said "Why should words be anything but a pleasure?" leaving out *sequence* altogether. But she chose the word *sequence* over a number of other possibilities, just as she chose to use the word *pleasure* over *gratification, satisfaction, joy, delight,* or any number of other words suggesting a positive experience.

This reminds us that any word we write is chosen from a list of synonyms or a list of words that are either more or less abstract. When I write "I got into my car," for instance, I could have used a much more abstract word such as vehicle or transportation. I got in my vehicle. I got in my transportation. Or I could have used a less abstract word such as *sedan* or *minivan*. I got in my sedan. I got in my minivan. Or I could have chosen an even less abstract, more precise word or term such as *Ford* or *Ford Fusion*. I got in my Ford Fusion. In this sense, each word we write in a sentence represents a choice from what we might think of as a vertical series of words above the word we choose, which would be more abstract, or below the word we choose, which would be more precise. Semanticists refer to this as the ladder of abstraction, and it reminds us that one of the important variables in our writing is the degree of precision in our choice of the words that we use.

The other choice we make when we write a sentence is the order in which we arrange the words we choose. For example, Stein could just as easily have made her question "Why should we get anything but pleasure from a sequence of words?" We might think of the order in which words appear in a sentence as choices made along that horizontal axis we call syntax.

Now that we've identified the three main factors that determine the style and effectiveness of our writing—propositional content, word choice, and syntax—let's go back to our sentence from Gertrude Stein one more time to see the most important assumption underlying this course: that the same words in different order have different meanings, or to put this another way, that style is content.

Most of us have been taught to think of style and meaning, or form and content, as two different things and, indeed, it is almost impossible to talk about language without resorting to this binary opposition. We think of content as the ideas or information our writing conveys, and we think of style as the way in which we present these ideas. Many aphorisms and metaphors have been used through the years to describe style, ranging from "Style is the man himself" to "Style is the dress of thought." Most of these metaphors confuse our understanding of style as much or more than they clarify it. If we have to use a metaphor to explain style, we might think of the onion, which consists of numerous layers of onion we can peel away until there's nothing left. The onion is its layers, and those layers don't contain a core of onionness, but they are themselves the onion.

Similarly, when we write a sentence, the way we choose to order its propositional content subtly affects that content so that the meaning changes ever so slightly with every vocabulary and syntactical choice we make. It's probably safe to say that all of us can agree that the point of Stein's "Why should a sequence of words be anything but a pleasure?" is that words should do more than just convey information, that language is itself an experience worth considering, quite apart from its reference. But do we really believe that "Why should a sequence of words be anything but a pleasure?" means exactly the same as:

> Why shouldn't words in sequence always be a pleasure?
> Shouldn't a sequence of words be always a pleasure?
> A sequence of words should always be a pleasure.
> Or my favorite, the Yoda variant:
> Always a pleasure words in sequence should be.

We read these sentences differently. Each reflects different stylistic choices, and each hits the reader just a little bit differently than does Stein's original sentence, which is dismissive of opposition, as only Gertrude Stein could be. Another way of looking at this assumption—that form is content, style is meaning—is to say that when we write, we are doing something with our sentences, and what we do unfolds in time, whether to our readers' eyes or ears. The summarizable or paraphrasable information conveyed in our sentences is only a part of their meaning, since what they do to a reader, the way they direct the reader's thinking and unfold information, may be as or more important than the information they contain.

The point of all of this is simply to remind us of something we never forget in speaking to one another—that the way we say things may be as or more important than what we say—but it's something we frequently forget when we are writing. However, when we write, we need to remember that the style of a sentence is its content. This inseparability of form from content was what poet Archibald MacLeish was trying to explain in his poem *Ars Poetica* when he famously noted that "a poem should not mean / but be." The same is true of sentences. Or, to put this another way, the informational or propositional content of a sentence is not the same as the sentence's meaning, since the sentence doesn't just carry information, like putting objects in a canister, but it does things with it and to it, shaping it to particular purposes and effects. In this important sense, sentences work like verbs, doing things, taking action, rather than like nouns that only name.

Understanding how sentences put propositions together is the first step in understanding how they do things, the ways in which they work, the ways they present information, and the ways they unfold their meanings, and to learn how to make them work for us. We will do this by studying the ways in which sentences combine information by coordinating it, subordinating it, or subsuming it in modification. We will look at the difference between sentences that combine information through loose syntax that puts the subject and the verb near the beginning of the sentence, and those that do so through periodic syntax, delaying the unfolding of the sentence's most important news until the very end, creating a sense of suspense that demands the reader's attention, sometimes to that very last word.

In the 18th century, this syntax of delay was seen as the gold standard of fine writing, a sign of the writer's care, control, and sophistication. Indeed, masterful 18th-century writers, such as Dr. Samuel Johnson, referred to the sentences they wrote not as sentences, but as periods. To escape that historical prejudice which hangs on in many composition manuals, but no longer holds true for our understanding and evaluation of sentence structure, I'll usually refer to periodic sentences—those sentences that delay the delivery of their most important information to the very end—as suspensive sentences. We will pay particular attention to the cumulative sentence, a special kind of loose syntax that can also function suspensively because it offers powerful generative or heuristic advantages to the writer who understands its forms.

We will study the sentence as a thing in motion, a thing alive, considering the strategies writers can use to give sentences pace and rhythm, particularly the duple rhythms of balance and the three-beat rhythms of serial constructions. In short, this course will reveal some of the syntactic strategies professional writers regularly employ. These are also strategies we can use in our writing to ensure that our sentences will be effective and possibly even elegant.

Grammar and Rhetoric
Lecture 2

Sentences are alive. We experience them in time, and we react to their
unfolding as they twist and turn, challenging us, teasing us, surprising
us, and sometimes boring or confusing us as we read them.

This lecture will examine some of the key terms we will be using as
we talk about sentences: *effectiveness, elegance, grammar, and
rhetoric.* Effectiveness will be explained in terms of situational
appropriateness and informational density, the assumption being that unless
the situation demands otherwise, sentences that convey more information are
more effective than those that convey less. Elegance will be explained in
terms of the mathematical concept of the elegant solution, with the important
difference that we frequently gain precision in language by adding words
rather than by subtracting. I will explain the difference between grammatical
and rhetorical terminology, offering a brief grammatical overview of
sentences and then contrasting it with a rhetorical view. This course will
focus on grammatical issues only insofar as they are helpful in explaining
rhetorical concerns, meaning our concern will always be with how sentences
work rather than with how to label their constituent parts.

John Steinbeck, in his introduction to *The Log from the Sea of Cortez*, points
out the difference between the "subjective relational reality" we might
have with a living fish and the technical, objective way we might need to
categorize or specifically identify the fish. This point seems to me to apply
equally to sentences. Most of the terms we use to identify sentences or to
label their parts treat the sentence as something dead, to be dissected, its
parts identified. Sentences are alive, we experience them in time, and we
react to how they unfold as we read them.

I want to start by looking at the term "elegant and effective writing." Both
these modifiers have everything to do with what Steinbeck was talking about
when he described the relational reality someone might have with a living
fish. Both effectiveness and elegance remain largely a matter of personal
taste. So let me tell you what I mean by those terms.

Effective writing anticipates, shapes, and satisfies a reader's need for information. Unless the situation demands otherwise, sentences that convey more information are generally more effective than those that convey less. Sentences that bring ideas and images into clearer focus by adding more useful details and explanations are generally more effective than those that are less clearly focused and offer fewer details. Many of us have been taught over the years that effective writing is simple and direct, a term generally associated with Strunk and White's legendary guidebook, *The Elements of Style*. Strunk and White do a great job of reminding us to avoid needless words but don't begin to consider all of the ways in which more words might be needed. My goal will be to explain why in many cases we actually need to add words to improve our writing. Effective writing is largely determined by how well the writer's efforts respond to the situation that occasioned the writing, to the writer's purpose in writing, and to the reader's needs.

One term I ought to mention is *style*, a concept so rich, so expansive, so subjective, and so contested that any attempt to define it immediately encounters resistance.

Most of us can agree on whether writing is effective or not. Elegant writing is much harder for us to agree upon. Strunk and White's guidebook and other guidebooks imply that elegant writing is gaudy writing, overly lush, opulent, and mannered—and therefore to be avoided. H. W. Fowler's *Modern English Usage* warns against "elegant variation" in prose style, which he characterized as the tendency of second-rate writers to concentrate more on "expressing themselves prettily" than on "conveying meaning clearly." I'm referring to elegant prose style in the same way that mathematicians refer to the elegant solution to a math problem. In math, elegant solutions are the most direct route to solving a problem, taking the fewest number of steps. In writing, elegance is indeed a matter of efficiency, but the problems a writer attempts to solve have an emotional or affective dimension not generally associated with mathematics.

The final two terms I want to discuss in this lecture, *grammatical* and *rhetorical*, are easier to define than are *effective* and *elegant*, and more important. Grammatical descriptions of the sentence are primarily concerned with identifying its parts. Rhetorical descriptions of the sentence are primarily concerned with identifying the relational reality established when a reader reads or hears it. Grammar has to do with classifying words by their function in a sentence. It deals with the rules underlying our understanding and use of language. Most of us recognize and use these phenomena every day, though few of us keep in mind all the definitions or rules. Nor do we need to. Grammar describes the machinery of the sentence, but doesn't teach us how to make the sentence go anywhere or do anything.

Through a history that no doubt dates from our earliest use of language, but that has been recorded from the 5th century B.C., rhetoric has been associated with persuasion. For my purposes, rhetoric has to do with motive and impact—the reasons why we use language to accomplish certain goals and the extent to which it accomplishes them. Rhetoric focuses on the producer of language—the speaker or writer—and on the receiver of language—the listener or reader. Rhetoric has to do with the purposes to which we put language and the consequences of our efforts. Rhetoric is about the best ways of getting and holding attention with language and shaping that attention to achieve particular outcomes.

Whenever possible, the terms I use in this course will refer to rhetorical phenomena rather than with grammatical phenomena. We have generated a lot of labels that are grammatical, such as categorizing sentences by the number and kinds of clauses they contain, leading us to describe sentences as simple, compound, or complex. But a simple sentence can create an incredibly complex reaction in a reader, and a complex sentence may have only a very simple impact. Accordingly, we will rely more on terms or labels that direct our attention to the ways in which sentences deliver their goods. Some of the terms we'll use are terms I made up simply because I couldn't find existing ones that directed our attention to the rhetorical phenomena I wanted to discuss. Effectiveness and elegance are both rhetorical issues; grammar alone can lead us to neither.

One term I ought to mention is *style*, a concept so rich, so expansive, so subjective, and so contested that any attempt to define it immediately encounters resistance. We may refer to the style of a period, the style of a literary form or genre, the style of a nation, the style of an individual writer, of a work by an individual writer, the style of a particular period in a writer's career, the style of a group or movement of writers, a period in a movement, and so on. The definition I use when I'm talking about sentences is: "Style is what the writer writes and/or what the reader reads." This definition refuses to distinguish style from content or meaning. As our course progresses I'll try to show why. ■

Questions to Consider

1. Pick the opening sentence from a newspaper or magazine article and rewrite it in a completely different style—try making it bare and spare, like Hemingway, or formal and ceremonious, or lushly descriptive, or more emotional.

2. What have your ideas about style been? Would thinking that style isn't a "garnish for the meat of prose" change the way you think about or approach the task of writing?

Grammar and Rhetoric

Lecture 2—Transcript

In the first lecture, we took a broad overview of the assumptions that will underlie this course, the goals that we'll pursue for improving writing, and some of the terms that we'll employ as we try to understand how sentences work and how we can make them work better. In this lecture, we'll look a bit more closely at key terms we'll be using, not because those terms are important in their own right, but because they give us better tools for describing sentences and for helping us understand and control the choices we make when we write.

I've always been fond of a distinction drawn by John Steinbeck in his "Introduction" to *The Log from the Sea of Cortez*, a little book describing a marine specimen-collecting trip that Steinbeck and his friend Ed Ricketts made in 1940. There, Steinbeck considers what it means to go on an expedition, and how each expedition inevitably shapes the reality it hopes to study. More specifically, he notes that one of the processes at the heart of studying marine biology, naming the parts of a fish and cataloging a fish in terms of its structure, doesn't actually tell the full story. As he explains, a fish can be rigorously identified by counting its spines:

> For example: the Mexican sierra has "XVII-15-IX" spines in the dorsal fin. These can be easily counted. But if the sierra strikes hard on the line so that our hands are burned, if the fish sounds and nearly escapes and finally comes in over the rail, his colors pulsing and his tail beating the air, a whole new relational externality has come into being—an entity which is more than the sum of the fish plus the fisherman. The only way to count the spines of the sierra unaffected by this second relational reality is to sit in a laboratory, open an evil-smelling jar, remove a stiff, colorless fish from a formalin solution, count the spines, and write the truth "D.XVII-15-IX." There you have recorded a reality which cannot be assailed—probably the least important reality concerning either the fish or yourself.

Sure, Steinbeck is slanting the case to stress the subjective relational reality we might have with a living fish over the quite technical, objective way we might need to categorize or specifically identify the fish. But I love his reminder about the great differences that exist between the way we encounter and experience a live fish in nature and the way we might encounter or experience a quite dead fish in the laboratory. And his point seems to me to also apply equally to sentences, and not just because they can also be slippery. Most of the terms we use to identify sentences or to label their parts treat the sentence as something dead, to be dissected, its parts identified. This ignores the fact that what Steinbeck terms a "relational reality" exists between sentences and readers, just as surely and much more frequently, with much more usually at stake, than exists between a fisherman and a fish.

Sentences are alive. We experience them in time, and we react to their unfolding as they twist and turn, challenging us, teasing us, surprising us, and sometimes boring or confusing us as we read them. Accordingly, whenever possible, I will use terms in this course that focus on the sentence as a thing in motion, an experience, something with which we form a relational reality when we read, rather than as something stiff and lifeless, whose parts can be counted or named. As I'll try to explain more fully in a moment, I see this distinction as primarily between viewing the sentence as a grammatical phenomenon or as a rhetorical phenomenon.

But before I get to the distinctions I see between grammatical and rhetorical concerns, I want to look at the phrase "elegant and effective writing." Both of those modifiers have everything to do with what Steinbeck was talking about when he described the relational reality someone might have with a living fish, and not much at all to do with labeling and categorizing with objective rigor. What one reader or writer may find elegant is not the same as what another reader or writer may find elegant, and while we may be able to measure effectiveness a bit more objectively than we can measure elegance, determining how effective writing is also remains largely a matter of personal taste. Let me tell you what I mean by these two important terms.

First, effective: For me, effective writing is writing that anticipates, shapes, and satisfies a reader's need for information. Effective writing gives the reader the information necessary for thoughtful consideration of the writer's purpose in introducing a subject. It anticipates the obvious questions an interested reader may form, and it accomplishes both the informational and emotional goals of the writer. Effective writing guides the reader's thinking, satisfies the reader's need for essential information, and implicitly assures the reader that he or she is in good hands, reading prose by a writer who anticipates both the reader's informational and emotional needs.

Accordingly, one of the assumptions shaping my approach to teaching writing is that unless the situation demands otherwise, sentences that convey more information are more effective than those that convey less. Sentences that anticipate and answer more questions that a reader might have are better than those that answer fewer questions. Sentences that bring ideas and images into clearer focus by adding more useful details and explanation are generally more effective than those that are less clearly focused and that offer fewer details. In practice, this means that I generally value longer sentences over shorter sentences, as long as the length accomplishes some of those important goals I've just mentioned.

Many of us have been exposed over the years to the idea that effective writing is simple and direct, a term generally associated with Strunk and White's legendary guidebook, *The Elements of Style*. Or we remember some of the slogans from that book, such as "Omit needless words." Unfortunately, it's a lot harder for us to remember that Strunk concluded his discussion of the mandate to omit needless words with this all-important qualifier: "This requires not that the writer make all sentences short or that he avoid all detail and treat subjects only in outline, but that every word tell." Indeed, Strunk's concern is specifically with words and phrases that do not add propositions to the sentence, phrases like "the reason why is that" used in place of "because," or "owing to the fact that" in place of "since." It's far easier to remember the term *simple and direct* as a summary of Jacques Barzun's advice in his *Simple & Direct: A Rhetoric for Writers* than it is to remember that simple does not mean simplistic, direct does not mean short, and simple and direct does not mean that we should all write like Ernest Hemingway in a hurry.

"Omit needless words" is great advice, but not when it gets reduced to the belief that shorter is always better, or that needless means any word without which the sentence can still make sense. And for those of us hypnotized and maddened by a recent TV advertisement for a headache remedy that just repeats its claim three times, "Apply directly to the forehead, apply directly to the forehead, apply directly to the forehead," we should remember that this odd and grating rhetorical strategy comes directly from the lecture practice of Professor Will Strunk circa 1919, as E. B. White reminds us in his introduction to Strunk's rules for plain English. So while I don't intend any advice I give about writing sentences to contradict the generally quite useful advice we can find in Strunk and White, I do want to suggest that it presents a very subjective aesthetic, as well as rules for better writing.

I like Faulkner as well as I like Hemingway, and I'd like to believe that even Professor Will Strunk and certainly E. B. White would not have tried to edit Faulkner out of existence. When Hemingway writes of an old waiter in "A Clean, Well-Lighted Place," "He disliked bars and bodegas," few of us would argue that his sentence is not simple and direct and not free of needless words. But when Faulkner writes about the boy who's the protagonist in "Barn Burning" it's hard to see how Strunk and White might apply:

> The boy, crouched on his nail keg at the back of the crowded room, knew he smelled cheese, and more: from where he sat he could see the ranked shelves close-packed with the solid, squat, dynamic shapes of tin cans whose labels his stomach read, not from the lettering which meant nothing to his mind but from the scarlet devils and the silver curve of fish—this, the cheese which he knew he smelled and the hermetic meat which his intestines believed he smelled coming in intermittent gusts momentary and brief between the other constant one, the smell and sense just a little of fear because mostly of despair and grief, the old fierce pull of the blood.

I'm not so sure about what may or may not be needless in this particular sentence, but simple and direct it most certainly is not. Both writers, Faulkner and Hemingway, introduce us to the thinking of their characters, but just as the thinking of Hemingway's old waiter is infinitely more tired and less active than the thinking of Faulkner's boy, the sentence each writer constructs is intended to hit us in very different ways for very different reasons. Start cutting out words and simplifying the syntax in Faulkner's sentence and we'll miss the complex thinking that haunts the boy throughout the story, and leads him ultimately to betray his father to keep him from burning another barn.

But even Hemingway, the poster boy for simple and direct, reminds us that a simple and direct sentence is not the same as one that is simplistic and short, as we can see from another earlier sentence from "A Clean, Well-Lighted Place": "In the daytime, the street was dusty, but at night the dew settled the dust and the old man liked to sit late because he was deaf and now at night it was quiet and he felt the difference."

To put this another way, Strunk and White do a great job of reminding us to avoid needless words, but they don't begin to consider all of the ways in which more words might actually be needed. My goal will be to explain why, in many cases, we need to add words to improve our writing, as Faulkner so frequently does, rather than trying to pare our writing down to some kind of telegraphic minimum, as is frequently the case with Hemingway.

While I'm mentioning Strunk and White, let me suggest that we could all do a lot worse than digging out that tattered copy we've had since high school or college, and giving it a fresh read. Then let me suggest you acquire and put on your bookshelf, right next to Strunk and White's *The Elements of Style*, Bill Walsh's *The Elephants of Style*, subtitled *A Trunkload of Tips on the Big Issues and Gray Areas of Contemporary American English*. Walsh, a writer for *The Washington Post*, offers a number of useful tips about writing, most of which are a whole lot funnier than the tips served up by Will Strunk and E. B. White.

Now, elegant: Effective writing is largely determined by how well the writer's efforts respond to the situation that occasioned the writing, the writer's purpose in writing, and the reader's needs. Most of us can agree whether writing is effective or not, although we may disagree widely about whether one kind of effective writing is preferable to another. Elegant writing is much harder for us to agree upon, and indeed, the implication of Strunk and White and of a number of other guidebooks about writing might be that elegant writing is gaudy writing, overly lush, opulent, and mannered, and therefore should be avoided. Indeed, in his celebrated *Modern English Usage*, H. W. Fowler specifically warned against "elegant variation" in prose style, what he characterized as the tendency of second-rate writers to concentrate more on "expressing themselves prettily" than on "conveying their meaning clearly."

I don't want to argue with Fowler any more than I want to argue with Strunk and White, so I need to state that I'm referring to "elegant prose style" in the same way mathematicians refer to the elegant solution to a math problem. In fact, elegant solutions in math are the most direct routes to solving a problem, taking the fewest number of steps, offering the solution which is seen as the simplest, neatest, or cleanest response to a problem, no matter how complex the problem is. It's crucial that we understand, however, that writing problems are very different from mathematical problems.

As Jacques Barzun reminds us, "Language is not an algebra," and there is no single right answer to any given predicament with words. In writing, elegance is indeed a matter of efficiency, but we need to remember that the problems a writer attempts to solve have an emotional or affective dimension not generally associated with mathematics. Accordingly, elegant sentences are those that efficiently accomplish what the writer wants them to accomplish, and while there may be only one elegant solution to a math problem, there may be many different elegant solutions to a problem we address with language.

All of which is simply to say that there may not be that much difference between writing we find effective and writing we find elegant, and the two terms, much as is the case with form and content, may actually be inextricably wrapped up with each other. Indeed, we might think of elegant writing as writing that is unusually effective. Both terms, however, are subjectively relational, having to do with the impact writing has on a reader, with the way the reader experiences writing, rather than objectively describable or prescribable.

When we refer to sentences as effective or as elegant, we refer to what they do, rather than to the parts they consist of, and no amount of sophisticated vocabulary or complicated syntax can make a sentence effective or elegant unless that sentence accomplishes the task it was intended to accomplish. Both Hemingway and Faulkner strike me as elegant writers because they're so good at accomplishing what they set out to do. It's hard to imagine the writer who could out-Hemingway Hemingway, or who could out-Faulkner Faulkner, and attempts to do so generally seem humorous, as each found the elegant solution to the problems he wanted to write about.

A reminder of this can be found in *The Best of Bad Faulkner: Choice Entries from the Faux Faulkner Contest*, a collection of Faulkner parodies, including one by John Ruemmler entitled "Bran Burning." In it, we find a sentence that is vaguely familiar:

> He could see through the square of the glass into the oven, and though he could not read the recipe on the counter—the black lettering meant nothing to him, like history—he knew he smelled in the steady wash of warm air and unwashed family another smell, a scent of fear and decay and grief—for he was a full-blooded Snopes, blind to the truth and chained to the past, whether he knew it or not—and the rush of blood to his head made him woozy like his brothers Heck and I.O.U., who were anxious to confess their guilt and leave the kitchen (where no good ever originated, not the way their mother cooked) and to run to town for Coca Colas and Ding Dongs and some conversation at Homer Barren's 7-Eleven (which was only open 9 am till 7 pm, when Homer went home for supper) but their father would not let up, not for one minute, for he fancied himself wise as Solomon who never put to death an honest man, for who among us is honest or ever was 'cept Him Who died on the cross?

Effective? Yes, as a parody. Elegant? Not so much.

The final two terms I want to discuss in this lecture, grammatical and rhetorical, are both easier to define than are effective and elegant, and they're both more important. If we remember Steinbeck's discussion of different ways of looking at and thinking about the Mexican sierra, we might say that grammatical descriptions of the sentence are primarily concerned with identifying its parts, while rhetorical descriptions of the sentence are primarily concerned with identifying that relational reality established when a reader reads or hears the sentence.

Grammar has to do with relationships among words, largely irrespective of their meaning. Grammar has to do with classifying words by their function in a sentence, by what part of speech a word may be, how we refer to its tense if it's a verb, whether a noun is singular or plural, and agrees with the verb: The doctor is a woman. The swimmers are men. Grammar deals with the rules underlying our understanding and use of language. Most of these rules we've unconsciously known ever since we learned to speak.

Some of these rules are not rules at all, but simply reflect majority values or practices, and can be broken without any real harm to making ourselves understood, as in a phrase frequently attributed to Winston Churchill. The story goes that Churchill slyly reminded us how silly it is to make a rule that we have to obey that precludes ending a sentence with a preposition as Churchill put it, by referring to the things "up with which he would not put."

The Harbrace College Handbook I was required to purchase as a college freshman contains a "Glossary of Grammatical Terms" that runs on for some 24 pages. Included are terms such as parts of speech, nouns, pronouns, verbs, adverbs, adjectives, prepositions, participles, conjunctions, gerunds, and so on. Also included are grammatical terms that refer to groups of words, such as clauses, phrases, subordinate clauses, predicates, and so on. Most of us will recognize and we regularly use most of these grammatical phenomena every day, although only a few of us can remember or keep in mind all of the specifics of each definition or all of the rules governing the correct use of each of them, nor do we really need to.

The dirty little secret of correct grammar is that it allows a writer to avoid grammatical mistakes, but the most perfect adherence to all the rules of grammar will not necessarily produce writing that is either effective or elegant. Grammar describes the machinery of the sentence, but it doesn't teach us how to make the sentence go anywhere or do anything. In other words, grammar is more than a little bit like counting the spines of a dead fish.

I'll use some grammatical terms as this course proceeds, simply because that's the easiest way for me to suggest how to get our sentences to do some of the things we want them to do. But knowing grammar backward and forward is not in itself a step toward better writing. In fact, it can and frequently does lead to boring or ineffective writing that is grammatically correct, but not good for much of anything else. My interest has to do much, much more with rhetoric.

Through a history that no doubt dates from our earliest use of language, but that has been recorded from the 5th century B.C., rhetoric has been associated with persuasion. For my purposes, rhetoric, unlike grammar, has to do with both motive and impact, the reasons why we use language to accomplish certain goals, and the extent to which it accomplishes them. Or to put this another way, grammar has to do with words, while rhetoric has to do with the way we do things with words. Rhetoric focuses on the producer of language, in our case the speaker or writer, and on the receiver of language, the listener or reader. Grammar has to do with words as objects which can be labeled and classified, while rhetoric has to do with the purposes to which we put language, and to the consequences of our efforts.

Richard Lanham is a maverick rhetorician and author of *Style: An Anti-Textbook*, a book to which we'll return later in the course. Lanham is trying to get at this crucial aspect of rhetoric when he rehearses the many different understandings of the term rhetoric over its 2,500-year history, only to conclude that a contemporary understanding of rhetoric best describes it as the "science of human attention-structures." Rhetoric is about the best ways of getting and holding attention with language, and shaping that attention to achieve particular outcomes. Whenever possible, the terms I use in this course will refer to rhetorical phenomena, things having to do with the way sentences work, rather than with grammatical phenomena, what we label the parts of a sentence, and how we understand the relationships among those parts.

We've generated a lot of labels that are grammatical, such as categorizing sentences by the number and kinds of clauses they contain, leading us to describe sentences as simple, compound, or complex. But a simple sentence can create an incredibly complex reaction in a reader, and a complex sentence may have only a very simple impact. Accordingly, we will rely more on terms or labels that direct our attention to the ways in which sentences deliver their goods, remembering that what they deliver is emotional impact, as well as information. And to be honest, some of the terms I'll use to describe the way sentences work, for example, referring to suspensive, intensive, or interruptive sentences, are terms I made up simply because I couldn't find existing terms that directed our attention to the rhetorical phenomena I wanted to discuss.

The main point to remember here is that effectiveness and elegance in writing are both rhetorical issues, and grammar alone can lead us to neither.

Oh yes, there's one other term I really ought to mention, although having gone this far without discussing it, I'm tempted to see if I can get away with not discussing it at all. That term is, of course, *style*. Style is a concept so rich, so expansive, so subjective, and so contested that any attempt to define it immediately encounters resistance, if not outright hostility. We refer to the style of a period, the style of a literary form or genre, the style of a nation, the style of an individual writer, the style of a work by an individual writer, the style of a particular period in a writer's career as in early or late Henry James, the style of a group or movement of writers, the style of a particular period in a movement as in early or late modernism, the style of a particular kind of sentence, and so on.

Obviously style means something different in each of these cases, not to mention that it can refer to features consciously chosen by the writer, or consciously sought for and found by the reader. Just one word is used to describe or focus our attention on so many different aspects of writing.

So with a mixture of desperation and ingenuity, I've come up with a definition of style that I use when talking about sentences: Style is what the writer writes and/or what the reader reads. That's about as inclusive a definition of style as one can get. It's also a definition that refuses to distinguish style from content or meaning. I made the case earlier for the notion that style is content, but while we've been referring to Strunk and White, let me add E. B. White's considerable authority to this argument.

In his brief essay, "An Approach to Style," which he appended to Will Strunk's rules, White admits that there is no satisfactory explanation of style, but does make clear his belief:

> Young writers often suppose that style is a garnish for the meat of prose, a sauce by which a dull dish is made palatable. Style has no such separate entity. It is nondetachable, unfilterable.

As our course progresses, I'll try to show why I so strongly agree with White, and why I believe this assumption is central to any serious attempt to improve our writing.

Propositions and Meaning
Lecture 3

Most of us have been taught that the base clause of a sentence, the sentence's subject and predicate, is responsible for advancing its most important proposition, and this is simply not the case. Propositions carry emotional or effective impact that has nothing to do with the grammatical expression or surface structure that advances that proposition in a sentence. It is only when we consider the emotional effect of the way we order and combine the propositions that underlie the sentences we speak or write that we can consider ourselves in control of our writing.

What we generally think of as the style of a sentence is largely a matter of the way in which its words represent and organize its underlying propositions. Rather than expressing a complete thought or idea or feeling, a sentence expresses a number of thoughts or ideas or feelings either stated or implied in the propositions that underlie and give rise to the surface structure of the sentence's words and syntax. In 17th-century France, the Port Royal Grammarians illustrated this concept with the sentence "Invisible God created the visible world." A sentence's underlying propositions may actually trump or override the grammatical and syntactic cues of its surface language.

In 1926 H. W. Fowler, the legendary English lexicographer and philologist, complained that "proposition" was a "jack-of-all-trades" word that had come to be used in so many different ways that it really had no meaning. What so bothered Fowler was that this term, so clearly tied to propounding or setting forth an idea in philosophy, had come to be used to refer to commercial proposals, tasks, jobs, problems, occupation, trade, opponent, prospect, enterprise worth undertaking, area, field—and most galling of all, when used as a verb, to make an "amatory advance." In the study of logic, a proposition is a statement in which the subject is affirmed or denied by the predicate. As far as possible, I like to think of a proposition as a kind of basic or elementary statement that can't easily be broken down into constituent propositions.

In 1966 Noam Chomsky famously made a 17th-century discussion of propositions by the Port-Royal Grammarians one of the central arguments for his theory of deep structure and transformational grammar. For my purposes, what matters in Chomsky's discussion is the example of the relation between a sentence and its underlying proposition—an example that he cites from *The Port-Royal Grammar*, published in 1660. The sentence Chomsky cites is *"Dieu invisible a créé le monde visible,"* or "Invisible God created the visible world." *The Port-Royal Grammar* noted that this sentence actually advanced not just one, but three different propositions: that God is invisible, that God created the world, and that the world is visible. As Chomsky summed up this argument, there exists a deep structure, an unwritten or unspoken "underlying mental reality" (unwritten propositions) below the surface structure of the spoken or written form of the sentence. Chomsky concludes that "the deep structure consists of a system of propositions, and it does not receive a direct, point-by-point expression in the actual physical object (the sentence) that is produced. To form an actual sentence from such an underlying system of elementary propositions, we apply certain rules (in modern terms, grammatical transformations)."

The style of our sentences is determined by the ways in which we combine propositions.

The key here is to think of a sentence as being a visible piece of writing and the propositions it advances as assumptions and ideas not necessarily written out. The basic unit of writing sentences is the proposition, not the word or even a sequence of words. The style of our sentences is determined by the ways in which we combine propositions. The sentence rests upon a number of unstated, unwritten propositions that might have been implied or acknowledged by writing this sentence a number of different ways.

Let's see how the order in which underlying propositions are advanced by the written sentence can make a big difference in the way the sentence works. This is an important step for writers to take because they can take control of that order to better accomplish their purpose for the sentence.

When a sentence works like a mini-narrative, telling a kind of story that has a surprise ending, I think it will almost always catch a reader's attention and remind the reader of the creative mind that crafted that sentence. The point here is not that the end of the sentence is where we should place the word or words we most want to emphasize, but that the power of underlying propositions is not tied to the traditional way we look at sentences.

Most of us have been taught that the base clause of a sentence is responsible for advancing its most important proposition, and this is simply not the case. Only when we consider the emotional effect of the way we order and combine the propositions that underlie the sentences we speak or write can we consider ourselves in control of our writing. An example from Joseph Conrad's *The Secret Sharer* can suggest the way underlying propositions may actually carry more weight or have a greater impact on the reception of a sentence than does its surface. Richard Ohmann, in an article, "Literature as Sentences," published in *College English* in 1966, made the case that "most sentences directly and obliquely put more linguistic apparatus into operation than is readily apparent." He illustrates his argument with the striking final sentence of *The Secret Sharer*:

> Walking to the taffrail, I was in time to make out, on the very edge of a darkness thrown by a towering black mass like the very gateway of Erebus—yes, I was in time to catch an evanescent glimpse of my white hat left behind to mark the spot where the secret sharer of my cabin and of my thoughts, as though he were my second self, had lowered himself into the water to take his punishment: a free man, a proud swimmer striking out for a new destiny.

Ohmann refers to the propositional underpinning of this sentence as one of "extraordinary density," and density is one of the writing values I will argue for in this course. ■

1. Choose a long, fairly complicated sentence: You can find these in technical articles, academic research articles, legal documents, or a 17th-century poem. (If the sentence is in verse form, simply ignore the line breaks). Identify the base clause in the sentence and count the number of modifiers attached to it.

2. Write a sentence that, using cumulative syntax and adding as much detail as you can stand, describes a dramatic situation. Identify the base clause of the sentence. Move the base clause three times and observe how you like each new placement.

Propositions and Meaning
Lecture 3—Transcript

In 1926, H. W. Fowler, the legendary English lexicographer and philologist, writing in his authoritative *Modern English Usage*, complained vociferously that proposition was a "Jack-of-all-trades" word that had come to be used in so many different ways that it really had no meaning. Disdainfully noting that misuse of this term had apparently spread from America to England, Fowler thundered:

> It won its popularity partly because it combined the charms of novelty and length …; there is less trouble in using it than in choosing a more suitable word from the dozen or so whose places it is apt to usurp.

What so bothered Fowler was that this term, so clearly tied to propounding or setting forth an idea in philosophy, had come to be used to refer to commercial proposals, tasks, jobs, problems, occupations, trade, opponent, prospect, enterprise worth undertaking, area, field, and most galling of all, when used as a verb, to make an "amatory advance." I mention Fowler's diatribe simply to give some context to the way I will use this term when talking about sentences.

In the study of logic, a proposition is a statement in which the subject is affirmed or denied by the predicate. In the first lecture, I suggested that for my purposes, a proposition, which is usually expressed in the form of a sentence, is a statement about reality that can be accepted or rejected. And so far as possible, I like to think of a proposition as a kind of basic or elementary statement that can't easily be broken down into constituent propositions. "I live" is thus a proposition, but "I am tired and hungry" actually expresses two basic propositions, "I am tired" and "I am hungry."

Moreover, in rigorous logical or philosophical terms, each of those propositions can actually be broken down further into propositions: that there is something called an "I"; that I am in the category of those things; that there's a category of physical or emotional condition known as being tired, that my physical or emotional condition falls into that category, and so on.

But this kind of rigor will make us crazy and doesn't help us to write better sentences, so I generally won't push things past identifying the propositions directly indicated by visible words in a sentence.

So I'll call "I am tired" a proposition, "I am hungry" a proposition, and say that the sentence "I am tired and hungry" expresses two propositions, and these two propositions can be expressed or advanced a number of different ways. I might say "I, who am tired, am also hungry" or "I, being tired, am also hungry" or I might boil the two propositions down to single-word modifiers that let me start a sentence with, "Tired and hungry" and then take it from there: "Tired and hungry, just back from a week in the bush, I limped into the mess hall, hoping the food lines were still open." Now, that's a sentence that advances a bunch of propositions, and one that I think is a big improvement on just saying, "I'm tired and hungry." Much more on this later.

Fowler probably wouldn't approve of the way I'm using the term proposition, but Noam Chomsky probably would. In 1966, Chomsky famously made a 17th-centry discussion of propositions by the Port Royal Grammarians one of the central arguments for his theory of deep structure and transformational grammar. Chomsky's *Cartesian Linguistics: A Chapter in the History of Rationalist Thought* claimed that the loose association of 17th-century French scholars known as the Port Royal Logicians or Grammarians had developed the framework for his discussion of language formation in terms of deep and surface structure, and the transformative steps that lead from the former to the latter.

Chomsky's claims in *Cartesian Linguistics* were immediately challenged, and his linguistic theories remain a site of controversy. For my purposes, however, those controversies are beside the point, since my concern is not with linguistic theories about the formation of language, a process that seems to take place largely at the unconscious level, but with theories of composition that focus on conscious decisions we make when we write sentences.

For my purposes, what matters in Chomsky's discussion is the example of the relation between a sentence and its underlying propositions, as he cites from *The Port-Royal Grammar* published in 1660. The sentence Chomsky cites is *"Dieu invisible a créé le monde visible."* My forays into French are always an adventure, as you can tell, but this sentence in English is "Invisible God created the visible world." *The Port-Royal Grammar* noted that this sentence actually advanced not just one, but three different propositions: that God is invisible, that God created the world, and that the world is visible, with the second proposition—that God created the world—being the most important.

As Chomsky summed up his argument:

> In other words, the deep structure underlying the proposition Invisible God created the visible world consists of three abstract propositions, each expressing a certain simple judgment, although its surface form expresses only the subject-attribute structure.

Or, as he puts it another way, there exists a deep structure, an unwritten or unspoken "underlying mental reality," the unwritten propositions, below the surface structure of the spoken or written form of the sentence. He concludes that "the deep structure consists of a system of propositions, and it does not receive a direct, point-by-point expression in the actual physical object (the sentence) that is produced."

As I noted before, I'm borrowing Chomsky's example and applying it to the conscious choices we make in writing sentences, and I'm neither endorsing nor challenging his theories of transformational grammar. His concerns are quite different from mine. The key here is to think of a sentence as being a visible piece of writing, and the propositions it advances as assumptions and ideas not necessarily visible or written out. As I previously suggested, the easiest way of thinking about this relationship is to say that a written sentence usually rests on or contains a number of underlying propositions, most of which the sentence simply assumes, and which would be too basic or simple-sounding to actually write out. As I've noted before, I like to think of the written sentence as the part of the iceberg you see above the water, while many of its underlying propositions remain out of sight, underwater.

The point here is simply that the basic unit of writing sentences is the proposition, not the word or even a sequence of words, and we build sentences by putting propositions together. The style of our sentences is determined by the ways in which we combine not words, but the propositions those words stand for or refer to. Sentences convey information, organizing it into propositions or statements, and then combining those propositions through syntactical arrangements that establish the logical relationships between and among them.

Thus, sentences join together propositions: sometimes just coordinating them by putting them side by side, for example, "I like to read and I like to write"; sometimes by subordinating one to another, for example, "I, who like to write, also like to read"; and sometimes marking temporal or causal relationships, for example, "Because I like to write I like to read" or "After I enjoy reading something, I like to start writing."

Let's return to that sentence from *The Port-Royal Grammar*: "Invisible God created the visible world." Chomsky, like the authors of *The Port-Royal Grammar*, argued that this sentence actually puts forward three propositions: that God is invisible, that God created the world, and that the world is visible. But let's look a bit more closely at the underlying propositions neither Chomsky nor the Port-Royal Grammarians thought deserving of mention.

First, that God exists, there is a God, and that the world exists, there is a world. Certainly that first proposition remains a subject of some debate today, and at least among some philosophies, the proposition that the world exists also remains an active question. And underlying the notion that God created the world is the proposition that God is powerful enough to have done so. I'm stretching a point, but what I hope you'll see is that the sentence "Invisible God created the visible world" actually rests upon a number of unstated, unwritten propositions. Moreover, those propositions might have been implied or acknowledged by writing this sentence in a number of different ways.

For instance, the sentence might have been written, "God is invisible, and the world is visible, and God created the world"; or "God is invisible, and God created the world, and the world is visible"; or "God, who is invisible, created the world, which is visible"; or "God, being invisible, created the world, it being visible"; or "Being invisible, God created the world, which is visible." Or we could have shifted the focus of the sentence from God to the world: "The world is visible and it was created by God, and God is invisible" or "The world is visible, and God is invisible, and the world was created by God" or "The visible world was created by invisible God" or "The world, which is visible, was created by God, who is invisible" or "Being visible, the world was created by invisible God" and so on.

Even more of the underlying propositions might have been brought to the surface of the sentence. For instance, "There is a God, and God is invisible, and God created the world" or "There is a world and the world is visible, and there is a God and God is invisible, and God created the world" or "There is a God who is invisible and God created the world, which is visible" or "There is a God who is invisible, and there is a world, which is visible, and God created the world" or "There is a world which is visible and the world was created by God, who is invisible."

There's no way to predict all the differences and how these variations might actually hit a reader, but it seems safe to assume that a sentence mentioning God three times and the world once will have a slightly different impact on a reader than a sentence that mentions the world three times and God twice. And there surely must be some difference between a sentence that simply assumes God exists and one that chooses to make that claim explicitly.

But let's leave the theologically complicated territory of this particular sentence to see how E. B. White approached the same phenomenon in his afterword to William Strunk's *The Elements of Style*. White suggests to his readers, "If you doubt that style is something of a mystery, try rewriting a familiar sentence and see what happens." The sentence he chooses is Thomas Paine's famous, "These are the times that try men's souls." And the variations he considers are "Times like these try men's souls" or "How trying it is to live in these times!" or "These are trying times for men's souls" and my favorite, "Soulwise, these are trying times." White dryly concludes, "It seems unlikely that Thomas Paine could have made his sentiment stick if he had couched it in any of these forms."

Or to consider these variations in the terms we've been developing in this lecture, while each different form of Thomas Paine's celebrated sentence seems to advance the same underlying propositions, and all could be summarized in pretty much the same way, each sentence hits us differently, and only Paine's version has the power that makes it appeal to our ears and stick in our minds.

Let's take one step further the idea that a written sentence is the surface expression of one or more underlying and unwritten propositions. Let's see how the order in which those underlying propositions are advanced by the written sentence can make a big difference in the way the sentence works. This is an important step for writers to take because once it becomes clear that the order in which propositions appear in a sentence directly affects the way the sentence works, writers can take conscious control of that order to better accomplish their purpose for the sentence.

Consider this sentence: "He drove the car carefully, his shaggy hair whipped by the wind, his eyes hidden behind wraparound mirror shades, his mouth set in a grim smile, a .38 Police Special on the seat beside him, the corpse stuffed in the trunk." I think most of us would agree that the punch of this sentence comes at the end, and that the most significant proposition it advances is that there's a corpse in the trunk. But that's only one of the propositions the sentence advances. Those propositions and the order in which they appear are:

1. He drove the car.
2. He drove carefully.
3. He had shaggy hair.
4. The wind whipped his shaggy hair.
5. His eyes were hidden.
6. Wraparound mirror shades hid them.
7. His mouth was set in a smile.
8. The smile was grim.
9. There was a .38 Police Special.
10. It was on the seat by him.
11. There was a corpse in the trunk.

We could argue about whether "He drove the car carefully" should count as one proposition or as two, or whether a grim smile suggests one proposition or two, or whether the detail that the corpse in the trunk had been stuffed there should add another proposition, but these distinctions don't really matter and shouldn't bother us. The point is that this sentence rests on a bunch of propositions, one of which seems considerably more significant and certainly is more dramatic than are the others. That such a more dramatic proposition is not revealed until the very end of the sentence builds suspense and might almost be thought of as a surprise ending.

If we look at the surface of the sentence, we see that it reveals or unfolds its underlying propositions, however many we choose to count, through six distinct steps or chunks or discrete sequences of words; one clause, "He drove the car carefully," followed by five modifying phrases. "He drove the car carefully" is the base clause, "his shaggy hair whipped by the wind" a modifying phrase, "his eyes hidden behind wraparound mirror shades" another modifying phrase, and "his mouth set in a grim smile, a .38 Police Special on the seat beside him, the corpse stuffed in the trunk." The clause "He drove the car carefully" contains a subject *He* and a verb *drove* and could stand alone as a sentence.

Each modifying phrase contains or suggests a verb form, but not an active verb, and none of the modifying phrases can stand by itself as a sentence, even though each represents one of the propositions underlying the sentence. And because these particular modifying phrases can be moved around and still make sense since all of them modify some aspect of the base clause, we call them free modifiers. Like Legos, free modifiers can be stuck together lots of different ways. For instance, our sentence might be rearranged by moving the base clause deeper, but keeping the modifying phrases in their original order.

> His shaggy hair whipped by the wind, he drove the car carefully, his eyes hidden behind wraparound mirror shades, his mouth set in a grim smile, a .38 Police Special on the seat beside him, the corpse stuffed in the trunk.

Or we can move it deeper still:

> His shaggy hair whipped by the wind, his eyes hidden behind wraparound mirror shades, he drove the car carefully, his mouth set

in a grim smile, a .38 Police Special on the seat beside him, the corpse stuffed in the trunk.

And so on, moving the base clause step by step deeper into the sentence until we finally get to:

His shaggy hair whipped by the wind, his eyes hidden behind wraparound mirror shades, his mouth set in a grim smile, a .38 Police Special on the seat beside him, the corpse stuffed in the trunk, he drove the car carefully.

Or we might switch around the order of the modifying phrases:

He drove the car carefully, his eyes hidden behind wraparound mirror shades, his shaggy hair whipped by the wind, his mouth set in a grim smile, a .38 Police Special on the seat beside him, the corpse stuffed in the trunk.

Or:

He drove the car carefully, the corpse stuffed in the trunk, a .38 Police Special on the seat beside him, his shaggy hair whipped by the wind, his eyes hidden behind wraparound mirror shades, his mouth set in a grim smile.

And so on.

In fact, if I remember the formula for possible combinations of items correctly, and if we think of this base clause plus five modifying phrases as consisting of six items, we could write six factorial or 720 variations on this sentence, representing 720 different orders in which we might arrange its propositions. But let's not try that. While everything I know about prose style tells me that each of those ever so slightly different word orders would ever so slightly change the emphasis and the impact of the sentence, I think I can make the point I hope to make with just two variations.

The first is the sentence we started with:

> He drove the car carefully, his shaggy hair whipped by the wind, his eyes hidden behind wraparound mirror shades, his mouth set in a grim smile, a .38 Police Special on the seat beside him, the corpse stuffed in the trunk.

The second would invert the order of the sentence, placing the final modifying phrase first, and putting the base clause last:

> The corpse stuffed in the trunk, a .38 Police Special on the seat beside him, his mouth set in a grim smile, his eyes hidden behind wraparound mirror shades, his shaggy hair whipped by the wind, he drove the car carefully.

No doubt it's a matter of personal taste, but I enjoy or appreciate that first sentence, where the corpse in the trunk comes as a complete surprise, a lot more than I enjoy or appreciate the second one, where the first thing we learn is that there is a corpse in the trunk, and the last thing we learn is that someone drove carefully. Indeed, I don't think my preference is idiosyncratic since even Professor Strunk suggests, "The proper place in the sentence for the word or group of words that the writer desires to make most prominent is usually the end." Put in the context of whatever sentences might precede our corpse in the trunk sentence, and whatever sentences might follow it, that second version might actually be more appropriate, but I somehow doubt that it would ever be more effective. When a sentence works like a mini-narrative, telling a kind of story that has a surprise ending, I think it will almost always catch a reader's attention and remind the reader of the creative mind that crafted that sentence, and that's one of the functions of style: to remind us of the mind behind the sentences we read. The point I think most important here is not that the end of the sentence is where we should place the word or words we most want to emphasize, but that the power of underlying propositions is not tied to the traditional ways we look at sentences.

Most of us have been taught that the base clause of a sentence, the sentence's subject and predicate, is responsible for advancing its most important proposition, and this is simply not the case. Propositions carry emotional or effective impact that has nothing to do with the grammatical expression or surface structure that advances that proposition in a sentence. It is only when we consider the emotional effect of the way we order and combine the propositions that underlie the sentences we speak or write that we can consider ourselves in control of our writing. Or to locate this phenomenon in the terminology I discussed in the last lecture: The way we give voice to the propositions that underlie the tip of the iceberg we see as a sentence has to do with the sentence's rhetorical functioning much more than with its grammatical description. Perhaps an example from Joseph Conrad's *The Secret Sharer* can suggest the way underlying propositions may actually carry more weight or have a greater impact on the reception of a sentence than does its surface. In an article "Literature as Sentences" published in *College English* in 1966, Richard Ohman chose the noteworthy final sentence from Conrad's celebrated story to make the case that apprehension of a literary work begins with sentences, that sentence structures have a good deal to do with our experience of a literary work, and roughly following Chomsky's lead, that "most sentences directly and obliquely put more linguistic apparatus into operation than is readily apparent." Ohman illustrates his argument with the striking final sentence of *The Secret Sharer*:

> Walking to the taffrail, I was in time to make out, on the very edge of a darkness thrown by a towering black mass like the very gateway of Erebus—yes, I was in time to catch an evanescent glimpse of my white hat left behind to mark the spot where the secret sharer of my cabin and of my thoughts, as though he were my second self, had lowered himself into the water to take his punishment: a free man, a proud swimmer striking out for a new destiny.

We can almost hear the music swell as Conrad's narrator marks the departure of Leggatt, whom the narrator has helped escape formal trial for a murder at sea, having decided that Leggatt's action was justified by an extreme set of circumstances, an early brief for situational ethics. Ohman sees in this sentence a just representation of its author's mind "energetically stretching to subdue a dazzling experience outside the self." Ohman then notes that the base clause of this sentence "I was in time," which is repeated, is expanded by the embedded or supporting propositions "I walked to the taffrail," "I made out," and "I caught," ostensibly focusing our attention on the narrator, who is the subject of those five clauses.

Not so fast, says Ohman, who calls our attention to the fact that no less than seven of the embedded sentences, underlying propositions, have sharer as grammatical subject. In another three, the subject is a noun linked to sharer by the copula, a be verb, and in two, sharer is the direct object, and in two more, share is actually the verb. Thus, as Ohman sees it, 13 propositions go to the semantic emphasis on the secret sharer, even though the surface of the sentence seems to emphasize the narrator's agency. In a fundamental way, Ohman concludes, the sentence is mainly about Leggatt, although the surface structure indicates otherwise. Yet the surface structure does not simply throw a false scent, Ohman quickly notes, since its syntactic focus shifts from *I* in seven underlying propositions to *hat*, also the focus of seven propositions, to finally arrive at sharer. Ohman suggests:

> This progression in the deep structure rather precisely mirrors both the rhetorical movement of the sentence from the narrator to Leggatt via the hat that links them, and the thematic effect of the sentence, which is to transfer Leggatt's experience to the narrator via the narrator's vicarious and actual [experience] in it.

Ohman never claims that this kind of propositional analysis is necessary for us to understand Conrad's style, nor do I want to claim that writers need to be this aware of the propositions underlying their sentences to give those sentences more effective shape. But it is a useful reminder that the surface structure of a sentence may rest on a large number of unwritten propositions, and that the style of a sentence includes the way it invokes, suggests, or assumes some of those propositions, as well as the way it explicitly represents others.

Nor will we always agree on how those underlying propositions affect surface meaning. For example, I look at the same propositional unpacking that Ohman offers for this sentence, and what I notice is that the narrator seems to want to hold onto the idea of the sharer as long as he can, as we frequently do with our most elaborate fantasies. When I teach this story, I focus on the clear evidence that our narrator has an active imagination, and get my students to at least consider how convenient Leggatt is as a kind of imaginary friend at precisely the moment our narrator most needs one. Now I think I'll start using Ohman's analysis as another bit of evidence that might support such a reading. Mainly I offer Ohman's reading of this sentence to call attention one more time to the way written sentences represent the combination of underlying propositions, not all of which are directly apparent in the surface of the sentence. He refers to the propositional underpinning of this sentence as one of "extraordinary density," and density is precisely one of the writing values I will argue for in this course.

In the next lecture, we'll focus on the surprisingly few basic ways in which we can combine propositions in our writing to achieve greater density of the positive kind, highlighted by Ohman. One final note: The sentence about that corpse in the trunk I've discussed at such length—although remember, I did spare you at least some of its 720 variations—represents a kind of loose sentence we call cumulative. The cumulative sentence generally posits a brief base clause—he drove the car carefully—then follows it with free modifying phrases that really carry the sentence's most useful or most informative propositions. I like everything that a cumulative sentence does, from the way it allows us to add detail or information to a base clause, to the way its distinctive rhythm calls attention to the sentence as a thing in motion, making it particularly effective for capturing actions. It's no accident that sportswriters and writers of hardboiled detective stories use cumulative syntax for all its worth.

I think cumulative syntax gives the writer an invaluable and multifaceted tool. For my money, cumulative syntax is the Swiss Army knife of sentence structure, and in subsequent lectures, I'll attempt to show why I think that mastering cumulative syntax is the first and singly most important step we can take toward improving our writing.

How Sentences Grow
Lecture 4

A kernel sentence is one of those multitasking terms we can't seem to avoid when talking about sentence style, a term that can refer to quite different sentences, depending on the situation of their use.

Sentence growth starts with what we'll call a *kernel sentence*, the initial building block to which we will add information. A kernel sentence may consist of a single word—such as General McAuliffe's answer of "Nuts!" to the German demand that he surrender during the Battle of the Bulge. The kernel sentence is simply about as short as it can be, and each proposition we add to it seems to turn the sentence in a new direction. The sentence may take several turns before it becomes clear what it is trying to do.

In yet another situation, the kernel sentence gives us more propositional information and follows the common sentence pattern of providing a subject, a verb, and an object. It is this second sense of the term *kernel sentence* that we will face most frequently as we improve our writing. The kernel sentence serves as an invitation for more propositional content, implying questions about the subject, the verb, or the object; when we answer any of those implicit questions by adding information to the sentence, we will make it more effective.

Another situation exists at the opposite end of the continuum from those irreducibly short kernel sentences. This last situation is most frequently faced by writers who hope to improve their sentences. This is the situation of almost any sentence of almost any length or complexity. This sentence may already advance a number of propositions, but it advances propositions to which we can still add useful detail or clarification. Most of the sentences we write aren't actually that long or that complicated; most can be improved by adding propositions that help explain the sentence or by adding details that clarify information it advances—as long as the additions we make are helpful, logical, and easy to follow. Even a longish sentence can become a kernel sentence if we use it as the starting point for an even longer sentence that advances more propositions.

Kernel sentences can themselves create a writing style. Kernel sentences that simply posit information without detail or explanation offer the most basic form of predication. These sentences state something and then leave it to subsequent sentences to add information, if information is ever to be added. This is macho-speak that bluntly posits information without reflecting upon it or elaborating on it, and we find it exactly where we might expect it, as in the opening to David Morrell's 1972 novel *First Blood*. We refer to these short, simple sentences and simple compound sentences as *predicative* and they are characteristic of the style Walker Gibson calls "tough," a style frequently associated with some of Ernest Hemingway's best-known fiction. This style is effective when creating characters who act, but don't think much about what they do. Needless to say, the highly predicative style is not one I'll be advocating for effective writing—unless you want to write tough-guy narratives. I'm much more concerned with how we move beyond a highly predicative style than I am with offering it as a goal.

Even a longish sentence can become a kernel sentence if we use it as the starting point for an even longer sentence that advances more propositions.

Once we have a kernel sentence—of any length—there are three basic approaches we can take to building it. We can add propositional information simply by using conjunctions or other connective words, like adding boxcars to a train. Sentences we build using this strategy simply add information. We can call this strategy *connective*. We can add propositional information by subordinating some parts of the sentence to other parts. We can call this strategy *subordinative*. We can add propositional information by using modifying words and phrases that turn underlying propositions into modifiers. We can call this strategy *adjectival*. Most of my emphasis in this course will be on learning to use adjectival strategies to write more effectively, but it's important to remember that this strategy is just one of three.

The pioneering poet and style theorist Josephine Miles gave a lot of thought to the way in which we might think of sentences as a series of steps. In her 1967 book *Style and Proportion: The Language of Prose and Poetry*, Miles wrote: "Prose proceeds forward in time by steps less closely measured, but not less propelling, than the steps of verse." Poetry, Miles explains, calls attention to its movement by meter, by line stops, by sentences, by rhyme schemes, and by stanzas, while prose measures its unfolding in ways much less obvious, but no less certain. She offers as an example the following sentence: "Early in the morning, in a small town, near the highway, because he was hungry and though he was in danger, the young boy, looking neither to [the] left nor to [the] right, climbed the path to the city hall."

Analyzing the way the sentence moves forward, Miles notes that "if the qualifiers and connectives in this sentence are transferred back to their root predications, we would read: "The time was early. The time was morning. The place was a town. The town was small. The town was near the highway. The boy was young. The boy was hungry. The boy was in danger. The boy did not look to the left. The boy did not look to the right. The boy climbed the path. The path belonged to the city hall." Miles explains what she's doing by referring to the celebrated sentence from the Port-Royal Grammarians: "Invisible God created the visible world." What results from her unpacking of the propositions is a highly predicative version.

At the other extreme, she shows what might happen if the phrases and clauses were to be reduced to qualifiers, resulting in a highly adjectival style. "Early this morning in a small highway town, hungry and in danger, the young boy, looking neither left nor right, climbed the city-hall path." Miles characterizes the version of this sentence we started with as a mixture of connective and subordinative strategies. Accordingly, she suggests that we can think of prose as having three primary modes of progression—three primary ways in which it takes its steps: the predicative, the connective-subordinative, and the adjectival. I've slightly modified her overview by calling the predicative style the starting point from which we build longer sentences, choosing among and/or mixing three strategies: the connective, the subordinative, or the adjectival. What I want to take away from Miles's approach to sentence style is simply the idea that the sentence unfolds in time by taking steps, and that these steps fall into three categories of added propositional information.

In future lectures, I'll focus on the particular types of steps the cumulative sentence takes, and try to make my case for the advantages it offers the writer. ∎

1. Generate a single-step or kernel sentence, and then generate three more single-step or kernel sentences that add information to your original sentence. That will give you four predicative sentences. Your task is to join these four kernel sentences in as many ways possible within the framework of our broad categories of Connective, Subordinative, and Adjectival modes of progression.

2. Find a cumulative sentence in a story or essay. Treat it as a kernel sentence by adding more modifiers to it.

    Example: Kernel—My shoes are Nikes. Additions—My Nikes are designed for playing tennis. My Nikes have air soles. I like their weight.

    Example: Breakfast is my favorite meal. Additions—I like hot food for breakfast. I prefer eggs and bacon to oatmeal. A good breakfast always starts my day off right.

How Sentences Grow
Lecture 4—Transcript

This is the lecture in which we really get down to the business of seeing how sentences grow, or to be even more precise, how we can grow our sentences. That agricultural metaphor is actually appropriate because sentence growth starts with what we'll call a *kernel sentence*. And here I go again, introducing a term that's a little confusing because we will use it to refer to several different situations, each presenting the sentence in a different way, or to put the case another way, we'll use the term kernel sentence not to refer to the formal characteristics of a sentence such as length or degree of complexity or the number of the propositions the sentence advances. Instead, we'll use this term to refer to different situations in which the kernel is the initial building block to which we will add information.

Confused yet? I am just a little bit, and it's my term. But here's what I mean by different situations in which the kernel sentence is the starting point for building longer and more effective sentences. A kernel sentence may consist of but a single word. Remember General McAuliffe's answer of "Nuts!" to the German demand that he surrender during the Battle of the Bulge? But McAuliffe's single-word reply obviously worked as a sentence, and not just as a noun. I'm not sure whether his message to the Germans was meant to be understood as "You must be nuts to think I'm going to surrender" or "Nuts to you" or something similar, but his celebrated answer reminds us that a kernel sentence can contain only a single word.

We probably shouldn't mess with kernel sentences of the single-word variety, since they almost certainly are most important and most effective precisely because of their dramatic terseness. In a slightly different situation, the kernel sentence is simply about as short as it can be, and each proposition we add to it seems to turn the sentence in a new direction, with it taking several of these turns before it becomes clear what the sentence is trying to do. For example, given the kernel sentence "They slept," almost anything we add to it will make it more satisfying in terms of propositional information. "They slept, having finally found a campsite, sheltered from the freezing rain." "They slept, the man simply collapsing on the bed, the woman first seeing what TV channels were available." "They slept and they dreamed." "They slept, a sleep deeper and more relaxing than they had even dreamed possible, a sleep that was itself undisturbed by dreams." "They, who had never before considered sleep a luxury, slept."

In these cases, the kernel sentence only advances a kernel of information, so what we might add to the sentence can turn it in a number of different directions. Frankly, kernel sentences this short and this stark also probably serve a dramatic function that's more important than adding information might be, but it is good to remember that a sentence so short it can't be made any shorter—They slept—is the most extreme example of a kernel sentence. In yet another situation, the kernel sentence gives us more propositional information and follows the common sentence pattern of providing a subject, a verb, and an object.

For example, "The girl raised the flag." In this case, the kernel sentence provides us with four obvious opportunities to provide more propositional information focused on the entire base clause, "The girl raised the flag"; on its subject, the girl; on its verb, raised; or on its object, flag. Adding to this kernel, we might get "The girl raised the flag because she knew that doing so would inspire her compatriots," or "The girl, who had just realized she was the only survivor, raised the flag," or "The girl raised the flag, triumphantly racing it up to the top of the flagpole," or "The girl raised the flag, its green striped fabric tattered and torn by bullets," or finally, "The girl raised the flag and was proud to see it waving once again over the town square."

In this situation, a kernel sentence provides us with great starting points for elaboration and clarification. It's this second sense of the term kernel sentence we will face most frequently as we improve our writing. Here, the kernel sentence serves as an invitation for more propositional content, implying questions about the subject, the verb, or the object, and when we answer any of those implicit questions by adding information to the sentence, we will make it more effective.

And still another situation exists at the opposite end of the continuum from those irreducibly short kernel sentences, such as "They slept." As a matter of fact, this last main situation is one most frequently faced by writers who hope to improve their sentences. This is the situation of almost any sentence of almost any length or complexity. This sentence may already advance a number of propositions, but it advances propositions to which we can still add useful detail or clarification. The fact is that most of the sentences we write aren't actually that long or that complicated. Most can be improved by adding propositions that help explain the sentence, or by adding details that clarify information it advances. In this sense, a relatively lengthy and complicated sentence should not necessarily discourage us from making it even longer and even more complicated, as long as the additions we make are helpful, logical, and easy to follow.

Consider the sentence: "Cumulative sentences fascinate me with their ability to add information that actually makes the sentence easier to read and more satisfying, flying in the face of the received idea that cutting words rather than adding them is the most effective way to improve writing." This rather complicated sentence of over 40 words becomes a kernel sentence if we use it as the starting point for an even longer sentence that advances even more propositions. Thus, we might build from this kernel sentence the following: "Cumulative sentences, those loose sentences that quickly posit a base clause and then elaborate it by adding modifying words and phrases, fascinate me with their ability to add information that actually makes the sentence easier to read and more satisfying, answering questions as it provides more detail and explanation, flying in the face of the received idea that cutting words rather than adding them is the most effective way to improve writing."

Or we might write: "Cumulative sentences that start with a brief base clause and then start picking up new information, much as a snowball gets larger as it rolls downhill, fascinate me with their ability to add information that actually makes the sentence easier to read and more satisfying because it starts answering questions as quickly as an inquisitive reader might think of them, using each modifying phrase to clarify what has gone before, and to reduce the need for subsequent explanatory sentences, flying in the face of the received idea that cutting words rather than adding them is the most effective way to improve writing, reminding us that while in some cases, less is indeed more, in many cases, more is more, and more is what our writing needs."

I can't prove that either of those extended examples is actually a better sentence than the one we started with, but I would argue that neither is hard to follow and both contain extra propositional information which adds to their effectiveness. But that's neither here nor there. The point is that both of these examples build from a kernel sentence that functions as a kernel by being the starting point for adding propositions. We need the term kernel in this situation only to remind us of the sentence we started with.

Accordingly, depending on the situation, a kernel sentence may be: (1) the shortest possible sentence, possibly consisting of only one or two words, usually a sentence so dependent on its brevity for drama that we don't really want to add to it; (2) a very brief sentence containing a subject and a verb that may need to remain brief for dramatic effect, but that calls for at least some development in subsequent sentences before it makes much sense; (3) a predicative sentence that has a subject, a verb, and possibly an object, but nothing more—this is a sentence that invites development because it leaves so much unsaid; (4) a sentence of any length that we take as a starting point for adding information, for developing the sentence by elaborating on the steps it already takes.

A kernel sentence is one of those multitasking terms we can't seem to avoid when talking about sentence style, a term that can refer to quite different sentences, depending on the situation of their use. Kernel sentences can themselves create a kind of writing style. In fact, we might think of this style as the starting point for all other styles. Kernel sentences that simply posit information without detail or explanation offer the most basic form of predication. These sentences state something and then leave it to subsequent sentences to add information, if indeed information is ever going to be added.

Highly predicative prose isn't long on explanations. It has a kind of take-it-or-leave-it quality. This is macho-speak that bluntly posits information without reflecting upon it or elaborating it, and we find it exactly where we might expect to find it:

> His name was Rambo, and he was just some nothing kid for all anybody knew, standing by the pump of a gas station at the outskirts of Madison, Kentucky. He had a long, heavy beard, and his hair was

hanging down over his ears to his neck, and he had a hand out trying to thumb a ride from a car that was stopped at the pump.

This is how David Morrell began his 1972 novel, *First Blood*, and his famous protagonist shares his narrator's preference for simple declarations. Later in the novel, when Rambo briefly considers surrendering to the authorities who are hunting him, he quickly dismisses the thought:

> Then he would throw down his rifle and hold up his hands and yell that he was surrendering. The idea revolted him. He couldn't let himself merely stand and wait for them. He'd never done it before. It was disgusting.

We refer to these short, simple sentences and simple compound sentences as being predicative, and they are characteristic of the style Walker Gibson calls "tough"—a style frequently associated with some of Ernest Hemingway's best-know fiction. In his 1966 study, "Tough, Sweet, & Stuffy: An Essay on Modern American Prose Styles," Gibson closely examines the celebrated first paragraph of Hemingway's *A Farewell to Arms*:

> In the late summer of that year, we lived in a house in a village that looked across the river and the plain to the mountains. In the bed of the river, there were pebbles and boulders, dry and white in the sun, and the water was clear and swiftly moving and blue in the channels. Troops went by the house and down the road and the dust they raised powdered the leaves of the trees. The trunks of the trees were dusty and the leaves fell early that year and we saw the troops marching along the road and the dust rising and leaves, stirred by the breeze, falling and the soldiers marching and afterward the road bare and white except for the leaves.

Gibson explains this highly predicative style is tough because its speaker, Frederick Henry, Hemingway's protagonist, says only what he could see or directly experience during a limited period of time, linking observations primarily with conjunctions, stating information without processing it. This predicative style is very effective when creating tough-guy characters, men and women who act, but don't think much about what they do. It's a style that Will Strunk would be hard-pressed to criticize, although I doubt he ever wanted any of his students to write exactly this way.

Needless to say, the strongly predicative style is not one I'll be advocating for effective writing, unless you want to write tough-guy narratives. The highly predicative style seems to me to introduce the reader to a mind that is amazingly unreflective, almost anesthetized, or so focused on one purpose that it simply refuses to think about anything else or consider alternate points of view. That mindset is great for Rambo, but I don't think that's the mind we most want to introduce to our readers, unless our goal is to intimidate them. Accordingly, I'm much more concerned with how we move beyond a highly predicative style than I am with offering it as a goal, and the rest of this lecture will focus on the ways in which we can move beyond the tough-guy rhetoric of strong predication.

Once we have a kernel sentence of any length, there are three—and only three—basic approaches we can take to building it: (1) We can add propositional information simply by using conjunctions or other connective words to add to the sentence in much the same way we might add more boxcars to a train; (2) we can add propositional information by subordinating some parts of the sentence to other parts; (3) we can add propositional information by using modifying words and phrases that turn underlying propositions into modifiers.

Our earlier discussion of kernel sentences has already given us examples of these three fundamental strategies. Given that kernel sentence, "The girl raised the flag," we can see an example of the first strategy in the sentence "The girl raised the flag and was proud to see it waving once again over the town square." The conjunction "and" here adds a new proposition, that the girl was proud to see the flag waving once again over the town square, to give us a compound sentence. Similarly, we might use a connective word such as "because" to get a new extended sentence that not only advances the proposition that she raised the flag, but also explains why: "The girl raised the flag because she knew that doing so would inspire her compatriots." Sentences we build using this strategy simply add on information, and we can call our syntactic strategy or move connective.

The second strategy for building a sentence is to add new information, but to make it subordinate to information in the kernel. So given the kernel "The girl raised the flag," we can add the proposition that the girl had just realized she was the only survivor by putting that information in a subordinate relative clause: "The girl, who had just realized she was the only survivor, raised the flag." Similarly, we might have added new information about the flag by putting it in a subordinate relative clause: "The girl raised the flag that had long been a symbol of the resistance movement." When we subordinate information by putting it in clauses introduced by relative pronouns, such as who, which, or that, we create sentences in which we can call our syntactic strategy subordinative.

And the third main strategy for building a sentence is to add new information to it by boiling that information down to a single modifying word or to a modifying phrase. For instance, we can add the proposition that the girl was young simply by writing "The young girl raised the flag." Or we can add information in modifying phrases that follow the base clause: "The girl raised the flag, a triumphant grin on her face, the flag's green striped fabric tattered and torn by bullets, her bravery an inspiration to her compatriots."

When we extend a sentence primarily by adding modifying words and phrases, we adopt a syntactic strategy we might call adjectival. Of course, we can, and usually do, combine two or even all three of these strategies when we build a longer sentence, but it's fascinating to me that there are only three main ways in which we can build more effective sentences, and we term those three main strategies connective, subordinative, and adjectival.

As it happens, most of my emphasis in this course will be on learning to use adjectival strategies to write more effectively, but I think it's very important that adjectival strategies are only one of three main ways in which we can build longer sentences. Let's try to put this notion of three main strategies for lengthening sentences toward an even more useful sense of how sentences work. These three strategies point toward three different ways that a sentence can take a step forward, making new information a part of the way we experience it.

Pioneering poet and style theorist Josephine Miles, the first woman to gain tenure in the English Department at Berkeley, has given a lot of thought to the way in which we might think of sentences as a series of steps, and I am greatly indebted to her for this important insight. In her 1967 book *Style and Proportion: The Language of Prose and Poetry*, Miles herself employed a stunning sentence to introduce us to a new way of thinking about sentences: "Prose proceeds forward in time by steps less closely measured, but not less propelling, than the steps of verse."

She explained:

> While every few feet, verse reverses, repeats, and reassesses the pattern of its progression, prose picks up momentum toward its forward goal in strides variably adapted to its burdens and purposes. Both use steps; neither merely flows; each may be perceived and followed by its own stages of articulation.

Leave it to a poet to literalize the practice of measuring poetic meter in terms of feet, and to remind us that feet take steps. More importantly, Miles reminds us that the language of prose moves forward in time, one word following another, just as surely as does the language of poetry. Poetry calls attention to its movement by meter, by line stops, by sentences, by rhyme schemes, by stanzas, while prose measures its unfolding in ways much less obvious, but no less certain.

She offers as an example the following sentence:

> Early in the morning, in a small town, near the highway, because he was hungry and though he was in danger, the young boy, looking neither to the left, nor to right, climbed the path to the city hall.

Miles marks the steps this sentence takes typographically, putting spaces between its steps.

> Early in the morning, in a small town, near the highway, because he was hungry, and though he was in danger, the young boy, looking, neither to left, nor to right, climbed the path, to the city hall.

61

She then analyzes the way this sentence moves forward. As she says:

> The sentence takes a step: its verb locates itself in time and relation, the boy climbed the path; subject acts upon object, in past tense. The rest of the material of the sentence is additional: specifically linked by the links in, near, because, though, neither, nor, to. The only other terms not so linked are the words of modification, the single adverbs and adjectives early, small, happy, looking, young. First we get one of these, the single word early, then a phrase of time; then two phrases of place; then two contrasting clauses of consequence; then the subject qualified, first by an adjective and then by a participle controlling two disjunctive alternative phrases; finally, the verb and its object, with a qualifying phrase of location. All this variety can be ordered into three parts: the basic section, the predication of subject, the boy climbed the path; the qualifying phrases and clauses, signalized by connectives in, near, because, and so on, and the adjectives that assume rather than predicate.

That description is fairly technical and it is a bit hard to follow, but Miles then translates her analysis into the underlying propositions it describes. By now, this move to unpack unwritten propositions should feel pretty familiar to us. She notes that if the qualifiers and connectives in this sentence are transformed back to their root predications, we would read:

> The time was early.
> The time was morning.
> The place was a town.
> The town was small.
> The town was near a highway.
> The boy was young.
> The boy was hungry.
> The boy was in danger.
> The boy did not look to the left.
> The boy did not look to the right.
> The boy climbed the path.
> The path belonged to the city hall.

Indeed, Miles explains what she's doing by referring to—you've guessed it—that celebrated sentence from the Port Royal Grammarians, "Invisible God created the visible world." What results from her propositional unpacking is, of course, a highly predicative version. At the other extreme, she shows what might happen if the phrases and clauses of this sentence were to be reduced to qualifiers, resulting in a highly adjectival style: "Early this morning in a small highway town, hungry and in danger, the young boy, looking neither left nor right, climbed the city-hall path." Miles characterizes the version of this sentence we started with as a mixture of connective and subordinative strategies.

Accordingly, she suggests that we can think of prose as having three primary modes of progression, three primary ways in which it takes its steps: the predicative, the connective-subordinative, and the adjectival. In other words, these represent different modes of progression for a sentence in which "a defining feature is the delivery of the goods." I've slightly modified Miles's overview by calling the predicative style the starting point from which we build longer sentences, and then stating that there are three main ways in which we can go about that building or growing, choosing among and/or mixing three strategies for adding propositional information, those strategies being the connective, the subordinative, and the adjectival.

Miles starts from her idea that sentences proceed forward in time by taking syntactic steps to develop a very complicated typology of prose styles, described by the proportion of parts of speech in the sentence. Counting the ratio of adjective to noun to verb to connective, she then analyzes larger units of prose from various writers and various periods in history, using her proportional findings to characterize the style of a historical period. However, since our concern is with building better sentences rather than characterizing the typical sentence structure of 17th- or 19th-century English, I mention that only in passing.

What I want to take away from Miles's approach to sentence style is simply the idea that the sentence unfolds in time by taking steps, and that these steps broadly fall into three strategies of adding propositional information. In future lectures, I'll focus on the particular kind of steps the cumulative sentence takes, and try to make my case for the advantages it offers the writer. For now, you might want to experiment with each broad strategy to see how natural or unnatural it feels. By the way, these exercises are in your Guidebook. Generate a single-step or kernel sentence, and then generate three more single-step or kernel sentences that add information to your original sentence. That will give you four predicative sentences. Your task then is to join these four kernel sentences in as many ways as possible within the framework of our broad categories of connective, subordinative, and adjectival modes of progression. Of course, you may also want to consider the possibilities when you create sentences that employ various combinations of these strategies.

The point of such an exercise is simply to focus your attention on the fact that we make sentences longer not just by adding words, but by choosing among these three broad syntactic strategies. Here's an example of how this might go. You start with a kernel sentence, "My shoes are Nikes" and then you add "My Nikes are designed for playing tennis. My Nikes have air soles. I like their weight." Here's another example. You start with a kernel "Breakfast is my favorite meal" and for additions, you add "I like hot food for breakfast. I prefer eggs and bacon to oatmeal. A good breakfast always starts my day off right." You'll probably discover that some of these propositions just don't lend themselves to adjectival combination, but there's almost always a workaround that lets us express a proposition as a modifying phrase, and it's well worth our trouble to find that option since these workarounds soon become familiar to us, and we unconsciously add them to the tools we bring to our writing.

Adjectival Steps

Lecture 5

Sentences so clotted up by bound modifiers with embedded prepositional phrases and relative clauses are really beyond help. These are sentences not even a mother could love, and the only real way to improve them is to start over, trying to figure a relatively short base clause at the heart of each, and then ways of expanding and explaining that base clause with modifying phrases.

This lecture will make the case for choosing adjectival steps to increase the informational efficiency and effectiveness of our sentences. One of the most efficient moves we can make in writing sentences is to boil down subordinate clauses to single modifying words, shifting the sentence from a subordinate to an adjectival pattern. In this way "The boy who was hungry sat down at the table" can be boiled down to "The hungry boy sat down at the table." Generally speaking, the more we can reduce the incidence of subordinate clauses introduced by pronouns such as *who, that,* or *which*, the more we minimize possible confusion or uncertainty about the noun that that pronoun refers to, and in doing this we buy ourselves the opportunity to add useful information to the sentence without as much risk that the sentence will become hard to follow. Not all propositions can be effectively boiled down to single modifying words or short modifying phrases, but many can, and this boiling down process allows us to pack more information into each sentence, much like chefs boil down cooking liquids to create more taste-packed reductions.

An assumption exists that long sentences are bad, but it is usually the case that bad sentences are long. What's usually bad about a long sentence is not its length, but its logic—or lack thereof. There must be over half a million webpages that focus on long sentences in writing, almost all of which share the general view that long sentences are bad. There's even a poem titled "The Very Long Sentence" which rambles on for some 412 words.

Something about long sentences seems to catch our attention, and writers are being warned to avoid them. But that advice doesn't make sense. If stylistic theory doesn't agree on much else, it agrees that sentence length is simply not a very useful index to style. The length of a sentence doesn't take into account the relative complexity or sophistication or even the length of the words that make up that sentence, and vocabulary choices could make a huge difference in the sentence's readability or effectiveness. Moreover, to think in terms of the average length of a sentence is sheer madness. Stylistic theory says that writers should vary the length of their sentences, avoiding long strings of short sentences, just as surely as they might want to avoid long strings of long sentences.

An assumption exists that long sentences are bad, but it is usually the case that bad sentences are long.

Now that I've made several strong claims about sentence length, let me offer a few examples to support those claims. Ask anyone who has read much Hemingway whether his sentences were characteristically long or characteristically short, and the odds are they'll choose short. But consider this sentence from *Death in the Afternoon*:

> Once I remember Gertrude Stein talking of bullfights spoke of her admiration for Joselito and showed me some pictures of him in the ring and of herself and Alice Toklas sitting in the first row of the wooden barreras at the bull ring at Valencia with Joselito and his brother Gallo below, and I had just come from the Near East, where the Greeks broke the legs of their baggage and transport animals and drove and shoved them off the quay into the shallow water when they abandoned the city of Smyrna, and I remember saying that I did not like the bullfights because of the poor horses.

My point is that Hemingway wrote tons of long sentences. It may be precisely those long sentences he wrote that make us remember the short ones. What has given long sentences such a bad rep is not their length, but their over-reliance on bound modifiers rather than on the free modifiers used so effectively by Hemingway.

Lecture 5: Adjectival Steps

Virginia Tufte calls attention to this problem in her study *Artful Sentences: Syntax as Style*, offering examples of sentences that rely too heavily on bound modifiers in prepositional phrases and long noun phrases. As Tufte explains, these sentences are bad "mostly because of what goes into them, not because of how much there is." We can make sentences like these a little easier to read by trying to rethink them as a short sentence followed by modifying information. Rewriting these sentences to get as much of their information into free modifying phrases that follow a relatively simple base clause makes it much more clear when each sentence takes a step forward.

So the first step in writing long sentences is to start from a relatively short and simple base clause and then build the longer sentence around it. The second step is to remember that almost any relative clause can be boiled down to a modifying phrase that, if not shorter, is easier to follow than a series of clauses calling our attention to information tied to *that* or to *who* or to *whom* or to *which*.

The beauty of free modifiers is that they can be placed at the beginning of a sentence or in the middle of a sentence just as well as at its end, the only requirement is that the placement make sense by being close enough to what it modifies so as to preclude confusion. While it is not important that we make our sentences shorter, it is important that we make their constituent elements or steps as short as possible whenever doing so doesn't conflict with some other goal. Generally speaking, turning relative clauses into modifying words and phrases and then stringing these modifiers together around a base clause will allow us to write longer sentences that are more effective, because their length results from detail and explanation that adds propositional content. This satisfies the reader's desire to learn and gratifies the reader's confidence that he or she is in the good hands of a thoughtful writer. ■

1. How many free modifiers can you find in this sentence?

The room was fragrant with the smell of punch, a tumbler of which grateful compound stood upon a small round table, convenient to the hand of Mr. Mould; so deftly mixed that as his eye looked down into the cool transparent drink, another eye, peering brightly from behind the crisp lemon-peel, looked up at him, and twinkled like a star.

—Charles Dickens, *Martin Chuzzlewit.*

2. Find three bound modifiers in this sentence.

For our continued influxes of feeling are modified and directed by our thoughts, which are indeed the representatives of all our past feelings; and, as by contemplating the relation of these general representatives to each other, we discover what is really important to men, so, by the repetition and continuance of this act, our feelings will be connected with important subjects, till at length, if we be originally possessed of much sensibility, such habits of mind will be produced, that, by obeying blindly and mechanically the impulses of those habits, we shall describe objects, and utter sentiments, of such a nature, and in such connexion with each other, that the understanding of the Reader must necessarily be in some degree enlightened, and his affections strengthened and purified.

—William Wordsworth, "Preface to the Lyrical Ballads."

Adjectival Steps

Lecture 5—Transcript

Google "long sentences" and you get some fascinating results. Weed out the websites that refer to long sentences of the prison term, time-behind-bars type, and there must still be over half a million webpages that focus on long sentences in writing, almost all of which share the general view that long sentences are bad. Indeed, many are, but the point these zillions of webpages obscure is that while many long sentences are bad, it's usually the case that bad sentences are long, or to put this another way, what's usually bad about a long sentence is not its length, but their logic or lack thereof. More on this in a moment or two.

One website offers a 630-word example from a document describing the plans of a borough council in the United Kingdom to move a path. To save my life, I couldn't tell you whether they want to move it just a few meters or to the other side of town. Equally unreadable is a 516-word sentence from a legal contract, but this website assures us both of these horrific long sentences are pikers when compared to a sentence from Jonathan Coe's 2001 novel *The Rotters' Club*, which stakes its claim to being the longest sentence in English, coming in at 13,955 words. And then there are those seven or eight humungous sentences that make up Molly Bloom's soliloquy in *Ulysses*, one of which we're told contains 4,491 words. I haven't read *The Rotters' Club*, but I'll guarantee that 13,955-word sentences simply lack punctuation. I have read Molly's soliloquy, and I know that's the case there.

This website claims that Faulkner's *Absalom, Absalom!* contains the longest properly punctuated sentence, a whopper of 1,287 words, and that may well be true, although something tells me that a sentence 1,000 words long has stopped being a sentence and has become something we don't have a word for. It comes as no surprise that this website is the official voice of something called the Plain English Campaign, the crusading lifework of one Chrissie Maher, a spirited 69-year-old community organizer, whose advice to writers is "You should always try to avoid long sentences."

Another webpage devoted to overly long sentences tells us that "A recommended sentence length is anywhere from 17 to 24 words" and assures us that sentences of over 40 words are generally ineffective. There's even a poem titled "The Very Long Sentence," which rambles on for some 412 words. Clearly something about long sentences seems to catch our attention, and it's equally clear that writers are being warned to avoid them, but that advice doesn't make sense if we think about it. In the first place, if stylistic theory doesn't agree on much else, it does agree that sentence length is simply not a very useful index to style. The length of a sentence doesn't take into account the relative complexity or sophistication, or even the length of the words that make up that sentence, and vocabulary choice could make a huge difference in the sentence's readability or effectiveness.

Moreover, to think in terms of the average length of a sentence is sheer madness. Take a monster like the 630-word sentence about moving a path I mentioned earlier. Follow it with an extremely short sentence, such as "Jesus wept"—and Jesus might well have wept had he ever read a 630-word sentence—and you have two sentences that add up to 632 words, for an average sentence length of 316 words. That average might point to something worth knowing about the length of one of those two sentences, but it completely misses the point and effectiveness of the short sentence, "Jesus wept." More important, it misses what stylistic theory says is much more important than sentence length, and that is that writers should vary the length of their sentences, avoiding long strings of short sentences, just as surely as they might want to avoid long strings of long sentences.

And if variety of sentence length is deemed important, and I agree that it is important, don't we need to know how to write effective long sentences so we can throw them in and mix them up with all those short sentences we're being encouraged to go for? So let's just stop thinking about the average length of our sentences and, in particular, let's forget that bit of hoo-ha that says that a sentence of over 40 words is generally ineffective. I don't know who came up with that magic number and I can't begin to imagine how it was arrived at, but I can tell you that this advice is completely arbitrary, way too simplistic, and it actually discourages some of the skills an effective writer needs to develop.

I'm with Ursula K. Le Guin when it comes to the subject of long sentences. Le Guin, herself one of our finest writers, devotes an entire chapter to sentence length and complexity in her fine and wonderfully titled creative writing guidebook *Steering the Craft: Exercises and Discussions on Story Writing for the Lone Navigator or the Mutinous Crew*. In that chapter, which celebrates the glories of long and complicated sentences, Le Guin writes:

> Teachers trying to get school kids to write clearly, and journalists with their weird rules of writing, have filled a lot of heads with the notion that the only good sentence is a short sentence. This is true for convicted criminals.

She goes on to deflate the myth that short-sentence prose is more like the way we speak, and concludes: "To avoid long sentences and the marvelously supple connections of a complex syntax is to deprive your prose of an essential quality."

Now that I've made several strong claims about sentence length, let me offer a few examples to support those claims. Ask anyone who has read much Hemingway whether his sentences were characteristically long or characteristically short, and the odds are they'll choose short. Indeed, Hemingway has become something of the poster child for short sentences. Okay, the image most of us have of grizzled Papa Hemingway doesn't fit the poster child metaphor all that well, but consider this sentence from *Death in the Afternoon*:

> Once I remember Gertrude Stein talking of bullfights spoke of her admiration for Joselito and showed me some pictures of him in the ring and of herself and Alice Toklas sitting in the first row of the wooden barreras at the bull ring at Valencia with Joselito and his brother Gallo below, and I had just come from the Near East, where the Greeks broke the legs of their baggage and transport animals and drove and shoved them off the quay into the shallow water when they abandoned the city of Smyrna, and I remember saying that I did not like the bullfights because of the poor horses.

For any of you who were counting, that's 108 words. And here's another celebrated Hemingway sentence that left that supposed upper limit of 40 words in the rear view mirror.

So far, about morals, I know only that what is moral is what you feel good after and what is immoral is what you feel bad after and judged by these moral standards, which I do not defend, the bullfight is very moral to me because I feel very fine while it is going on and have a feeling of life and death and mortality and immortality, and after it is over I feel very sad but very fine.

Those Hemingway sentences were clearly written under the influence of Gertrude Stein, but here's one that's pure action:

George was coming down in the telemark position, kneeling, one leg forward and bent, the other trailing, his sticks hanging like some insect's thin legs, kicking up puffs of snow, and finally the whole kneeling, trailing figure coming around in a beautiful right curve, crouching, the legs shot forward and back, the body leaning out against the swing, the sticks accenting the curve like points of light, all in a wild cloud of snow.

My point is simply that Hemingway wrote tons of long sentences. It's just that most of them aren't particularly memorable. Indeed, it may be precisely those long sentences he wrote that make us remember the short ones. Similarly, William Faulkner wrote tons of short sentences, but it's the long ones we tend to remember. What matters most in the case of both writers is not the length of their sentences, but the ways in which they made their sentences long. For instance, there's almost a sense of exhilarating speed and ease to that Hemingway sentence about skiing for the simple reason that it relies exclusively on free modifying phrases that seem to race downhill after a short base clause. This great example of cumulative syntax is 74 words long, but I doubt that anyone on hearing it or on reading it would think of this as a long sentence. This is a fast sentence.

What has given long sentences such a bad rep is not their length, but their over-reliance on bound modifiers rather than on the free modifiers used so very effectively by Hemingway. Virginia Tufte calls attention to this problem in her fine study *Artful Sentences: Syntax as Style*. She offers the example of a sentence that relies too heavily on bound modifiers in prepositional phrases and in long noun phrases.

Here we go:

> Neglect of this rich mine of information is due in part to the difficulty one faces in attempting to establish a suitable model in this area for modern quantification techniques that have contributed immeasurably to the formulation of historic generalizations in such areas as economic history and voting patterns.

My eyes glaze over. My ears glaze over. Later, Tufte gives us three more examples of the unfortunate results of relying on bound modifiers to advance the propositional content of a sentence.

Here we go again:

> The control of these fundamental protective systems and the channeling of them into team play and individual effort that possess logic and reason acceptable to the individual's culture represent the mental hygiene of athletic endeavor.

Here's another:

> It is encouraging to note the progress made by beekeeping to meet the challenging times, particularly in connection with the difficult problem of pesticides as they relate to the keeping of bees in the highly cultivated areas where bees are needed for pollination.

And:

> At the time I surveyed a major portion of the work written on gene structure and I was struck by the numerous instances of independent discovery, periods of obscurity, and spurious philosophic attitudes that subsisted underneath the apparently smooth transition of ideas and experimental progress that reviews and text alike tend to produce.

Admittedly, these sentences lack the clear action and time focus of the Hemingway sentence as they advance ideas rather than action, but they make those ideas almost painful to think about. As Tufte explains, these sentences are bad mostly because of what goes into them, not because of how much there is. Part of the problem is that when we try to figure out the base clause at the heart of each, we find that the subject of the sentence is not a single word or two, but a lengthy noun phrase containing numerous propositions. For instance, the subject of that sentence about athletic injuries is the noun phrase "the control of these fundamental protective systems and the channeling of them into team play and individual effort that possess logic and reason acceptable to the individual's culture." This means that of that 35-word sentence—I know it seemed like more, didn't it?—its subject required 28 words. When a subject takes 28 words, what's left for a predicate to do?

Sentences so clotted up by bound modifiers with embedded prepositional phrases and relative clauses are really beyond help. These are sentences not even a mother could love, and the only real way to improve them is to start over, trying to figure a relatively short base clause at the heart of each, and then ways of expanding and explaining that base clause with modifying phrases. Nevertheless, we can make them a little easier to read by trying to rethink them as a short sentence, followed by modifying information.

In this way, we might rewrite that first sentence about athletic injuries. Remember, it read:

The control of these fundamental protective systems and the channeling of them into team play and individual effort that possess logic and reason acceptable to the individual's culture represent the mental hygiene of athletic endeavor.

We might rewrite this:

> This is the mental hygiene of athletic endeavor,
>   controlling these fundamental protective systems,
>   channeling them into team play and individual effort,
>   both possessing logic,
>   both acceptable to the individual's culture.

That sentence about beekeeping, remember it?

It is encouraging to note the progress made by beekeeping to meet the challenging times, particularly in connection with the difficult problem of pesticides as they relate to the keeping of bees in the highly cultivated areas where bees are needed for pollination.

We might rewrite this one to read:

> Beekeeping is making encouraging progress,
> responding to challenging times,
> facing challenges such as the difficult problem of pesticides,
>   the problem being to keep bees in the highly cultivated areas where bees are needed for pollination.

And that sentence about gene structure, remember it?

> At the time, I surveyed a major portion of the work written on gene structure and I was struck by the numerous instances of independent discovery, periods of obscurity, and spurious philosophic attitudes that subsisted underneath the apparently smooth transition of ideas and experimental progress that reviews and texts alike tend to produce.

We could rewrite that one to read:

> When I surveyed a major portion of the work written on gene structure
> I was struck by numerous instances of independent discovery, periods of obscurity, and spurious philosophic attitudes,
>   all subsisting underneath the apparently smooth transition of ideas and experimental progress,
>   a smooth transition that reviews and texts both tended to produce.

I've attempted to typographically represent the fact that rewriting these sentences to get as much of their information as possible into free modifying phrases that follow a relatively simple base clause makes it much more clear when each sentence takes a step forward. These steps are more signs of logical progression than of unfolding actions in a sequence, but they remind us that a sentence can give us a sense of movement, even when it is not describing motion. In fact, that's what was wrong with those original versions—there was no sense of movement. You couldn't tell when the sentence was taking a step. In fact, those original sentences were so cramped up they didn't seem to take any steps at all.

The first step in writing long sentences is to start from a relatively short and simple base clause, and then build the longer sentence around it. Chris Anderson emphasizes this point in his really helpful writing text, *Free Style: A Direct Approach to Writing*. Like me and like Virginia Tufte, Anderson is a fan of cumulative sentences, and puts at the center of his advice for improving writing:

> Say things directly, the subject first and then what the subject is doing. Then trail the modifiers, putting the modifying phrases at the end of the straightforward declarations, expanding and contracting them, adjusting their rhythm as you need to, creating texture, refining with detail.

As that last sentence so effectively illustrates, Anderson practices what he preaches, and his formula for the cumulative sentence, centered on adding free modifying phrases to a short base clause, explains how the cumulative creates both a conceptual pattern and a sound pattern, his sentence doing precisely what it describes. The second step is to remember that almost any relative clause can be boiled down to a modifying phrase that, if not shorter, is easier to follow than a series of clauses calling our attention to information tied to that or to who or to whom or to which.

It may be helpful here to remember that classic Mother Goose poem, "This is the House that Jack Built":

> This is the house that Jack built.
> This is the malt
> That lay in the house that Jack built.
> This is the rat,
> That ate the malt

That lay in the house that Jack built.
This is the cat,
That killed the rat,
That ate the malt
That lay in the house that Jack built.
This is dog
That worried the cat
That killed the rat
That ate the malt
That lay in the house that Jack built.

And so on, until we reach a final verse that could stand as an ode to the relative clause:

This is the farmer sowing his corn,
That kept the cock that crowed in the morn,
That waked the priest all shaven and shorn,
That married the man all tattered and torn,
That kissed the maiden all forlorn,
That milked the cow with the crumpled horn,
That tossed the dog,
That worried the cat,
That killed the rat,
That ate the malt
That lay in the house that Jack built.

I'd love to know whether or not the unknown author of that poem was a frustrated writing teacher, but its cascade of "That" clauses certainly suggests that the author had gotten his or her fill of relative clauses, and so should we. Instead of relying on little clauses that have *who* or *that* or *which* as their subject and that tell us something about the subject, we should boil that relative clause down to a modifying word or phrase. Indeed, the author of "This is the House that Jack Built" starts doing this, whether out of inspiration or desperation, in the poem's final stanza. Instead of "This is the farmer that sows his corn" we get "This is the farmer sowing his corn." Instead of "That waked the priest that was all shaven and shorn" or "The man that was all tattered and torn" or "The maiden that was all forlorn," we get modifiers that omit both the relative pronoun and the verb.

It's important to remember, as Virginia Tufte points out, using a sentence from Charles W. Morton, that relative clauses can kill the movement of a sentence by being too long, just as surely as they can by being too numerous. Tufte offers the example:

> I still count the little preamble that begins as the houselights go down and the footlights glow and goes on to accompany the slow rise of the curtain on the opening scene of *Carmen* as the most cunningly contrived passage of descriptive music I have ever heard.

It seems that there are a number of ways in which relative clauses can go amiss, and their main claim to utility is that they seem committed to specification. While specification is generally a fine goal in writing, we should remember that the rhetoric of specification is the rhetoric of the law and of legal documents. In her 1971 book *Grammar as Style: Exercises in Creativity*, Virginia Tufte challenged writers to use free modifiers to craft a sentence from the raw material of the six following propositions:

> He went to speak to Mrs. Bean.
> She was tiny among the pillows.
> Her small toothless mouth was open like an O.
> Her skin was stretched thin and white over her bones.
> Her huge eye sockets and eyes were in a fixed infant-like stare.
> And her sparse white hair was short and straggling over her brow.

If those propositions sound unusually specific to you, it's because Tufte had extracted them from a sentence in *Momento Mori* by Muriel Spark. The sentence reads:

> He went to speak to Mrs. Bean, tiny among the pillows, her small toothless mouth open like an "O," her skin stretched thin and white over her bones, her huge eye sockets and eyes in a fixed, infant-like stare, and her sparse white hair short and straggling over her brow.

Tufte, probably our most accomplished current student of sentence structure, is a big fan of adding propositions to sentences by adding free modifying words and phrases following a short base clause, noting again and again in her writing how this technique allows us to write sentences that can grow to considerable length without becoming hard to follow or unpleasant to the ear.

So, to sum up, if we have a number of propositions concerning a boy who sits down at a table, we can reduce all, or at least most, of those propositions to modifiers, and probably improve our writing if we do so. If we want to work with these propositions:

> The boy sat down at the table.
> The boy was young.
> The boy was out of breath from running.
> He sat down quickly.
> He sat down dramatically.
> He plopped into his chair.
> The table was covered with steaming dishes of food.
> The table was made of heavy oak.
> The boy looked around the room.

We might be tempted to write something semi-barbarous, along the lines of:

> The boy, who was young and who was out of breath from running, sat down at the table, whose heavy oak surface was covered with dishes of food that were steaming, plopping into his chair in a way that was quick and dramatic, and then looked around the room.

That's not a terrible sentence, but a much better one would be:

> Out of breath from running, plopping into his chair quickly, dramatically, the young boy sat down at the table, its heavy oak surface covered by steaming dishes of food, only then looking around the room.

You'll notice that I've fudged the recommended form just a bit, placing several modifiers before the base clause but, as I'll explain in a subsequent lecture, the beauty of free modifiers is that they can be placed at the beginning of a sentence or in the middle of a sentence just as well as at its end, the only requirement being that the placement make sense by being close enough to what it modifies as to preclude confusion. Not all propositions can be effectively boiled down to single modifying words or short modifying phrases, but many can, and this boiling down process allows us to pack more information into each sentence, much like chefs boil down cooking liquids to create more taste-packed reductions.

So while it is not important that we make our sentences shorter, it is important that we make their constituent elements or steps as short as possible, whenever doing so doesn't conflict with some other goal. For example, there may be very good reasons for not boiling down "The man, who had always believed that violence was not a solution to any problem, clenched his fists and headed back into the bar." And we might not want to boil this down to "The pacifist clenched his fists and headed back into the bar." Somehow reducing the noun phrase "The man who had always believed that violence was not a solution to any problem" to the single word "pacifist" just doesn't seem to do justice to the drama of the situation of this sentence.

Generally speaking, however, turning relative clauses into modifying words and phrases, and then stringing those modifiers together around a base clause, will allow us to write longer sentences that are more effective because their length results from detail and explanation that add propositional content, both satisfying the reader's desire to learn, and gratifying the reader's confidence that he or she is in the good hands of a thoughtful writer. Years ago, there was an advertising jingle—I think for some brand of cigarettes—that went, "It's not how long you make it, but how you make it long." At the risk of reminding us how this jingle was almost immediately re-appropriated by wags as sex advice, I want to suggest that we remember it when we construct longer sentences. The way to make our sentences longer is with free modifiers, and the resulting cumulative syntax has a number of other advantages for the writer, advantages I'll describe in upcoming lectures.

The Rhythm of Cumulative Syntax
Lecture 6

Work with cumulative sentences and soon their rhythms become seductive, urging us to keep adding modifying phrases, their very sound reminding us of the limitless detail and explanation we can add to each sentence we write.

The cumulative syntax, first codified and best explained by Francis Christensen, adds information to an initial base clause in unbound or free modifying phrases, all of which point back to, expand, and add to information presented in the base clause. The cumulative sentence is a form of a loose sentence, as opposed to periodic sentences that delay completion of their meaning until the end of the sentence. Cumulative sentences are easy to write, a process of adding modifying phrases to the base clause of the sentence, each phrase adding to our understanding or sharpening our visualization of the preceding phrase or of the base clause, taking us through increasingly specific sentence levels, each level another step for the sentence. Cumulative sentences lend themselves to numerous writing moves that almost guarantee our writing will become more effective, and subsequent lectures will explore a number of those moves. This is not to say that cumulative sentences are better than other sentences, nor is it to claim that what they accomplish can only be accomplished by this syntax, but it is to claim that the cumulative syntax gives us a kind of Swiss Army knife for our writing, a multipurpose tool that can be useful in a wide range of situations.

I've been peppering the preceding lectures with references to cumulative sentences and with examples of what they can do. If I haven't managed to establish the form these sentences take, I have managed to alert your ears to their characteristic rhythms. The examples we've seen contain rhythms within rhythms, setting up parallels and repetitions, balancing sound against sound, the product not of conscious choice so much as it is the natural benefit of the cumulative syntax, itself a rhythm so powerful that it encourages us to find other rhythms within it. After a while you can almost hear these rhythms coming, knowing that a free modifying phrase starting with a participle, usually an -*ing* form of a verb, might come next, or an adverb such as a -*ly* word, or a phrase started with a possessive pronoun—*his, her,* or *its,* or a phrase that backtracks, picking up and repeating a word from the base clause before adding new information. In this way, we get cumulative rhythms such as: The chef prepared the fish, carefully, stuffing it with wild rice, sautéing it briefly, its sweet aroma blending smoothly with the other enticing odors in the kitchen, the fish becoming more than a food item, ascending to the status of art.

That we now know so much about cumulative syntax is a tribute to the pioneering work of Francis Christensen, an English professor at the University of Southern California, who in the 1960s stopped repeating received truths about what made for good writing and actually started looking at the way professional writers wrote. Much of his influence can be traced back to a single essay, "A Generative Rhetoric of the Sentence," first published in *College Composition and Communication* in 1962, and then republished in Christensen's collection of essays *Notes Toward a New Rhetoric: 6 Essays for Teachers* in 1967. What so distinguished Christensen's approach to teaching writing was first the belief that writing should really matter and second, that writing improves most obviously and most quickly when we add information to our sentences in free modifiers following or surrounding a base clause. Christensen saw sentences as a means to a crucial end more important than clarity or effectiveness. His second, or more instrumental, belief was that traditional writing instruction had missed the point by advocating the subordinate clause and the complex sentence, and that "we should concentrate instead on the sentence modifiers, or free modifiers." Equally important to his approach to teaching writing was his concern with its sound; he noted that "the rhythm of good modern prose comes about equally from the multiple-tracking of coordinate constructions and the downshifting and backtracking of free modifiers."

Christensen seems to have found inspiration for his approach to the cumulative sentence in a little-known essay by novelist and educator John Erskine. In 1946 Erskine had contributed an essay, "The Craft of Writing,"

What makes me such a fan of the cumulative syntax is that this goal can be achieved so easily.

to a collection of essays titled *Twentieth Century English*, edited by William S. Knickerbocker. Neither Erskine's essay nor the collection in which it appeared is remembered much today, but in his essay Erskine struck a note that served as the foundation for Christenson's theory of the cumulative sentence. Erskine noted that while grammar concedes that "speech is a process of addition," grammar then confuses things by making it seem that the substantive (i.e., nouns), since it can stand alone, is more important than the adjective; that the verb is more important than the adverb; that the main clause is more important than the subordinate. Erskine maintained that the modifiers were "the essential part of any sentence," and explained, "In practice, therefore, the sentence proceeds from something the reader may be expected to know already toward that ever new thing we wish to tell him. We proceed by addition."

From Erskine's observation about the importance of adding information through the use of modifiers, Christensen developed four principles for understanding and developing cumulative sentences. The first principle is that composition is essentially a process of addition. The second principle is that the information we add to sentences in modifying phrases gives the sentence a direction of modification or a direction of movement. This principle of direction of modification has sometimes been suggested by others who use the term *left-branching sentence* to describe modification that comes to the left of or before the main clause, or *right-branching sentence* to describe modification that comes to the right or after the main clause. In the left-branching sentence, the movement of modification is forward; in the right-branching sentence the movement of modification is backward.

The third principle is that cumulative sentences tend to develop by downshifting through increasingly detailed or specific levels of generality or levels of abstraction. Christensen's fourth principle is that cumulative sentences add texture to the propositional content of a sentence. Greater texture or density of information is one of the most important keys to better writing. The plain style that has been the goal of so much writing instruction is a style that devalues texture in favor of simplicity.

And there you have it—a generative rhetoric of the cumulative sentence based on just four principles: addition, movement, levels of generality, and texture. Consider the cumulative syntax in the terms of the steps suggested by Josephine Miles, and we get the idea of a sentence that takes a new step with each new modifying phrase we add, that adds a new level or degree of specificity with each of these steps. What makes me such a fan of the cumulative syntax is that this goal can be achieved so easily, just by practicing the basic moves of the cumulative sentence until we internalize its rhythms and start to produce them without thinking. In the next two or three lectures. I'll be focusing specifically on those rhythms. ■

Questions to Consider

1. "The end is to enhance life—to give the self (the soul) body by wedding it to the world, to give the world life by wedding it to the self. Or, more simply, to teach to see, for that, as Conrad maintained, is everything."

—Francis Christensen.

How might writing better help a person to see better? Or, to put it another way, which comes first: seeing as a writer, or writing?

2. Write a cumulative sentence that adds increasing specificity of detail to the subject or to the verb of the base clause, or to the base clause itself, with free modifiers, and has a surprise ending.

The Rhythm of Cumulative Syntax
Lecture 6—Transcript

Finally! This is the lecture I've been waiting for, the one where I get to introduce the structure of cumulative sentences, the syntax at the very heart of my approach to teaching writing. Of course, it's misleading to say that I'm about to introduce you to the cumulative syntax since I've been peppering the preceding lectures with references to cumulatives and with examples of what they can do. If I haven't yet managed to clearly establish the form these sentences take, I bet I have managed to alert your ears to their characteristic rhythms. Just listen to a few of the cumulative sentences I've used in previous lectures:

> George was coming down in the telemark position, kneeling, one leg forward and bent, the other trailing, his sticks hanging like some insect's thin legs, kicking up puffs of snow, and finally the whole kneeling, trailing figure coming around in a beautiful right curve, crouching, the legs shot forward and back, the body leaning out against the swing, the sticks accenting the curve like points of light, all in a wild cloud of snow.

> He went to speak to Mrs. Bean, tiny among the pillows, her small toothless mouth open like an "O," her skin stretched thin and white over her bones, her huge eye sockets and eyes in a fixed infant-like stare, and her sparse white hair short and straggling over her brow.

> Out of breath from running, plopping into his chair quickly, dramatically, the young boy sat down at the table, its heavy oak surface covered by steaming dishes of food, only then looking around the room.

> They slept, the man simply collapsing on the bed, the woman first seeing what TV channels were available.

> He drove the car carefully, his shaggy hair whipped by the wind, his eyes hidden behind wraparound mirror shades, his mouth set in

a grim smile, a .38 Police Special on the seat beside him, the corpse stuffed in the trunk.

Here are a couple of new ones from Faulkner's "Barn Burning":

> Again he could not see, whirling; there was a face in a red haze, moonlike, bigger than the full moon, the owner of it half again his size, he leaping in the red haze toward the face, feeling no blow, feeling no shock when his head struck the earth, scrabbling up and leaping again, feeling no blow this time either and tasting no blood, scrabbling up to see the other boy in full flight and himself already leaping into pursuit as his father's hand jerked him back, the harsh, cold voice speaking above him: "Go get in the wagon."

Or another one from Faulkner:

> His father struck him with the flat of his hand on the side of the head, hard but without heat, exactly as he had struck the two mules at the store, exactly as he would strike either of them with any stick in order to kill a horse fly, his voice still without heat or anger.

And here are a couple of sentences from Don DeLillo, starting with a great description of a laugh:

> He crossed his arms on his midsection, bent against the wall, laughing. It was a staccato laugh, building on itself, broadening in the end to a breathless gasp, the laughter that marks a pause in the progress of the world, the laughter we hear once in 20 years.

And then a DeLillo description of wind:

> Some nights the wind never stops, beginning in a clean shrill pitch that broadens and deepens to a careless and suspenseful force, rattling shutters, knocking things off balconies, creating a pause in one's mind, a waiting-for-the-full-force-to-hit.

I love the sound of these sentences. I love the stop-and-go rhythms they set up with each syntactic step they take, moving us forward, preparing our ears for what will come next, just as they add to our knowledge of what came before. And the examples I've just read contain rhythms within rhythms, setting up parallels and repetitions, balancing sound against sound, the product, not of conscious choice so much as it is the natural benefit of the cumulative syntax, itself a rhythm so powerful that it encourages us to find other rhythms within it.

After a while, you can almost hear these rhythms coming, knowing that a free modifying phrase starting with a participle, usually an -*ing* form of a verb, might come next, or an adverb, such as a -*ly* word, or a phrase started with a possessive pronoun, *his* or *her* or *its*, or a phrase that backtracks, picking up and repeating a word from the base clause before adding new information.

In this way, we get cumulative rhythms such as:

> The chef prepared the fish, carefully, stuffing it with wild rice, sautéing it briefly, its sweet aroma blending smoothly with the other enticing odors in the kitchen, the fish becoming more than a food item, ascending to the status of art.

Work with cumulative sentences and soon their rhythms become seductive, urging us to keep adding modifying phrases, their very sound reminding us of the limitless detail and explanation we can add to each sentence we write. That we now know so much about the cumulative syntax is a tribute to the pioneering work of Francis Christensen, an English professor at USC who, in the 1960s, stopped repeating received truths about what made for good writing, and actually started looking at the way professional writers wrote. Christensen, who died in 1970, was an incredibly influential rhetorician, and his impact on the teaching of writing has been profound.

Much of his influence can be traced back to a single essay, "A Generative Rhetoric of the Sentence," first published in *College Composition and Communication* back in 1963, and then republished in Christensen's collection of essays *Notes Toward a New Rhetoric: 6 Essays for Teachers* published in 1967. What so distinguished Christensen's approach to teaching writing was first, the belief that writing should really matter, and second, that writing improves most obviously and most quickly when we add information to our sentences in free modifiers, following or surrounding a base clause.

When I say that Christensen thought that writing really mattered, I mean that he saw sentences as means to a crucial end, much more important than clarity or effectiveness. As he put it:

> The end is to enhance life—to give the self (the soul) body by wedding it to the world, to give the world life by wedding it to the self. Or, more simply, to teach to see, for that, as Conrad maintained, is everything.

His second, and more instrumental, belief was that traditional writing instruction had missed the point by advocating the subordinate clause and the complex sentence, and that "we should concentrate instead on the sentence modifiers, or free modifiers."

And equally important to his approach to teaching writing was his concern with sound. As he noted:

> … the rhythm of good modern prose comes about equally from the multiple-tracking of coordinate constructions and the downshifting and backtracking of free modifiers.

What a great description, "downshifting and backtracking of free modifiers." If you'll think back to those cumulative sentences I read just a moment ago, you can hear that their rhythm is indeed one of downshifting and backtracking. The free modifiers point back to the base clause and shift down to a greater level of detail or specificity. They backtrack by picking up and expanding on some aspect of the base clause, giving the sentence, as Christensen points out, "a flowing and ebbing movement, advancing to a new position and then pausing to consolidate it, leaping and lingering as the popular ballad does."

Christensen seems to have found inspiration for his approach to the cumulative sentence in a little-known essay by the novelist and educator John Erskine. A longtime professor of literature at Columbia, Erskine had been largely responsible for the development of Columbia's signature humanities course, a great books course that has been the model for many general education literature courses across the country. In 1946, Erskine had contributed an essay, "The Craft of Writing," to a collection of essays titled *Twentieth Century English*, edited by William S. Knickerbocker. Neither Erskine's essay nor the collection in which it appeared is remembered much today, but in his essay Erskine struck a note that served as the foundation for Christensen's theory of the cumulative sentence.

Almost as a throwaway observation, Erskine wrote:

> Let me suggest here one principle of the writer's craft, which though known to practitioners I have never seen discussed in print. The principle is this: When you write, you make a point not by subtracting as though you sharpened a pencil, but by adding. When you put one word after another, your statement should be more precise the more you add. If the result is otherwise, you have added the wrong thing, or you have added more than was needed.

Erskine then noted that while grammar loosely concedes that "speech is a process of addition," it then confuses things by making it seem that the substantive (nouns), since it can stand alone, is more important than the adjective; that the verb is more important than the adverb; that the main clause is more important than the subordinate. Not so, wrote Erskine:

> What you wish to say is found not in the noun but in what you add to qualify the noun. The noun is only a grappling iron to hitch your mind to the reader's. The noun by itself adds nothing to the reader's information; it is the name of something he knows already, and if he does not know it, you cannot do business with him. The noun, the verb, and the main clause serve merely as a base on which meaning will rise. The modifier is the essential part of any sentence ... In practice, therefore, the sentence proceeds from something the reader may be expected to know already toward whatever new thing we wish to tell him. We proceed by addition.

In a wonderfully sly swipe at those writing gurus who put all their weight behind omitting all modifiers and confining ourselves to nouns, pronouns, and verbs, Erskine notes that "The best tombstone and monumental descriptions follow this style, but here it should be noted the intention is to commemorate, to remind, rather than to say anything new." From Erskine's observation about the importance of adding information through the use of modifiers, Christensen developed four principles for understanding and writing cumulative sentences, and he emphasized that these principles were intended as a heuristic, as a prompt to the writer to inspire more effective writing, rather than as rules for writing that was simply utilitarian and error-free. In this way, he saw his approach to the cumulative sentence as a generative rhetoric, a means of spurring on and producing better sentences.

His first principle is that composition is essentially a process of addition. To a base clause, such as "They turned on the radio," we add information, such as "ceaselessly turning the dial back and forth, trying to find a clear station, hoping for some news of the election."

The second principle is that the information we add to sentences in modifying phrases gives the sentence a direction of modification or a direction of movement. As Christensen explains:

> The main clause, which may or may not have a sentence modifier before it, advances the discussion, but the additions move backward, as in this clause, to modify the statement of the main clause or more often, to explicate or exemplify it so that the sentence has a flowing and ebbing movement, advancing to a new position and then pausing to consolidate it, leaping and lingering as the popular ballad does.

This principle of direction of modification has sometimes been suggested by others who use the term *left-branching sentence* to describe modification that comes to the left of or before the main clause, or *right-branching sentence* to describe modification that comes to the right of or after the main clause. In the left-branching sentence, the movement of modification is forward. In the right-branching sentence, it is backward. The cumulative sentence makes good use of both movements, but the cumulative sentences Christensen focuses the most attention on have modifiers that generally point or move backward.

As he puts it:

> The additions stay with the same idea, probing its bearings and implications, exemplifying it or seeking an analogy or metaphor for it, or reducing it to details. Thus the mere form of the sentence generates ideas. It serves the needs of both the writer and the reader, the writer by compelling him to examine his thought, the reader by letting him into the writer's thought.

I'd put this a bit differently, noting that the cumulative form urges the writer to give more information to the reader, and it suggests to the reader that the writer is doing her or his best to make things as clear and as satisfying as possible. This is the syntax that sends the signal that the writer is doing her or his level best to communicate fully and effectively, trying harder than other writers.

The third principle is that cumulative sentences tend to develop by downshifting through increasingly detailed or specific levels of generality or levels of abstraction. Several lectures ago, I noted that every word in a sentence is chosen from an imaginary vertical or paradigmatic axis, along which each word is more precise than a number of alternate choices above it on the ladder of abstraction, and less precise than choices below it. Cumulative sentences tend to extend this principle to the entire sentence, usually modifying the base clause with a phrase that gives it more precision, and then frequently downshifting once again to a second-level modifying phrase that adds precision to the first one.

As Christensen explains this:

> With the main clause stated, the forward movement of the sentence stops, the writer shifts down to a lower level of generality or abstraction or to singular terms, and goes back over the same ground at this lower level.

We can see how this principle operates in a sentence where the base clause introduces a compound subject, and subsequent modifying clauses break it down into its constituent parts, as in:

> They sat down, the young man cautiously, as if he might decide not to sit at all; the young woman hurriedly, as if this were something she wanted to finish as quickly as possible.

Or we can see it in a sentence in which each new layer—remember that each new layer or modifying phrase can be thought of as a step the sentence takes—refines the information of the preceding step:

> This room looks like a disaster area, its walls pocked with holes, holes that suggest the room had been the site of a violent fight, a fight in which sledgehammers had been the weapons of choice.

Or using a rough form of diagramming to indicate sentence levels, with the base clause always the first level, we might write:

(1) Cumulative sentences can take any number of forms,

   (2) detailing both frozen or static scenes and moving processes,

   (2) their insistent rhythm always asking for another modifying phrase,

      (3) allowing us to achieve ever-greater degrees of specificity and precision,

         (4) a process of focusing the sentence in much the same way a movie camera can focus and refocus on a scene,

            (5) zooming in for a close-up to reveal almost microscopic detail,

            (5) panning back to offer a wide-angle panorama,

(5) offering new angles or perspectives from which to examine a scene or consider an idea.

Christensen's fourth principle is that cumulative sentences add texture to the propositional content of a sentence. You may remember that one of the key assumptions underlying this course is my belief that greater texture or density of information is one of the most important keys to better writing. The plain style that has been the goal of so much writing instruction is a style that devalues texture in favor of simplicity.

Christensen notes:

> The writing of most of our students is thin—even threadbare. But if he adds frequently or much or both [to his nouns, verbs and main clauses], the texture may be said to be dense or rich. One of the marks of an effective style, especially in narrative, is variety in the texture, the texture varying with the change in pace, the variation in texture producing the change in pace ... In our classes, we have to work for greater density and variety in texture and greater concreteness and particularity in what is added.

The cumulative sentence encourages us to do exactly this, and pretty much without stopping to think about what we need to do. Christensen points to a striking example of this kind of texture in a magnificent sentence by Loren Eiseley that warns of unbridled atomic power, developing that warning through six memorable levels of generality, producing a sentence that unfolds in 11 distinct steps:

(1) It is with the coming of man that a vast hole seems to open in nature,

(2) a vast black whirlpool spinning faster and faster,

(3) consuming flesh, stones, soil, minerals,

(3) sucking down the lightning,

(3) wrenching power from the atom,

(4) until the ancient sounds of nature are drowned out in the cacophony of something which is no longer nature,

(5) something instead which is loose and knocking at the world's heart,

(5) something demonic and no longer planned—

(6) escaped it may be—

(6) spewed out of nature,

(6) contending in a final giant's game against its master.

And there you have it, a generative rhetoric of the cumulative sentence, based on just four principles: addition, movement, levels of generality, and texture. Consider the cumulative syntax in the terms of the steps suggested by Josephine Miles, and we get the idea of a sentence that takes a new step with each modifying phrase we add, that adds a new level or degree of specificity or clarity with each of these steps. Consequently, we can start thinking about improving the effectiveness of our sentences just by adding a single new modifying level, by making our sentences more effective still with each new modifying level we add beyond that.

Christensen said of his own teaching:

> I try in narrative sentences to push to level after level, not just two or three, but four, five, or six, even more as far as the students' powers of observation will take them. I want them to become sentence acrobats, to dazzle by their syntactic dexterity.

I couldn't agree more. What a great goal for writers, "to become sentence acrobats, to dazzle by their syntactic dexterity." And what makes me such a fan of the cumulative syntax is that this goal can be achieved so easily, just by practicing the basic moves of the cumulative sentence until we internalize its rhythms and start to produce them without thinking. In the next two or three lectures, I'll be focusing specifically on those rhythms, on the basic moves we can make with cumulatives. For now, I just want to leave you with their sound, with how easy this syntax makes it for us to add information to our sentences, to make them longer, but to make them more satisfying as we do so.

The following examples are sentences composed by students over the years, and they are sentences of which any writer should be proud:

(1) They sat down at the table,

   (2) he resignedly slumping into the straight-backed chair,

      (3) his tired face a picture of dejection,

      (3) his hands shaking uncontrollably,

   (2) she stiffly taking her seat with exaggerated formality,

      (3) her eyes cold and hard and locked on his,

      (3) her thin lipped smile at once triumphant and condescending,

   (2) the table piled high with stock reports and financial statements,

      (3) its surface completely covered with documents of desperation,

      (3) its jumble of information now completely useless,

   (2) the overall scene suggesting an abandoned battleground.

Here's another:

   Monique went down the stairs, walking on tip-toe, trying to keep her weight evenly distributed, trying not to touch the walls, muttering, "Vector forces," breathing in sharply every time she heard a noise, hoping desperately that the building was not going to collapse.

And another:

> He stepped up to home plate, the chalk lines barely visible, wiping the sweat from his face, taking one last deep breath of the crisp autumn air, a look of determination in his eyes, the crowd rhythmically chanting his name, knowing that he represented the last ray of hope for his team.

Another one:

> We navigated Nashville's back roads, hooping ourselves horse up and over the hills, feeling our weight alternately light and heavy on our seats, leaning right and left as the roads forked, wondering if we would ever escape the shade of the trees, laughing at the clock, longing for the North Star.

Or:

> A lamp was burning on the table, flickering slightly, casting a dim light on the shabby room, leaving the corners dark, providing no comfort to the lonesome inhabitant of the shelter, promising him nothing.

> She called him, picking up the phone, hoping he would be home, scared of what he would say, praying that they would work things out, wishing he'd call her first, trying to get a grip on her emotions.

And here's an even cooler thing about cumulatives: they build upon each other, setting up an insistent rhythm among, as well as within, sentences. Here are just a couple of examples of what I refer to as cumulative clumps, several cumulative sentences in a row that feed on each other, build on each other. I asked my students to use some of these cumulative clumps to write about crying, and here's some of what I got:

> I forced the knife through the onion, exposing its flesh, releasing a distinct aroma into my hallway of a kitchen; seconds later, my eyeballs began to burn, tiny fires blazing each time I blinked, a

watery film coating the insides of my eyelids, my vision blurred, causing me to blindly put down the knife, leaving me no option, other than to stumble to the freezer and stick my entire head inside, remembering the onion remedy I once saw in a magazine.

Here's another:

The little girl is standing in the aisle, hands on hips, foot tapping, bottom lip twitching up and down with her brow scrunched together, her small arms wrapping themselves as far around the doll still in the box as possible, slowly, one by one, tiny tears roll out of the corners of her eyes, bright blue eyes, staring up at her father; the tears start out quiet, almost silent, quickly turning into a foot-stomping tantrum, doll on the ground, arms smacking the sides of her thighs, ponytail flopping as her head rocks back and forth, the tears, having stopped somewhere in the middle, have turned to an all-encompassing fit of rage.

And finally:

The old man waited for the music to begin, gazing over the crowd, his eyes meeting none of theirs, shifting his weight from hip to hip; with the first notes of the procession reverberating off the high ceiling, he took the first steps down the long aisle, the crowd now standing, faces turning, smiling eyes meeting, poring into one another, a sensation of weightlessness growing in his stomach, engulfing his chest, clutching his throat, inhaling only short, stilted huffs as though anticipating a sneeze, procuring a handkerchief, he dabbed the perspiration from his forehead and the tears from the tip of his nose, walking with his granddaughter, the bride-to-be.

The writers of these sentences have learned some of the seductive secrets of cumulative syntax, and now you know too.

Direction of Modification
Lecture 7

In this and subsequent lectures, I'll continue to try to point out the many reasons why I think cumulative syntax is the greatest thing since sliced bread, and the surest way for writers to immediately improve the effectiveness of their sentences.

While the cumulative form celebrated by Francis Christensen focused on modifying phrases added at the end of base clauses, cumulative sentences can also employ modifying words and phrases before the base clause or in the middle of the base clause. Each placement changes the meaning of the sentence and changes the way the sentence works. In this way, the cumulative modifying phrases may open, close, or appear in the middle of the sentence. For example, given *boy* as the object of modification and *crying loudly* as the modifying phrase, we might construct a sentence with that phrase in the initial slot (Crying loudly, the boy left.), the final slot (The boy left, crying loudly.), or the medial slot (The boy, crying loudly, left). This lecture will explore the rhetorical implications of each of these placement options.

In the last lecture I outlined what I believe are the broad advantages of cumulative syntax:

- Focusing on the clarity of logical relations this syntax establishes among parts of sentences.

- Focusing on the ebb-and-flow rhythms it promotes, almost guaranteeing that cumulative syntax will appeal to the ear.

- Perhaps most importantly, I showed how the cumulative syntax functions heuristically, prompting writers to make sentences more satisfying and effective by adding detail and explanation in free modifying phrases.

- Each new modifying phrase answers a question that a reader might have about the preceding clause or phrase.

I will need to review some grammar to help us distinguish cumulative sentences from those that are not cumulative. A cumulative sentence gets its name from the fact that it accumulates information, gathering new details as it goes. A cumulative sentence has two main parts: The first part, the base clause, contains the sentence's main subject and main verb. The second part of a cumulative sentence consists of one or more modifying phrases. Unlike a clause, a phrase does not contain a subject and a verb, and can't stand alone as a sentence. Most modifying phrases can be classified as participial phrases, gerund phrases, infinitive phrases, or prepositional phrases. Cumulative sentences frequently contain participial phrases or prepositional phrases that contain participles.

Unlike a clause, a phrase does not contain a subject and a verb, and can't stand alone as a sentence.

The crucial point here is that these contain verbals and not active or passive verbs. We might think of verbals as "verbs lite," or as verbs drained of their power to make anything happen. A phrase may contain a verb form—a participle—that actually works like a modifying adjective or adverb, to modify nouns or pronouns. Modifying phrases may add information about the subject or the verb of the main clause (or the object, if it contains an object), or they may simply add to our understanding of the entire clause. The distinction between a clause and a phrase is crucial to understanding the cumulative sentence; students trying to write cumulatives for the first time often produce comma splices.

The cumulative sentence might be thought of as a major kind of adjectival sentence (to use the term suggested by Josephine Miles). The main feature of this sentence pattern is that it packages modifiers as unbound words or phrases—in ways that usually allow them to appear in the sentences in different positions, rather than bound to the words they modify. Modifying phrases may open, close, or appear in the middle of the sentence. Some writing scholars, such as Virginia Tufte, describe the positioning of modifying phrases as left-branching (before the base clause) or right-branching (after the base clause). I prefer to use Francis Christensen's original terms: *initial, medial,* or *final.* Free modifiers are free to be moved around, and they are also free to be mixed and matched.

Cumulative sentences featuring modifying phrases in the initial or medial positions carry a couple of risks. Initial modifying phrases run the risk of being misplaced modifiers, when the modifying phrase doesn't match up with what it tells about. The classic example is "Having eaten lunch, the bus left the station." The problem is that the modifying phrase doesn't really have a logical object of modification in the base clause: People eat lunch; buses don't. The sentence fails to provide logical agents who could be modified by the phrase "having eaten lunch." To call this modifier misplaced suggests that the sentence can be corrected by moving the modifying phrase to the correct place in the sentence, but no such place exists. The problem with this sentence is not placement of the modifying phrase, but that there's nothing for that phrase to modify.

To clean this sentence up, we would need to add a word or phrase to the base clause that would provide an object of modification—or that might provide something that the modifying phrase can answer a question about—in this case, "Who ate lunch?" So-called misplaced modifiers can occur anywhere in the sentence, but for some reason I don't understand, starting a sentence with an initial modifying phrase seems to lead writers to make this mistake. So whenever you begin a sentence with a modifying phrase, be sure that the base clause contains a word or words that the phrase can logically modify, and if possible, put it as close to the start of the base clause as possible.

There's also a risk we need to be aware of when we put modifying phrases in the medial position, between the subject of the base clause and its verb. If it's only a single modifying word or phrase, there's no problem, but if we start dumping modifying phrases in the middle of a base clause, we risk making the sentence hard to follow or transforming it into a suspensive sentence. When this happens, the sentence may be cumulative in a grammatical sense, but loses many of the sound and sense advantages of cumulative syntax.

The cumulative sentence is most typical and probably appears most frequently with the modifying phrase or phrases in the final position, since the whole idea behind the cumulative sentence is that it quickly posits a somewhat stark or kernel-like base clause (subject and verb, or subject, verb, object), then presents much more information about that base clause in subsequent modifying phrases. Accordingly, to give any sentence more of a cumulative form, simply replace its period with a comma and start adding modifying phrases. ■

Each of the following cumulative sentences is not quite as good as it could be. Some aren't even cumulative. For others, either the logic of the modifying scheme isn't completely clear, or the overlap with the preceding level isn't as insistent as it might be, or something just doesn't sound right when you read the sentence aloud. Figure out a way to improve each sentence by maximizing its cumulative potential.

1. The woman sang with a pitch that rang true and fire in her heart.

2. I caught a fish, hating the thought of eating it, she hated eating it too.

3. We caught the bus to go to the zoo on Sunday, shouting for the driver to stop, the driver with a look of annoyance.

4. He scrubbed the linoleum floor, his pants rolled up to his knees, a sombrero on his head, one his great uncle bestowed on him before running off with the circus.

5. The man looked at his wife, disappointed in her once again, the fifth time this month, at least the hundredth time this year.

Direction of Modification
Lecture 7—Transcript

In the last lecture, I outlined what I believe are the broad advantages of cumulative syntax, focusing both on the clarity of logical relations this syntax establishes among parts of sentences, and on the ebb-and-flow rhythms it promotes, almost guaranteeing that cumulative prose will appeal to the ear. Perhaps most importantly, I showed how the cumulative syntax functions heuristically, prompting writers to make sentences more satisfying and effective by adding detail and explanation in free modifying phrases.

The cumulative is, as Francis Christensen suggested, a generative syntax in the sense that it encourages writers to add information to their sentences, relying on free modifying phrases after the base clause, each new phrase a step forward for the sentence, each new phrase sharpening the sentence by adding new details or offering clarification or explanation for propositions advanced in the base clause or preceding modifying phrase.

One useful way of thinking of this feature of the cumulative is to see each new modifying phrase as answering a question that a reader might have about the preceding clause or phrase. Thus, if we start with a base clause "He was afraid," we might well expect a reader to wonder who he is, and why he might be afraid. Both questions are anticipated and answered by adding free modifying phrases that would give us the sentence, "He was afraid, a little boy separated from his mother in a large department store, fearing that he would never find her, feeling lost and abandoned in a world of strange and scary faces." My assumption here is that most of us start thinking about our sentences with fairly simple subject-verb-base clauses or kernel sentences that might not be as stark as "He was afraid," but are very rarely as developed as "He was afraid, a little boy separated from his mother in a large department store, fearing that he would never find her, feeling lost and abandoned in a world of strange and scary faces."

In this and subsequent lectures, I'll continue to try to point out the many reasons why I think cumulative syntax is the greatest thing since sliced bread, and the surest way for writers to immediately improve the effectiveness of their sentences. But first, we need to backtrack just a bit and be sure we understand the technical aspects of cumulative syntax. I'm going to try to keep grammatical descriptions to a minimum here, but I will need to review some grammar to help us distinguish cumulative sentences from those that are not cumulative. So for the next few minutes, you may feel like you're back in a 9th- or 10th-grade English class, but odds are that 9th- or 10th-grade English class was never this useful. I know mine weren't, and I deeply regret that I was not introduced to the cumulative sentence until I was in grad school.

So here goes: A cumulative sentence gets its name from the fact that it accumulates information, gathering new details as it goes, like a snowball that gets bigger and bigger and bigger as you roll it through snow. To write a cumulative sentence, all you have to do is turn the period at the end of one of your sentences into a comma, and start adding modifiers. As you add modifying details, you will bring your writing into focus, making your point sharper and sharper, your meaning more and more clear.

A cumulative sentence has two main parts. The first part is called the base clause. A base clause contains the sentence's main subject and main verb. A base clause can be thought of as a short, boiled-down sentence. For example, "The boy fainted." The verb in a base clause is called a finite verb. Verbs express an action or state of being. State-of-being verbs are also called linking verbs. An action verb expresses something that can be done. A linking verb points to more information. That is, it must be followed by another word that completes its information. True linking verbs include all forms of state-of-being verbs, and state-of-being verbs include all the forms of the verb *be*. These are heavily used in our writing, as in "He is," "I am," "We are," "It was," "They were," "It has been," "We might have been," "I will become," "It seems," and so on.

You'll notice that none of the above combinations of a subject and a linking verb offer any really useful information. That's because each linking verb needs a verb complement that explains the specific nature of a particular state of being; thus, "He is hungry," "I am eating," "We are singing," "It has been educational," "I seem to have lost my billfold" and so on. Forms of state-of-being verbs are almost always linking verbs, although very rarely they can function independently, signaling being as existence, as in, "I think, therefore I am."

But we also have a group of verbs that can function either as linking verbs, needing a complement to complete their meaning, or that can function independently as action verbs. The context of the sentence, the way they function in the sentence, will determine whether they are action or linking verbs. There are too many of these multitasking verbs to list, but the category includes such verbs as *appear*, which can be used interchangeably with the linking verb *seem* or *feel*, which can be used in many cases that we might use the linking verb *am*: "I am sick" or "I feel sick" and so on.

A number of verbs in this category are very close to linking verbs in meaning. For example, verbs such as *remain* or *continue* clearly can refer to states of being, but can function independently as action verbs, as in "The building remains" or "The drama continues." Action verbs also can be subdivided into those that need an object to complete their meaning, and those that do not. If the verb requires or even if it just can be used with a direct object, we call it a transitive verb. If the verb cannot take a direct object, we call it an intransitive verb.

Here are some examples: The boy fainted: action verb, intransitive. The boy is tired: linking verb. The boy kicked the ball: action verb, transitive.

There are almost an infinite number of both kinds of verbs, and many verbs can function either intransitively, as in "He eats" or "He is eating," or transitively, as in "He eats lasagna" or "He is eating lunch." So much for the base clause.

The second part of a cumulative sentence consists of one or more modifying phrases. Unlike a clause, a phrase does not contain a subject and a verb, and it cannot stand alone as a sentence. Here are some examples of phrases: his face turning white, a goofy looking sixth-grader, muscles turning to jelly. Most modifying phrases can be classified as participial phrases, gerund phrases, infinitive phrases, or prepositional phrases.

Participial phrases are particularly important for cumulative sentences, and we'll consider them more fully in just a moment. To start with, however, going back to those four categories of phrases, participial phrases contain a verb that has been turned into an adjective. For example:

The boy fainted, exhausted by his long run.
The boy fainted, fainting as if he had been shot.
The boy fainted, slumping to the ground.
The boy fainted, stricken with grief.
The boy fainted, lost for the rest of the race.
The boy fainted, his face turning a sickly white.

Now, for the second kind of phrase: Gerund phrases are somewhat similar to participial phrases, with the difference that they contain a verb that's been turned into a noun: "Eating ice cream too fast makes my forehead hurt," "Eating ice cream too fast is what I always try to avoid," and "His eating ice cream proved to be his undoing." In much the same way that a participle is a verb drained of power, a gerund is a verb with -*ing* added to turn it into a noun, using it as we use a noun to name a person, place, or thing. Just as a noun functions, a gerund can be the subject of a sentence, the direct object of the verb in a sentence, a subject complement, or the object of a preposition.

Here are some examples. First of all, gerund as subject: "Cheating might become a habit." Now, gerund as direct object: "They do not understand my cheating." Gerund as subject complement: "My biggest problem is cheating." Gerund as object of a preposition: "The coach chewed him out for cheating." Gerunds can serve in cumulative modifying phrases as appositives, substitutes for previous nouns or pronouns, and they can serve in combination with participles, as in "Fainting having become something of a problem for troops in formation, the general tried to finish his inspection as quickly as possible."

Now, infinitive phrases: "The boy wanted to faint." "Fainting is the problem to be overcome." "To faint or not to faint was the question." Infinitives function much like gerunds and frequently appear in cumulative modifying levels, accompanied by a participle: "Thinking he needed to find a job, the ex-super hero started scouring the want ads."

And finally, prepositional phrases: "The boy fainted after finishing the race." "The boy fainted as his shocked parents watched." "The boy fainted in front of his parents." "The boy fainted with no warning." Common prepositions that begin prepositional phrases are *across, after, as, at, because of, before, between, by, for, from, in, in front of, in regard to, like, near, of, on, over, through, to, together with, under, until, up,* and *with.* The crucial point here is that all four kinds of phrases can appear as steps in cumulative sentences, but it is crucial that these phrases contain verbals and not active or passive verbs. We might think of verbals as verbs lite, or as verbs drained of their power to make anything happen, serving only to modify something.

Back to participial phrases: Since participles are in effect adjectives made from verbs, participial phrases function in a sentence in all the ways an adjective might function, primarily modifying nouns or pronouns. Participles that refer to ongoing actions or processes are called present participles. Participles that refer to past or completed actions or processes are called past participles. Present participles end in *-ing.* Past participles can take more forms, but generally are verbs that can function as verbals in their forms, ending in *-d, -ed, -en, -t* or *-n,* as in the words confused, marked, eaten, recovered, dealt, and written. Here are some examples: "The boy slumped to the floor, dropping his books." Dropping is a present participle. "The boy slumped to the floor, scared witless by what he saw." Scared is a past participle. "The boy slumped to the floor, driven past his physical limits." That's another past participle.

Modifying phrases may add information about the subject or the verb of the base clause or the object, if it contains an object, or they may simply add to our understanding of the entire base clause. For example, "The boy kicked the ball, hitting it squarely with the toe of his soccer shoe." Another example: "The boy kicked the ball, a tattered and worn old football." "The boy kicked the ball, grim determination clear in his every move." "The boy kicked the ball, his friends yelling their encouragement."

Base clause plus modifying phrases makes a cumulative sentence, and we get as a result something like:

> The boy fainted, a goofy-looking sixth-grader, his face turning white, muscles turning to jelly, dropping his books, uttering a kind of pained squeak, scared witless by what he saw.

This cumulative sentence packs a lot of information. Indeed, when we unpack its underlying propositions, we see that it does the work of at least seven different sentences:

1. The boy fainted.
2. The boy was a goofy-looking sixth-grader.
3. When he fainted, the boy's face turned white.
4. When he fainted, the boy's muscles turned to jelly.
5. When he fainted, the boy dropped his books.
6. When he fainted, the boy uttered a kind of pained squeak.
7. The boy fainted because he was scared witless by what he saw.

Because the cumulative sentence does pack so much detail and because it is easy to follow, professional writers use it very frequently. In fact, it has been estimated that professional writers put their modifiers at the end of their sentences two-thirds of the time.

That was a basic description of cumulative syntax. I've actually used that description to try to explain the cumulative to students in a junior high class—without much success, I have to admit—but I also use it in my prose style class at Iowa, frequently discovering that my English majors have never been taught the difference between a clause and a phrase. That distinction is crucial, since students trying to write cumulatives for the first time often produce comma splices, following the base clause with a comma, but then adding another base clause rather than a modifying phrase. Thus, instead of getting the cumulative sentence "The boy fainted, his face turning white" we get something like "The boy fainted, his face turned white," which is called a comma splice because a comma is simply not a strong enough mark of punctuation to join together two base clauses.

The crucial difference between these two sentences is that the cumulative sentence follows the subject and verb of the base clause, with a verbal in a modifying phrase. Let's stay with the example I started with, "The boy fainted, his face turning white." The difference between "his face turned white" and "his face turning white" becomes pretty clear when we remember that "his face turned white" could stand alone as a sentence in its own right, a sure sign that it is a clause, while "his face turning white" cannot stand alone as a sentence, a sure sign that it is a phrase.

Let's try to think about the technical aspects of the cumulative sentence in somewhat more sophisticated terms. As I noted in the last lecture, the philosophy of the cumulative sentence was codified by Francis Christensen in his "A Generative Rhetoric of the Sentence," first published in *College Composition and Communication* in October 1963. Christensen credited novelist John Erskine with inspiring this philosophy in a 1946 essay published in *Twentieth Century English*. That essay, entitled "A Note on the Writer's Craft," directly challenged the simple and direct school of composition that stressed the paring down of writing, and championed modification instead. As I noted in the last lecture, Erskine took the unique tack of arguing, "When you write, you make a point not by subtracting as though you sharpened a pencil, but by adding." And this insight led him to his radical conclusion that "The modifier is the essential part of any sentence."

With its emphasis on modifying phrases, the cumulative sentence might be thought of as a major kind of adjectival sentence, to use the term suggested by Josephine Miles. The main feature of this sentence pattern is that it packages modifiers as unbound words or phrases—that is, in ways that will usually allow them to appear in the sentence in different positions, rather than bound to the word or words they modify. In this way, the cumulative modifying phrase may open, close, or appear in the middle of the sentence. For example, given "boy" as the object of modification and "crying loudly" as the modifying phrase, we might construct a sentence with that phrase in the initial slot, "Crying loudly, the boy left;" the final slot, "The boy left, crying loudly;" or the medial slot, "The boy, crying loudly, left."

As I previously noted, some writing scholars, such as Virginia Tufte, describe the positioning of modifying phrases as left-branching or right-branching. If the modifying phrase comes before the base clause or to the left of it on the page, it's called a left-branching sentence. If the modifying phrase comes after the base clause or to the right of it on the page, it is called a right-branching sentence, and if the modifying phrase comes in the middle of the base clause, it is called mid-branching. But what's important here is not the terminology, but that a free modifying phrase can be placed in each of these three positions. That's the point of calling them free modifiers—they are free to be moved around.

And they are free to be mixed and matched, since we can write cumulative sentences that feature modifying phrases in all three positions at once. For example, "Having cleared customs, the elegantly dressed old man, a gleeful smile on his face, hailed a cab, instructing its driver to take him to the nearest casino."

It is important to note, however, that cumulative sentences featuring modifying phrases in the initial or medial positions carry a couple of risks. Initial modifying phrases run the risk of becoming misplaced modifiers.

We have a misplaced modifier—sometimes called a dangling modifier or a dangling participle—when the modifying phrase doesn't match up with what it tells about. I bet more than a few of us remember the classic example of a misplaced modifier: "Having eaten lunch, the bus left the station." Obviously the bus did not eat lunch, but that's what this sentence suggests. The problem is that the modifying phrase doesn't really have a logical object of modification in the base clause. People eat lunch. Buses don't. More specifically, the people who were riding on the bus ate lunch, but the base clause, "The bus left the station," doesn't mention people, doesn't mention bus riders, doesn't mention anyone who could conceivably eat anything.

What this sentence fails to do is to provide logical agents who could be modified by the phrase "having eaten lunch." In other words, the base clause lacks any clue as to who did the eating. Once we figure out that the sentence fails to provide a logical object of modification for the modifying phrase, we realize that the term that is usually applied to this mistake—misplaced modifier—is itself not really correct. Misplaced suggests that the sentence can be corrected simply by moving the modifying phrase to the correct or logical place in the sentence, but no such place exists. "The bus left the station, having eaten lunch" doesn't make a bit more sense, nor does "The bus, having eaten lunch, left the station." The problem with this sentence is not placement of the modifying phrase, but that there's nothing for that phrase to modify.

To clean this sentence up, we would need to add a word or phrase to the base clause that would provide an object of modification, or in the terms I've suggested, that might provide something that the modifying phrase can answer a question about; in this case, who ate lunch? Consequently, a satisfying and logical cumulative sentence might read, "After the passengers ate lunch, the bus left the station."

Remember, a misplaced or dangling modifier is a word or phrase that modifies a word not clearly stated in the sentence. These modifiers aren't actually misplaced. They need something to modify. Frequently, a misplaced modifier modifies an agent, someone doing something, but that agent is not specified in the sentence. For example, "After running the race so well, fainting was a disappointment." Cumulative sentences are all about specificity, and both the agents responsible for action in a cumulative sentence and the objects of action must be clearly identified. We need to know who it was that fainted.

"Having forgetfully left his backpack in the restaurant, his absentmindedness caused his friends to make fun of him." Or, "Having forgetfully left his backpack in the restaurant, the hapless freshman invited the ridicule of his friends." In the first sentence, there's no clear indication of whom or what is performing the action expressed in the participial phrase "Having forgetfully left his backpack in the restaurant." "Having forgetfully left" can't logically modify "his" or "his absentmindedness" or his forgetfulness or anything else, and since there is no clearly specified object for "Having forgetfully left his backpack" to modify, we call this a misplaced modifier or a dangling modifier. We might think of dangling modifiers as a participial phrase that's all dressed up with no place to go, since there's nothing specifically present in the sentence for it to point to.

So-called misplaced modifiers can occur anywhere in the sentence, but for some reason I don't understand, starting a sentence with an initial modifying phrase or left-branching sentences seems to particularly lead writers to make this mistake. So whenever you begin a sentence with a modifying phrase, be sure that the base clause contains a word or words that phrase can logically modify and, if possible, put that object of modification as close to the start of the base clause as possible.

And there's also a risk we need to be aware of when we put modifying phrases in the medial position, usually interposing them between the subject of the base clause and its verb. If we only separate subject from verb by a single modifying word or phrase, there's no problem. However, if we start dumping modifying phrases in the middle of a base clause, we run the risk of either making the sentence hard to follow, or of transforming it into a suspensive sentence, where delaying its completion becomes the dominant aspect, sacrificing the strong sense of cumulative movement for a sense that the sentence is putting off whatever may be at its end, either to build suspense or to add maximum emphasis to its final word. Here's an example of what can happen:

> The bus, an ancient yellow relic, a vehicle so old and undependable that even our strapped-for-cash school district would no longer use it, a monument to questionable design in its beginnings, and of poor maintenance near the end of its service, left the station.

There's nothing really wrong with that sentence, and it is grammatically cumulative, but its cumulative modifying phrases add motion with no movement, its rhythm somehow stuck, and the reason for using cumulative form not at all clear.

To sum up, the cumulative sentence is most typical and probably appears most frequently when the modifying phrase or phrases appear in the final position, since the whole idea behind the cumulative sentence is that it quickly posits a somewhat stark or kernel-like base clause—subject and verb, subject, verb, object—then presents much more information about that base clause in subsequent modifying phrases. For example:

> They drank their coffees, the old man downing his in one quick gulp, spilling several drops on his faded shirt, the finely dressed young woman nursing hers along quite slowly, carefully raising and lowering the cup to her lips as if it contained nitroglycerine rather than coffee, a stiffly mechanical process that suggested her nervousness more than her control.

We've seen that cumulative modifying phrases can start a sentence, can interrupt a base clause by coming between the subject and the verb, or can follow the base clause. And of course, there's no reason why a single cumulative sentence can't use modifying phrases in all three positions. And remember, to give any sentence more of a cumulative form, simply replace its period with a comma and start adding modifying phrases. Just like that, you're on your way.

Coordinate, Subordinate, and Mixed Patterns
Lecture 8

In coordinate patterns, all modifying phrases refer back to the base clause. In subordinate patterns, each modifying phrase refers to the immediately preceding clause or phrase, and we can mix these two patterns by adding subordinate levels to coordinate patterns, or coordinate levels to subordinate patterns, with one or the other pattern predominating.

This lecture will explain and discuss the rhetorical implications of the options available when we want to add more than one cumulative modifying phrase to a base clause. Cumulative phrases can be strung together, each new phrase adding or clarifying information about the base clause or about the immediately preceding modifying phrase. When we employ more than a single modifying phrase in a cumulative sentence, we can choose to combine them in patterns that are coordinate, subordinate, or mixed. In coordinate patterns, all modifying phrases refer to the base clause. In subordinate patterns, each modifying phrase refers to the preceding clause or phrase. And we can mix these two patterns by adding subordinate levels to coordinate patterns or coordinate levels to subordinate patterns, with one or the other pattern predominating.

Subordinate levels move the focus of the sentence forward, moving from general to specific, zooming in like a movie camera.

We've seen that cumulative sentences can be described in terms of whether their free modifying phrases come at the beginning of the sentence—before the base clause—in the initial or left-branching position, in the medial position between the subject and verb of the base clause, at the end of the sentence—after the base clause—in the final or right-branching position, or some combination of the three positions. It may help to think of this aspect of cumulative form as being syntagmatic, a term we've previously applied to the way in which a sentence unfolds its meaning horizontally, to the eye of the reader, from left to right. There is also what can be called a *paradigmatic* or *vertical aspect* of cumulative sentences. This aspect is conceptual or logical, rather than visual, as it focuses on the discursive relationship between and among cumulative free modifying phrases, irrespective of their placement. Or, to put this another way, the syntagmatic aspect or characteristic of cumulative sentences is strictly *formal*, determined by where a modifying phrase is placed, while the paradigmatic aspect is strictly *functional*, determined by what each modifying phrase does.

Each cumulative modifying phrase means that the sentence takes another step, but we need to realize that each step has two aspects or dimensions or purposes. Each step moves the sentence toward the period at its end, but each step also adds a new level of detail or explanation. Consider the sentence: "Having sold all of her boxes of cookies, the elated Girl Scout went home." In syntagmatic terms, we would describe this cumulative sentence as having its modifying phrase ("Having sold all of her boxes of cookies") in the initial or left-branching position. In *paradigmatic* terms, we would describe this cumulative level as having two *levels*, the first being the base clause, the second being its single modifying phrase.

Cumulative syntax also makes possible two other patterns of logical relationships among base clauses and modifying phrases. The three paradigmatic patterns of the cumulative sentence are called *coordinate, subordinate*, and *mixed*. In coordinate patterns, as you'll remember from the previous example, all modifying phrases refer to the base clause.

(1)   The elated Girl Scout went home,
    (2)   having sold all of her boxes of cookies,
    (2)   having knocked on every door in her neighborhood,
    (2)   so excited she could barely explain her success to her mother,
    (2)   so proud of her accomplishment she immediately wanted to get more cookies to sell.

In subordinate patterns, each modifying phrase refers to the preceding clause or phrase.

> (1) The elated Girl Scout went home,
>   (2) having sold all of her boxes of cookies,
>   (3) those inescapable icons of capitalism,
>   (4) its methods and assumptions hardwiring our children to value the power of selling in almost their every activity,
>   (5) methods and assumptions championed by some and resisted by others.

We can mix these two patterns by adding subordinate levels to coordinate patterns or coordinate levels toff subordinate patterns, with one or the other predominating.

> (1) The elated Girl Scout went home
>   (2) so excited she could barely explain her success to her mother,
>   (2) having sold all of her boxes of cookies,
>   (3) those inescapable icons of capitalism,
>   (3) those irresistible sugar bombs,
>   (2) having knocked on every door in her neighborhood,
>   (3) recognizing some who came to their doors as friends of her parents,
>   (3) remembering some houses where she had gotten particularly wonderful Halloween treats,
>   (4) figuring both categories of potential buyers would find it hard to say no to a cute little girl participating in one of America's best-established cultural rituals.

Coordinate levels can be thought of as modifying the entire base clause, or as focusing on one of its elements. Subordinate levels move the focus of the sentence forward, moving from general to specific, zooming in like a movie camera.

The main appeal and power of coordinate cumulative construction come from its distinctive rhythm and the very simple logical relations among the steps the sentence takes. It tends to be repetitive, both in sound and in sense. All the new information added by each coordinate level adds detail, helps explain the base clause, but never moves it forward. And yet, a coordinate sentence whose modifying phrases follow a sequence can seem to move, indeed can display what I think is the most seductive prose rhythm of cumulative form.

The main appeal of subordinate cumulative construction comes from its ability to advance the sentence into new territory, making it particularly effective when used to describe a process or to follow something that unfolds in time. Pure subordinate cumulative sentences, particularly those that develop through more than three levels, are difficult to find because the circumstances that call for such a pure construction are as rare as they are hard to imagine. Accordingly, most subordinate cumulative sentences are really just dominantly subordinate.

The main appeal of mixed cumulative construction is that it combines the strength of both the coordinate and subordinate forms, allowing the sentence to move forward in time and open up new ideas, while maintaining intensity and focus.

In this lecture I've tried to show how the steps cumulative sentences take—each modifying phrase a new step—fall into three main categories. We've looked at coordinate cumulative sentences where all the modifying phrases point back to the base clause, and any one of which makes sense if moved just before or just after the base clause. These coordinate cumulatives can be thought of as two-level sentences, with all of their second-level modifying phrases pointing back to the first level of the base clause. We've seen subordinate cumulative sentences where the modifying phrases are pretty much locked in place below or after the level of the sentence they modify, with modifying phrases after the second level each taking the phrase before it to a new level of information or explanation. And we've seen mixed cumulative sentences, where some modifying phrases follow the mixed pattern and follow the subordinate pattern.

Understanding the way each of these three cumulative patterns works makes it easier for us to write extended cumulative sentences. Understanding the concept of sentence levels can be very important, immediately giving writers reachable goals for improving their own writing. It may be a bit of an oversimplification, but generally speaking, one mark of inexperienced or ineffective writing is that it relies heavily on sentences of only one or two levels. Just adding one new level of information to our sentences means that our sentences will contain more information, more detail, and a better explanation. ■

Questions to Consider

1. Diagram this sentence, indicating levels of coordination and subordination:

He comes into a room with one of these documents in his hand, with the air of a schoolmaster and a quack doctor mixed, asks very kindly how you do, and on hearing you are still in an indifferent state of health owing to bad digestion, instantly turns round and observes that "All that will be remedied in his plan; that indeed he thinks too much attention has been paid to the mind, and not enough to the body; that in his system, which he has now perfected and which will shortly be generally adopted, he has provided effectually for both; that he has been long of opinion that the mind depends altogether on the physical organisation, and where the latter is neglected or disordered the former must languish and want its due vigour; that exercise is therefore a part of his system, with full liberty to develop every faculty of mind and body; that two Objections had been made to his *New View of Society*, viz. its want of relaxation from labour, and its want of variety; but the first of these, the too great restraint, he trusted he had already answered, for where the powers of mind and body were freely exercised and brought out, surely liberty must be allowed to exist in the highest degree; and as to the second, the monotony which would be produced by a regular and general plan of co-operation, he conceived he had proved in his *New View* and *Addresses to the Higher Classes,* that the co-operation he had recommended was necessarily conducive to the most extensive improvement of the ideas and faculties, and where this was the case there must be the greatest possible variety instead of a want of it.

—William Hazlitt, "On People with One Idea."

2. Write a subordinate cumulative sentence, in which there is a base clause and three modifying phrases, and in which each modifying phrase modifies something in the phrase that preceded it.

Coordinate, Subordinate, and Mixed Patterns
Lecture 8—Transcript

We've seen that cumulative sentences can be described in terms of whether their free modifying phrases come at the beginning of the sentence, before the base clause, in the initial or left-branching position; in the medial position between the subject and the verb of the base clause; at the end of the sentence, after the base clause, in the final or right-branching position; or in some combination of these three positions. It may help to think of this aspect of cumulative form as being syntagmatic, a term we've previously applied to the way in which a sentence unfolds its meaning horizontally to the eye of the reader, from the left of the page to the right.

There's also what can be called a paradigmatic or vertical aspect of cumulative sentences. This aspect is conceptual or logical, rather than visual, as it focuses on the discursive relationship between and among cumulative free modifying phrases, irrespective of their placement. Or, to put this another way, the syntagmatic aspect or characteristic of cumulative sentences is strictly formal, determined by where a modifying phrase is placed, while the paradigmatic aspect is strictly functional, determined by what each modifying phrase does.

I realize this may sound both a little confusing and unnecessarily technical, but it really does help us understand how to build cumulative sentences if we understand these two important aspects. Each cumulative modifying phrase means that the sentence takes another step, but we need to realize that each step itself has two aspects or dimensions or purposes. Each step moves the sentence toward the period at the sentence's end, but each step also adds a new level of detail or explanation. I think an example can really help here.

Consider the sentence: "Having sold all of her boxes of cookies, the elated Girl Scout went home." In syntagmatic terms, we would describe this cumulative sentence as having its modifying phrase, "Having sold all of her boxes of cookies," in the initial or left-branching position. In paradigmatic terms, we would describe this cumulative sentence as having two levels, the first being the base clause, the second being its single modifying phrase "Having sold all of her boxes of cookies." Each level of a cumulative sentence adds to its information, making the sentence both more specific and more intellectually satisfying—so far, so good. I'm pretty sure the previous example helps us understand the difference between the syntagmatic and the paradigmatic aspects of cumulative sentences.

But now we need to look at another example that may complicate things again. Consider a more extended or elaborated version of our Girl Scout cookie sentence. Instead of just having one modifying phrase, "Having sold all of her boxes of cookies, the elated Girl Scout went home," let's give our reader more information. Let's say, "Having sold all of her boxes of cookies, the elated Girl Scout went home, so excited she could barely explain her success to her mother." In syntagmatic terms, we now have a sentence with cumulative modifying phrases in both the initial and the final position, but in paradigmatic terms, we now have a sentence with two second-level modifying phrases.

Let's try to diagram this relation using a simple diagramming scheme I introduced several lectures ago. In this scheme, the base clause of the sentence is always the first level, and we indicate this by starting at our left margin and putting a (1) before the base clause, wherever it appears in the sentence. Any modifying phrase that modifies part or all of the base clause is the second level, and we indicate this by indenting and putting a (2) before that modifying phrase, and before however many other modifying phrases there may be that also modify part of or all of the base clause. Accordingly, we could visually represent our original sentence as:

(2) Having sold all of her boxes of cookies,

(1) the elated Girl Scout went home.

And our extended sentence would look like this:

(2) Having sold all of her boxes of cookies,

(1) the elated Girl Scout went home,

(2) so excited she could barely explain her success to her mother.

As long as our modifying phrases all point to or modify part or all of the base clause, we just repeat this pattern, no matter how many second-level phrases there are. For instance, we could have:

(2) Having sold all of her boxes of cookies,

(2) having knocked on every door in her neighborhood,

(1) the elated Girl Scout went home,

(2) so excited she could barely explain her success to her mother,

(2) so proud of her accomplishment she immediately wanted to get more cookies to sell.

We still have a two-level cumulative, but now with four second-level modifying phrases, and here's where we need a new term. We call a cumulative sentence with more than one second-level modifying phrase a coordinate cumulative sentence. All of its modifying phrases point back to the base clause, and any one of them would make sense if moved to any of the three syntagmatic positions; the initial (before the base clause), the medial (in the middle of the base clause), or the final (just after the base clause). So we could rearrange the steps of the above sentence in more ways than I'm about to demonstrate, but just to give you an idea of the possibilities, we might write:

(1) The elated Girl Scout went home,

(2) having sold all of her boxes of cookies,

(2) having knocked on every door in her neighborhood,

(2) so excited she could barely explain her success to her mother,

(2) so proud of her accomplishment she immediately wanted to get more cookies to sell.

Or we could do it this way:

(2) Having sold all of her boxes of cookies,

(2) having knocked on every door in her neighborhood,

(2) so excited she could barely explain her success to her mother,

(2) so proud of her accomplishment she immediately wanted to get more cookies to sell,

(1) the elated Girl Scout went home.

There are all sorts of variations that would be in between these extremes, such as:

(2) Having sold all of her boxes of cookies,

(2) having knocked on every door in her neighborhood,

(2) so excited she could barely explain her success to her mother,

(1) the elated Girl Scout went home,

(2) so proud of her accomplishment she immediately wanted to get more cookies to sell.

No matter how much we rearrange the syntagmatic order of this sentence's steps, the paradigmatic order remains the same. It's a two-level sentence, with four second-level modifying phrases. So why is this important to know? First of all, we need to call this pattern something because cumulative syntax also makes possible two other patterns of logical relationships among base clauses and modifying phrases, and each pattern is more effective in some situations and for some purposes than it is for others. The three paradigmatic patterns of the cumulative sentence are called coordinate, subordinate, and mixed.

In coordinate patterns, all modifying phrases refer back to the base clause. In subordinate patterns, each modifying phrase refers to the immediately preceding clause or phrase, and we can mix these two patterns by adding subordinate levels to coordinate patterns, or coordinate levels to subordinate patterns, with one or the other pattern predominating.

Secondly, what's true of both patterns is that they show us how to add levels of new meaning to our sentences. You'll remember that a coordinate cumulative sentence looks like this when diagrammed:

(1) The elated Girl Scout went home,

    (2) having sold all of her boxes of cookies,

    (2) having knocked on every door in her neighborhood,

    (2) so excited she could barely explain her success to her mother, (

    (2) so proud of her accomplishment she immediately wanted to get more cookies to sell.

The subordinate pattern goes a little bit differently.

(1) The elated Girl Scout went home,

    (2) having sold all of her boxes of cookies,

        (3) those inescapable icons of capitalism,

            (4) its methods and assumptions hardwiring our children to value the power of selling in almost their every activity,

                (5) methods and assumptions championed by some and resisted by others.

You'll notice that both of these sentences take four steps after the base clause, but each step in the first sentence just gives it another second level, while each step in the second sentence adds a new level of meaning, ultimately developing the sentence through five levels of specificity. Of course, for the mixed version of a cumulative sentence, we would get:

(1) The elated Girl Scout went home,

    (2) so excited she could barely explain her success to her mother,

    (2) having sold all of her boxes of cookies,

        (3) those inescapable icons of capitalism,

        (3) those irresistible sugar bombs,

    (2) having knocked on every door in her neighborhood,

        (3) recognizing some who came to their doors as friends of her parents,

        (3) remembering some houses where she had gotten particularly wonderful Halloween treats,

            (4) figuring both categories of potential buyers would find it hard to say no to a cute little girl participating in one of America's best-established cultural rituals.

Now that you've seen what these three patterns look like when roughly diagrammed in terms of their levels, let's describe them and think about them a little bit more thoroughly. Coordinate levels can be thought of as modifying the entire base clause, or as focusing on one of its elements. Given a base clause containing a subject, a verb, and a direct object, the coordinate modifying levels may sharpen or focus on the whole clause, on its subject, on its verb, or on its object. Coordinate levels keep the sentence running in place as more information is added to its load.

I've used some of these examples before, but now I hope you'll see them in a new light, representing not just the cumulative sentence, but the coordinate cumulative sentence. Here are some examples:

He drove the car carefully, never speeding, never running red lights, always looking both ways at intersections, always defensive.

He drove the car, turning down the old country road, shifting into first gear as his speed slowed, absently glancing at the farms on either side of him, desperately wondering what to do next.

He drove the car, his shaggy hair whipped by the wind, his eyes hidden behind wraparound mirror shades, his mouth set in a grim smile, a .38 Police Special on the seat beside him, and you-know-what stuffed in that trunk.

He drove the car, a rusted old yellow-and-cream-colored Rambler, a relic from the days when a car's weight meant as much as did its mileage, a purchase he had often questioned, an impulse buy he had never really understood, but had never regretted.

And of course, if we add more information to the base clause, we give ourselves more targets for modification, more opportunities for adding modifying phrases as we would get if the base clause, for instance, instead of reading "He drove carefully" would read "He carefully drove the rented car back toward town."

Subordinate levels move the focus of the sentence forward, moving from general to specific, zooming in like a movie camera. They can also break a whole into its constituent parts, accomplishing the same end as do some uses of the colon. Subordinate levels can also lead us into new thoughts, nudging us to be ever more specific, to refine and/or detail whatever we have just written. However, these subordinate levels can also run amok, taking us away from our subject, diverting attention to subsidiary, incidental, even irrelevant details, details for which we have no real need or use, being ever mindful of our reader's time and patience, patience we run the risk of sorely taxing with sentences such as this one, sentences that seem to go on and on, moving us further and further from what we started to say, making the subordinate form seem more and more aimless.

He drove carefully, trying to protect his old Rambler, a rusted yellow-and-cream-colored classic sedan, one with Rambler's legendary reclining seats, seats intended to make driving more relaxing, a good design intention with a number of side effects, some not relaxing at all, side effects that made him the envy of every boy in his high school class.

He drove carefully, one hand on the wheel, the other hand holding a sandwich, a ham and cheese fossil, a strangely colored lump made three days before by his sister, a simple, trusting woman, someone who deserved a better life than fate had dealt her, a life of happiness, if not of success, the basic happiness of feeling loved and needed.

He drove carefully, his thoughts drifting back to other trips, fondly remembered Sunday outings, outings made wonderful by his mother and father, warm and humorous parents he would never see again.

They drove carefully, he with hands on the wheel in the prescribed position at 10 and 2, his eyes riveted to the road, a road almost invisible beyond the sheets of rain that pelted the windshield, she checking and rechecking the map, calling out town names and possible landmarks, landmarks neither could possibly see, both growing more tense and worried by the minute, neither able to say anything soothing or encouraging, their vacation dissolving into a nightmare of bad weather and wrong turns.

The main appeal and power of coordinate cumulative construction comes from its distinctive rhythm and very simple logical relations among the steps the sentence takes. The coordinate cumulative sentence tends to be repetitive, both in sound and in sense, and as Gertrude Stein rightly pointed out, repetition in language takes on an insistent quality. Moreover, the coordinate cumulative sentence is sort of like a car stopped at a stop light, but revving its motor. All the new information added by each coordinate level adds detail to, helps explain the base clause, but never moves it forward. Call it motion without movement. The coordinate syntax is essentially static, going over the same information again and again, refining it or clarifying it with each new pass or each new modifying phrase, backfilling rather than moving forward. And yet a coordinate sentence whose modifying phrases follow a sequence can seem to move, indeed can display what I think is the most seductive prose rhythm of cumulative form.

Christensen singles out a sentence from E. B. White to illustrate this strength:

> We caught two bass, hauling them in briskly as though they were mackerel, pulling them over the side of the boat in a businesslike manner without any landing net, and stunning them with a blow on the back of the head.

I love the sound of this sentence and I love the way it reminds me of that John Steinbeck discussion of two ways of looking at the Mexican sierra that I cited in my second lecture. This is clearly a sentence that evokes the experiential relationship between fish and fisherman, rather than resorting to labeling the dead, stiff, formalin-smelling fish by counting its spines.

Joan Didion is a master of the cumulative sentence in general, and here's a fine coordinate cumulative sentence from her:

> Mysteriously and rather giddily splendid, hidden in a grove of sycamores just above the Pacific Coast Highway in Malibu, a commemoration of high culture so immediately productive of crowds and jammed traffic that it can now be approached by appointment only, the 17-million-dollar villa built by the late J. Paul Getty to house his antiquities and paintings and furniture manages to strike a peculiar nerve in almost everyone who sees it.

The main appeal of subordinate cumulative construction comes from its ability to advance the sentence into new territory, making it particularly effective when used to describe a process or to follow something that unfolds in time. As opposed to the rigid and unmovable logic of the coordinate cumulative sentence, where every new modifying phrase ties back to the base clause, the subordinate cumulative sentence is loosey-goosey and can move on to new information. Of course, as I mentioned before, that freedom to move forward can reach a point of diminishing returns, when or if subordinate modifying phrases move so far away from the base clause that it looks as if the sentence has run wild.

It turns out it's actually hard to find pure examples of subordinate cumulative sentences, where every new modifying phrase adds a new level to the sentence. Indeed, Christensen only came up with a couple of examples of pure subordinate construction, although his first example from Sinclair Lewis is quite impressive:

(1) He dipped his hands in the bichloride solution and shook them,

   (2) a quick shake,

      (3) fingers down,

         (4) like the fingers of a pianist above the keys.

That's a four-level subordinate cumulative sentence.

Pure subordinate cumulative sentences, particularly those that develop through more than three levels, are difficult to find, in part because the circumstances that call for such a pure construction are as rare as they are hard to imagine. Accordingly, most subordinate cumulative sentences are really just dominantly or primarily subordinate, rather than exclusively so.

Two examples—the first from A. S. Byatt, the second from Toni Morrison—show what I mean. Here's the Byatt sentence:

> He lit on an image, a woman in a library, a woman not naked but voluminously clothed, concealed in rustling silk and petticoats, fingers folded over the place where the tight black silk bodice met the springing skirts, a woman whose face was sweet and sad, a stiff bonnet framing loops of thick hair.

Here's the Toni Morrison sentence:

> The clarinets had trouble because the brass was cut so fine, not lowdown the way they love to do it, but high and fine like a young girl singing by the side of a creek, passing time, her ankles cold in the water.

The main appeal of mixed cumulative construction is that it combines the strength of both coordinate and subordinate forms, allowing the sentence to move forward in time and open up new ideas, while also maintaining its intensity and focus. Here's a mixed cumulative sentence from Joseph Heller that shows what I mean:

> He worked without pause, taking the faucet apart, spreading all the tiny pieces out carefully, counting and then studying each one interminably as though he had never seen anything remotely similar before, and then reassembling the whole small apparatus, over and over and over again, with no loss of patience or interest, no sign of fatigue, no indication of ever concluding.

It's worth noting that the mixed cumulative form can easily draw from the sound and logical advantages of coordinate form, most obviously when the mixed cumulative sentence stresses parallelism of sound or structure. In *Free Style*, Chris Anderson cites a Loren Eiseley sentence that sounds and feels more coordinate than mixed, precisely because its six modifying phrases balance three parallel second levels against three parallel third levels:

(1) I used to park my car on a hill and sit silently observant,

   (2) listening to the talk ringing out from neighbor to neighbor,

   (2) seeing the inhabitants drowsing in their doorways,

   (2) taking it all in with nostalgia—

      (3) the sage smell of the wind,

(3) the sunlight without time,

(3) the village without destiny.

It should be apparent to some of your ears by now that I'm a real fan of balanced or duplc rhythms in prose. I love their sound and firmly believe that balance appeals to the mind, as well as the ear, its extended parallels and match-ups easy to follow and hard to forget. One of the many benefits of cumulative syntax is that it points us toward parallel constructions, and actually generates sound balances. That sentence by Eiseley is the kind of thing that starts happening with ever-greater frequency as we write more cumulative sentences.

But for my money, the real master of mixed cumulative rhythms is F. Scott Fitzgerald, as we can hear in the following stunning sentences from *The Great Gatsby*:

> Her face was sad and lovely with bright things in it, bright eyes and a bright passionate mouth, but there was an excitement in her voice that men who had cared for her found difficult to forget: a singing compulsion, a whispered "Listen," a promise that she had done gay, exciting things just a while since and that there were gay, exciting things hovering in the next hour.

Here's another great one:

> Slenderly, languidly, their hands set lightly on their hips, the two young women preceded us out onto a rosy-colored porch, open toward the sunset, where four candles flickered on the table in the diminished wind.

And another:

> Perhaps some unbelievable guest would arrive, a person infinitely rare and to be marveled at, some authentically radiant young girl who with one fresh glance at Gatsby, one moment of magical encounter, would blot out those five years of unwavering devotion.

And:

There was a ripe mystery about it, a hint of bedrooms upstairs more beautiful and cool than other bedrooms, of gay and radiant activities taking place through its corridors, and of romances that were not musty and laid away already in lavender, but fresh and breathing and redolent of this year's shining motorcars and of dances whose flowers were scarcely withered.

And believe me, there are plenty more where those came from.

In this lecture, I've tried to show how the steps cumulative sentences take, each modifying phrase a new step, fall into three main categories, each category displaying different logical relations between and among the base clause and modifying phrases, each category having different rhythms and different strengths. We've looked at coordinate cumulative sentences where all the modifying phrases point back to the base clause, and any one of which makes sense if moved just before or just after the base clause. These coordinate cumulatives can be thought of as two-level sentences, with all of their second-level modifying phrases pointing back to the first level of the base clause.

If we try to visually represent coordinate cumulative sentences, numbering their levels, they look like this:

(1) He grabbed her hand, (first level)

    (2) his heart pounding, (second level)

    (2) his knees shaking, (second level)

    (2) his head spinning, (second level)

    (2) his palms sweating, (second level)

    (2) his fright slowly fading away. (second level)

Or they look like this:

(2) The game and the entire season on the line,

(1) he stepped up to the home plate,

    (2) a hulking giant who suddenly seemed a bit smaller,

    (2) the chalk lines around the plate barely visible to his squinting eyes,

    (2) his face dripping nervous sweat,

    (2) grim determination evidence in his every move,

    (2) barely hearing the crowd chant his name,

    (2) tightly gripping his bat,

    (2) all too aware that in a few moments he would be a hero or a heel.

We've seen subordinate cumulative sentences where the modifying phrases are pretty much locked in place below or after the level of the sentence they modify, with modifying phrases after the second level each taking the phrase before it to a new level of information or explanation. If we try to visually represent subordinate cumulative sentences, numbering their levels, they look like this, their levels looking much like stair steps:

(1) His business plan was a joke,

    (2) little more than a childish dream, first formed when he was eight,

        (3) old enough to realize the advantage of having lots of money,

            (4) advantages such as being able to buy every comic book in the store,

    (5) the comic store itself representing to his young mind fabulous success.

And we've seen mixed cumulative sentences, where some modifying phrases follow the coordinate pattern, and some follow the subordinate pattern. If we try to visually represent mixed cumulative sentences, numbering their levels, they look like this:

(1) Cumulative sentences can take any number of forms,

    (2) detailing both frozen or static scenes and moving processes,

    (2) their insistent rhythm always asking for another modifying phrase,

        (3) allowing us to achieve ever-greater degrees of specificity and precision,

            (4) a process of focusing the sentence in much the same way a movie camera can focus and refocus on a scene,

                (5) zooming in for a close-up to reveal almost microscopic detail,

                (5) panning back to offer a wide-angle panorama,

                (5) offering new angles or perspectives from which to examine a scene or consider an idea.

Understanding the way each of these three cumulative patterns works makes it easier for us to write extended cumulative sentences. Perhaps more importantly, understanding the concept of sentence levels can be very important, immediately giving writers reachable goals for improving their writing. It may be a bit of an oversimplification, but generally speaking, one mark of inexperienced or ineffective writing is that it relies heavily on sentences of only one or two levels. Just adding one new level of information to our sentences, whether the modifying phrase we add follows the coordinate or the subordinate pattern, means that our sentences will contain more information, more detail, better explanation.

In short, adding even a single new level to our characteristic sentences will make them more effective, both in terms of their sound and in terms of their sense. This is as close to magic as writing gets, and if we can start composing the occasional cumulative sentence that contains several more modifying phrases and/or several new levels, we start thinking and writing much more effectively, and frequently much more elegantly.

Coordinate Cumulative Sentences
Lecture 9

One of the great beauties of the cumulative sentence is that it always presents us with a number of different workarounds that will smooth over rough spots in the way the sentence sounds or in the logical relationships of its parts.

Coordinate levels can be thought of as modifying the entire base clause, or as focusing on one of its elements. Given a base clause containing a subject, a verb, and a direct object, the coordinate modifying levels may sharpen/focus on the whole clause, its subject, verb, or object. Coordinate levels keep the sentence running in place as more information is added to its load. It is helpful to diagram cumulative sentences in a way that reveals the relationship of multiple modifying phrases. Such a diagram assigns a (1) to the base clause, and then numbers subsequent phrases in terms of the level each modifies. Thus, the coordinate cumulative sentence "This room looks like a disaster area, its ratty carpet stained and worn thin in many spots, its sheetrock walls pocked with cracks and holes, its broken and splintered furniture good only for firewood" might be diagrammed as follows:

> (1) This room looks like a disaster area,
>   (2) its ratty carpet stained and worn thin in many spots,
>   (2) its sheetrock walls pocked with cracks and holes,
>   (2) its broken and splintered furniture good only for firewood.

This lecture will be shorter on terms and descriptions and longer on considering the kinds of writing tasks that coordinate cumulative construction seems tailor-made for. It's easier to write cumulative sentences if we understand their basic grammar and logical construction, but one of the beauties of this syntax is that we don't have to think very much about their design once we become familiar with their distinctive rhythms. Probably the best and most useful advice I can give to anyone who wants to master writing cumulative sentences is this: Read them aloud. Your ear will detect problems or awkwardnesses or alert you to the need to add more information to your sentence because the parts that sound "clunky" or go "bump" when you read them aloud almost always sound bad because the logic of the sentence needs tweaking. Our eyes are very forgiving, but our ears almost never let us down, alerting us to something that needs fixing, even if we can't describe the problem.

Let's consider some of the advantages of coordinate cumulative sentences. Coordinate cumulative sentences pile up a number of modifying phrases, all of which point back to or modify either the entire base clause or some part (or word) in the base clause. A cumulative sentence with only a single second level is more satisfying than would be the sentence without a second level, but a single cumulative modifying phrase only begins to tap the advantages of cumulative syntax. If a sentence only takes a single cumulative step, it can't really be said to be either coordinate or subordinate, since we need at least two modifying phrases before we can make that determination. Accordingly, while a cumulative sentence with only a single modifying phrase does take the important step that gives the sentence a second level of meaning or texture, such a sentence does not plug into either the sound or logical advantages of longer, more pronounced cumulative sentences.

Probably the best and most useful advice I can give to anyone who wants to master writing cumulative sentences is this: Read them aloud.

However, the coordinate cumulative sentence with two second-level modifying phrases, such as those we just saw from Carl Klaus, offers writers a number of opportunities for parallels and parallel rhythms, for insistent repetitions and backtracking overlaps, and allows writers to make clear their control of this important syntax. When writers take the next step, adding a third modifying phrase to their sentences, their prose becomes even more effective, their control of syntax even more impressive. One of the most effective moves writers can make in cumulative sentences with three or more modifying phrases is to make the final phrase either a kind of summation or make it a simile or metaphor that nails down or drives home the idea the preceding phrases build toward. Writing pure coordinate sentences in which there are only second-level modifying phrases, all modifying the base clause, is never a goal in itself, just a reminder that the intrinsic strength of the coordinate form is most pronounced when that pure form is achieved. Specific context is much more important than following any abstract blueprint for a particular syntactical pattern.

We might think of the coordinate cumulative sentence as establishing a sense of what Gertrude Stein called "the continuous present," describing a process that we know must unfold in time, but presenting it as a series of components or constituent actions that are themselves free from time markers that would impose chronological order on them. In this way, coordinate cumulative sentences slow readers down, forcing them to pause as a process or action is broken down into discrete parts, the sentence lingering to deepen detail, going back to elaborate the base clause rather than moving on to completely new propositions. Without making too big a point of it here, I'd note that the coordinate form also lends itself to the description of rhythmic processes.

Now, before we move on in the next lecture to subordinate and mixed cumulative sentences, I need to offer one important reminder and one small caveat. The reminder is that while the examples of coordinate structure I've offered in this lecture have all been examples of right-branching sentences where the modifying phrases all come after the base clause, coordinate cumulatives can also be left-branching, where the modifying phrases come before the base clause, or mid-branching, where the modifying phrases interrupt the base clause, coming between its subject and its verb. The caveat is that not all coordinate modifying phrases work exactly in the way grammar tells us they can work. So-called free modifiers can be stuck in particular places by the needs of spatial, temporal, causal, and agental logic. Once more, we are reminded that the so-called rules of grammar should really be thought of as guidelines, some of them quite loose. The bottom line is that language is inherently rebellious, chafing against any authority that would attempt to limit what it can and cannot do. Finding these pressure points where the rules simply don't work is part of what makes writing so much fun! ■

1. Write or find a sentence that you feel moves quickly through an action or a sequence of actions. Rewrite the content of the sentence, adding whatever modifying phrases you need to slow down the pace, to downshift the reader's attention. Possible ways to downshift: add detail, anticipate conflict or consequences and set up a dramatic scene, add introspection (by the narrator or by a character) or exploration of broader meaning.

2. Write a coordinate cumulative sentence in which the free modifiers have to be in a certain sequence but are still free.

Coordinate Cumulative Sentences
Lecture 9—Transcript

The last lecture contained a lot of fairly technical discussions and used a number of terms to describe the differing mechanics of coordinate and subordinate and mixed cumulative sentences. This lecture will be shorter on terms and descriptions, and longer on considering the kinds of writing tasks that coordinate cumulative construction seems tailor-made for. But the really good news I have for those of you whose eyes glaze over when someone gets into the intricacies of grammatical description is that you really need to remember very, very few of the terms, labels, and definitions I've introduced in the past couple of lectures, and will add to from time to time in this and subsequent lectures.

I think it's easier to write cumulative sentences if we understand their basic grammar and logical construction, but one of the beauties of this syntax is that we don't have to think very much about their design once we become familiar with their distinctive rhythms. This is probably not what Joyce's Stephen Dedalus was thinking about in *Ulysses* when he meditated on the "ineluctable modality of the visible." But the point of his meditation on the difference between sight and sound, eyes and ears, applies perfectly here. Our eyes may glaze over when assaulted by sentence-level diagram after sentence-level diagram, but when we read these sentences aloud, our ear picks up the rhythms formed by the logical relationships between and among their base clause and modifying phrases. Or to put this another way, once your ear picks up the insistent rhythms of these sentences, those very rhythms can generate new cumulative levels.

I don't mean to suggest there's anything murky or mystical about this process. Instead, it's really very similar to what happens when we learn to ride a bicycle. We can read all the instructions and rules in the world for riding a bicycle, but nothing takes the place of actually getting on a bike and going through the exhilarating and scary process of learning that our body balances us without any conscious thought on our part. Our bodies learn the rhythm, the feel of riding a bike, and once we've internalized that knowledge, we never need to think about instructions or rules for balancing on a bike again. Never again, that is, until we need to teach our children how to ride, and then we go through the frequently frustrating experience of trying to teach them by explaining what they need to do, all the while knowing we just have to push them and let them fall until their bodies get it the way ours did.

All of which is to say that probably the best and most useful advice I can give to anyone who wants to master writing cumulative sentences is this: Read them aloud. Read every sentence you write aloud, read every example of cumulative form you find aloud. Read them aloud in the bathroom or in a closet if reading aloud makes you self-conscious, but trust your ear to understand cumulative rhythm before you consciously understand all the principles involved in its construction. This is such a simple, immediate, and surefire way to improve our writing that it amazes me every year when I have a tough time getting all of my students to do this. It's easy to tell who does and who does not read their sentences aloud before class. When I have them read their work aloud in class, it almost never fails that they pause or stop dead at precisely the point where, had they read the sentence aloud in private, their ear would have told them it needed work. I just smile knowingly at those moments, and over the course of the semester, these telltale moments usually diminish in frequency, and then disappear altogether.

As I said before, there's nothing mystical about this process. Your ear will detect problems or awkwardness, or alert you to the need to add more information to your sentences because the parts that sound clunky or go bump when you read them aloud almost always sound bad because the logic of the sentence needs tweaking. Either the modifying phrase needs a clear target or object of modification, or the agent of an action needs to be specified, or the modifying phrase needs more overlap with the word it modifies, etc. Our eyes are very forgiving and frequently fail to catch these problems, but our ears almost never let us down, alerting us to something that needs fixing in the sentence even if we can't easily describe the problem.

For me, this most frequently means I'll think a sentence needs an extra beat, an extra word to smooth out its rhythm, and it's almost always the case that what my ear hears as the need for an extra beat turns out to be that the modifying phrase needs to be more specific or to make its connection to the preceding phrase more clear by backtracking to point more clearly to what it modifies, or moving forward to add new information.

For example, if I hear the following sentences, I hear something in each that doesn't quite ring true or that needs just a bit of tweaking. See if you hear what I hear:

> A large hand grabbed my hair, sharply forcing my head back, jarring my neck, muscles stretched tautly.

> The lumberjack's axe split the base, toppling the tree, crashing to the ground.

> The rough concrete tore through my jeans, embedding small pieces of gravel into my knee, ruining another pair of pants, a wonder they lasted this long.

> I started to run, something large landing on my back, getting nowhere.

The first of these sentences moves along nicely until that final modifying phrase: "A large hand grabbed my hair, sharply forcing my head back, jarring my neck, muscles stretched tautly." That final phrase "muscles stretched tautly" sounds odd because it doesn't make clear whether those taut muscles belong to the speaker of the sentence or to the person whose large hand grabbed the speaker's hair. Accordingly, we need to tweak the sentence to clear up that ambiguity, and we do it this way: "A large hand grabbed my hair, sharply forcing my head back, jarring my neck, tautly stretching my muscles." Or even better because it picks up and re-emphasizes "neck" with the overlapping word "throat": "A large hand grabbed my hair, sharply forcing my head back, jarring my neck, tautly stretching the muscles in my throat."

And better still if we honor Professor Strunk's injunction to "omit needless words" and cut both "sharply" and "tautly" since both are already implicit: "A large hand grabbed my hair, forcing my head back, jarring my neck, stretching the muscles in my throat." Remember that second sentence? "The lumberjack's axe split the base, toppling the tree, crashing to the ground."

It sounds a bit odd when it gets to that final modifying phrase because "crashing" doesn't really have anything to modify. If it's supposed to modify "axe" or the entire base clause, the sentence should read something like: "The lumberjack's axe split the base, toppling the tree, the split causing it to crash to the ground." If "crashing to the ground" is supposed to modify "base," the sentence should read something like: "The lumberjack's axe split the base, toppling the tree, sending the base crashing to the ground."

Or if this is really meant to be a subordinate cumulative sentence with "crashing to the ground" modifying the preceding phrase "toppling the tree," then the sentence should read something like: "The lumberjack's axe split the base, toppling the tree, crashing the tree to the ground." Or better still because it adds important information and smoothes out the rhythm a bit: "The lumberjack's axe split the base, toppling the tree, sending the massive oak crashing to the ground."

Similarly, and I bet you can see why, I'd want to improve those last two sentences by making them read something like this. Remember, the original was: "The rough concrete tore through my jeans, embedding small pieces of gravel into my knee, ruining another pair of pants, a wonder they lasted this long."

And I'd revise this to read: "The rough concrete tore through my jeans, embedding small pieces of gravel into my knee, ruining another pair of pants, the wonder being that they had lasted this long." Remember the other original? "I started to run, something large landing on my back, getting nowhere." I'd revise this to read: "I started to run, something large suddenly landing on my back, preventing me from escaping."

These are only a few of the ways in which the original sentences could be made to sound better, the improvement in the way they sound resulting from our tightening up the logical relationships within the sentences, providing missing objects of modification, or clarifying some aspect of what is being described. One of the great beauties of the cumulative sentence is that it always presents us with a number of different workarounds that will smooth over rough spots in the way the sentence sounds or in the logical relationships of its parts.

One final example of the point I'm trying to make: If I hear the sentence "He became a pirate, a murderous rogue," I may well want to improve the sound and the sense of the sentence by backtracking and focusing a moment longer on "pirate," and then making what I mean by "murderous rogue" a bit more specific. So I'm likely to revise my sentence to read: "He became a pirate, one of those scourges of the sea, a murderous rogue, indiscriminately killing both passengers and crew of the ships he captured."

I like the sound of this extended sentence more than the sound of the one I started with, but more importantly, this sentence now displays the kind of overlap or redundancy of information that gives the cumulative sentence its clarity and insistent force. Now, readers not only see that "He became a pirate," but that the pirate he became was a "scourge of the seas" and a "murderous rogue," and also learn why he might be called a murderous rogue.

Years ago, I had a wise colleague who liked to explain that the difference between students who loved to read literature and students who became English majors was like the difference between folks who wanted their cars to take them places, and those who insisted on knowing and understanding what was actually under the hood. I think that having at least a rough idea of what's under the hood in cumulative sentences makes it easier to write them, but I also think that recognizing the distinctive sounds and rhythms of cumulative sentences is more than enough to allow most writers to drive them wherever they want to go.

Having said that, it's time for us to go back under the hood for a few more minutes. More specifically, let's consider some of the advantages of coordinate cumulative sentences. In the last lecture, I explained that coordinate cumulative sentences pile up a number of modifying phrases, all of which point back to or modify either the entire base clause or some part or word in the base clause. Given a base clause containing a subject, a verb, and a direct object, the coordinate modifying levels may sharpen or focus on the whole clause, its subject, its verb, or its object. Coordinate levels keep the sentence running in place as more information is added to its load.

My former colleague at Iowa, Carl Klaus, one of the most important influences on my understanding of prose style, and a masterful stylist in his own right, offers these examples of coordinate cumulative sentences written by his students, each with two second-level modifying phrases:

The dog lunged toward him, fangs bared, eyes rolled back in anger.

The guillotine falls, slicing the air, heads rolling on the ground.

The storm raged on, a brutal assault, indiscriminate in its destruction.

Her hair hung long and loose down her back, blue-black in the stage lights, flowing with each animated gestured as she played the piano solo.

He bought a mattress at Goodwill, lumpy and ancient, tiny bugs hiding in its springs.

She served the dessert, a French pastry affair, dripping with dark chocolate.

The armored men hurled themselves into battle, metal crashing, screams fading.

She was a classical musician, a second violinist, scorned by her fiddle-playing brothers.

I photographed her against the sunset, a goddess, her white gauze robe glowing blonde with mellow light.

Most cumulative sentences don't have more than a couple of modifying phrases, and in some ways, the cumulative sentence with two modifying phrases isn't a bad goal for writers hoping to make their sentences more effective. A cumulative sentence with only a single second level is more satisfying than would be the sentence without a second level, but a single cumulative modifying phrase only begins to tap the advantages of cumulative syntax. If a sentence only takes a single cumulative step, it can't really be said to be either coordinate or subordinate, since we need at least two modifying phrases before we can make that determination. Accordingly, while a cumulative sentence with only a single modifying phrase does take the important step that gives the sentence a second level of meaning or texture, such a sentence does not plug into either the sound or logical advantages of longer, more pronounced cumulative sentences.

However, the coordinate cumulative sentence with two second-level modifying phrases, such as those we just saw from Carl Klaus, offers writers a number of opportunities for parallels and parallel rhythms, for insistent repetitions, and backtracking overlaps, and allows writers to make clear their control of this important syntax. Like Francis Christensen, I'd love for my writing students to become "sentence acrobats" who can "dazzle by their syntactic dexterity," but I feel like I've given them a valuable skill if they simply start incorporating into their writing a few cumulative sentences with at least two modifying phrases.

When writers take the next step, adding a third modifying phrase to their sentences, their prose becomes even more effective, their control of syntax even more impressive. The beauty of the coordinate cumulative syntax is that this next step does not require mastery of any new principles. It just asks the writers to add one more modifying phrase, similar to or even almost identical with the first two second-level modifying phrases they've used. For example, returning for a moment to two examples we borrowed from Carl Klaus, we can easily add a third modifying phrase to each. To the sentence "The dog lunged toward him, fangs bared, eyes rolled back in anger," we can simply add "his attack swift and unexpected." To the sentence "The storm raged on, a brutal assault, indiscriminate in its destruction," we can easily add a third modifying phrase, "flattening houses as if they were made of matchsticks."

But adding a third cumulative modifying phrase also gives us a chance to use that phrase as a comment on or a summing up of the previous two phrases, as we can again see in these examples, provided by Carl Klaus:

> Before the bonfire, she dips and sways to the talk of the bongos, long skirt swirling, snapping castanets in time to the beat of the drums, a frenzied rhythm sweeping her far into the night.

Or:

> I walked with him hand-in-hand down the quiet neighborhood street that spring evening, the air heady with the scent of lilacs, past lawn sprinklers that sounded like gentle waterfalls, in love for the first time.

One of the most effective moves writers can make in cumulative sentences with three or more modifying phrases is to make the final phrase either a kind of summation, or make it a simile or metaphor that nails down or drives home the idea the preceding phrases build toward.

Consider these examples, each of which uses that final modifying phrase to comment on or characterize earlier phrases:

> He drove the car, carefully, never speeding, never running red lights, always looking both ways at intersections, always defensive.

> The small girl rose from her seat, determined, head held high, demanding attention, like a queen.

> It was a heartbreaking moment, both lovers feeling deep emotion, a combination of bewilderment and sadness, a time when words are no use at all, the awkward silence marking a final farewell.

Now that we've looked at and listened to a number of coordinate cumulative sentences, I'd like to briefly consider a couple of the distinctive forms they take, with which most of us are already familiar, although we may not have previously thought of them in quite these terms.

The first is a pattern we hear particularly during political races, since the coordinate cumulative sentence has both the repetitive parallelism and the insistent repetition favored in political rhetoric. I bet you'll recognize this pattern, or you may want to think of it as a distinctive rhythm:

(1) I am proud to place in nomination the name of one of Iowa's native daughters,

    (2) a woman who has served this state in various public offices for over 15 years,

    (2) a woman who attended the University of Iowa and then Drake Law School,

    (2) a woman whose name has become synonymous with working to keep Iowa green,

    (2) a woman who has fought tirelessly to protect the rights and livelihood of Iowa farmers,

    (2) a woman who stands for all that makes Iowa great,

    (2) a woman who will never forget her Iowa roots or her Iowa values …

And so on, and on, and on, and on.

Here's another pattern or rhythm I bet will sound familiar:

(1) He raced through the airport,

    (2) running faster than he ever had before,

    (2) dodging slower-moving travelers,

    (2) weaving around baby carriages and wheelchairs,

    (2) trying to listen to departure announcements,

    (2) hoping against hope that his plane was still boarding,

    (2) wondering what had possessed him to have that second margarita.

Virginia Tufte offers another and distinctly more literary example of this coordinate pattern, featuring a string of second-level modifying phrases, all beginning with an *-ing* participle:

(1) Their trim boots prattled as they stood on the steps of the colonnade,

    (2) talking quietly and gaily,

    (2) glancing at the clouds,

    (2) holding their umbrellas at cunning angles against the few last raindrops,

       (3) closing them again,

    (2) holding their skirts demurely.

You undoubtedly noticed that this example from Joyce's *Portrait of the Artist as a Young Man* actually sneaks in one subordinate third-level modifying phrase, "closing them again," which can only make sense if it refers to the umbrellas in the preceding phrase. This is a good time for me to stress that writing pure coordinate sentences, in which there are only second-level modifying phrases, all modifying the base clause, is almost never a goal in itself, just a reminder that the intrinsic strengths of the coordinate form are most pronounced when that pure form is achieved. It may well be the case that a brief digression from the pure coordinate structure, as we see in Joyce's sentence, makes more sense and works better than would the sentence without that fleeting third level.

As is always the case in writing effective sentences, specific context is much more important than is following any abstract blueprint for a particular syntactical pattern. In the case of Joyce's sentence, as Tufte points out, all those *-ing* participial phrases have "a vigorous narrative impact," building our sense of "an ongoing feeling or process." We might think of the coordinate cumulative sentence as establishing a sense of what Gertrude Stein called "the continuous present," describing a process that we know must unfold in time, but presenting it as a series of components or constituent actions that are themselves free from time markers that would impose chronological order on them. In this way, coordinate cumulative sentences slow readers down, forcing them to pause as a process or action is broken down into discrete parts, the sentence lingering to deepen detail, going back to elaborate the base clause, rather than moving on to completely new propositions.

Christensen offers us another example of this effect, citing a sentence from Walter Van Tilburg Clark, best known for writing *The Ox-Bow Incident*, that memorably describes a flying predator:

(1) He could sail for hours,

   (2) searching the blanched grass below him with his telescopic eyes,

   (2) gaining height against the wind,

   (2) descending in mile-long, gently declining swoops when he curved and rode back,

   (2) never beating a wing.

Without making too big a point of it here, I'd note that the coordinate form also lends itself to the description of rhythmic processes, as the above sentence itself seems to follow the rising and descending motion of the bird flight it describes. Its sense of a kind of continuous present, composed of actions of searching, gaining, descending, and never beating also tends to add a kind of experiential or visceral dimension to the flat statement of the base clause that this bird "could sail for hours." We have long recognized the ability of poets to have their poems seem to do what they are about, but it is equally the case that fine prose writers routinely and largely unconsciously craft sentences whose rhythms reinforce the propositional content of the sentence, adding to its impact.

Before we move on in the next lecture to subordinate and mixed cumulative sentences, I need to offer one important reminder and one small caveat. The reminder is that while the examples of coordinate structure I've offered in this lecture have all been of right-branching sentences, where the modifying phrases all come after the base clause, coordinate cumulatives can also be left-branching, where the modifying phrase comes before the base clause, or mid-branching, where the modifying phrase interrupts the base clause, coming between its subject and its verb. Of course, all kinds of mixes of these structures are also possible. I've limited myself to right-branching examples just because they're easier to follow, easier to diagram, and I hope, easier to remember.

Consider the following example:

> Rubbing his hands together, running his hungry eyes over the steaming food, he sat down, anticipating the feast, savoring its aromas, stunned by his good fortune, realizing an opportunity like this might never come again.

This sentence reminds us that true coordinate second-level modifying phrases are free modifiers and can be placed in any order around the base clause. In many cases, the cumulative modifying phrases can come between the subject and the verb of the base clause, as is the case with this sentence:

> Cressler, exhausted from having gone three days without sleep, discouraged by his failure to find even a single clue to his client's murder, suspecting that he would never be able to solve this case, went home.

The caveat is that not all coordinate modifying phrases work exactly in the way grammar tells us they can or should work. Even though coordinate modifying phrases are technically free modifiers, meaning we should be able to move them around in any combination, not all of them are completely free, being tied to a specific place in the sentence by the logic of their propositions. Most coordinate cumulative sentences work like the example I gave above:

> Rubbing his hands together, running his hungry eyes over the steaming food, he sat down, anticipating the feast, savoring its aromas, stunned by his good fortune, realizing an opportunity like this might never come again.

Those five coordinate second-level modifying phrases can be shuffled and reshuffled into any order around the base clause, "he sat down." We can write the sentence, making it entirely left branching: "Rubbing his hands together, running his hungry eyes over the steaming food," and so on until you get to the base clause.

We can make it completely right branching: "He sat down, rubbing his hands together, running his hungry eyes over the steaming food, anticipating the feast," and so on.

Or we can do anything in between. We can mix and match the cumulative phrases. That's the way free modifiers are supposed to work. But so-called free modifiers can be stuck in particular places in the sentence by the needs of spatial, temporal, causal, and agential logic. Here's what I mean. Consider these two sentences:

(1) He got up early,

    (2) waking long before sunrise,

    (2) always looking for an edge,

    (2) always trying harder than anyone else,

    (2) believing sleep a waste of time,

        (3) motivated by insecurity and greed.

And another version:

(1) He got up early,

    (2) waking long before sunrise,

    (2) going for his daily two-mile run before breakfast,

(2) usually limiting his morning meal to coffee and a single piece of toast,

(2) showering and dressing quickly,

(2) leaving for work shortly before 8:00 a.m.

In the first sentence, we might find some order of those coordinate modifying phrases more effective than others, but the phrases are indeed free and they can be written in any order. In the second sentence, the coordinate modifying phrases are grammatically free, since each of them could be placed immediately after the base clause and make perfect sense, but they are not free to be shuffled around because they're logically tied to a chronological order. The subject can't leave for work before his morning run, before breakfast, etc. Accordingly, we need to be sure that our coordinate cumulative modifiers always make sense in the order we place them, honoring progressions or sequences in time and space, their order tracking through time, from large to small, right to left, cause before effect, tying agent to action, and so on.

Once more, we're reminded that the so-called rules of grammar should really be thought of as guidelines, some of them quite loose. The bottom line is that language is inherently rebellious, chafing against any authority that would attempt to limit what it can and cannot do. Finding these pressure points where the rules simply don't work is part of what makes writing so much fun.

Subordinate and Mixed Cumulatives
Lecture 10

One of the strengths of the coordinate cumulative form is that it suggests a writer who is very concerned with the reader, and who wants to give that reader a satisfying amount of information in a sentence form that makes a lot of information easy to process.

As we've discussed, subordinate levels move the focus of the sentence forward, moving from general to specific, zooming in like a movie camera. They can also break a whole into its constituent parts, accomplishing the same end as do some uses of the colon. Subordinate levels can also lead us into new thoughts, nudging us to be ever more specific, to refine and/or detail whatever we have just written. Thus: "He drove carefully, one hand on the wheel, the other hand holding a sandwich, a ham and cheese fossil, a strangely colored lump made three days before by his sister, a simple, trusting woman, someone who deserved a better life than fate had dealt her, a life of happiness if not of success, the basic happiness of feeling loved and needed." Mixed patterns obviously can tap both the repetitive, "running in place" emphasis of coordinate levels and the progressive potential of subordinate levels. Thus: "They drove carefully, he with hands on the wheel in the prescribed position at ten and two, his eyes riveted to the road, a road almost invisible beyond the sheets of rain that pelted the windshield, she checking and rechecking the map, calling out town names and possible landmarks, landmarks neither could possibly see, both growing more tense and worried by the minute, neither able to say anything."

As we saw in the last lecture, coordinate cumulative modifying phrases can be quite powerful, returning again and again to the base clause to add detail or explanation, offering a kind of "continuous present." One drawback of the coordinate form, however, is that it calls attention to itself through its pronounced repetitions and parallels to such an extent that writers must be careful not to rely too heavily on the form.

Fortunately, cumulative syntax provides us with almost unlimited patterns of modification, so we can avoid relying too heavily on any single pattern or rhythm. The coordinate cumulative form represents one extreme of the cumulative syntax, the extreme where the sentence seems to run in place, adding more detail to the propositional content of the base clause. The subordinate cumulative pattern represents the opposite extreme, where the sentence seems constantly moving forward, leaving the base clause behind. It moves the focus of the sentence forward, from general to specific. The identifying characteristic of a coordinate cumulative sentence is that any of its modifying phrases will make sense if placed directly before or after the base clause. The identifying characteristic of the subordinate cumulative sentence is that none of its modifying phrases after the second level will make sense if placed directly before or after the base clause.

In an earlier lecture, I pointed out that it's actually hard to find pure examples of subordinate cumulative sentences, where each new modifying phrase is a new level. Sentences that consist entirely of subordinate cumulative modifying phrases, particularly those that develop through more than three levels, are difficult to find in part because the circumstances that call for such a pure construction are as rare as they are hard to imagine. Once again I should stress that purity of syntactic form is rarely, if ever, something writers should be concerned with in real-life writing situations.

As long as we understand the general principles of cumulative syntax, precise labeling or classification isn't necessary for writers to use the form effectively.

Writers will almost certainly rely more heavily on cumulative sentences that mix coordinate and subordinate modifying patterns. You may remember some of the mixed-form cumulative sentences we've seen in earlier lectures. There was the wonderful sentence by Loren Eiseley that clearly stresses the repetitions of the coordinate pattern over the forward motion of the subordinate. As is true of so many aspects of the cumulative sentence, we might not agree which rhythm or pattern dominates in any of these sentences, and we might not agree with the way a sentence is diagrammed. But I can't stress too strongly that disagreements like this are beside the point: They just don't matter! As long as we understand the general principles of cumulative syntax, precise labeling or classification isn't necessary for writers to use the form effectively.

Now it's time for us to make sure we understand all, or at least most, of the ways we can get the job done by adding cumulative modifying phrases to our sentences. Accordingly, I want to take a minute to review the basic patterns that a cumulative modifying phrase can take. Once again, while I'll offer a brief grammatical description of each pattern, you don't need to remember the grammatical terms if you recognize and remember the way each pattern sounds. Indeed, I strongly urge you *not* to worry about the grammatical descriptions, but simply to read these patterns aloud until they become familiar to you.

Here are the main possibilities for adding second-level modifying phrases to the base clause. These patterns will also work for adding subordinate levels to preceding phrases.

- Perhaps the easiest way to add a second level is to begin the modifying phrase with a verbal.

- A variation on this pattern is to begin the modifying level with a verbal plus another modifier (an adverb).

- You can begin the modifying phrase with an article plus one of the nouns (subject or object) from the base clause.

- You can begin the modifying phrase with an article plus an adjective plus one of the base clause nouns.

- You can begin the modifying phrase with an article plus an adjective plus almost any noun followed by a prepositional phrase.

- You can begin the modifying phrase with an article plus an appositive for one of the base clause nouns or a noun phrase appositive for the action of the clause.

- You can begin the modifying phrase with a possessive pronoun referring to either subject, object, or to the sense of the entire base clause.

- You can begin the modifying phrase with an adverb or an article plus an adverb.

- You can begin the modifying phrase with an article plus entirely new information, including even relative non sequiturs.

- You can begin the modifying phrase with almost anything followed by a simile or metaphor that details all or part of the base clause.

There are other patterns that modifying phrases can follow, but these are the most prevalent ones I can think of. I have my students repeat this exercise with a base clause of their own choosing simply to help them realize just how many different ways there are to write cumulative modifying phrases. My guess is that each of them will, consciously or unconsciously, gravitate toward using some of the above patterns much more frequently than others, but what is most important is that we remember not just how many patterns there are but that they can be combined in an almost infinite number of variations.

I ask my students to respond to the challenge of following structural prompts. Now, obviously an exercise such as this has no direct application to any real-world writing situation, but almost without fail, once my students realize they can control that much information using cumulative syntax and produce sentences that sound that good, they realize how easily they can produce similarly complex and rhythmic sentences of their own. Once my students make that discovery they usually become enthusiastic and impressive masters of cumulative syntax, giving themselves over to its seductive rhythms, logical strength, and generative magic. My hope is that their experience will become yours as well. ■

1. Choose a base clause. Modify it with base clauses following the ten patterns for adding second-level modifying phrases.

2. Finish the sentences below, making your own modifying phrases.

   (1) Big Al headed back into the bar,

       (2) a _____,

       (2) his _____,

           (3) _____,

           (3) _____.

   (1) They sat down at the table,

       (2) he _____,

           (3) his _____,

           (3) his _____,

       (2) she _____,

           (3) her _____,

           (3) her _____,

       (2) the table _____,

           (3) its _____,

           (3) its _____,

       (2) the overall scene suggesting _____.

Subordinate and Mixed Cumulatives
Lecture 10—Transcript

As we saw in the last lecture, coordinate cumulative modifying phrases can be quite powerful, returning again and again to the base clause to add detail or explanation, offering a kind of continuous present where the sentence seems to linger on a statement, trying to get it fully detailed, almost as if the writer keeps remembering one more important thing to say before moving on. Accordingly, one of the strengths of the coordinate cumulative form is that it suggests a writer who is very concerned with the reader, and who wants to give that reader a satisfying amount of information in a sentence form that makes a lot of information easy to process.

One drawback of the coordinate form, however, is that it calls attention to itself through its pronounced repetitions and parallels, sometimes to such an extent that writers must be careful not to rely too heavily on the form. The repetitions in a single coordinate cumulative sentence focus our attention on the base clause in a way that makes the sentence stick in our minds, But, as is always the danger with repetition, too many coordinate cumulative sentences become repetitious, and they run the risk of becoming boring.

Fortunately, cumulative syntax provides us with almost unlimited patterns of modification, so we can avoid relying too heavily on any single pattern or rhythm. If the coordinate cumulative form represents one extreme of the cumulative syntax, the extreme where the sentence seems to run in place, adding more detail or explanation to the propositional content of the base clause, but not moving the focus of the sentence to new information, then the subordinate cumulative pattern represents the opposite extreme, where the sentence seems constantly moving forward, leaving the base clause in the dust.

Subordinate modifying levels move the focus of the sentence forward, moving from general to specific, zooming in like a movie camera. They can also break a whole into its constituent parts, which is pretty much the same thing that a colon can do. Subordinate levels can also lead us into new thoughts, nudging us to be ever more specific, to refine and/or detail whatever we've just written. As I previously noted, the main appeal of subordinate cumulative construction comes from its ability to advance the sentence into new territory, making it particularly effective when used to describe a process or to follow something that unfolds in time.

As opposed to the tightly progressive logic of the coordinate cumulative sentence, where every new modifying phrase ties back to the base clause, the subordinate cumulative sentence seems able to ramble, moving almost randomly to new information. Thus, we can get a sentence like, "He drove carefully, one hand on the wheel, the other hand holding a sandwich, a ham and cheese fossil, a strangely colored lump made three days before by his sister, a simple, trusting woman, someone who deserved a better life than fate had dealt her, a life of happiness if not of success, the basic happiness of feeling loved and needed."

And we can easily see the movement of this sentence if we diagram its levels:

(1) He drove carefully,

    (2) one hand on the wheel,

        (3) the other hand holding a sandwich,

            (4) a ham and cheese fossil,

                (5) a strangely colored lump made three days before by his sister,

                    (6) a simple, trusting woman,

                        (7) someone who deserved a better life than fate had dealt her,

                            (8) a life of happiness if not of success,

                                (9) the basic happiness of feeling loved and needed.

Sure, that sentence is a stretch. It seems to race forward on the edge of being out of control. It's hard to imagine a writing situation that would call for such an exaggerated and extended subordinate form, but it is good to know that the subordinate form can make any single sentence tell a story, moving the focus or action of the sentence forward. Just as the identifying characteristic of a coordinate cumulative sentence is that any of its modifying phrases will make sense if placed directly before or after the base clause because all of its second-level modifying phrases point back to the base clause, the identifying characteristic of the subordinate cumulative sentence is that none of its modifying phrases after the second level will make sense if placed directly before or after the base clause.

It doesn't make sense, for instance, to write "He drove carefully, a ham and cheese fossil." We can't write "He drove carefully, the other hand holding a sandwich" and we can't write "He drove carefully, the basic happiness of feeling loved and needed." The above subordinate cumulative sentence moves through nine levels of modification, and clearly pushes the form to and probably past a point of diminishing effectiveness.

But subordinate sentences of only four or five levels don't run into that problem. For instance, few of us would think anything strange about a sentence that read "He drove carefully, one hand on the wheel, the other hand holding a sandwich, a ham and cheese fossil, a strangely colored lump made three days before by his sister." That sentence clearly prepares us for a shift of focus to the sister, revealing that one of the strengths of the subordinate cumulative form is that it provides clear transitions from one sentence to another, virtually guaranteeing that our writing will never sound choppy because it's hard to tell how it moves from one sentence to another.

In an earlier lecture, I pointed out that it's actually hard to find pure examples of subordinate cumulative sentences, where each new modifying phrase is a new level in the sentence. I offered one example from Sinclair Lewis:

(1) He dipped his hands in the bichloride solution and shook them,

    (2) a quick shake,

(3) fingers down,

(4) like the fingers of a pianist above the keys.

And here are two examples from Josephine Miles:

(1) From literal to figurative is one range that a word may take:

(2) from *foot* of a person to *foot* of a mountain,

(3) a substituted or metaphoric use.

And the second sentence:

(1) From concrete to abstract is another range:

(2) from *foot* to *extremity*,

(3) stressing one of the abstract characteristics of foot,

(4) a contrast for which the terms *image* and *symbol* as distinguished from *concept* are also used."

Sentences that consist entirely of subordinate cumulative modifying phrases, particularly those that develop through more than three levels, are difficult to find, in part because the circumstances that call for such a pure construction are as rare as they are hard to imagine. Once again, I should stress that purity of syntactic form is rarely, if ever, something writers should be concerned with in real-life writing situations. As is consistently the case in my approach to writing, I try to present the most pure or most extreme form of sentence syntax, only to suggest the point where the inherent strengths or advantages of that form are at their greatest.

Most of us most of the time will approach, but rarely reach, the exaggerated limit of pure syntactic form. Indeed, most subordinate cumulative sentences are really just dominantly subordinate, rather than exclusively so. By that, I mean that their distinctive rhythm has a bit more to do with moving the sentence forward than having it run in place, as coordinate form suggests. Or to put this another way, writers will almost certainly rely more heavily on cumulative sentences that mix coordinate and subordinate modifying patterns than on those that exclusively present just one form or the other.

You may remember some of the mixed form cumulative sentences we've seen in earlier lectures. There was a wonderful sentence from Loren Eiseley that combines coordinate and subordinate modification, but does so in a way that clearly stresses the repetitions of the coordinate pattern over the forward motion of the subordinate. Here's the sentence:

(1) I used to park my car on a hill and sit silently observant,

    (2) listening to the talk ringing out from neighbor to neighbor,

    (2) seeing the inhabitants drowsing in their doorways,

    (2) taking it all in with nostalgia—

        (3) the sage smell of the wind,

        (3) the sunlight without time,

        (3) the village without destiny.

And here's a mixed cumulative in which the subordinate rhythm seems to dominate, a characteristically stunning sentence from Joseph Conrad's *Heart of Darkness*, yet another reminder of Conrad's stylistic genius:

(1) The great wall of vegetation,

    (2) an exuberant and entangled mass of trunks, branches, leaves, boughs, festoons,

        (3) motionless in the moonlight,

(1) was like a rioting invasion of soundless life,

   (2) a rolling wave of plants piled up,

      (3) crested,

      (3) ready to topple over the creek,

      (3) [ready] to sweep every little man of us out of his little existence.

As is true of so many aspects of the cumulative sentence, we might not agree which rhythm or pattern dominates in these sentences and we might not agree with the way a sentence is diagrammed, since in many cases, there's actually some doubt about whether a modifying phrase is subordinate or coordinate, a result we get when the phrase can make sense as either. But I can't stress too strongly that disagreements such as these are beside the point: They just don't matter. As long as we understand the general principles of cumulative syntax, precise labeling or classification isn't necessary for writers to use the form effectively.

We should think of cumulative form much as we think of the human hand, which functions in an infinite number of ways, depending on what we need it to do. Sentences are like hands. We use both to meet the needs of particular situations, and the point is almost never how we label or classify either our sentences when we set them to particular tasks, or what a hand does when we use it to point or pick up or squeeze or gesture or sort or hold, or do any of the infinite number of tasks a hand routinely performs. The point is simply to get the job done.

And now it's time for us to make sure we understand all, or at least most, of the ways we can get the job done by adding cumulative modifying phrases to our sentences. It is particularly important when we write subordinate or mixed cumulative sentences that we have a good idea of all the forms a modifying phrase can take. This is so because while the coordinate cumulative form invites repetition and may actually have greater impact or power when all of the modifying phrases are of the same kind, subordinate and mixed cumulative form rewards variety in modifying phrases. When four or five second-level coordinate modifying phrases all start with, for instance, an *-ing* participial phrase, the repetition and predictability of that single form strengthens the sentence, but that same degree of repetition and predictability simply won't work well in subordinate or mixed cumulative sentences where we need variety.

Accordingly, I want to take just a minute to review the basic patterns that a cumulative modifying phrase can take, and once again, while I'll offer a brief grammatical description of each pattern, you don't need to remember the grammatical terms if you recognize and remember the way each pattern sounds. Indeed, I strongly urge you not to worry about the grammatical descriptions, but simply to read these patterns aloud until they become familiar to your ear.

Remember, while no set formulas can anticipate the problems or opportunities posed by the situations in which sentences develop, there are several general patterns for adding cumulative modifying levels to base clauses. Given a base clause containing a subject, a verb, and an object, we know three immediate targets for further modification by cumulative phrases. Depending on the object of modification, those cumulative phrases may appear in the initial, medial, or final modifying slots. But as I've done in most of my lectures, the examples I offer will all appear in the final position.

You'll notice that in many cases, the cumulative pattern produces adjectival information that might otherwise have been subordinated in relative clauses, that in several cases the cumulative pattern may actually subsume a relative clause, and that the cumulative pattern sometimes encourages us to figure out relationships between seemingly unrelated bits of information. Some of these patterns will sound natural only when we follow them with one or more other cumulative levels.

Given the base clause "The woman closed the door," here are the 10 main possibilities for adding second-level modifying phrases to that base clause, and these patterns will also work for adding subordinate levels to preceding phrases. I know that what follows will sound really repetitive, but I think the patterns are far easier to see, hear, and understand when we use the same base clause for all of them, so here goes:

Perhaps the easiest way to add a second level is to begin the modifying phrase with a verbal. The easiest way to do this is base clause, verb plus -*ing*: "The woman closed the door, closing it with a bang." We can also do it with any verb plus -*ing*: "The woman closed the door, catching her heel on the step." We can use almost any verb plus -*ed*: "The woman closed the door, blinded by the dust." Or we can start it with almost any past participle: "The woman closed the door, driven by the wind."

A variation on this pattern is to begin the modifying level with a verbal plus another modifier, an adverb for instance: "The woman closed the door, grinning crazily." "The woman closed the door, moving crisply." "The woman closed the door, distracted momentarily."

Or you can begin the modifying phrase with an article plus one of the nouns, either the subject or the object from the base clause: "The woman closed the door, a door made of carved oak." "The woman closed the door, the door she had never before dared close." "The woman closed the door, a woman eerily dressed entirely in white." "The woman closed the door, the woman the world would soon know so well."

You can begin the modifying phrase with an article plus an adjective plus one of the base clause nouns: "The woman closed the door, a magnificent door." "The woman closed the door, a magnificent woman." "The woman closed the door, the ominous door." "The woman closed the door, the ominous woman."

You can begin the modifying phrase with an article plus an adjective plus almost any noun, followed by a prepositional phrase: "The woman closed the door, a crazy grin on her face." "The woman closed the door, a gaping hole in its central panel." "The woman closed the door, the billowing snow behind her." "The woman closed the door, an awful look in her eyes." "The woman closed the door, the silver doorknob between her thumb and index finger."

You can begin the modifying phrase with an article plus an appositive for one of the base clause nouns or a noun phrase appositive for the action of the clause. An appositive is a noun substitute that refers to the same thing as the original noun or sense of the entire clause, but considers it from a somewhat different viewpoint: "The woman closed the door, an enraged mother ready to confront her son's tormentors." "The woman closed the door, a crudely framed exit to the garage." "The woman closed the door, the only obstacle to the madman's rage." "The woman closed the door, a determined politician ready to begin work." "The woman closed the door, an action she would long remember and never regret." "The woman closed the door, a clear sign of her insistence on privacy."

You can begin the modifying phrase with a possessive pronoun referring to either subject, object, or to the sense of the entire base clause: "The woman closed the door, its massive hinges creaking eerily." "The woman closed the door, her massive fingers choking its doorknob." "The woman closed the door, its doorknob helpless in the vice of her grip." "The woman closed the door, her face a study in triumph." "The woman closed the door, its closing her final act of rebellion." "The woman closed the door, her effort little short of heroic." "The woman closed the door, her decision no longer a mystery."

You can begin the modifying phrase with an adverb or an article plus an adverb: "The woman closed the door, madly fleeing the swarm of wasps." "The woman closed the door, cheerfully determined to retype her article." "The woman closed the door, quietly securing its three different locks." "The woman closed the door, carelessly slamming it behind her." "The woman closed the door, the soothingly quiet night luring her into its darkness."

You can begin the modifying phrase with an article plus entirely new information, including even relative non sequiturs. I'm not really sure how this works, but it does work. "The woman closed the door, the stormy night swallowing its solid thud." "The woman closed the door, a radio blaring in the background." "The woman closed the door, the ice cream cone in her hand beginning to melt." "The woman closed the door, a threadbare coat draped over her right shoulder." "The woman closed the door, an entire morning wasted by senseless meetings."

At last, here's the 10th and final way of doing this: You can begin the modifying phrase with almost anything followed by a simile or metaphor that details all or part of the base clause: "The woman closed the door, grinning like the proverbial Cheshire cat." "The woman closed the door, sounding like a thunderbolt." "The woman closed the door, her action as fresh as a wet kiss." "The woman closed the door, Pandora with a second chance."

And remember, each of these 10 patterns for adding a second level can in turn be followed by one or more modifying levels that follow any of the 10 patterns. Mix-and-match is the name of this game. And there are other patterns that modifying phrases can follow, but these are the most prevalent ones I can think of.

I'm pretty sure by now you're even more tired than I am of hearing "The woman closed the door," but I had my students repeat this exercise with a base clause of their own choosing, simply to help them realize just how many different ways there are to write cumulative modifying phrases. My guess is that each of us will consciously or unconsciously gravitate toward using some of the above 10 patterns much more frequently than others, but what's most important is that we remember not just how many patterns there are, but that they can be combined in an almost infinite number of variations. If we write our cumulative sentences using only one or two modifying patterns, our sentences will start sounding too repetitive, even sing-songy. But if we understand the range of options we have available to us for crafting modifying phrases, we can rely very heavily on cumulative sentences without it ever becoming apparent how heavily we are relying on a single syntax.

We've now reached the point where the possible patterns for modification in mixed cumulative sentences are far too numerous for us to categorize them. Accordingly, I'll just offer a number of examples, hoping to indicate the almost infinite possibilities in rhythms of the mixed form. I'll start with some prescriptive formulas I ask my students to follow on a worksheet that presents the structural diagram for a mixed sentence, without saying anything about content. I ask my students to respond to the challenge of the following structural prompts. This is going to be a bit hard to describe if you're not looking at the exercise, which is reproduced in your guidebook, but I'll try to give you an idea of the prompts I then expect my students to finish on their own, adding their own modifying phrases.

For instance, I'll give them the base clause "Big Al headed back into the bar," first level, and then I'll say, okay, I want two second-level modifying phrases, the first starting with the word *a*, the second starting with *his*. And then I want two third-level modifying phrases, and you can do them any way you want.

(1) Big Al headed back into the bar,

    (2) a _____,

    (2) his _____,

       (3) _____,

       (3) _____.

Or I'll give them the base clause "They sat down at the table," and I'll say, I want a second-level modifying phrase that starts with *he*, and then a third-level that starts with *his*, another third-level that starts with *his*, another second-level that starts with *she*, a third-level that starts with *her*, another third-level starting with *her*, then another second-level going back to that base clause and picking up the other part of it, the table, and then two third-levels, starting with the possessive pronoun *its*. And then finally another second-level, a kind of summative thing here, the overall scene suggesting blank, and then I let them fill in the blanks.

(1) They sat down at the table,

    (2) he _____,

       (3) his _____,

       (3) his _____,

    (2) she _____,

       (3) her _____,

       (3) her _____,

(2) the table _____,

 (3) its _____,

 (3) its _____,

(2) the overall scene suggesting _____.

When I give this exercise, I get fabulous sentences like these in response, and I love some of these sentences:

(1) Big Al headed back into the bar, a demented grin twisting his scarred face,

 (2) his bloodshot eyes narrowed to a fierce squint,

 (2) looking around the dim and smoke-filled interior,

  (3) scanning the terrified inhabitants for any of his tormentors.

Here's another:

(1) Big Al headed back into the bar,

 (2) a Louisville Slugger baseball bat clutched in his hands,

 (2) his menacing stance better for chopping wood than for batting practice,

  (3) arms directly above his head,

  (3) the bat slowly making small circles as he decided on his target.

Here's the other one:

(1) They sat down at the table,

(2) he resignedly slumping into the straight-backed chair,

   (3) his tired face a picture of dejection,

   (3) his hands shaking uncontrollably,

(2) she stiffly taking her seat with exaggerated formality,

   (3) her eyes cold and hard and locked on his,

   (3) her thin lips' smile at once triumphant and condescending,

(2) the table piled high with stock reports and financial statements,

   (3) its surface completely covered with documents of desperation,

   (3) its jumble of information now completely useless,

(2) the overall scene suggesting an abandoned battleground.

Wow, that's a sentence. Here's another form:

(1) They sat down at the table,

   (2) he quietly awed by the restaurant's fabled elegance,

      (3) his left hand admiringly rubbing the silk tablecloth, his right hand tracing the etching on a fine crystal goblet,

   (2) she distracted by and obviously more interested in the other diners,

      (3) her eyes drawn to tables at which sat well-known celebrities,

      (3) her imagination running wild about others she didn't recognize,

   (2) the table an altar to excess,

(3) its place settings sporting no less than four different kinds of forks,

(3) its intricately patterned china giving off a kind of radiance,

(2) the overall scene suggesting what it might be like to dine at a restaurant in heaven.

Obviously an exercise such as this has absolutely no direct application to any real-world writing situation, but almost without fail, once my students realize they can control that much information using cumulative syntax, and once they realize they can produce sentences that sound that good, they realize how easily they can produce similarly complex and rhythmic sentences of their own. Once my students make that discovery, they usually become enthusiastic and impressive masters of the cumulative syntax, giving themselves over to its seductive rhythms, its logical strength, and its generative magic. My hope is that their experience will become yours as well.

Prompts of Comparison
Lecture 11

This will be the first of two lectures suggesting ways in which cumulative syntax can be employed to remind us of sentence moves that almost always improve our writing. Professional writers rely heavily on figurative language—similes and metaphors—to make their sentences at once more informative and more interesting; more informative by suggesting clarifying comparisons, more interestingw by turning the sentence in a more vivid, engaging, or speculative direction. Similes and metaphors can pop up anywhere in our sentences, but we can prompt ourselves to make figurative language a constant attraction in our writing by adding *like, as if,* or *as though* to the end of a sentence and then completing that prompt by deciding on an effective comparison to complete the simile. Each of these prompts commits the sentence to taking another step, and the steps introduced by these words will add both information and imaginative appeal to the sentence.

This lecture will discuss the advantages of incorporating similes into cumulative sentences. The next lecture will focus on the advantages of using speculative phrases, usually beginning with words such as *because* or *possibly* or *perhaps*. Similes and metaphors both make comparisons, asking us to think of something in terms that may at first seem surprising. A simile explicitly compares two things of different kind or quality, usually introducing the comparison of two things of different kind or quality, but implying introducing the comparison with *like* or *as*. A metaphor is a kind of stealth simile, offering a comparison of two things of different kind or quality, but implying or assuming the comparison and not introducing it with *like* or *as*. Both similes and metaphors quickly and powerfully suggest comparisons that might be impossible to explain in any literal way. Professional writers rely heavily on figurative language—similes and metaphors—to make their sentences at once more informative and more interesting, more informative by suggesting clarifying comparisons, more interesting by turning the sentence in a more vivid, engaging, or speculative direction.

Professional writers rely heavily on figurative language—similes and metaphors.

In the past you may have encountered a writing teacher who warned you against relying heavily on similes and metaphors, apparently viewing these lively figures of speech as mere ornament, adding superficial flair but no important contribution. E. B. White, in the "List of Reminders" in "An Approach to Style" chapter, which he added to Professor Strunk's advice in *The Elements of Style,* sounds a warning against the heavy use of similes: "The simile is a common device and a useful one, but similes coming in rapid fire, one right on top of another, are more distracting than illuminating. The reader needs time to catch his breath; he can't be expected to compare everything with something else, and no relief in sight." Now, I don't know what kind of writers Mr. White was thinking of when he wrote this warning, but the last thing I worry about with my writing students today is that they might use too many similes, overwhelming their readers with a cascade of comparisons. I urge my students to think of the simile as an important way to forge an emotional link with their readers, giving readers a glimpse into the way the writer thinks, as opposed to just what the writer sees or reports.

I think that in most writing situations it is not just advantageous but is crucial that writers reveal their distinctive individuality—their personality as sound thinkers—through their writing. Accordingly, I try to get my students to see the importance of processing information rather than just presenting it. Cumulative syntax offers us great opportunities of writing with style.

- It gives us an effective way of organizing the information and opinion we present in our writing.

- It suggests to our readers that we take pains to keep the logical relationships clear among the propositions our sentences advance.

- It suggests to our readers that we are attuned to the rhythmic pleasures of language as well as to its utilitarian functions.

- It forges a kind of implicit contract with our readers in which they can be confident that we are doing our level best to communicate as fully and clearly with them as we possibly can.

- Cumulative syntax also gives us great opportunities to make even more distinctive similes a part of our writing practice.

- As a generative syntax, it offers us prompts, inviting us to use similes to sum up or look back on previous information or details from a new vantage point.

More importantly, when writers add a simile to their cumulative sentence, they give the sentence a distinctive touch, making a comparison that may be surprising, revealing something important, individualistic, and possibly unique about the way the writer's mind works.

Whatever we understand a writer's style to be, one key to the nature of that style is likely to be found in the writer's use of figurative language. Our use of figurative language is one of the acts of self-definition that goes into creating the style of our writing. Indeed, the distinctive cumulative rhythm particularly invites—and rewards—our use of similes. The cumulative syntax provides an armature on which we can almost always tack a simile. Of course, the simile doesn't have to come at the end of the sentence, but can be introduced before or after or in the middle of the base clause—as is true of free modifying phrases in general.

Thomas Pynchon incorporates similes into some of his characteristically cumulative sentences in his novel *Against the Day*. These sentences are noteworthy in a number of different ways. They are marked by insistent cumulative rhythms, even if they are not always punctuated in ways that emphasize their essentially cumulative structure. You can't miss their essential ambiguity; none of these sentences out of context makes it clear what's going on, but all suggest a kind of mysterious, numinous quality to the semblance of Pynchon's novel. Finally, while the similes he uses may not be dramatic show-stoppers, they are arguably not comparisons any of us would have thought of, thus serving to reinforce the uniqueness of Pynchon's novelistic vision.

Pynchon frequently places his similes as the last of a number of sentence steps, using that final *as if* as a kind of summary comment on what has come before. He also uses the simile as a kind of hinge earlier in the sentence, a step which turns the sentence in a new direction, with subsequent cumulative modifying phrases pointing back to, elaborating, and/or explaining the simile itself. We can see something similar going on in Joyce Carol Oates's frequently anthologized creepy short story "Where Are You Going, Where Have You Been?" She creates the mood of her story in part by using simile-clinched sentences.

Similes, while technically not always cumulative modifying phrases, can work exactly like the way cumulative modifying phrases work. Our writing benefits when we use similes (and metaphors) to reveal more about the way we think or feel about what we are writing. ■

Questions to Consider

1. Using this base clause anywhere it works best for you, write a sentence that adds narrative detail and concludes with an *as if* simile:

   The music came from somewhere in the woods...

2. Using this base clause anywhere it works best for you, write a sentence that adds narrative detail and concludes with a speculative phrase that begins with *as if*:

   Louise opened the window and looked down the street ...

Prompts of Comparison
Lecture 11—Transcript

This will be the first of two lectures suggesting ways in which cumulative syntax can be employed to remind us of sentence moves that almost always improve our writing. This lecture will discuss the advantages of incorporating similes into cumulative sentences. Similes generally describe something in terms of something else, the comparison being signaled by *like* or *as* or the phrases *as if* or *as though*. The next lecture will focus on the advantages of using speculative phrases, usually beginning with words such as *because, possibly*, or *perhaps*.

But I'm going to throw you a wee bit of a curve in both of these lectures because technically, most of the sentence moves I'll be describing are not exactly cumulative. However, it ought to be clear by now that I'm much more interested in the way a sentence works, the way it does what it does, than in naming its parts or holding it to strict grammatical standards. Accordingly, in both this lecture and the next one, we'll be talking about steps a sentence can take that may not be cumulative in a strict grammatical sense, but that work cumulatively, plugging into cumulative rhythms and offering the same kind of overlap and repetitive emphasis we expect of cumulative modifying phrases.

The bottom line here is that no matter what we call them, these sentence moves can make our writing more effective. Possibly more importantly, by adding steps to our sentences that give our readers a new way of looking at what we are writing about, we make our writing more distinctive, more clearly the product of a unique consciousness—our own—a reflection of our individuality, a sign of our originality. And whatever prose style is, that's one of its important functions.

I'm sure we all remember the basic definition of a simile as one of two primary figures of speech, similes and metaphors, both of which make comparisons, asking us to think of something in terms that may at first seem surprising. A simile explicitly compares two things of different kind or quality, usually introducing the comparison with *like* or *as*. A metaphor is a kind of stealth simile, offering a comparison of two things of different kinds or quality, but implying or assuming the comparison, and not introducing it explicitly with words such as *like* or *as*. Thus, "She ran like a gazelle" is a simile, comparing a girl to a famously fast and graceful animal, and introducing the comparison with *like*. But "She gazelled her way across the field" would be a metaphor, the comparison implicit in a verb that suggests her movement had qualities that might be associated with a gazelle.

Not every simile is a metaphor, since some similes simply make comparisons and do not ask us to think of one situation or thing as being something else, but every metaphor inherently implies the comparison we find in a simile. Both similes and metaphors make our writing more interesting and more effective. Both quickly and powerfully suggest comparisons that might be impossible to explain in any literal way. Years ago, S. I. Hayakawa noted in his classic textbook *Language in Thought and Action* that similes don't actually compare two apparently dissimilar things or situations as much as they compare our feelings toward those two things or situations, thus offering a window into the way we feel, as well as to the way we think.

As Hayakawa puts it: "The simile ... is something of a compromise stage between the direct, unreflective expression of feeling and the report, but of course closer to the former than the latter." He goes on to suggest that "The imaginative process by which phrases such as these [similes] are coined is the same as that by which poets arrive at poetry. In poetry, there is the same love of seeing things in scientifically outrageous but emotionally expressive language."

I mention Hayakawa's view not only because I think it gets directly at the way similes work in our writing, but also because, like Josephine Miles, he reminds us that prose and poetry are not so different in their appeals, both taking steps that have more in common than we might at first think, both offering effective platforms for the use of similes to strengthen the relationship between writers and their readers. For instance, "He endured a firestorm of criticism" gets and holds our attention more effectively—at least, I think—than "He endured intense criticism," although what he endured didn't actually involve either smoke or fire, but the metaphor "a firestorm of criticism," or the simile "The criticism he faced hit him like a firestorm" both have an emotional aspect that reveals something of the writer's sense of the intensity and drama of the situation in which someone is being criticized, not just the fact that someone is being criticized.

When we say "She ran like a gazelle," we probably don't literally mean that she was as fast as that particular animal, that she ran on all fours and so on, but we are expressing a kind of visceral admiration at the way she runs. Professional writers rely heavily on figurative language—similes and metaphors—to make their sentences at once more informative and more interesting; more informative by suggesting clarifying comparisons, more interesting by turning the sentence into a more vivid, engaging, or speculative direction. In the past, you may have encountered a writing teacher who warned you against relying heavily on similes and metaphors, apparently viewing these lively figures of speech as "mere ornament, touches that might add superficial flair to our writing, but that make no important contribution."

Indeed, E. B. White, in the "List of Reminders" included in his "An Approach to Style" chapter, which he added to Professor Strunk's advice in their combined book *The Elements of Style*, seems to belong to this particular school of thought, sounding a warning against heavy use of similes. We can almost hear him sniff when Mr. White dismissively writes:

> The simile is a common device and a useful one, but similes coming in rapid fire, one right on top of another, are more distracting than illuminating. The reader needs time to catch his breath; he can't be expected to compare everything with something else, with no relief in sight.

I don't know what kind of writers Mr. White was thinking of when he wrote this warning, but the last thing I worry about with my writing students today is that they might use too many similes, overwhelming their readers with a cascade of comparisons. Indeed, I have to labor mightily to get my students to use any similes. I urge them to think of the simile as an important way to forge an emotional link with their readers, at once suggesting to readers that the writer is doing his or her level best to make clear what he or she is trying to describe or explain, and giving readers a glimpse into the way the writer thinks, as opposed to just what the writer sees or reports.

Our choice of similes shows how we process information, how we think about the information we're passing along to our readers, how we organize it, how we understand it, our attitudes toward it. As Aristotle suggested in his *Rhetoric*, the ability to make comparisons between things that are unlike and seemingly far apart is "a sign of sound intuition in a philosopher," one mark of a sharp and distinctive mind. I think that in most writing situations, it is not just advantageous, but is in fact crucial that writers reveal their distinctive individuality, their personality as sound thinkers, through their writing. Accordingly, I try to get my students to see the importance of processing information rather than just presenting it.

A security camera in a convenience store can present what happens in front of its lens, but that security camera is just like every other security camera in every other convenience store. We might prefer to have the information that camera presents to not having the information, but we have no reason whatsoever to value what it records and presents over what any other or every other security camera would record and present. I see writing in much the same way. I think one of the most important goals of our writing is to reveal the nature of the writer's mind at work, a process in which the writer wants readers to value the writer's thoroughness, accuracy, and logic, but also the writer's unique way of looking at and understanding the world. That's really what's at stake when we talk about a writer's style, and I try to get my students to see the importance of writing with style rather than writing as if they were an unthinking and unfeeling security camera.

And cumulative syntax offers us great opportunities to do exactly that. The cumulative sentence gives us an effective way of organizing the information and opinion we present in our writing, suggesting to our readers that we do take pains to keep the logical relationships clear among the propositions our sentences advance, suggesting to our readers that we are attuned to the rhythmic pleasures of language as well as to its utilitarian functions, forging a kind of implicit contract with our readers in which they can be confident that we're doing our level best to communicate as fully and clearly with them as we possibly can. And, more to the point of this lecture, cumulative syntax also gives us great opportunities to make even more distinctive similes a part of our writing practice.

Indeed, this is in keeping with the way in which we can think of cumulative syntax as a generative syntax, offering us prompts, inviting us to use similes to sum up or look back on previous information or details from a new vantage point. More importantly, when writers add a simile to their cumulative sentence, they give the sentence a distinctive touch, making a comparison that may be surprising, revealing something important, individualistic, and possibly unique about the way the writer's mind works.

Listen to the striking opening sentence of Joseph Conrad's *The Secret Sharer*:

> On my right hand there were lines of fishing stakes[,] resembling a mysterious system of half-submerged bamboo fences, incomprehensible in its division of the domain of tropical fishes, and crazy of aspect[,] as if abandoned forever by some nomad tribe of fishermen[,] now gone to the other end of the ocean; for there was no sign of human habitation as far as the eye could reach.

I've slightly re-punctuated this sentence to emphasize its cumulative rhythms, but I cite it here to note how it is only when we get to the simile "as if abandoned forever by some nomad tribe of fisherman" that we fully understand the extent to which Conrad's narrator has a very active imagination, and loves to use it to make stories out of what he sees. In other words, while mastery of coordinate, subordinate, and mixed cumulative forms is an important goal and may tell us a lot about a writer's syntactic skill and versatility, it doesn't do much to distinguish the skill and versatility of one writer who writes great cumulative sentences from the skill and versatility of another writer who also can write great cumulative sentences. However, the similes these two writers will think of, the comparisons they will make, will almost certainly be different, each writer drawing from different knowledge, different experiences, and revealing different interests. In this way, the similes these writers choose may tell us much more about the way each thinks and sees the world than does the sentence structure each favors.

Whatever we understand a writer's style to be, one key to the nature of that style is likely to be found in the writer's use of figurative language. This is an important part of what Walker Gibson is getting at when he writes in his classic study of style, *Tough, Sweet, & Stuffy*, that:

(A) style is not simply a response to a particular kind of subject matter, nor is it entirely a matter of the writer's situation and his presumed audience. It is partly a matter of sheer individual will, a desire for a particular kind of self-definition no matter what the circumstances.

Our use of figurative language is one of the acts of self-definition that goes into creating the style of our writing. And while our use of the cumulative syntax is itself an act of self-definition that goes toward establishing the style of our writing, that cumulative syntax also lends itself to our using both similes and metaphors in our writing. Indeed, the distinctive cumulative rhythm particularly invites and rewards our use of similes.

Consider the following sentences some seen and heard before, but now see them taking a new step with the addition of a simile: "The boy sat down at the table, eagerly anticipating the feast, never suspecting it would be the last meal he would eat, acting as carefree as a lark." Okay, I'm not at all sure that larks are really carefree and I am sure that "carefree as a lark" is a much overused cliché, but this simile adds a sense of closure to the sentence, a final comment that sums up all that has gone before it. Imagine how much more effective a more original simile would work here, possibly something along the lines of "as unconcerned with his future as a pig in mud." Better make that "as a shark in a feeding frenzy." Well, you get the idea.

Try this one: "Tired and hungry, just back from a week in the bush, I limped into the mess hall, hoping the food lines were still open, feeling like the fool it seemed I had become." Or this one: "The chef prepared the fish, carefully, stuffing it with wild rice, sautéing it briefly, its sweet aroma blending smoothly with the other enticing odors in the kitchen, the fish becoming more than a food item, ascending to the status of art, as if transformed by magic." Or this: "The boy fainted, a goofy-looking sixth grader, his face turning white, muscles turning to jelly, dropping his books, uttering a kind of pained squeak, scared witless by what he saw, seeming to shrivel up like a deflating balloon."

As it happens, I'm not proud of or even satisfied with any of the above sentences. The similes I've added in final modifying phrases aren't very original, they aren't very striking, and they aren't very effective. In great part,

181

that is the case because they were arbitrarily tacked onto the end of already completed sentences, rather than growing out of the logic of the sentences as it developed. I offer these examples only as a rather crude reminder that the cumulative syntax provides an armature on which we can almost always tack a simile.

In much the same way that any sentence can be turned into a cumulative sentence if we only change the period at its end to a comma and start adding free modifying phrases, any cumulative sentence can be summed up or clinched by adding one more modifying phrase that contains a comparison introduced by *like* or *as*, *as if* or *as though*. And, of course, the simile doesn't have to come at the end of the sentence, but can be introduced before or after or in the middle of the base clause, as is true of free modifying phrases in general.

Here's the way Thomas Pynchon incorporates similes into some of his characteristically cumulative sentences in his recent novel *Against the Day*:

> They loomed out there in black mystery above the bright interiors and the faro players and insatiably desirable girls, and sometimes shadowy figures could be seen kneeling, reaching out to touch one of these slag piles, reverently as if, like some counter-Christian Eucharist, it represented the body of an otherworldly beloved.

Here's another:

> With the sun at this angle, the Kara Tagh looked like a stone city, broken into gray crystalline repetitions of city blocks and buildings windowless as if inhabited by that which was past sight, past light, past all need for distinguishing outside from in. Kit found he could not look at this country directly for more than a minute or so—as if its ruling spirits might properly demand obliquity of gaze as a condition of passage.

Or:

> She would return to her deck chair out of breath, sweating, exhilarated for no reason, as if she had just escaped some organized threat to her safety.

> After running madly round and round in the same tight circle at top speed a number of times, the vessel, as if getting a grip on itself, finally slowed down, easing back to vertical and steadying on to a new course southeast by east.

These sentences are noteworthy in a number of different ways. First of all, I hope you hear their insistent cumulative rhythms, even if they're not always punctuated in ways that emphasize their essentially cumulative structure. Second, I'm pretty sure you can't miss their essential ambiguity. None of these sentences out of context makes it clear what's going on, but all suggest a kind of mysterious, numinous quality to the semblance of Pynchon's novel. Each *as if* suggests the possibility that something is going on other than what seems to be the case, that a report of what characters can see or seem to understand may not be enough to capture the indeterminacy of Pynchon's world. And finally, while the similes he uses may not be dramatic showstoppers, so striking they will stick in our minds long after we've closed the pages of Pynchon's novel, they are arguably not comparisons any of us would have thought of, thus serving to reinforce—as if it really needed reinforcing—the uniqueness of Thomas Pynchon's novelistic vision.

Indeed, consider for just a moment some of the other numerous similes Pynchon uses. And here, both to save time and to focus more intensely, I'll just reproduce the similes, stripped from the sentences in which they appear: "as if the division between the singers were more than the width of a valley"; "as if they were protecting themselves against future gringo mischief"; "as if in the breeze from an undefined wing passing his face"; "as if emerging from the resolute blankness of history"; "as if this were a message from a realm with which he had done business"; "as if parties to a secret whose terrible face was somehow, conveniently, set to one side"; "as if it were not a fellow's appearance so much as his odor she wished to appear indifferent to"; "as if there were something up here to be gotten through as a point of honor."

Pynchon's *Against the Day* teems with similes such as these, just as it teems with elaborately extended cumulative sentences. Indeed, I think it's safe to say that *Against the Day* contains more similes and more cumulative sentences than has any American novel written in the past 50 years. Of course, when we remember that *Against the Day* is a whopping 1,085 pages long, it probably has a formidable head start in both categories, with competition possible from only a few other massive novels, such as David Foster Wallace's *Infinite Jest* or Neal Stephenson's *Cryptonomicon*.

My point is not to plug Pynchon's novel—although I think it quite remarkable and rewarding, both for students of American fiction and for students of the sentence—but to note how his characteristic similes fit so well into his characteristically cumulative sentences. Pynchon frequently places his similes as the last of a number of sentence steps, using that final *as if* as a kind of summary comment on what has come before, but he also uses the simile as a kind of hinge earlier in the sentence, a step which turns the sentence in a new direction, with subsequent cumulative modifying phrases pointing back to, elaborating, and/or explaining the simile itself.

And of course, Pynchon is far from being alone in employing similes in this fashion and to this effect. For instance, we can see something similar going on in Joyce Carol Oates's frequently anthologized creepy short story "Where Are You Going, Where Have You Been?" There, Oates introduces the very threatening Arnold Friend, who may be a serial killer, may be the devil, or just "an old fiend," as rearranging the letters of his name suggests. And she creates the mood of her story in part by using simile-clinched sentences such as these:

> They went up through the maze of parked and cruising cars to the bright-lit, fly-infested restaurant, their faces pleased and expectant as if they were entering a sacred building that loomed [up] out of the night to give them what haven and what blessing they yearned for.

> He was standing in a strange way, leaning back against the car as if he were balancing himself.

He stood there so stiffly relaxed, pretending to be relaxed, with one hand idly on the door handle as if he were keeping himself up that way and had no intention of ever moving again.

She watched this smile come, awkward as if he were smiling from inside a mask.

Once again, I want to call attention to the way in which these similes lend themselves to cumulative rhythm, giving the sentence another distinctive step, even when that step is not emphasized by punctuation. So far, most of the examples of similes I've offered have introduced their explicit comparisons with the words *as if*, even though we know that similes are frequently, if not most frequently, identified by the use of *like* to indicate a comparison. For example, he spoke like a robot. She looked like a troublemaker. They huddled together like sheep. Nor have I given many examples in which the comparison is introduced by *as though*, which grammatical expert after grammatical expert assures us—incorrectly I believe—means exactly the same thing as does *as if*. More on this distinction in a moment. I've focused on *as if* similes because they most powerfully lend themselves to cumulative rhythm.

Similes introduced by *like* need to be processed a bit before they fit as well into cumulative sentences. "He spoke like a robot" shows no sign of cumulative syntax, but with the addition of just a bit more information, always a good thing in my view, the simile can become a cumulative step: "He spoke slowly, mechanically, without inflection, like a robot." We even start to plug into the strength of cumulative syntax in a much shorter version of this sentence that would read: "He spoke slowly, like a robot." Or better still: "He spoke slowly, sounding like a robot."

The point I want to make here is that similes, while not always technically cumulative modifying phrases, can work exactly like a cumulative modifying phrase works. If the sentence clearly takes a step, indicated either by punctuation, usually a comma or a dash, or by the distinctive rhythm of cumulative progression, then I'm happy to call the simile a cumulative step, and I'm happier still when I come across these steps in the writing of my students.

Bottom line is that our writing benefits when we use similes and metaphors to reveal more about the way we think or feel about what we're writing, and I think our writing benefits even more when we incorporate the similes we use into cumulative syntax. I should stress that I don't value similes more than I value metaphors. It's just the case that metaphors come in so many varieties, I can't generalize about how they might be used in conjunction with the characteristic advantages offered the writer who controls cumulative syntax.

And here, once again, we see how the cumulative syntax can function generatively, acting as a heuristic prompt to urge us to make our sentences more detailed, better explained, more individualistic, more effective. I do not believe that mechanical, by-the-numbers sentence construction is the key to producing more effective sentences, but I do believe that the writer who understands a full range of syntactic and rhetorical options is much more likely to take advantage of opportunities where those options might apply than is the writer who does not command the full range of tools provided by a thorough knowledge of cumulative syntax.

Prompts of Explanation

Lecture 12

Writing is one of the most distinctly human activities, and ... like all human knowledge, it inherently, inevitably, and gloriously involves acts of interpretation.

Sentences are purpose-driven. We use them to get things done—to answer questions, to advance opinions, to explain ideas that are not clear, to show our thinking as we attempt to solve problems. Sometimes our sentence moves can help focus our attention on the value of pushing ourselves to explain more and to explain more effectively the information and propositions we advance in our writing. And heuristic prompts, syntactic challenges to add to and improve our explanations of ourselves and the world around us, can help us make our writing more effective. Three useful heuristic prompts are the words *because, perhaps,* and *possibly*. Each word can be used in many different ways and in many different places when we are writing, but, when added to the end of a base clause, each can challenge us to move beyond what we have written. We can add to or better account for what we have written in the base clause by adding a new clause introduced by the conjunction *because*. Or we can more tentatively suggest causes, motives, or explanations which we think likely but not certain with cumulative phrases introduced by *perhaps* or *possibly*.

The most effective prose establishes a relationship between writer and reader. If our writing doesn't offer some glimpses of writers as personalities, it's hard to say that it has a style, much less that its style will appeal to readers. If our writing displays no more of the way we think—the ways in which we process information—than does objective technology, it probably doesn't matter that what we write accurately records and reports information.

Our writing is purpose-driven, and almost always we have multiple purposes when we write. We write to accomplish a wide variety of goals, and very rarely is our primary goal only to record or report. We record and report in order to accomplish larger purposes, and those larger purposes shape the way in which we approach the task of recording and reporting, choosing what to include, choosing what to exclude, organizing our presentation of information to best suit our purposes. One of the important purposes that we should always have when we write is, as Joan Didion so powerfully put it in her celebrated essay "On Keeping A Notebook": "Remember what it was to be me." If we scale down this large philosophical assumption to the level of the sentences we write, it suggests we should be concerned not just with the accuracy and clarity of what we write, but that we should also be concerned with making our writing a reflection of who we are, how we think, and what we value.

Our writing is purpose-driven, and almost always we have multiple purposes when we write.

We signal that we are processing information in our writing in a number of ways, several of which we've already been exploring in this course. The cumulative syntax itself signals our determination to get it right—to extend the detail and explanation in our writing further, to take one more crack at making as clear as possible what we are trying to communicate, using cumulative modifying phrases to sharpen our images and to better reveal our reasoning. The cumulative syntax can also prompt us to include similes and metaphors in our writing—particularly similes—that compare what we are writing about with something else, the comparison both offering another perspective on or way of thinking about our subject and offering a window into the way our own thinking works, a glimpse of our intellectual personality, our individuality—our style.

Now, I want to suggest another way in which the cumulative syntax can serve to prompt us to reveal more about our thinking, more about the characteristic ways in which we process information. One step beyond making the comparisons, as similes do, between two things or situations that are different, and sometimes quite different, is to speculate about that which is not known. We signal such speculation in lots of different ways, but I'll focus on three of those signals: the words *because*, *possibly*, and *perhaps*. These words lend themselves to the step-logic and downshifting rhythms of the cumulative syntax. They also lend themselves to becoming generative challenges or heuristic prompts.

Adding speculation concerning motive behind, cause of, or interpretation of the events or actions we write about helps forge the connection between reader and writer as two minds at work. Knowing how easily we can add speculation to our writing may encourage us to put a bit more of the way we think into our writing. Here, of course, I'm thinking of writing situations where it is as important to present our judgment, our ability to interpret, our commitment to understanding as it is to present unprocessed information.

Linguistic theory tells us that the last or next-to-last step or slot in the sentence generally is the place in the sentence where we place the most intonational stress. As Martha Kolln explains in her chapter on sentence rhythm in her *Rhetorical Grammar: Grammatical Choices, Rhetorical Effects*, this well-recognized rhythm pattern is called *end focus*, and it gives rhythmic emphasis to information at the end or near the end of the sentence. The truth is we can shape our sentences so that we can emphasize any part of them we want to—and that emphasis is rhetorical rather than grammatical, determined by the context and purpose of the sentence rather than by its grammatical form.

The point we need to remember is that position, by itself, may or may not place emphasis, but the end position does lend itself to emphasis. That's why, in this lecture, I'm suggesting the advantages of using the final step of a cumulative sentence for speculation about motive or likely consequences or cause—speculation signaled by *because, possibly,* or *perhaps*. The cumulative syntax also invites the placement of speculative phrases in the initial or medial slots in the sentence, but I've focused on the final slot simply to take full advantage of the generative power of the cumulative. Nor do the heuristic prompts I've singled out exhaust the possibilities for introducing such speculation. Indeed, *for* and *as* can be used interchangeably with *because*. I suspect that each of us gravitates toward one of these options more than the other two, and I further suspect we do so because we sense at least connotative differences among the three.

And should we wish to move beyond speculation to offer an explanation between our thinking and apparent or received truth, we might wish to introduce our summative cumulative modifying phrase with a word such as *likely*, a phrase such as *more likely*, or a word as insistent as *actually*. The verbs most frequently associated with the kind of writerly speculation

I'm advocating are *seems* and *appears*, the verbal, participial forms of both, *seeming* and *appearing* custom-made for introducing speculative cumulative modifying phrases.

By this point in the lecture I must seem less and less concerned with the production and inclusion in our writing of cumulative sentences and more and more concerned with ways in which we foreground ourselves in our writing as thinkers, developing the ethical appeal of our writing. Obviously there are an almost infinite number of ways we can call attention to ourselves as the consciousness, the personality, behind what we write. Perhaps I should acknowledge once again that my approach to teaching writing does value very highly the *ethos* aspect of rhetorical situations, in part because those other two classic components of rhetoric, *logos* and *pathos*, strike me as much more beyond the reach of writing instruction since they are context-dependent.

We are now fast approaching an important turning point in this course. It's time now for us to turn our attention to the delaying strategies of periodic or suspensive sentences and to the powerful rhythmic appeal and emphatic power of balanced forms and serial constructions. We will discover that the versatility of the cumulative sentence can also be extended to help us master these new forms, although cumulative syntax will now become only one of many different means to the end of making our writing more effective. ■

Question to Consider

1. Write a smooth-sounding cumulative sentence that uses no less than 100 words. Your sentence should sound as smooth and natural as possible. It may also be compound, with modifying levels for each of two or more base clauses joined by conjunctions. It's more fun, though, to see if you can construct your 100-word sentence around a single base clause.

Prompts of Explanation
Lecture 12—Transcript

One of the most important assumptions of this course is that the most effective prose establishes a relationship between writer and reader. That's a relationship between two people, two distinct personalities. If our writing doesn't offer some glimpses of writers as personalities, it's hard to say that it has a style, much less that its style will appeal to readers. As I noted in the last lecture, if our writing displays no more of the way we think, the ways in which we process information, than does objective technology, such as that we might find in a security camera at a convenience store, it probably doesn't matter that what we write accurately records and reports information. That's the difference between a writer and a security camera: The security camera only records what takes place in front of its lens, while the writer thinks about, reflects upon, forms opinions about, and frequently comments on what he or she is writing about.

Another way of putting this assumption is for me to argue that our writing is purpose-driven, and almost always we have multiple purposes when we write. We write to accomplish a wide variety of goals, and very, very rarely is our primary goal only to record or to report. We record and report in order to accomplish larger purposes, and those larger purposes shape the way in which we approach the task of recording and reporting, choosing what to include, choosing what to exclude, organizing our presentation of information to best suit our purposes. One of the important purposes that we should always have in mind when we write is, as Joan Didion so powerfully put it in her celebrated essay "On Keeping A Notebook," "Remember what it was to be me: that is always the point."

Didion was specifically meditating on keeping a notebook or a journal and not on writing in general, but I think her reminder serves all writers in good stead, applying to greater or lesser degree to almost everything we write. She was definitely not offering a brief for solipsism, even in notebook writing, or even arguing that the writers should primarily be concerned with remembering and conveying their personality in everything they write. She was, I believe, reminding herself and us that writing is one of the most distinctly human activities, and that, like all human knowledge, it inherently, inevitably, and gloriously involves acts of interpretation. If that were not the case, there would be no difference between the human writer and the mechanical security camera.

If we scale down this large philosophical assumption to the level of the sentences we write, it suggests we should be concerned not just with the accuracy and clarity of what we write, but that we should also be concerned with making our writing a reflection of who we are, how we think, what we value. The style of our writing is determined by a huge number of variables, but one aspect of that style should always be that our writing present us as individual consciousnesses, as personalities who process the information we pass on in our writing, rather than as automatons who only record, report, or summarize information, as if it were being spewed out by a machine, or even worse, by a committee.

Sure, there are some writing situations where we want to submerge our individuality in the collective prose of a committee, and there are some situations when we might want our writing to pretend to the accuracy and objectivity of a mechanical recording device, although I'm hard-pressed to think of situations where we would want that to be the case. But here, as elsewhere in this course, I'm referring to writing as a discovery process in which writers find out things about themselves, even as they write for specific audiences with specific purposes in mind. My definition of writing always includes the processing of information by the writer's mind, a requirement that distinguishes writing from copying, from repeating, from mere recording and reporting.

We signal that we're processing information in our writing in a number of ways, several of which we've already been exploring in this course. The cumulative syntax itself signals our determination to get it right, to extend the detail and explanation in our writing further, to take one more crack at making as clear as possible what we're trying to communicate, using cumulative modifying phrases to sharpen our images and to better reveal our reasoning. In the last lecture, I suggested that the cumulative syntax can also prompt us to include similes and metaphors in our writing, particularly similes that compare what we are writing about with something else, the comparison both offering another perspective on our way of thinking about our subject, and offering a window onto the way our own thinking works, a glimpse of our intellectual personality, our individuality, our style.

I want to suggest another way in which cumulative syntax can serve to prompt us to reveal more about our thinking, more about the characteristic ways in which we process information. One step beyond making the comparisons, as similes do, between two things or situations that are different, and sometimes quite different, is for us to speculate about that which is not known. Some similes are already well on their way beyond comparison and into speculation, as we can see in this passage from John Updike's well-known short story "A&P," where the protagonist Sammy is describing a striking young girl in a bathing suit, who, along with two friends, has just entered the grocery store where he's a checker:

> She didn't look around, not this queen, she just walked straight on slowly, on these long white-prima-donna legs. She came down a little hard on her heels, as if she didn't walk in her bare feet [that] much, putting down her heels and then letting the weight move along to her toes as if she was testing the floor with every step, putting a little deliberate extra action into it.

Both of the "as if" comparisons Updike offers in this last sentence reveal Sammy's speculation as he tries to account for the girl's noteworthy way of walking. Both of these similes are actually offered more tentatively than authoritatively, presented as possible comparisons, possible explanations. Two sentences from Joyce Carol Oates's "Where Have You Been, Where Are You Going?" suggest the degrees of difference between a simile that primarily advances a comparison and one that primarily advances a speculation:

"He spoke in a simple lilting voice, exactly as if he were reciting the words to a song."

That seems firmly grounded in an easily visualized comparison, but consider this sentence:

"She looked at it for a while as if the words meant something to her that she did not yet know."

That seems to be a simile of a quite different sort, offering much more speculation than it offers actual comparison. We signal such speculation in lots of different ways, but I'll just focus on three of these signals: the words *because, possibly,* and *perhaps.* I've chosen these words because they also lend themselves to the step logic and downshifting rhythms of the cumulative syntax, and that also means that they lend themselves to becoming generative challenges or heuristic prompts in the way the cumulative syntax does so distinctively and so well.

Consider these sentences:

> The dog froze in place, ears up to detect the slightest sound, eyes riveted on the clump of brush, possibly sensing danger.

Or:

> Cumulative syntax prompts us to add information to our sentences, reminding us that there's always more to say, more detail or explanation that will make our writing more clear, possibly serving as a silent voice, a kind of personal writing trainer, urging us to go for that extra level of meaning, to push ourselves to anticipate a reader's possible questions about what we've just written, always thinking about the benefits of having our sentences take that extra step.

Or:

> He suddenly ran off the stage, possibly because he had forgotten his lines, possibly because he had just noticed the audience for the first time, perhaps even because he was in some physical distress.

Each of these sentences goes beyond stating what is known to suggest motivations or causes that remain speculative. Each sentence attempts to explain the image, idea, or situation it references, revealing that the writer wants to be helpful, wants to account for things as well as possible, wants to further engage the reader in the effort to make the best sense possible of the information provided by the sentence. Each sentence gives us a glimpse of the way the writer thinks about the world in general, and the subject of his or her writing in particular.

My pitch is that adding speculation concerning motive behind, cause of, or interpretation of the events or actions we write about helps forge the connection between reader and writer as two minds at work. Obviously, speculations introduced by words such as *possibly* or *perhaps* will not be appropriate in many writing situations, but knowing how well the cumulative syntax lends itself to speculative phrases introduced by these words may prompt us to consider whether or not to use them. After all, just knowing how easily we can add speculation to our writing may encourage us to put a bit more of the way we think into our writing, possibly forging a stronger relationship with a reader who appreciates our willingness to go beyond the "Just the facts, Ma'am" literalness of Sgt. Joe Friday in *Dragnet*, perhaps signaling our readers that it is as important to wonder why and how things happen as it is to know what happens.

Here, of course, I'm thinking of writing situations where it is as important to present our judgment, our ability to interpret, our commitment to understanding as it is to present unprocessed information. In this advocacy for making cumulative-step speculation an option in our writing, I'm applying to writing the advice Margaret Atwood gives to readers in her didactic short story, "Happy Endings." In that minimalist meditation on possible plots involving various relationships among briefly sketched lovers, Atwood urges readers to focus less on plots, which she describes as "just one thing after another, a what and a what and a what." Her advice is "Now try How and Why." I think that's great advice for writers as well, and in the cases when the how and why of a situation have not been and possibly cannot be determined, it frequently benefits the writer to move beyond the known to speculate about the likely or even just the possible.

Consider these sentences:

> The fire spread quickly, its flames fanned by the stiff breeze, consuming the small apartment in minutes, possibly the result of a candle left burning too close to blowing curtains.

Some cumulative sentences place a second-level modifying phrase just after the first clause in a compound sentence and just before the second clause, as in this sentence from E. B. White:

> They damned the falls, shutting out the tide, and dug a pit so deep you could look down and see China.

White is possibly using that middle modifying phrase as a kind of hinge, turning the sentence in a new direction.

Thomas Berger remains one of America's most celebrated under-read authors, a writer whose books enjoy rave reviews, but whose sales and numbers rarely rise above respectable, possibly because his fiction consistently resists the twin sentimentalities of idealism and despair.

Linguistic theory tells us that the last or the next-to-last step or slot in the sentence generally is the place in the sentence where we want to put the most intonational stress. As Martha Kolln explains in her chapter on sentence rhythm in her *Rhetorical Grammar: Grammatical Choices, Rhetorical Effects*, this well-recognized rhythm pattern is called end focus, and it gives rhythmic emphasis to information at the end or near the end of the sentence. Professor Strunk had already intuited this principle in 1919 as his 22nd and final "Principle of Composition" in his "little book." It was, "Place the emphatic words of a sentence at the end."

I have mixed feelings about this advice, particularly when it is used to make the claim that periodic or suspensive sentences are somehow superior to loose or right-branching cumulative sentences. The truth is, we can shape our sentences so that we can emphasize any part of them we want to, and that emphasis is rhetorical rather than grammatical, determined by the context and purpose of the sentence rather than by its grammatical form. To his great credit, Professor Strunk acknowledged that truth by qualifying his "end-of-sentence" advice, explaining, "The proper place in the sentence for the word or group of words that the writer desires to make most prominent is *usually* the end," emphasis mine. Moreover, shortly thereafter he adds that "… the *other* prominent position in the sentence is the *beginning*," emphasis mine again. The point we need to remember is that position by itself may or may not place emphasis, but the end position does generally tend to lend itself to emphasis.

And that's why, in the last lecture, I suggested the advantages of using the final step of a cumulative sentence for a summative simile or a simile that recasts previous information in more dramatic and memorable form. That's why, in this lecture, I'm suggesting the advantages of using the final step of a cumulative sentence for speculation about motive or likely consequences or cause, speculation signaled by the words *because, possibly,* or *perhaps*. Of these heuristic prompts, *because* sounds a lot more certain than does *possibly* or *perhaps*, and *because* is a subordinating conjunction, almost always introducing a subordinate clause rather than a modifying phrase. I group these words together because they serve very similar informational functions, and they so frequently appear in combination.

We can see how they work in combination in sentences such as "The guard fainted, dropping his rifle, crumpling at the feet of the Queen, perhaps because he had been standing in the blazing sun for hours," or as in "We all dropped the class, possibly because we couldn't see how it would help us make our fortunes, possibly because its instructor spoke very rapidly in a shrill, high voice, possibly because we were not convinced of the value of deconstructing old episodes of *Buffy the Vampire Slayer*, or possibly because it was at 7:30 in the morning."

Of course, the cumulative syntax also invites the placement of speculative phrases in the initial or medial slots of the sentence, but as has been my practice so far, I've focused on the final slot simply to take full advantage of the generative power of the cumulative, its final modifying phrase always reminding us of the option of coming up with a simile or speculation that might provide a new perspective, or offer a summation of what has gone before in the sentence, both options also giving us a chance to reveal more of the way we process information in our writing.

Nor do the heuristic prompts I've singled out exhaust the possibilities for introducing such speculation. *For* and *as* can be used interchangeably with *because*:

He knew that calling for help was useless, a waste of breath, because no one lived for miles around.

He knew that calling for help was useless, a waste of breath, for no one lived for miles around.

He knew that calling for help was useless, a waste of breath, as no one lived for miles around.

Obviously, none of these variations is a cumulative phrase in strict grammatical sense, but if the clause introduced by *because* or by causal uses of *for* or *as* come to us at the end of phrases that have established the cumulative rhythm, they work cumulatively, plugging into the rhetorical advantages and opportunities cumulative syntax offers us. I'm also not sure that any significant difference exists among these three sentences, but I suspect each of us gravitates toward one of these options more than we use the other two, and I further suspect we do so because we sense at least connotative differences among the three. To my ear, *for* in place of *because* sounds just a bit old, archaic, possibly poetic. At the very least, using *for* in place of *because*, that is, using it as a conjunction, may lead to some confusion if a second *for* appears in the sentence, this time serving as a preposition.

We can see this happen in a sentence from Joan Didion's essay "On Keeping a Notebook." Responding to complaints from members of her family that her memories of shared events are frequently in error, she acknowledges:

> Very likely they are right, for not only have I always had trouble distinguishing between what happened and what merely might have happened, but I remain unconvinced that the distinction, for my purposes, matters.

As in place of *because* sounds a tad smug to me. "She didn't come to the party, as we had not invited her." As a matter of fact, *as* is a word with as many different uses as to stun those of us who don't think systematically, perhaps obsessively, about language. Fowler's *Modern English Usage* identifies a whopping 13 different ways or senses in which the word *as* can be used. I mention this only because it is from little choices, such as those concerning our choice between *as* and *for*, that we build individual writing styles, and as much as is possible, I'd like my own writing style to be the result of conscious choices that I can, if need be, explain, even though those choices have become so habitual or so natural for me that I certainly am no longer conscious of them when I write.

Nor, of course, are *possibly* or *perhaps* the only words we can use to signal speculation. *Maybe* would serve the same purpose, or we might choose *probably* to signal a greater degree of confidence in our speculation. Should we wish to move beyond speculation to offer an explanation that puts distance between our thinking and apparent or received truth, we might wish to introduce our summative cumulative modifying phrase with a word such as *likely*, a phrase such as *more likely*, or a word as insistent as *actually*. Here are examples:

> The guard fainted, dropping his rifle, crumpling at the feet of the Queen, likely a casualty of poor training and poor conditioning.

> The guard fainted, dropping his rifle, crumpling at the feet of the Queen, more likely a sign of his nervousness than of exhaustion.

> The guard fainted, dropping his rifle, crumpling at the feet of the Queen, actually reinforcing the view widely held by the press that these ceremonial inspections were pointless.

And, of course, the verbs most frequently associated with the kind of writerly speculation I'm advocating are *seems* and *appears*, the verbal participial forms of both *seeming* and *appearing*, custom-made for introducing speculative cumulative modifying phrases. Here's an example:

> Each essay explored another of the writer's fears, seeming to reveal an almost infinite number of pathologies, each appearing more threatening than the last.

Another example:

> She built her business slowly, opening a new store only when its success was certain, seemingly incapable of miscalculations when assessing likely profits.

Or another:

> The young novelist produced bestseller after bestseller, appearing to have stumbled on some magic formula for literary success.

By this point in the lecture, I must seem less and less concerned with the production and inclusion in our writing just of cumulative sentences, and more and more concerned with ways in which we foreground ourselves in our writing as thinkers, developing the ethical appeal of our writing. I've only begun to skim the surface of ways in which we can foreground ourselves in our writing as thinkers, as information processors. Obviously, there are an almost infinite number of ways we can call attention to ourselves as the consciousness, the personality behind what we write. We can use verbs of intellectual agency, verbs such as *I think, I believe, I know*, or *it seems to me*. We can use phrases that self-consciously foreground our thinking, phrases such as *in my opinion* or *the way I see it*.

There are other ways, probably beyond counting, and certainly beyond systematic study, to accomplish this important goal. For instance, listen to the way E. B. White makes his opinion very clear about the ethics of mining companies in this sentence from his essay "Letter From the East":

"The mining company soon milked the place dry of copper and zinc and got out, the way mining companies do."

If his choice of "milked" as a verb didn't establish his view of mining companies, the final cumulative modifying phrase "the way mining companies do" makes his disdain unmistakable. I'm betting that each of us could come up with quite a list of ways in which we can signal in our writing the individuality of our thinking. What's more, I bet our lists would be quite different, yet another tribute to the diversity and multiplicity of language.

Perhaps I should acknowledge once again that my approach to teaching writing does value very highly the ethos aspect of rhetorical situations, in part because those other two classic components of rhetoric, logos and pathos, strike me as much more beyond the effective reach of writing instruction since they are always so context-dependent. We may not be able to anticipate the logical or emotional context in which we must write, but we do always bring the same creative consciousness to the process of writing. We can always remember, as Joan Didion put it, "what it meant to be me," or what it means to be me, and how we want to communicate to our readers our personality, our individuality, as the creative mind behind what we write.

We are now fast approaching an important turning point in this course. In the next lecture, I will make a final pass at stressing the importance of the rhythm of our sentences, particularly as cumulative syntax provides us with some fairly predictable ready-made rhythms. In Lecture Fourteen, we'll shift our focus from the cumulative syntax as a versatile and powerful armature on which we can build our writing style, and begin looking at other syntax opportunities, some of which can still be approached through cumulative techniques, but some of which are nearly completely antithetical to the cumulative assumptions and practices to which I've devoted the first half of this course.

It's time now for us to turn our attention to the delaying strategies of periodic or suspensive sentences, and to the powerful rhythmic appeal and emphatic power of balanced forms and serial constructions. This does not mean, however, that we will suddenly abandon the cumulative moves we've been exploring. Instead, we will discover that the versatility of the cumulative sentence can also be extended to help us master these new forms, although cumulative syntax will now become only one of the many different means to the end of making our writing more effective.

The Riddle of Prose Rhythm
Lecture 13

The topic of prose rhythm is tremendously more complicated and tremendously less understood, much less agreed upon, than is the topic of rhythm in dance or music or even in poetry.

Most of us recognize distinctive rhythms in prose but have never stopped to think about them in terms of the relationship between the long and short steps by which our sentences move forward in time. One way of thinking about these rhythmic relationships is to compare them with the dih/dah or dot/dash rhythms of Morse code. For example, writers who use cumulative modifying levels frequently alternate between long and short modifying levels, with a single word producing the effect of the Morse Code dot. Thus, "Slowly, he opened the book, thumbing through its pages, stroking its cover" might be thought of as dot—dash—dash—dash." And that rhythm can be compared with that of "He opened the book, slowly, thumbing through its pages, stroking its cover," or dash—dot—dash—dash. Each rhythm slightly changes the sentence and can create almost hypnotic effects, as we can see in this sentence from *The Great Gatsby*: "Slenderly, languidly, their hands set lightly on their hips, the two young women preceded us out onto a rosy-colored porch, open toward the sunset, where four candles flickered on the table in the diminished wind." Dot—dot—dash—dash—dash—dash.

I can't dance, but while my sense of rhythm is pretty hopeless when it comes to dancing, I think I have a very good ear for rhythm in prose. I recognize it when I am reading silently. I think I do a good job of invoking it when I read prose aloud, and I can be equally hypnotized by Virginia Woolf's gentle and carefully crafted rhythms and by the sometimes manically varied rhythms found in Thomas Berger's fiction. I've chosen passages from Woolf and Berger to suggest the possible range of prose rhythms. Notice that these passages are rhythmical, but not musical or even metrical—the result of how each proceeds forward in steps rather than of syllable count or meter. As Ursula K. Le Guin reminds us in her writing text, *Steering the Craft*, "The sound of language is where it all begins and what it all comes back to. The basic elements of language are physical; the noise words make and the rhythm of their relationships. This is just as true of written prose as of poetry." My writing students may at first roll their eyes when I tell them that a sentence they've written needs an extra beat or needs to be slowed down or speeded up, but they almost always agree with me once we start working on the sentence.

The basic elements of language are physical; the noise words make and the rhythm of their relationships.

I'm going to focus this lecture on the important but unsettled topic of prose rhythm. I'll give a very brief overview of the history of attempts to study, measure, explain, or theorize prose rhythm. I'll offer a couple of ways of thinking about the importance of prose rhythm. I'll offer a modest way of thinking about prose rhythm in the cumulative sentences we've been working with, including a very modest model for describing the rhythms of some cumulative sentences.

Aristotle seems to have been one of the earliest to weigh in on this topic of prose rhythm. He prescribed that "prose should not be metrical, nor should it be without rhythm." As he explained this dictum, "Metrical prose is unconvincing because it betrays artifice" and also because it "distracts the hearer, who is led to look for the recurrence of a similar metrical pattern." But after saying that prose should not be metrical, Aristotle goes on to discuss prose rhythms in exclusively metrical terms. We can't transfer Aristotle's pronouncements about rhythms in Greek prose to rhythms in English prose.

Prose rhythms are simply too diverse—too variable and unpredictable—to be treated metrically, at least in the terms we use to analyze poetry: feet and syllables, stressed and unstressed. Yet the history of attempts to analyze prose rhythm shows that they are largely prone to doing just that: dividing prose passages into feet, marking accented and unaccented syllables, and identifying the meter revealed by the scan in exactly the way we identify the meter of poetry. Apart from accepting and passing along the assumption that prose rhythm is essentially just a watered-down version of poetic rhythm, most early-20th-century efforts to describe rhythm in prose manage to agree that very little agreement exists in their enterprise.

Metrical theories give us labels for metrical phenomena we can indeed find, on occasion, in prose, but those labels tell us absolutely nothing about the way prose rhythm works—about the relational realities it establishes between writers and readers. Only slightly more helpful are the related attempts to treat prose essentially as song lyrics and to describe it with musical time notations. We don't fare much better when we move to the experiential end of the continuum, where descriptions of prose rhythm invoke the rhythms of nature and the rhythms of the Bible.

One step in the right direction of understanding prose rhythm comes in another early-20th-century study, William Morris Patterson's *The Rhythm of Prose*. Patterson's study was supplemented by "voice photographs" of the wave patterns made by recordings of subjects uttering certain words and phrases. What strikes me about the Patterson study is its emphasis not only on rhythm as an experience but as inherently subjective experience. Patterson explains, "Rhythm is tangled up with our sense of time and our sense of intensity, both of which are not only tricky, but multifarious."

Patterson gives me a couple of terms I want to put to my own use. The first is his concept of the "aggressively rhythmic individual." I may be at sea on the dance floor, but when I read prose—particularly when I read prose aloud—I don the mask and cape of the "aggressively rhythmic individual," and I create in my reading the rhythms I most value. In Patterson's references to *spaced prose*, I hear an opportunity to invoke, once again, both the cumulative sentence and Josephine Miles's understanding that "prose proceeds forwards by steps less closely measured, but not less propelling, than the steps of verse."

Most of us recognize distinctive rhythms in prose but have never stopped to think about them in terms of the relationship of the long and short steps by which our sentences move forward in time. One way of thinking about these rhythmic relationships is to compare them with the dih/dah or dot/dash rhythms of Morse Code. For example, writers who use cumulative modifying levels frequently alternate between long and short modifying levels, with a single word producing the effect of the Morse Code dot. Thus, "Slowly, he opened the book, thumbing through its pages, stroking its cover" might be thought of as "dot—dash—dash—dash." To be honest, I'm still not completely sure what use we make of the insight that cumulative sentences seem to become more dramatic when they alter phrase steps with very short, single-word steps. But once you have this pattern pointed out to you, you'll start noticing it in more and more cases as a device used by a wide range of writers. ■

Question to Consider

1. Find five sentences (or sequences of sentences) whose effectiveness comes from variation in sentence length or in the length of modifying phrases.

The Riddle of Prose Rhythm
Lecture 13—Transcript

I'm really fond of the old Jerome Kern/Oscar Hammerstein song that goes "I can't dance, don't ask me." Only, as I suspect a number of you may already be thinking, that isn't exactly the way the song goes. The title of the song is "I Won't Dance," and the lyrics go "I *won't* dance, don't ask me." I'm not sure when I confused the lyrics or how I managed to remember "can't dance" from a show-stopping song and dance number performed by Fred Astaire, who—somewhat famously—*could* dance. Of course, it may be that my misremembering dates not from watching Astaire and Ginger Rogers in the 1935 musical *Roberta* but instead dates from the equally memorable performances by Kermit and Miss Piggy in an episode of *The Muppet Show*. And, after all, some confusion may be understandable here, since it seems that the original lyrics for the Jerome Kern/Oscar Hammerstein version of "I Won't Dance" were completely rewritten by the songwriting team of Dorothy Fields and Jimmy McHugh, and it's their lyrics we remember—or in my case misremember—today.

And, indeed, even though it is Fred Astaire who sang the song in *Roberta*—while spectacularly dancing—the lyrics do at least hint at problems with dancing, including, "I won't dance, why should I? / I won't dance, how could I?"

If you're wondering why I've suddenly gone all musical-trivia on you, there is a reason. You see, I can't dance. I have absolutely no sense of rhythm. Sure, I can shuffle around enough to fake it for a minute or two at weddings, bat mitzvahs, anniversary celebrations, and the like, but I simply can't dance. And, to judge from the anguished admissions I kept coming across on the Internet when I was trying to track down the song whose lyrics I so tellingly misremembered, I'm not alone. The number of my fellow sufferers, all of us rhythmically challenged, is legion! Moreover, I was grateful to discover that I am far from being alone in misremembering "I won't dance" as "I can't dance." Indeed, many of the references to this song on the Web make that very same mistake.

But here's the funny thing: While my sense of rhythm is pretty close to hopeless when it comes to dancing—or even to clapping in time with music—I think I have a very good ear for rhythm in prose. I recognize it even when reading silently, think I do a good job of invoking it when I read prose aloud, and I can be equally hypnotized by the gentle and carefully crafted rhythms of prose written by Virginia Woolf or the sometimes manically varied prose rhythms found in the fiction of Thomas Berger.

Listen to this justly celebrated, exquisitely measured passage from Virginia Woolf's *Mrs. Dalloway*:

> Quiet descended on her, calm, content, as her needle, drawing the silk smoothly to its gentle pause, collected the green folds together and attached them, very lightly, to the belt. So on a summer's day waves collect, overbalance, and fall; collect and fall; and the whole world seems to be saying "that is all" more and more ponderously, until even the heart in the body which lies in the sun on the beach says too, That is all. Fear no more, says the heart. Fear no more, says the heart, committing its burden to some sea, which sighs collectively for all sorrows, and renews, begins, collects, lets fall. And the body alone listens to the passing bee; the wave breaking; the dog barking, far away barking and barking.

And here are two very different-sounding sentences from two of Thomas Berger's novels. The first is from his classic *Little Big Man* and is in the inimitable voice of Jack Crabb:

> As I say, none of us understood the situation, but me and Caroline was considerably better off than the chief, because we only looked to him for our upkeep in the foreseeable future, whereas he at last decided we was demons and only waiting for dark to steal the wits from his head; and while riding along he muttered prayers and incantations to bring us bad medicine, but so ran his luck that he never saw any of the animal brothers that assisted his magic—such as Rattlesnake or Prairie Dog—but rather only Jackrabbit, who had a grudge against him of longstanding because he once had

kept a prairie fire off his camp by exhorting it to burn the hares' home instead.

The second example is from Berger's retelling of the "matter of Britain" in his *Arthur Rex* and sounds more than a bit like Sir Thomas Mallory—but like a Mallory who has just mastered the cumulative sentence:

> Now the abominable Sir Meliagrant took Guinevere to a kingdom that was not very distant from Britain but was cunningly concealed, tucked into a valley amongst mountains, entrance to which could be gained only by one pass not easily found, and before this pass was a rushing river over which was but one bridge, the narrowest in the world, for it was made of one long sword, the weapon of a giant, the which was mounted horizontally, keen edge upwards.

I've chosen these particular passages to share with you to suggest the range of prose rhythms we can hear in Woolf's finely architected prose, Berger's mastery of American vernacular prose rhythms, and Berger's ability to invoke the sound of Sir Thomas Mallory's prose, but in a book whose prose is also thorough-goingly modern. Notice that these passages are rhythmical, but not musical or even metrical—the result of the way each proceeds forward in steps rather than of syllable count or meter. As Ursula K. Le Guin reminds us in her delightful writing text, *Steering the Craft*, "The sound of language is where it all begins and what it all comes back to. The basic elements of language are physical; the noise words make and the rhythm of their relationships. This is just as true of written prose as it is of poetry."

Or as Virginia Woolf so perfectly put it in an excerpt from one of her letters that Le Guin cites:

> Style is a very simple matter; it is all rhythm. Once you get that, you can't use the wrong words.... Now this is very profound, what rhythm is, and goes far deeper than words. A sight, an emotion, creates this wave in the mind, long before it makes words to fit it.

My writing students may at first roll their eyes when I tell them that a sentence they've written needs an extra beat or needs to be slowed down or speeded up, but they almost always agree with me once we start working on the sentence. And once I get them thinking about prose rhythm, they credit that not only with helping them improve their own writing, but also with making their reading more enjoyable, as they start finding delight in writers at the level of the sentence that may help them understand why they are attracted to a writer's "larger" characteristics such as plot or theme or character.

What's funny about this seeming contradiction—no sense of rhythm when it comes to dancing, pretty good ear for rhythm when it comes to prose— is that the topic of prose rhythm is tremendously more complicated and tremendously less understood, much less agreed upon, than is the topic of rhythm in dance or music or even in poetry. Questions about the nature of prose rhythm are even peskier than are questions about the nature of prose style, and of course, there's every reason to suspect that prose rhythm plays a very important role in determining prose style—whatever we decide prose style is.

Accordingly, I'm going to focus this lecture on the oh-so-important but oh-so-unsettled topic of prose rhythm. It's too important for me not to mention it, too complicated and conflicted for me to do much more than suggest some of the complexities. So I'm going to give a very brief overview of the history of attempts to study, measure, explain, or theorize prose rhythm. I'm going to offer a couple of ways of thinking about the importance of prose rhythm. And finally, I'm going to offer a very modest way of thinking about prose rhythm in the cumulative sentences we've been working with, including a very, very modest model for describing the rhythms of some cumulative sentences.

As is frequently the case with matters pertaining to rhetoric and poetics, Aristotle seems to have been one of the earliest to weigh in on the topic of prose rhythm. Aristotle laid down a kind of "golden mean" law that prescribed "prose should not be metrical, nor should it be without rhythm." As he explained this dictum, "Metrical prose is unconvincing because it betrays artifice" and also because it "distracts the hearer who is led to look for the recurrence of a similar metrical pattern." Once prose becomes metrical, it becomes predictable, Aristotle argued, leading even children to anticipate what will come next in highly metrical prose.

So far, so good. Most of us would agree with his reasoning today, even though our attitude toward artifice in language, our understanding of the range of metrical patterns, and our sense of prose rhythms are all almost certainly quite different from those held by Aristotle. It's what he said next that still proves problematic: "Prose without rhythm is formless, and it should have form, but not meter. The indefinite and formless is displeasing and cannot be known. ... Prose then must have a rhythm but not meter, for if it has meter it will be a poem."

The problem is that after saying prose rhythm should not be metrical, Aristotle then goes on to discuss prose rhythms in exclusively metrical terms, just as if he were discussing poetry, referring to the "heroic" rhythm driven by dactyls and spondees, the "conversational" rhythm built into the iambic foot, and then the paeon with its parts in a ratio of two to three—none of which I'm going to try to explain, because it is all hopeless hooey. First of all, when we try to transfer Aristotle's pronouncements about rhythms in Greek prose to rhythms in English prose; and second of all because prose rhythms are simply too diverse, too variable, too unpredictable to be treated metrically, at least in the same way that we analyze poetry in terms of feet and syllables, stressed and unstressed.

Yet the history of attempts to analyze prose rhythm are largely prone to doing just that—dividing prose passages into feet, marking accented and unaccented syllables, and identifying the meter revealed by the scan in exactly the way we identify the meter of poetry.

Aristotle may have started us down this unproductive path, but it was British critic George Saintsbury who more than any other single authority doomed us to this approach with his 1912 magnum opus, *History of English Prose Rhythm*. Not only did Saintsbury largely follow Aristotle's lead, but he scoured the books for even more esoteric meters than those usually discussed in poetry and swelled the list of possible prose rhythms with impossibly arcane meters such as "amphibrach," "molossus," "proceleusmatic."

Saintsbury's efforts to describe English prose rhythms marked a period in the early decades of the 20th century during which there appeared a veritable stampede of theories and studies of rhythm in general and prose rhythm in particular. Somewhat typical was Albert C. Clark's lecture "Prose Rhythm in English," published by Oxford in 1913. Clark held:

> For the origin of prose rhythm we must go to Cicero. Nature, he tells us, has placed in the ears a register which tells us if a rhythm is good or bad, just as by the same means we are enabled to distinguish notes in music. Men first observed that particular sounds gave pleasure to the ear, then they repeated them for this end. ... The rhythm of prose is based on the same principle as that of verse. This in ancient prose was the distribution of long and short syllables; in our own tongue it is the arrangement of stressed and unstressed syllables.

A related attempt to describe prose rhythm in metrical terms was associated with Morris W. Croll, whose 1919 "The Cadence of English Oratorical Prose" and 1966 book *Style, Rhetoric, and Rhythm* advocated identifying prose rhythms according to a typology of clause endings used in medieval Latin. To the Latin meters identified as *planus*, *tardus*, *velox*, and *trispondaic*, Croll added some new endings he thought he had discovered in English prose. Once again, I hope you'll understand why I'm not going to try to explain this system, beyond noting its almost desperate desire to tie contemporary English prose rhythms to the classification system used in an ancient language that was not English.

Even more desperate seeming is the longing in these attempts to find a way of describing prose as essentially regular in its rhythms, with one particular beat or meter predominating throughout a single piece of prose or the prose of a single writer—this notwithstanding the repeated unflattering references from Aristotle to the present to Greek audiences that found the rhythms of some Greek orators so predictable they could not resist beating time like dancers with the speaker, "not apparently from any wish to ridicule him, but unable to resist the temptation and infection," claimed Saintsbury. While classical commentators from Aristotle to Quintilian to Cicero seem to agree that "variety" should be at the heart of effective prose rhythm, those commentators seem hopelessly tied to the notion that "variety" should occur at some level higher than that of the sentence, whose feet must necessarily manifest some regular meter, after the manner of poetry. Of course, today much poetry no longer regularly manifests meter, which makes it even harder to understand the persistent efforts to describe prose rhythm in terms of poetic meter.

Apart from simply accepting and passing along the assumption that prose rhythm is essentially just a watered-down version of poetic rhythm, most early-20th-century efforts to describe rhythm in prose manage to agree that very little agreement exists in their enterprise. E. A. Sonnenschein began his 1925 study, *What is Rhythm?*, with the somewhat discouraged observation:

> The large number of works on metre and prosody published during recent years in Europe and America bear eloquent testimony to the existence of a world-wide interest in the problem of rhythm, and to a deep-seated dissatisfaction with the results hitherto arrived at by enquirers. For it is evident not only that there is no accepted theory of rhythm in the field, but that there is no common understanding among enquirers as to the very nature of the thing called "rhythm."

Attempting to rectify this sad state of affairs, Professor Sonnenschein finally gets around to offering his own definition of rhythm: "Rhythm is that property of a sequence of events in time which produces on the mind of an observer the impression of proportion between the durations of the several events or groups of events of which the sequence is composed."

Phew! I'm glad we cleared that up. But, as generally unhelpful as I find this—and most other—takes on rhythm, I'm going to return to Sonnenschein's definition in just a minute to consider one part I think he got very right—the part that locates the order or pattern or structure of rhythm not in the language of the speaker or writer but locates rhythm only as that which "produces *on the mind of an observer* the impression of order or proportion."

I'm not a student of prosody, but as far as I can tell, Sonnenschein's description from 1925 pretty much describes the state of agreement—or disagreement—concerning prose rhythms that we still have today.

But not to worry! Remember that John Steinbeck quotation about spine counting? Metrical theories of prose rhythm strike me as the worst kind of spine counting. The good news is that they give us labels for metrical phenomena we can indeed find, on occasion, in prose; the bad news is that those labels tell us absolutely nothing about the way prose rhythm works—about the relational realities it establishes between writers and readers. And only slightly more productive are the related attempts to treat prose essentially as song lyrics and to describe it with musical time notations. Particularly for those of us who can't dance, this approach is not very promising, and while it may produce results for prose we widely recognize as "musical," it has little or no descriptive power for the vast majority of prose we encounter.

Unfortunately, we don't fare a lot better when we move to the experiential end of the descriptive continuum, where descriptions of prose rhythm invoke the rhythms of nature and the rhythms of the Bible. The ninth edition of the *Encyclopedia Britannica*, the famous "Scholar's edition" published between 1875 and 1889, has this to say about prose rhythm:

> Perhaps it may be said that deeper than all the rhythms of art is that rhythm which art would fain catch, the rhythm of nature; for the rhythm of nature is the rhythm of life itself. This rhythm can be caught by prose as well as by poetry, such prose, for instance, as that of the English Bible … Being rhythm, it is of course governed by law, but it is a law which transcends in subtlety the conscious art of the metricist, and is only caught by the poet in his most inspired moods, a law which, being part of nature's own sanctions, can of course never be formulated, but only expressed as it is expressed in the melody of the bird, in the inscrutable harmony of the entire bird-chorus of a thicket, in the whisper of the leaves of the tree, and in the song or wail of wind and sea …

I'm not sure what I gain when I trade in my metronome for the rhythms of birds and the wind and the sea, although I suspect it's a step in the right direction. And I've come across another step in the right direction of understanding prose rhythm in another early-20th-century study. I've been fascinated by the approach and findings of William Morrison Patterson's *The Rhythm of Prose: An Experimental Investigation of Individual Difference in the Sense of Rhythm*. Patterson was an English professor at Columbia, and his study, aided by the Columbia Department of Psychology, was published by Columbia University Press in 1917. His study was supplemented by "voice photographs" of the wave patterns made by recordings of subjects uttering certain words and phrases—including poet Amy Lowell reading from her own *vers libre* poetry.

What strikes me about the Patterson study is its emphasis not only on rhythm *as an experience*, but as an *inherently subjective* experience. Calling rhythm "one of the most 'individually different' of human experiences," Patterson explains "Rhythm is tangled up with our sense of time and our sense of intensity, both of which are not only tricky, but multifarious." He then followed this observation with a credo that sounds both modern and right, some 90 years after he wrote it:

> Nothing is more preposterous, therefore, than that an author, the organization of whose temporal impressions is confessedly vague [do I hear a faint hint here of "I can't dance"?], should undertake to present to humanity at large a comprehensive and final statement on the art of versification. His own particular code might easily be read with interest as a document, but could hardly be expected to serve as a universal guide. On the other hand, it would be equally misleading for the experiences of an aggressively rhythmic individual, with a relatively accurate sense of temporal values, strong motor reactions, and subtle powers of discrimination in pitch and stress, to be set forth as if they were thoroughly usual. The psychologists have long since recognized that rhythm is the result of a complex process, whose operation can never be reduced to any one short formula.

Apart from providing me with a useful and persuasive "Get Out of Jail Free" card when it comes to making systematic pronouncements about prose rhythm, Patterson also gives me a couple of terms I want to put to my own use. You may have noticed his reference in the quotation I just read to "an aggressively rhythmic individual." According to Patterson, "rhythmic experience, rather than so-called objective rhythm" is what we should be studying. And "rhythmic experience" tends to vary from individual to individual, with the "aggressively rhythmic individual" the one who has "the ability to organize subjectively into a sort of rhythmic tune any haphazard series of sounds, provided they are not too close to be distinguished or too far apart to be held together in one wave of attention." Or, to put this bluntly, rhythm is what we make it, something we construct rather than something we "find" or "discover." This is what I found so promising but unfulfilled in Sonnenschein's definition of rhythm as "that property of a sequence of events in time which produces *on the mind of an observer* the impression of proportion between the durations of the several events or groups of events of which the sequence is composed."

That's the first thing I want to borrow from Patterson, the idea of the "aggressively rhythmic individual." I may be at sea on the dance floor, but when I read prose—particularly when I read prose aloud—I don the mask and cape of the "aggressively rhythmic individual" and I create in my reading the rhythms I most value. The second term I want to borrow from Patterson is one he applied, apparently in some desperation, to the way Amy Lowell read her poetry. Noting that her reading of her free verse emphasized phrases rather than feet or meter, he suggested that her reading reminds us "gently but inevitably: 'This is a phrase! This is a phrase!'" Lowell's free verse, Patterson concluded, "lifts us necessarily out of prose experience. ... What is achieved, as a rule, in Miss Lowell's case," Patterson claims, "is emotional prose, emphatically phrased, excellent and moving. 'Spaced prose,' we may call it."

You will not be surprised to learn that in Patterson's references to Lowell's insistence "This is a phrase! This is a phrase!" as well as in his reference to her "spaced prose," I hear an opportunity to invoke, once again, both the cumulative sentence and Josephine Miles's understanding that "prose proceeds forward in time *by steps* less closely measured, but not less propelling, than the steps of verse." What I realized is that, for me, prose rhythm is a matter not of feet or regular metrical beat but of steps—the sound a sentence makes each time it takes a step forward with a phrase or a clause. And, of course, I've made no secret of my fondness for the particular kind of step forward the cumulative syntax urges us to take. And, unlike my feeling on the dance floor, where I always think I'm missing something everyone else is hearing, when it comes to prose style I think I hear—or at any rate think I create—rhythms everyone else is missing. The big difference is that my lack of a sense of rhythm in dancing comes from my perception, right or wrong, that regularity is the name of the game in dancing, but when it comes to prose, I figure variation is the name of the game. And, just as prose guidebook after prose guidebook tells us that the key to effective prose rhythm lies in varying the length of our sentences, I think it equally true that the key to effective prose rhythm lies in varying the length of our phrases or *steps* within the sentence.

And the cumulative sentence, quite apart from its distinctive backward and forward conceptual rhythm, its ability to backtrack and downshift to greater levels of specificity and detail, invites—indeed *encourages*—variety in the length of the cumulative phrases we add to the end of a base clause. Noted fiction writer Harold Brodkey once began an essay with the wonderfully suspensive sentence: "Sometimes in New York, I can create a zone of amusement and doubt around me by saying that I was a Boy Scout." As it happens, much the same holds true for an English professor at the University of Iowa. I mention this because the very modest way I'm about to propose for thinking about one of the prose rhythms we find ourselves using when we write cumulative sentences is directly tied to my experience as a Boy Scout with Morse code.

Most of us recognize distinctive rhythms in prose but have never stopped to think about them in terms of the relationship of the long and short steps by which our sentences move forward in time. One way of thinking about these rhythmic relationships is to compare them with the dih/dah or dot/dash rhythms of Morse code. For example, writers who use cumulative modifying levels frequently alternate between long and short modifying levels, with a single word producing the effect of the Morse code dot. Thus, "Slowly, he opened the book, thumbing through its pages, stroking its cover" might be thought of as dot—dash—dash—dash. And that rhythm can be compared with that of, "He opened the book, slowly, thumbing through its pages, stroking its cover," or dash—dot—dash—dash. Each rhythm slightly changes the sentence and can create almost hypnotic effects, as we can see in this great sentence from *The Great Gatsby*: "Slenderly, languidly, their hands set lightly on their hips, the two young women preceded us out onto a rosy-colored porch, open toward the sunset, where four candles flickered on the table in the diminished wind." Dot—dot—dash—dash—dash—dash.

Thus we might get a sentence: "He sprang to his feet, trembling, more excited than fearful," and we might ask ourselves how the rhythm of the sentence might actually change its meaning were we to move from the dash—dot—dash rhythm of the version I just read to the dot—dash—dash version of "Trembling, he sprang to his feet, more excited than fearful," or the dash—dash—dot version "He sprang to his feet, more excited than fearful, trembling," and so on through all the possible positionings.

To be honest, I'm still not completely sure what use we make of the insight that cumulative sentences seem to become more dramatic when they alternate longer steps with very short, single-word steps, but I'll guarantee that once you have this pattern pointed out to you, you'll start noticing it in more and more cases, a device used by a wide range of writers. And you may want to start utilizing this or other simple rhythms in your own writing.

Cumulative Syntax to Create Suspense
Lecture 14

In grammatical terms, sentences fall into just two main categories: sentences that are loose, putting the subject and the verb near the beginning of the sentence, and sentences that are periodic, delaying the unfolding of the sentence's most important news until its very end, demanding the reader's close attention—sometimes to the last word.

This lecture will complicate the binary opposition between *loose* and *periodic* sentences by demonstrating that sentences take their place in a continuum of delay and can best be thought of not as *types* but in terms of their degree of *suspensiveness*. The degree of suspensiveness of a cumulative sentence can be manipulated by the placement of its base clause. Thus we can start with a loose cumulative sentence. ("He sat down, rubbing his hands together, running his hungry eyes over the steaming food, anticipating the feast, savoring its aromas, stunned by his good fortune, realizing an opportunity like this might never come again.") and move its base clause toward the end of the sentence one phrase at a time, ending with a periodic cumulative sentence ("Rubbing his hands together, running his hungry eyes over the steaming food, anticipating the feast, savoring its aromas, stunned by his good fortune, realizing an opportunity like this might never come again, he sat down.") Thinking of degrees of suspense in our writing gives us much greater control over our sentences than does thinking of a kind of sentence that is loose and is the opposite of a kind of sentence that is periodic.

Most of the sentences we've worked with so far in this course have been, in grammatical terms, "loose sentences." They complete the basic pattern of subject and predicate early on, keeping subject and verb near the beginning of the sentence and close together. Most cumulative sentences are forms of loose syntax, quickly positing an initial base clause, then adding to it in modifying phrases that follow. The opposite of a loose sentence is a "periodic sentence" that delays or suspends the completion of its subject-verb clause until the very end. The periodic sentence seems particularly useful in periodic discourse, where "if ... then" constructions are frequently found.

Grammatical terminology stacks the deck against loose syntax when its opposite is not *tight* but *periodic* syntax. Even if we have no idea what "periodic" means, it sounds more formal, more businesslike, more impressive than *loose*. That's exactly the way most writing guides have constructed this opposition, associating loose sentences with simple or simplistic expression and equating periodic sentences with more sophisticated, complex thinking. Accordingly, many writing texts until the past few years have implied, if not prescribed, that writers should aspire to the formal maturity of the periodic sentence. In his 22nd principle of composition, Professor Strunk explains that "the effectiveness of the periodic sentence arises from the prominence it gives the main statement" by placing it at the end of the sentence. E. B. White certainly uses periodic technique and shows that the suspense it can build may be quite anticlimactic. My old *Harbrace College Handbook* (7th ed.) urges the writer to "gain emphasis by changing loose sentences into periodic sentences." Both Strunk and White and the *Harbrace Handbook* make difficulty of comprehension somehow a virtue in writing. But as we are about to see, the dichotomy long perceived between loose and periodic sentences is largely a false one.

For the moment I want to consider the history of the periodic sentence and to complicate the binary opposition between loose and periodic, demonstrating that sentences take their place in a continuum of delay and are best thought of not as types but in terms of their "degree of suspensiveness." The word "period" comes from the Greek word *periodos*, which had to do with cycles or coming back to or going around in a circle. Aristotle stressed the recurrent or reflexive nature of the periodic style as a style "that turns back on itself," citing as examples the antistrophes of the old poets and even suggesting that a period offered an antithetical opposition. Missing from Aristotle's view was the emphasis on interruption or delay that we now associate with periodic form. As Matthew Clark points out in his 2002 study, *A Matter of Style*, this identification of the periodic with antithesis—or with what we now think of as a balanced form—seems peculiar to Aristotle. All experts agree that the great classical master of the periodic sentence and of periodic style was the Roman orator Cicero. Ciceronian style is periodic style, as we understand the term today, particularly as it suggests delay, building to a dramatic conclusion at the end of the sentence.

Richard Lanham finds fault with both terms, *loose* and *periodic*, but notes that these terms do refer to different conceptual processes—a basic difference in how one human intelligence presents itself to another. "To imitate the mind in real-time interaction with the world is to write in some form of running style," he suggests, explaining, "Such a syntax models the mind in the act of coping with the world." Conversely, the periodic style dramatizes "a mind which has dominated experience and reworked it to its liking." Lanham reminds us that "to 'go with the flow' is as human as to oppose it, that humankind's bewilderment before raw event is as characteristic as the will to impose order on it." Lanham also notes that at the end of the Renaissance "a reaction set in against periodic structure as the ideal sentence shape." The revolt against the periodic sentence at the end of the Renaissance was only a mixed success, since, while most writing guidebooks today do warn against unrelieved strings of periodic sentences, they still suggest that the periodic sentence is what aspiring writers should try to write.

Think of suspensiveness as a continuum along which sentences fall.

I'm giving so much prominence to Lanham because I want to question the classic binary opposition between what Lanham identifies as "running" and "periodic" sentences or what is most frequently described as the opposition between loose and periodic syntax. Francis Christensen has helped us challenge this opposition with his theory of the cumulative sentence, which introduces us to one particular kind of loose sentence that grows tighter as it generates parallels, balances, even antitheses in its modifying phrases. By starting this course with the cumulative syntax and then moving on to the periodic syntax, I am not in any way suggesting that the latter somehow represents an advance or a refinement of or greater degree of sophistication than the other. I began this course with a focus on the cumulative sentence because it can provide a foundation for thinking about periodic sentences, while the reverse is not true. Nor do I want to suggest that the cumulative is somehow a superior syntax to be preferred over the periodic: My goal is to strip away several centuries of bias in favor of the periodic to celebrate these two syntaxes for their respective glories.

Let's look at some specific ways in which the grammatical distinction between cumulative and periodic sentences begin to break down. I'm going to stop using the term periodic, substituting for it suspensive, which has a connotative clean slate, only suggesting that the syntax builds suspense or suspends completion of the sentence's message to a greater or lesser degree. Winston Weathers and Otis Winchester explore this idea of degrees of suspensiveness (which they call "degrees of periodicity" in their book *The Strategy of Style*). Any sentence can be made more or less suspensive; think of suspensiveness as a continuum along which sentences fall. The more we are aware of this continuum and the more we master the sentence structures that constitute it, the more effective our writing will become. ■

Question to Consider

1. One of the great strengths of the suspensive syntax is that it allows us to write very long sentences, drawing out the final delivery of the most important information, delaying completion of the sentence by using a number of different strategies. Use this syntax to construct a smooth-sounding sentence containing not less than 100 words. Remember that the suspensive syntax can be constructed by employing within one sentence several different delaying strategies. Your sentence should sound as smooth and as natural as possible.

Cumulative Syntax to Create Suspense
Lecture 14—Transcript

Most of the sentences we've worked with so far in this course have been, in grammatical terms, "loose sentences." That means that they complete the basic pattern of subject and predicate early on, keeping subject and verb near the beginning of the sentence and keeping subject and verb close together. Most cumulative sentences are forms of loose syntax, quickly positing an initial base clause, then adding to it, detailing it, clarifying it in following modifying phrases. A sentence is considered loose no matter how long it is or how complex it is if it frontloads its subject and verb.

At least in grammatical terms, the opposite of a loose sentence is a "periodic sentence." Whereas the loose sentence wants to deliver its basic subject and verb information quickly, the periodic sentence wants to do just the opposite, delaying or suspending the completion of its subject-verb clause until the very end of the sentence. So in grammatical terms, sentences fall into just two main categories: sentences that are loose, putting the subject and the verb near the beginning of the sentence, and sentences that are periodic, delaying the unfolding of the sentence's most important news until its very end, demanding the reader's close attention—sometimes to the last word. Consider Midwesterner Nick Carraway's description of the East in *The Great Gatsby*:

> Even when the East excited me most, even when I was most keenly aware of its superiority to the bored, sprawling, swollen towns beyond the Ohio, with their interminable inquisitions which spared only the children and the very old—even then it had always for me a quality of …

"Distortion" is the word with which Nick ends his sentence, and until we get to that word, we really have no clear idea where his sentence is going. The East could have had a quality of lots of things for Nick—despair, unreality, sadness, pessimism, boredom, or any of an unlimited number of other negative descriptors, but it is only when we fill in that final blank with "distortion" that we fully comprehend what Nick is telling us.

That's a classic periodic sentence: "Even when the East excited me most, even when I was most keenly aware of its superiority to the bored, sprawling, swollen towns beyond the Ohio, with their interminable inquisitions which spared only the children and the very old—even then it had always for me a quality of distortion." And it's a really memorable, really emphatic sentence—it is striking, as many periodic sentences are.

And the periodic sentence seems particularly useful in philosophical discourse, where "if ... then" constructions are frequently found. Arguing that the universe "is not what I choose that it should be," Bertrand Russell explains:

> If it is indifferent to human desires, as it seems to be; if human life is a passing episode, hardly noticeable in the vastness of cosmic processes; if there is no superhuman purpose, and no hope of ultimate salvation, it is better to know and acknowledge this truth than to endeavor, in futile self-assertion, to order the universe to be what we find comfortable.

But before we start looking at some of the many other neat things periodic sentences can do, let's return for a moment to that idea that sentences fall into two main grammatical categories—loose and periodic.

If the terminology we have inherited for talking about sentences made any sense at all, the opposite of the loose sentence would be the "tight" sentence, not the periodic. And thinking of sentences as loose and tight would make it easier for us to decide which kind we prefer, with both terms having their positive and their negative connotations. But grammatical terminology immediately starts stacking the deck against loose syntax when its opposite is not tight but is periodic syntax. Even if we have no idea what "periodic" means, it sounds more formal, more businesslike, more impressive than "loose." And that's exactly the way most writing guides over the years have constructed this opposition, with loose sentences being equated with, or at least associated with, simple or simplistic expression and periodic sentences not just associated with but equated with more sophisticated, more complex thinking. Accordingly, many writing texts up until the past few years have strongly implied—if they have not openly prescribed—that writers should aspire to the formal maturity of the periodic sentence.

Number 18 of Professor Strunk's principles of composition in *The Elements of Style* is "Avoid a succession of loose sentences." Surprisingly enough, Professor Strunk did acknowledge that a writer could also err by using too many periodic sentences. He explained: "An occasional loose sentence prevents the style from becoming too formal and gives the reader a certain relief." However, there is no mistaking the put down in his description of loose sentences as "common in easy, unstudied writing" and in his dismissal that an "unskilled writer will sometimes construct a whole paragraph of sentences of this kind."

Later, in Professor Strunk's 22nd principle of composition, he explains that the "effectiveness of the periodic sentence arises from the prominence it gives the main statement" by placing it at the end of the sentence. He offers as an example:

> Four centuries ago, Christopher Columbus, one of the Italian mariners whom the decline of their own republics had put at the service of the world and of adventure, seeking for Spain a westward passage to the Indies to offset the achievement of Portuguese discoverers, lighted on America.

We all know where Columbus ended up, but we're not sure where that sentence is going to end until we come to its very last word. The "main statement" or base clause of the sentence is "Christopher Columbus lighted on America," but before we get to complete that thought, we are led on a rambling detour through the history of decline of Italy, Spain's desire for a westward passage to the Indies, and a reminder that mariners from Portugal were on a roll.

In his portion of *The Elements of Style*, E. B. White doesn't join Professor Strunk in warning against loose sentences, but in this noteworthy sentence from *Stuart Little* he certainly reveals his interest in periodic technique, and he reminds us both that the periodic sentence does not have to be overly complex and that the suspense it builds by delaying the completion of its message may ultimately be, in fact, quite anticlimactic:

> In the loveliest town of all, where the houses were white and high and the elm trees were green and higher than the houses, where the front yards were wide and pleasant and the back yards were bushy and worth finding out about, where the streets sloped down to the stream and the stream flowed quietly under the bridge, where the lawns ended in orchards and the orchards ended in fields and the fields ended in pastures and the pastures climbed the hill and disappeared over the top toward the wonderful wide sky, in this loveliest of all towns Stuart stopped to get a drink of sarsaparilla.

In a negatively prescriptive vein, similar to that adopted by Professor Strunk, my old *Harbrace College Handbook* (7th ed.) urges the writer to "gain emphasis by changing loose sentences into periodic sentences." Apparently, the problem with the loose sentence is that "it can be easily scanned, since the main idea comes toward the beginning," while "to get the meaning of a periodic sentence, however, the reader cannot stop until he reaches the period." Note how both Strunk and White and the *Harbrace Handbook* turn up their noses at writing that is "easy" or "easily scanned," as if difficulty of comprehension were somehow a virtue in writing. This was one of the bits of uncritically received writing "wisdom" against which Francis Christensen championed the cumulative syntax, although as we are about to see, the dichotomy long perceived between loose and periodic sentences is largely a false one.

In subsequent lectures we will look at the wide range of strategies that can produce periodic sentences and will consider some of the situations in which periodic sentences can be most effective. For the moment, however, I want to consider the history of this term; then I want to complicate the binary opposition between loose and periodic sentences by demonstrating that sentences take their place in a continuum of delay and can best be thought of not as "types" but in terms of their degree of "suspensiveness." Thinking of degrees of suspense in our writing gives us much greater control over our sentences than does thinking of a kind of sentence that is loose and is the opposite of a kind of sentence that is periodic.

As almost any history of rhetoric will note, the word "period" comes from the Greek term *periodos*, which had to do with cycles or coming back to or going around in a circle. Aristotle in particular stressed the recurrent or reflexive nature of the periodic style as a style "that turns back upon itself," citing as examples "the antistrophes of the old poets" and even more strongly suggesting that a period offered an antithetical opposition, such as we see in these examples from Aristotle:

> They benefited both those who had remained at home and those who had followed them; to the latter they secured more land than they had possessed at home, to the former they left land at home which was now adequate.

As Aristotle helpfully catalogues the antitheses or oppositions in this sentence, "those who remained at home" are opposed or balanced by "those who had followed them," "to the latter" is opposed by "to the former," "land they had possessed" is opposed by "left land at home," "more land" is opposed by "adequate," and so on.

Here are several more examples from Aristotle:

> It often happens in such cases that the wise fail and the fools succeed.

> Though citizens by birth, they were by law deprived of citizenship.

> As individuals we use barbarians as our servants, as citizens we tolerate many of our allies being enslaved.

For Aristotle, then, a periodic sentence was characterized by some form of "turning about," either through opposition of contrasting ideas or repetition—techniques which will delay our apprehension of the full meaning of the sentence until it has completed its turn or made clear its internal oppositions. But missing from Aristotle's view was the emphasis on interruption or delay that we now associate with periodic form. Also missing is the close association identified by George A. Kennedy in his *A New History of Classical Rhetoric* between periodic style and "writing in long, complex sentences not easily understood when first heard."

As Matthew Clark points out in his 2002 study *A Matter of Style*, this identification of the periodic with antithesis—or with what we now think of as balanced form—seems peculiar to Aristotle, since "in later rhetorical theory, a period is a long sentence that uses grammatical subordination, especially to create some sort of suspense of meaning." And all experts agree that the great classical master of the periodic sentence and of periodic style was the Roman orator Cicero. Ciceronian style is periodic style, as we understand the term today, particularly as it suggests delay, building to a dramatic conclusion at the end of the sentence.

I'm with Richard Lanham, who in some exasperation notes that periodic "is one of those traditional but confusing terms we ought to throw away but can't." As he discusses in his second edition of *Analyzing Prose*, Lanham reminds us that Aristotle referred to what we now call loose sentences as "strung-along sentences" or as "running sentences." The latter term actually seems to make more sense than "loose," since it suggests a sentence that just goes on, with no clear destination in sight, unless and until the subject matter runs out—as opposed to the period, which has to end just so. Lanham finds fault with both of the terms we have for describing sentences, finding "running" not much more helpful than "periodic." However, he notes that these terms do refer to different conceptual processes—a basic difference in how one human intelligence presents itself to another—if not to rigorously identifiable grammatical forms. "To imitate ... the mind in real-time interaction with the world is to write in some form of running style," he suggests, explaining "Such a syntax models the mind in the act of coping with the world." Conversely, the periodic style dramatizes "a mind which has dominated experience and reworked it to its liking, the mind showing itself after it has reasoned on the event; after it has sorted by concept and categorized by size; after it has imposed on the temporal flow the shapes through which that flow takes on a beginning, a middle, and an end."

If there seems to be an ideological ring to this description of the difference between loose and periodic sentences, an almost imperial imperative in which the writer is called upon to impose firm order on a messy world, Lanham quickly disavows that implication, reminding us that "to 'go with the flow' is as human as to oppose it, that humankind's bewilderment before raw event is as characteristic as the will to impose order on it." And you thought the difference between a loose and a periodic sentence was just a matter of where the base clause completes itself!

In historical terms, Lanham reminds us that at the end of the Renaissance, which he dates from about 1575, "a reaction set in against periodic structure as the ideal sentence shape; the call, under the banner of science, was for a new prose style that would more accurately reflect the world as it really was, not as it had been stuffed into the orderly and balanced mini-drama of the periodic sentence."

In some ways, that revolution against the periodic style at the end of the Renaissance was only a mixed success, since, while most writing guidebooks today do warn against unrelieved strings of periodic sentences, they still suggest that the periodic sentence is what aspiring writers should try to write. What I've been trying to show thus far in this lecture is the somewhat odd history on which that advice rests. And what I'll try to do in the remainder of this lecture is to further question the bias in favor of periodic sentences by suggesting that the chasm we've been told exists between loose and periodic sentences is not nearly as wide as we have been led to believe.

Once again, Richard Lanham, one of the true original thinkers in rhetorical and composition theory, reached this conclusion well before I did. Lanham ends the chapter on "The Periodic Style and the Running Style" in his 2003 second edition of *Analyzing Prose* with an acknowledgment that undercuts years of claims that periodic syntax was the true mark of a sophisticated writer:

> We can reason that the periodic style, like the noun style, shows thought to be static, organized into its component parts, and then flash-frozen; the running style, like the verb style, shows behavior still in progress, happening in the present, not the past. The contrast often proves a fruitful one, but it ought not to lead us to ignore the powerful internal dynamics the period can generate. If you add enough internal qualifications and parenthetical interruptions, it turns into a running style. The running style seems more naturally to represent the moody reflections of the private life. If, however, it is pervaded ... by a need for compound pairing and balance, for

syntactic regularity, it takes a turn toward the periodic, and even, in spots, toward antithetical compression or "point." Clearly "periodic" and "running" are two defining extremes within which the need to express action and stasis, emotion and concept, compression and expansion, finds many answerable prose patterns.

I'm giving so much prominence to Lanham because I want to seriously question—if not to deconstruct—the classic binary opposition between what Lanham identifies as running and periodic sentences or what is most frequently described as the opposition between loose and periodic syntax. Francis Christensen has helped us challenge this opposition with his theory of the cumulative sentence, which introduces us to one particular kind of loose sentence that grows progressively tighter or more like the periodic sentence as it generates parallels, balances, even antitheses in its modifying phrases. And one of the implications I want to avoid in this course is that, by starting the course with a focus on cumulative sentences and then moving on to periodic syntax, I am in any way suggesting that the latter somehow represents an advance over or refinement of or greater degree of sophistication than the former. Indeed, I began this course with a focus on the cumulative syntax because it can provide a foundation for thinking about periodic sentences, while the reverse is simply not true.

Nor do I want to suggest that the cumulative is somehow a superior syntax to be preferred over the periodic. My goal is to strip away several centuries of bias in favor of the periodic to celebrate these two syntaxes for their respective glories, without claiming that one shines more brightly than does the other. In this effort I think time is on my side, but the grip of the ancient and antique in rhetoric and composition theory is always difficult to overcome. There are hundreds if not thousands of books about writing gathering dust on library shelves throughout the land, and most of these books draw their examples of exemplary sentences from centuries not only before the 21st, but from before the 20th as well. I can't begin to prove it, but I bet that a good 75 percent to 85 percent of the examples of fine writing or distinguished prose in all the writing books that have been published are examples of periodic style, with most of those examples drawn from writers who lived before the 19th century. Whatever the figure, my point is that one of the important steps we need to take in order to make our writing more effective is to counteract the tons of bad, or at least of misleading, advice that has been faithfully and uncritically passed down to us through the ages. Cicero may have been the great master of periodic style, but the fact is few of us want to write like Cicero.

With that said, let's look at some specific ways in which the grammatical distinction between cumulative and periodic sentences begins to break down. Only, to move us another step away from the inherited bias in favor of periodic sentences, I'm also going to stop using the term "periodic" itself, substituting for it "suspensive." There's no difference really, since underlying both terms is the same aesthetic of delay, but "periodic" comes to us surrounded by connotations of length, complexity, and difficulty, whereas "suspensive" has a connotative clean slate, only suggesting that the syntax builds suspense or suspends completion of the sentence's message to a greater or lesser degree.

Suspensive sentences are the Hamlets of the writing world, and indeed, one of my favorite suspensive sentences comes from Hamlet himself: "To be or not to be, that is the question." And under the sign of delaying tactics, one of my all-time favorite suspensive sentences was written by one of my students years ago and says, quite simply: "I was, perhaps, stalling."

In earlier lectures I've already offered several examples of grammatically cumulative sentences that functioned suspensively. There was the "corpse in the trunk" sentence:

> He drove the car, his shaggy hair whipped by the wind, his eyes hidden behind wraparound mirror shades, his mouth set in a grim smile, a .38 Police Special on the seat beside him, the corpse stuffed in the trunk.

And I absolutely promise that is the *last* time I'll make you listen to that particular sentence!

There was also the boy sitting down to eat sentence, which is also grammatically cumulative, but which so delays the base clause by left-branching modifiers that it functions suspensively:

Rubbing his hands together, running his hungry eyes over the steaming food, anticipating the feast, savoring its aromas, stunned by his good fortune, realizing an opportunity like this might never come again, he sat down.

Let's take another example of a left-branching cumulative sentence that delivers the goods like a suspensive sentence to remind ourselves that suspense is always a matter of degree:

Having sharpened all of my pencils and lined them up together at least twice, having neatly placed beside my pencils a brand new yellow legal pad, having visited the bathroom for the third time in the past twenty minutes, having reminded myself that I now compose exclusively on the computer and not with pencil on yellow legal pad, having checked my e-mail one final time just to be sure there wasn't a note waiting for me from the MacArthur Foundation, having cranked up my iTunes Basil Poledouris soundtrack from *Conan the Barbarian* as loud as it would go, having done a final few deep knee bends, having drained my fourth cup of coffee (probably the reason for that third bathroom visit), desperately hoping that this time the magic would work, I sat down at my computer, ready to write.

That's a left-branching suspensive version of what could have been a right-branching cumulative sentence, or loose sentence, that would have read:

I sat down at my computer, ready to write, having sharpened all of my pencils and lined them up together at least twice, having neatly placed beside my pencils a brand new yellow legal pad, having visited the bathroom for the third time in the past twenty minutes, having reminded myself that I now compose exclusively on the computer and not with pencil on yellow legal pad, having checked my e-mail one final time just to be sure there wasn't a note waiting for me from the MacArthur Foundation, having cranked up my iTunes Basil Poledouris soundtrack from *Conan the Barbarian* as loud as it would go, having done a final few deep knee bends, having drained my fourth cup of coffee (probably the reason for that third bathroom visit), desperately hoping that this time the magic would work.

And, of course, I could reposition that base clause "I sat down at my computer" or its extended version "I sat down at my computer, ready to write" after any of those modifying phrases. For instance, if the base clause is moved roughly to the middle of the sentence, we get:

> Having sharpened all of my pencils and lined them up together at least twice, having neatly placed beside my pencils a brand new yellow legal pad, having visited the bathroom for the third time in the past twenty minutes, having reminded myself that I now compose exclusively on the computer and not with pencil on yellow legal pad, having checked my e-mail one final time just to be sure there wasn't a note waiting for me from the MacArthur Foundation, I sat down at my computer, ready to write, having cranked up my iTunes Basil Poledouris soundtrack from *Conan the Barbarian* as loud as it would go, having done a final few deep knee bends, having drained my fourth cup of coffee (probably the reason for that third bathroom visit), desperately hoping that this time the magic would work.

Winston Weathers and Otis Winchester explore this idea of degrees of suspensiveness (of course they insist on calling it "degrees of periodicity") in their *The Strategy of Style*, starting with the sentence "Red-tailed hawks hunt my meadow," then expanding it to "On those sheet metal days in February, red-tailed hawks hunt my meadow for rabbits and field mice."

Next they make it "somewhat more periodic": "On those sheet-metal days in February when the rabbits and field mice creep out to feed, red-tailed hawks hunt my meadow." And finally they make the sentence "almost wholly periodic": "Hunting my meadow for rabbits and field mice on those sheet-metal days in February was a pair of red-tailed hawks."

The point of their variations and of mine is simply to remind us that any sentence can be made more or less suspensive, and rather than think of the longstanding but essentially misleading dichotomy between loose and periodic sentences, it may reward the writer to think of suspensiveness as a continuum along which sentences fall. The more we are aware of this continuum and the more we master the sentence structures that constitute it, the more effective our writing will become.

Degrees of Suspensiveness
Lecture 15

> My interest in exploding rigid definitions and categories is in redirecting our attention to things that matter. Far too much thinking in traditional texts devoted to writing is obsessed with identifying or classifying language structures without ever wondering what those structures actually do, how they work.

If the sentence suspends completion of its message, whether by delaying its main clause until the very end, by splitting the subject from the verb with qualifying material, or by using any construction that refines, sharpens, or adds to initial information before putting it to final use, we call it periodic (or, as I suggested in the last lecture, suspensive). To be a complete stylist, to be able to display the syntactic versatility of the accomplished writer, to be able to control the rhythm of the sentence's delivery of information and shaping of affective impact, writers must have at their command each of the basic sentence patterns. The periodic/suspensive sentence reverses most of the qualities of most cumulative sentences, that it seems to suggest a greater degree of control (architectonic mastery) over the material it presents, that it almost always requires quite a few words before its rhythm is clear, and that it almost always slows the reader down should be fairly obvious. What is not so obvious is the fact that, when used effectively, the periodic/suspensive sentence can actually generate interest, combining conceptual complexity with syntactic suspense.

In the last lecture, I suggested that the two "primary kinds" of sentences aren't really two different kinds at all but represent the opposite ends of a continuum of degrees of suspense. In other words, instead of saying all sentences are either loose or periodic, it's actually more useful and more accurate to think of all sentences as making different demands on the reader's concentration and patience. Grammar and writing texts all faithfully note the differences among simple, compound, and complex sentences. None of them consider the different demands these kinds of sentences make upon readers or consider the affective difference between, say, two closely related simple sentences and a compound sentence that puts together the propositions in both. Most grammar and writing texts are much more interested, in Steinbeck's terms, in "spine counting" than in exploring relational realities, yet it is precisely the relational reality between writer and reader that determines effective prose. One of my goals in this course has been to question whenever possible the utility of pure categories of sentences.

Richard Lanham reminds us, "Prose styles rarely come in pure forms, 'purity' being usually a tacit assumption to ignore complications for the sake of analysis." One of the things that most fascinates me about suspensive syntax is that it can be achieved in so many different ways that any attempt to create rigid or pure categories of suspensive sentences would be a hopeless waste of time. In this lecture I want to survey some of the resting points along the continuum of suspense along which all sentences fall. My goal here is to free suspensive syntax from the longstanding assumption that periodic sentences, while marks of the writer's control and sophistication, are usually long and difficult to follow.

Powerfully suspensive sentences do not have to be all that long or all that complicated, but they do need skillful handling and they generally are most effective when consciously planned. Short suspensive sentences are all around us: "It's not just a job, it's an adventure." "It's not just footwear, it's equipment." Somewhat longer suspensive sentences are also bountiful: "Excuse me while I wipe the tears of laughter from my eyes and put a small but powerful handgun to my temple." Two somewhat opposite patterns frequently found in mid-length suspensive sentences are the post-colonic drumbeat of a final word to which the sentence has been building and the completely unexpected appearance at the end of the sentence of a word or phrase no one could have predicted. Suspensive sentences lend themselves to cataloguing as a means of delaying the completion of the sentence.

The critical discourse concerning periodic sentences notes that periodic style can be distributed across several sentences, as long as delay or suspense is the goal and the completion of the point of the period is suspended to the very end of the sequence of sentences it covers. Suspensive sentences do indeed align themselves along a continuum that runs from the very unsurprising to the very surprising, from the anticlimactic to the climactic. A variation on the one-two punch suspensive combo is simply to create a cascade of suspensive sentences, each building on the previous sentence, creating an atmosphere or climate in which delay and parenthetical digressions seem to become a kind of natural order of things. Suspensive syntax can delay our perception of the nature of the sentence as well as delaying our perception of the sentence's propositional content, as when the final step taken by the sentence reveals that it is asking a question.

Powerfully suspensive sentences do not have to be all that long or all that complicated, but they do need skillful handling.

In the preceding examples, we've seen that suspense comes in more shades than a certain ice cream chain has flavors, and we've seen that suspense created by syntactical delaying strategies can be put to many uses. Winston Weathers and Otis Winchester in *The Strategy of Style* suggest three main reasons for employing suspensive syntax: Varying your predominantly loose style and emphasizing your more important ideas, putting the important ideas at the end of the sentence, and sustaining interest in a long sentence. Richard Lanham shifts focus from the purposes of using suspensive style to its primary rhetorical strategies in the service of delay, identifying them as follows: suspension over a number of complex statements, parallelism of phrases and clauses, climax, and virtuoso display.

To these suggestions of characteristic purpose and rhetorical strategies, we should probably add a brief summary of the broad moves involved in creating suspensive syntax. If the sentence suspends completion of its message, whether by delaying its main clause until the very end, by splitting the subject from the verb with qualifying material, or by using any construction that refines, sharpens, or adds to initial information before putting it to final use, it has been historically termed a periodic sentence, but I think it more accurate to refer to it as a suspensive sentence. The fact that the periodic/suspensive sentence reverses most of the qualities of most cumulative sentences, that it seems to suggest a greater degree of control over the material it presents, that it almost always requires quite a few words before its rhythm is clear, and that it almost always slows the reader down should be fairly obvious. Not so obvious is the fact that when used effectively the periodic/suspensive sentence can actually generate interest, combining conceptual complexity with syntactic suspense.

Four broad delaying tactics mark the periodic/suspensive sentence, two of them relying on modifiers to delay completion of the base clause, the other two using initial clauses/phrases either as modifiers or as extended subjects.

- An inverted cumulative works periodically, forestalling the base clause by a number of modifying levels, keeping the distinctive cumulative rhythm but putting it to suspensive effect.

- Completion of the base clause can also be delayed, interposing modifying or qualifying material between the subject and the verb of the sentence, a splitting tactic that runs the risk of losing or alienating the reader; this is easily the least controlled or focused periodic form.

- Initial qualifying constructions lead to more complicated periodic structures, presenting information that becomes complete—safe to accept as final—only when joined with or reassessed in light of information in the base clause, a process signaled by opening words such as *although, even,* or *if.*

- Finally, an extended subject produces similar results, initially offering an infinitive or relative clause, bringing the sentence into focus only when it becomes clear that what at first may have looked like a complete sentence is actually no more than the subject of a much longer sentence.

Experiment with suspensive syntax, and I bet you'll generate sentences you'll find incredibly satisfying. ■

1. "Under the shadow of Boston State House, turning its back on the house of John Hancock, the little passage called Hancock Avenue runs, or ran, from Beacon Street, skirting the State House grounds, to Mount Vernon Street, on the summit of Beacon Hill; and there, in the third house below Mount Vernon Place, February 16, 1838, a child was born, and christened later by his uncle, the minister of the First Church after the tenets of Boston Unitarianism, as Henry Brooks Adams."

That's how Henry Adams began his famed autobiography, *The Education of Henry Adams*. He used the suspensive/periodic form to pack a wealth of information and atmosphere into his first sentence.

Here's how Leonard Woolf, Virginia Woolf's husband, began his autobiography: "Looking back at the eight of eighty-eight over the fifty-seven years of my political work in England, knowing what I aimed at and the results, meditating on the history of Britain and the world since 1914, I see clearly that I achieved practically nothing."

Write three possible first sentences for your autobiography, each one constructing or introducing your life story from a different angle. Each sentence should be highly suspensive/periodic, and each should try to follow Adams's example of packing as much information as possible into each sentences. It's up to you whether you choose to write in the first person, like Woolf, or in the third person, as Adams did.

Degrees of Suspensiveness
Lecture 15—Transcript

In the last lecture, I suggested that the two "primary kinds" of sentences aren't really two different "kinds" at all but represent the opposite ends of a continuum of degrees of suspense. In other words, instead of saying all sentences are either loose or periodic, it's actually more useful and more accurate to think of all sentences as making different demands on the reader's concentration and patience, some sentences delivering the goods of their messages as quickly as possible, others dragging out the process, finding any number of ways to delay the completion of the sentence. While I cheerfully admit to taking more than a little delight in finding pressure points where traditional grammatical definitions, explanations, and classifications long passed down to us as the received wisdom of writing where they don't seem to work as advertised—where received wisdom turns out to be a lot of hooey—I don't want to take too much pleasure in doing so. I don't want to be mistaken for the grammatical- or rhetorical-oriented version of the *Star Trek* continuity buffs who gloat when they point out that Scotty was holding his drink in his left hand just before the Klingon attack, but (Aha!) the drink is in his right hand in the very next shot.

My interest in exploding rigid definitions and categories is in redirecting our attention to things that matter. Far too much thinking in traditional texts devoted to writing is obsessed with identifying or classifying language structures without ever wondering what those structures actually do, how they work. For example, I can point to dozens of grammar and writing texts that identify adversative conjunctions such as "but" or "however" or "nevertheless," but I don't know of any discussions in writing books that consider the conceptual implications when a reader is given information that seems to be headed toward one destination, only to be undercut or reversed— its initial information effectively erased and replaced by information that is quite different, if not antithetical to the original propositional content of the sentence. For example: "We were excited about the chance to go to see a Hawkeye tennis match at our new tennis center and had planned our entire weekend around watching the Iowa women's team play Northwestern, but it rained and the match was cancelled." *Bump.*

Likewise, grammar and writing texts all faithfully note the differences among simple, compound, and complex sentences, but none of them consider the different demands these kinds of sentences make upon readers or consider the affective difference between two closely related simple sentences and a compound sentence that puts together the propositions in both. Most grammar and writing texts are much more interested, in John Steinbeck's terms, in spine counting than in exploring relational realities, yet it is precisely the relational reality between writer and reader that determines effective prose. And one of my goals in this course has been to question whenever possible the utility of "pure" categories of sentences. As Richard Lanham reminds us, "Prose styles rarely come in pure forms, 'purity' being usually a tacit assumption to ignore complications for the sake of analysis."

One of the things that most fascinates me about suspensive syntax is that it can be achieved in so many different ways that any attempt to create rigid or pure categories of suspensive sentences would be a hopeless waste of time. There are as many ways to suspend or delay the completion of a sentence's message as there are ways of putting off something we don't want to do. And in this sense of finding new reasons to delay what we don't want to do, we procrastinators are the most innovative and imaginative folks around. Fortunately, suspensive syntax gives us the opportunity to turn a vice into a virtue, as delay in a sentence can be a very good thing.

Accordingly, in this lecture I want to survey some of the resting points along the continuum of suspense along which all sentences fall. This survey will be somewhat haphazard, as many of these sentences defy categorization, having in common only their discovery of a way to delay the end of the sentence or to provide the end with some sort of surprise. My goal here is to free suspensive syntax from the longstanding assumption that periodic sentences, while marks of the writer's control and sophistication, are usually if not inevitably long and difficult to follow. Remember H. J. Rose's description of the periodic sentence as "the long and frequently involved type of sentence, needing skill to handle it properly, in which the construction begun with the first word is not completed until the last." Powerfully suspensive sentences do not have to be all that long or all that complicated, but they do need skillful handling and they generally are most effective when consciously planned.

Short suspensive sentences are all around us: "It's not just a job, it's an adventure." "It's not just footwear, it's equipment." "Read my lips: no new taxes." "I was, perhaps, stalling." "I came, I saw, I conquered." "Where she comes from, it turns out, is Arkansas." "When the going gets tough, the tough get going." Or this, from Anthony Bourdain in his *Cook's Tour*, "Cambodia is a dream come true for international losers."

And somewhat longer suspensive sentences are also bountiful: "Excuse me while I wipe the tears of laughter from my eyes and put a small but powerful handgun to my temple." And while we are on the subject of guns, notice the almost perverse turn taken by this sentence from William Kittredge in his book *Who Owns the West?*:

> After half a mile in soft rain on the slick hay-field stubble, I would crouch behind the levee and listen to the gentle clatter of the water birds, and surprise them into flight—maybe a half-dozen mallard hens and three green-headed drakes lifting in silhouetted loveliness against the November twilight, hanging only yards from the end of my shotgun.

Two somewhat opposite patterns frequently found in mid-length suspensive sentences are the post-colonic drumbeat of a final word to which the sentence has been building and the completely unexpected appearance at the end of the sentence of a word or phrase no one could have predicted. A classic *New York Times* article about political consultant Mark Penn illustrates the first of these patterns: "He remained for the second Clinton term and through Mr. Clinton's impeachment trial, demonstrating, among other things, one of the virtues that the Clintons prized most: loyalty." And the opposite pattern can be seen in a sentence from William C. Martin's essay on the inimitable Reverend Ike: "Reverend Ike has come a long way, honey." That "honey" comes out of nowhere and completely recasts all that has come before it in the sentence, adding a touch of aggressive emphasis to the comment, suggesting a quite unexpected attitude toward the reader. Many of us raised in the South will quickly associate this rhetorical pattern with the insidious Southern practice of erasing or mitigating a very critical, if not ugly, comment with the trailing phrase, "Bless her (or his) soul": "She dresses like a homeless person, bless her soul." And Gordon Parks gives us yet another variation on this pattern of slightly unsettling ending words or phrases when he tells us in an essay on Duke Ellington: "Edward Kennedy Ellington counted on going to heaven, have no doubt."

And we need to remember that the surprise at the end of a sentence that has been seemingly building to some dramatic conclusion may simply be anticlimactic, as we see in this sentence from Annie Dillard: "Late one night, while all this had been going on, and while the library was dark and locked as it had been all summer and I had accustomed myself to the eeriness of it, I left my carrel to cross the darkness and get a drink of water." Alexander Theroux managed to find a way to make a sentence featuring the Marquis de Sade end with a whimper rather than with a bang, when he wrote: "The notorious Marquis de Sade, ruminating on the subject of man's greatest torment, perversely concluded that it was the impossibility of offending nature."

Suspensive sentences lend themselves to cataloguing as a means of delaying the completion of the sentence, and cataloguing seems to lend itself to kicking off autobiographies, as we see in the celebrated first sentence of *The Education of Henry Adams*:

> Under the shadow of Boston State House, turning its back on the house of John Hancock, the little passage called Hancock Avenue runs, or ran, from Beacon Street, skirting the State House grounds, to Mount Vernon Street, on the summit of Beacon Hill; and there, in the third house below Mount Vernon Place, February 16, 1838, a child was born, and christened later by his uncle, the minister of the First Church after the tenets of Boston Unitarianism, as Henry Brooks Adams.

By the time Adams gets around to announcing his own birth, he's located his home in an enviable and eminently historical section of Boston, touched several geographical bases with iconic names, and identified not only his religion but also revealed that his uncle was a Unitarian minister. Talk about your auspicious beginnings!

Leonard Woolf struck a very different tone in opening his autobiography but, like Adams, he chose a highly suspensive sentence with which to begin his story:

> Looking back at the age of eighty-eight over the fifty-seven years of my political work in England, knowing what I aimed at and the results, meditating on the history of Britain and the world since 1914, I see clearly that I achieved practically nothing.

And Christopher Hitchens singles out a wonderfully suspensive sentence by another famous writer to explain how he had chronicled his own life: "In his 1991 *Memoirs*, Kingsley Amis stated roundly: 'I have already written an account of myself in twenty or more volumes, most of them called novels.'"

The point of these examples is that suspensive sentences do indeed align themselves along a continuum that runs from the very unsurprising to the very surprising, from the anticlimactic to the climactic. Suspensives can seem rambling, continuously digressing through interruption after interruption, parenthetical comment after parenthetical comment, finally reminding us of Mark Twain's celebrated story in *Roughing It* of the old ram, a story that never really starts and certainly never ends. Or suspensives may just sound incredibly fussy, exacting, determined to get things exactly right before proceeding to the end of the sentence, a quality famously associated with Henry James's later style.

It's also interesting to note that suspensive syntax sometimes requires more than a single sentence to create its effect. The critical discourse concerning periodic sentences notes that periodic style can be distributed across several sentences, as long as delay or suspense is the goal and the completion of the point of the period is suspended to the very end of the sequence of sentences it covers.

We can see this in a two-sentence combination from Art Buchwald in an essay about acid indigestion. Buchwald writes: "America is an abundant land that seems to have more of everything than anybody else." And he adds, "And if one were to ask what we have the most of, the answer would be acid indigestion." In the same collection of essays on "great American things,"

M. F. K. Fisher opens her essay on apple pie with a similar two-sentence one-two punch:

> It is as meaningless to say that something is 'as American as apple pie' as it is to assert proudly that a Swedish or Irish grandfather who emigrated to Minnesota was 'a first American.' Both the pie and the parent sprang from other cultures, and neither got here before the Indian.

And Edwin Newman also utilizes this two-sentence suspensive pattern to powerful effect in his essay on viable solutions:

> The day is not far off when someone about to join his family will excuse himself by saying that he does not want to keep his microcluster of structured role expectations waiting. True, I came upon this gem of social-scientific jargon in London, but that only shows how far our influence has spread and how determined the British are to join the Americans at the kill when the English language finally is done to death.

And the mother of all two-sentence suspensive combos must surely be the following pair of sentences by Ernest Hemingway in *Death in the Afternoon*:

> If you could make the yellow flames of candles in the sun; that shines on the steel of bayonets freshly oiled and yellow patent leather belts of those who guard the Host; or hunt in pairs through the scrub oak in the mountains for the ones who fell into the trap at Deva (it was a bad long way to come from the café Rotonde to be garroted in a drafty room with consolation of the church at order of the state, acquitted once and held until the captain general of the Burgos reversed the finding of the court) and in the same town where Loyola got his wound that made him think, the bravest of those who were betrayed that year dove from the balcony onto the paving of the court, head first, because he had sworn they would not kill him; (his mother tried to make him promise not to take his life because she worried most about his soul but he dove well and cleanly with his hands tied while they walked with him praying);

if I could make him; make a bishop; make Candido Tiebas and Toron; make clouds come fast in shadows moving over wheat and the small, careful stepping horses; the smell of olive oil; the feel of leather; rope soled shoes; the loops of twisted garlics; earthen pots; saddle bags carried across the shoulder; wine skins; the pitchforks made of natural wood (the tines were branches); the early morning smells; the cold mountain nights and long hot days of summer, with always trees and shade under the trees, then you would have a little of Navarra. But it's not in this book.

That first humongous and almost unreadable suspensive sentence from the acclaimed master of short sentences weighs in with no fewer than 272 words, all of which really just set up that short second punch: "But it's not in this book."

A variation on the one-two punch suspensive combo is simply to create a cascade of suspensive sentences, each building on the previous sentence, creating an atmosphere or climate in which delay and parenthetical digressions seem to become a kind of natural order of things, as Jean Stafford illustrates in an essay on Coca-Cola:

At one time there was a widely held belief among edgy mothers that Coca-Cola derived its name from cocaine, which was one of its principal ingredients (in the vernacular of the South and the West, it was referred to as "dope"), and that it was habit-forming. The pause that refreshes could lead quicker than you might think to the Big Sleep. My own mother had it on good authority ("Never mind who told me") that an aspirin tablet pulverized and added to a glass of Coca-Cola produced the same effect as a Mickey Finn: under the influence of this witch's brew, many unwitting girls had been despoiled ("stripped" was the way my mother put it) by concupiscent mountebanks posing as Fuller Brush men.

Suspensive syntax can delay our perception of the nature of the sentence as well as delaying our perception of the sentence's propositional content, as when the final step taken by the sentence reveals that it is asking a question. Renaissance scholar and clergyman Richard Hooker, a frequently cited master of suspensive syntax, provides a memorable example of this strategy in his 1593 work *Of the Laws of Ecclesiastical Polity*:

> Concerning faith, the principal object whereof is that eternal verity which hath discovered the treasures of hidden wisdom in Christ; concerning hope, the highest object whereof is that everlasting goodness which in Christ doth quicken the dead; concerning charity, the final object whereof is that incomprehensible beauty which shineth in the countenance of Christ the Son of the living God: concerning these virtues, the first of which beginning here with a weak apprehension of things not seen, endeth with the intuitive vision of God in the world to come; the second beginning here with a trembling expectation of things far removed and as yet but only heard of, endeth with real and actual fruition of that which no tongue can express; the third beginning here with a weak inclination of the heart towards him unto whom we are not able to approach, endeth with endless union, the mystery whereof is higher than the reach of the thoughts of men; concerning that faith, hope, and charity, without which there can be no salvation, was there ever any mention made saving only that in law which God himself hath from heaven revealed?

A couple of somewhat less antique examples of this pattern of turning the suspended sentence into a question at the very last moment might read:

> As I watched in horror the news clips of protesting students (the government called them rioters and hooligans) defiantly but hopelessly standing their ground against line after line of advancing soldiers, faces hidden by visors, their interlocked plastic shields reminding me of the battle tactics of Roman legions, I could only silently murmur again and again: what have we done?

> Although I am perhaps overly fond of footnotes, although I tend to weigh the value of authority not by the rigor of argument as much as by the writer's pedigree and the prestige of her publisher, does this make me a pedant?

In the same way that I earlier wondered what the affective impact is of a sentence that reverses course after an adversative conjunction, I wonder about the conceptual impact of a sentence that delays not only perception of the propositional goods it delivers, but also suspends realization until the end of the sentence that it will ask a question rather than make a statement.

In the preceding examples, we've seen that suspense comes in more shades than a certain ice cream chain has flavors, and we've seen that suspense created by syntactical delaying strategies can be put to many uses. Winston Weathers and Otis Winchester in their well-respected, rhetorically grounded writing text *The Strategy of Style* suggest three main reasons for employing suspensive syntax:

1. for varying your predominantly loose style and emphasizing your more important ideas,

2. for putting the important ideas at the end of the sentence, and

3. for sustaining interest in a long sentence.

Richard Lanham shifts focus from the purposes of using suspensive style to its primary rhetorical strategies in the service of delay, identifying them as *suspension* over a number of complex statements; *parallelism* of phrases and clauses; *balance*; *climax*; and what Lanham terms *virtuoso display*. Joan Didion touches all of these bases in her essay "Some Dreamers of the Golden Dream," with her suspensive account of a perplexing murder investigation:

> They set out to find it in accountants' ledgers and double-indemnity clauses and motel registers, set out to determine what might move a woman who believed in all the promises of the middle class—a woman who had been chairman of the Heart Fund and who always knew a reasonable little dressmaker and who had come out of the bleak wild of prairie fundamentalism to find what she imagined to be the good life—what should drive such a woman to sit on a street called Bella Vista and look out her new picture window into the empty California sun and calculate how to burn her husband alive in a Volkswagen.

To these suggestions of characteristic purpose and rhetorical strategies we should probably add a brief summary of the broad moves involved in creating suspensive syntax.

If the sentence suspends completion of its message, whether by delaying its main clause until the very end, by splitting the subject from the verb with qualifying material, or by using any construction that refines, sharpens, or adds to initial information before putting it to final use, it has been historically termed a periodic sentence, but I think it more accurate to refer to it as a suspensive sentence. To be a complete stylist, to be able to display the syntactic versatility of the accomplished writer, to be able to control the rhythm of the sentence's delivery of information or shaping of affective impact, writers must have at their command each of the basic sentence patterns. That the periodic/suspensive sentence reverses most of the qualities of most cumulative sentences, that it seems to suggest a greater degree of control (architectonic mastery) over the material it presents, that it almost always requires quite a few words before its rhythm is clear, and that it almost always slows the reader down should be fairly obvious. What is not so obvious is the fact that, when used effectively, the periodic/suspensive sentence can actually generate interest, combining conceptual complexity with syntactic suspense.

On the other hand, as Professor Carl Klaus has playfully noted:

> If you're a no-nonsense person, if you're a straightforward writer and you expect the same of others, if you don't have any patience with long-winded people—people, that is, who never come directly to the point, but instead waste your time in seemingly endless digressions, as if they were mentally incapable of putting first things first—then you will probably consider periodic sentences, such as the one you are reading right now, which looks like it may never come to an end, to be an exasperating waste of time.

As we'll explore in much greater detail in the next lecture, various delaying tactics mark the periodic/suspensive sentence, giving it a suspenseful quality, a sense of its constituent parts being juggled or scrambled until the very last moment, the "shot at the buzzer," finally falling into place at the very end of the sentence, resolved by the verb or modifier that allows us to process the information that has come before. Four broad tactics prevail, two of them relying on modifiers to delay completion of the base clause, the other two using initial clauses or phrases either as modifiers or as extended subjects.

Here's the first pattern: An inverted cumulative works periodically, forestalling the base clause by a number of modifying levels, keeping the distinctive cumulative rhythm, but putting it to suspensive effect. (Forestalling the base clause by a number of modifying levels, keeping the distinctive cumulative rhythm, but putting it to suspensive effect, an inverted cumulative works periodically.)

Secondly: Completion of the base clause can also be delayed, interposing modifying or qualifying material between the subject and the verb of the sentence, a splitting tactic that runs the risk of losing or alienating the reader—easily the least controlled or focused pattern of the periodic form.

Third pattern: Initial qualifying constructions lead to more complicated periodic structures, presenting information that becomes complete—safe to accept as final—only when joined with or reassessed in light of information in the base clause, a process signaled by opening words such as "although," "even," or "if."

Fourth pattern: An extended subject produces similar results, initially offering an infinitive or relative clause, bringing the sentence into focus only when it becomes clear that what at first may have looked like a complete sentence is actually no more than the subject of a much, much longer sentence—as I've done with a sentence from *The Great Gatsby*, designing my sentence to end on the same climactic word as did Fitzgerald's:

> "Even when the East excited me most, even when I was most keenly aware of its superiority to the bored, sprawling, swollen towns beyond the Ohio, with their interminable inquisitions which spared only the children and the very old—even then it had always for me a quality of distortion" was Fitzgerald's way of suspending his message to the very end of his sentence, a tantalizing way of foregrounding a word that functions on two levels, reminding us first

of Nick's ambivalence toward the world around him, then handing us on a rhetorical silver platter the one word that most accurately also characterizes Nick's own narration: distortion.

I'm proud of that sentence. In fact, it may be the best sentence I've ever written. That it is suspensive rather than cumulative both amazes and delights me. Experiment with suspensive syntax, and I bet you'll generate sentences you will find incredibly satisfying and of which you will be equally proud.

The Mechanics of Delay
Lecture 16

Punctuation may not exactly be big business, but it apparently is a large enough source of anxiety for enough of us to support a cottage industry of punctuation guides.

Various delaying tactics mark the periodic sentence, giving it a suspenseful quality, a sense of its constituent parts being juggled or scrambled until the very last moment, the "shot at the buzzer," finally falling into place at the very end of the sentence, resolved by the verb or modifier that allows us to process the information that has come before. We have seen four broad tactics thus far, two of them relying on modifiers to delay completion of the base clause, the other two using initial clauses/phrases either as modifiers or as extended subjects: first, inverting a cumulative sentence; second, delaying completion of the base clause; third, using initial qualifying constructions; and fourth, using an extended subject. This lecture introduces a fifth and final strategy: the sentence whose message is interrupted by a colon or semicolon, where the second clause inexorably deflates, inverts, or otherwise recasts the first clause's message. This is the classic balanced sentence.

In the last lecture, I noted that various delaying tactics mark the periodic/suspensive sentence. Five broad tactics prevail, two of them relying on modifiers to delay completion of the base clause, two using initial clauses/phrases either as modifiers or as extended subjects, and one balancing a second clause against a first, the two clauses linked by a semicolon, which is the classic structure of the balanced sentence. An inverted cumulative works periodically, forestalling the base clause by a number of modifying levels, keeping the distinctive cumulative rhythm, but putting it to suspensive effect. Completion of the base clause can also be delayed, interposing modifying or qualifying material between the subject and the verb of the sentence, a splitting tactic that runs the risk of losing or alienating the reader; this is easily the least controlled or focused periodic form.

Initial qualifying constructions lead to more complicated periodic structures, presenting information that becomes complete—safe to accept as final—only when joined with or reassessed in light of information in the base clause, a process signaled by opening words such as "although," "even," or "if." Starting a sentence with either "since" or "because" will always create some degree of suspense. *Although* and *when* (if used to indicate the satisfaction of a condition) create suspensive sentences. Indeed, there are any number of left-branching sentences that open with qualifying phrases or just plain prepositional phrases that will produce significant degrees of suspense.

An extended subject produces similar results, initially offering an infinitive or relative clause, bringing the sentence into focus only when it becomes clear that what at first may have looked like a complete sentence is actually no more than the subject of a much longer sentence. And now the fifth category of suspensive sentence: the sentence whose message is interrupted by a colon or a semicolon, but inexorably deflating, inverting, or otherwise recasting that message by the one that follows the colon or semicolon, often waiting until the last word of the second clause to spring the sentence's rhetorical trap. This is the classical form of the balanced sentence.

An inverted cumulative works periodically, forestalling the base clause by a number of modifying levels, keeping the distinctive cumulative rhythm, but putting it to suspensive effect.

This fifth and final strategy, with its specification of the importance of the semicolon and colon, brings us face to face with a subject I've so far neglected: punctuation—more specifically, the confusion, complexity, and anxiety surrounding the use of colons and semicolons. Punctuation may not exactly be big business, but it apparently is a large enough source of anxiety for enough of us to support a cottage industry of punctuation guides. Why are we being asked to think about punctuation now? The answer is pretty simple. While the cumulative sentence makes crucial use of commas, commas are pretty easy to use and pretty hard to misuse. Suspensive sentences, particularly long suspensive sentences, also make extensive use of commas, but the great majority of longer suspensive sentences would be impossible to parse without relying heavily on the semicolon and the colon. And semicolons and colons are not pretty easy to use and are distressingly easy to misuse.

First the semicolon. Those of us who aspire to write lengthy suspensive sentences or balanced sentences of any length don't have the luxury of avoiding semicolons. One of the easiest-to-understand uses of the semicolon is that it helps avoid confusion in sentences that contain numerous commas. Generally, when used between clauses in a compound sentence, a semicolon suggests a more complicated relationship than do conjunctions such as *and*; a semicolon signals the kind of conceptual reversal that follows adversative conjunctions such as *however* or *nonetheless*, and a semicolon also signals degree of relationship indicated by conjunctions such as *moreover*, or *similarly*.

Now the colon. Colons may have gotten a bad reputation as almost required components in the titles of academic publications—a phenomenon sometimes disparagingly referred to as "the post-colonic surge." The colon is a surprisingly emotional mark of punctuation. We've already seen how the colon can add emphasis to the final word in a suspensive sentence, as in "What worried me most was this: dying." We also know that the colon signals that some sort of explanation or enumeration is coming, that what follows the colon will break down or inventory something announced before the colon. As Gordon puts it, "What follows the colon further explains, illustrates, or restates, with precise, embellished, or loquacious variation, the words leading up to the colon. This is so often the case that if the goods are not delivered, you deserve to feel betrayed: forthcoming is the colon's middle name."

In a later lecture, we'll see how important the semicolon is in the construction of balanced sentences, and we'll consider further the kinds of relationships between clauses the semicolon can signal. ■

1. Using only sentences that display some form or forms of suspensive syntax, describe a process you know well, such as tying your shoes, reading the newspaper, eating a jelly donut, brushing your teeth, getting ready for bed, etc. Your description should be no more than two pages, no less than one. Be sure to vary the strategies of delay that produce your suspensive sentences, and produce a description that sounds as natural as possible.

The Mechanics of Delay
Lecture 16—Transcript

I wish I could open this lecture by fully sharing with you a remarkable essay by John D'Agata. The essay, "Notes Toward the Making of a Whole Human Being," appears in D'Agata's collection of essays *Halls of Fame*, published in 2001. I even wish I could just share with you the first sentence of this essay. But I can't. You see, the first sentence *is* the entire essay, or— to put this another way—the entire essay consists of a single, marvelous, suspensive sentence. On page 151, D'Agata jumps right into that sentence, actually offering it as a continuation of his title: "Notes Toward the Making of a Whole Human Being"; or:

> "Deep Springs"—being the incredible true story of twenty-five boys and their struggles to attain both bodies and souls at a small desert college in the American West (considered by some the best in the U.S.) for which young men at eighteen are plucked from the East and delivered to a campus surrounded by mountains, the size of Manhattan …

On page 155, D'Agata finally brings the many digressive flights of this monster sentence back to earth:

> … like holes in a map that is used too much, opened and folded, worn slowly down, torn and shredded, sinking continents along creases, draining whole seas, postponing America's great myth of frontier, as observed by the author, a former student and friend, assigned to tend the garden in this desert—is strange.

Got it? Four pages of subject finally allow the reader, after interminable delay, to get to the verb "is strange." Boil the sentence down to a base clause, and it reads "The incredible true story of twenty-five boys is strange."

Of course, that base clause reveals almost nothing of the real concerns of this suspensive essay, among which is its own extended form. Noting that the boys at the school tend to favor long sentences in their writing and in their speeches, D'Agata suggests that the experience of this odd school may itself somehow resemble the experience of the periodic sentence.

In D'Agata's contemplation of the affective dimensions of suspensive syntax I find exactly the kind of thoughtful, meaningful consideration that has so long been missing from the discourse of sentence structure in writing texts. Indeed, D'Agata's self-reflexive experiment with a massive periodic sentence should serve as an exciting model for taking suspensive syntax seriously— for exploring what it actually does, rather than for the thought-stopping normative claims that simply tell us it is a sign of a writer's mastery and sophistication. All of D'Agata's essays are interesting; this one is fascinating. But for now, we need to return to more mechanical concerns to survey some of the nuts-and-bolts strategies that actually produce suspensive sentences.

In the last lecture, I noted that various delaying tactics mark the periodic/ suspensive sentence, giving it a dramatic quality, a sense of its constituent parts being juggled or scrambled until the very last moment, finally falling into place at the very end of the sentence, resolved by the verb or modifier that allows us to process the information that has come before. Five broad tactics prevail, two of them relying on modifiers to delay completion of the base clause; two using initial clauses/phrases either as modifiers or as extended subjects; and one balancing a second clause against a first, the two clauses linked by a semicolon—the classic structure of the balanced sentence.

First tactic: An inverted cumulative works periodically, forestalling the base clause by a number of modifying levels, keeping the distinctive cumulative rhythm, but putting it to suspensive effect. Here's an example:

> His eyes weary from the road, his clothes tattered and dusty, his beard long and unkempt, looking as if not only insects but small animals might be nesting within its scraggly strands, Robert Coover's Wayfarer, the enigmatic protagonist of one of the mini-narratives in "Seven Exemplary Fictions," is hardly a character designed to attract our sympathy.

Second tactic: Completion of the base clause can also be delayed by interposing modifying or qualifying material between the subject and the verb of the sentence, a splitting tactic that runs the risk of losing or alienating the reader—easily the least controlled or focused periodic form.

This strategy, splitting the subject from the verb by interposing everything but the kitchen sink between them, bears more than passing resemblance to Mark Twain's description of the way the German language works—or doesn't work. As Twain put in one of his speeches:

> A verb has a hard enough time of it in this world when it is all together. It's downright inhuman to split it up. But that's what those Germans do. They take part of a verb and put it down here, like a stake, and they take the other part of it and put it away over yonder like another stake, and between these two limits they just shovel in German.

That's pretty much what this kind of suspensive strategy calls for—shoveling in anything and everything between the subject and the verb. Consider this example:

> The old mayor, after waving to the assembled reporters (a small crowd of harried, cynical-looking men and one stunningly calm-looking young woman), after whispering something in the ear of his sickly grinning administrative assistant, and after flashing a hollow version of his famed triumphant smile—a smile clearly patterned after that of Franklin Roosevelt's—and his equally well-known circle-the-wagons wave of his index finger, strode into the courtroom to play out the final act of his personal tragedy.

In *A Room of One's Own*, Virginia Woolf turns this process on its head by inverting the subject and verb of the following sentence but still keeping the verb apart from the subject by interposing all manner of exquisitely precise delaying information:

> And thus by degrees was lit, half-way down the spine, which is the seat of the soul, not that hard little electric light which we call brilliance, as it pops in and out upon our lips, but the more profound,

subtle, and subterranean glow which is the rich yellow flame of rational discourse.

Here's another inversion:

> In a small tar-paper shack, a forlornly leaning eyesore on the edge of the city dump farthest from its fly-guarded entrance, lives a curiously dignified, almost majestically independent, eighty-year-old retired garbage man, the unlikely hero of this story.

Third tactic: Initial qualifying constructions lead to more complicated periodic structures, presenting information that becomes complete—safe to accept as final—only when joined with or reassessed in light of information in the base clause, a process signaled by opening words such as "although," "even," or "if."

There are a number of conditional constructions that lead to suspensive sentences. The most obvious of these conditional sentence openers is "if." Here is *Texas Monthly* writer Jo Nick Patoski's conditional suspensive: "If you're at Big Bend Ranch State Park, you look for David Alloway, quick." It turns out that Alloway is the survival skills ranger, and Big Bend is a place where survival skills are more than an academic concern. And that final "quick" should also remind us of the suspensive phenomenon where the final word of the sentence receives extra emphasis either from a colon or from a totally unexpected final turn that serves to put in a new light what has come before.

Here's another example:

> If it can be proved that UFOs exist, and if it is revealed that the U.S. Government has indeed hidden evidence of extraterrestrial visitors, and even if it turns out that Bigfoot and Elvis do not live outside its lurid pages, the contribution of the *Weekly World News* to the history of journalism may have to be reassessed.

And here is an impressive use of conditionals that add emphasis to a feminist critique:

If I mow the lawn every Saturday, edge it to perfection and celebrate my victory over nature with a beer, if I stay on the pot for twenty minutes reading *Sports Illustrated* and return to the world bellowing a warning to stay clear of that end of the house, if I cuss and smoke and embarrass my friends with dirty jokes then laugh uproariously, if I play baseball in the park and spit out the car window two or three times on my way home, without hitting my own car, I still won't be treated as an equal.

Starting a sentence with either "since" or "because" will also always create some degree of suspense. Here's a wonderful example from Virginia Woolf:

Since he belonged, even at the age of six, to that great clan which cannot keep this feeling separate from that, but must let future prospects, with their joys and sorrows, cloud what is actually at hand, since to such people even in earliest childhood any turn in the wheel of sensation has the power to crystallise and transfix the moment upon which its gloom or radiance rests, James Ramsay, sitting on the floor cutting out pictures from the illustrated catalogue of the Army and Navy Stores, endowed the picture of a refrigerator, as his mother spoke, with heavenly bliss. [That, of course, from Woolf's *To the Lighthouse.*]

"Although" and "when," if used to indicate the satisfaction of a condition, also create suspensive sentences:

Although I am not disposed to maintain that the being born in a workhouse is in itself the most fortunate and enviable circumstances that can possibly befall a human being, I do mean to say that in this particular instance, it was the best thing for Oliver Twist that could by possibility have occurred.

And then we have another set of conditionals that are preceded by elaborations on the word "even": even when, even why, even if. Here's an example:

Even while I was trying to plug up the leak, desperately trying to wrap the ruptured pipe with duct tape and towels, yelling for my son to cut the water off to the house, wildly looking around for any container that might catch at least some of spurting water, I knew that my efforts were doomed to fail and that soon my basement would become Iowa City's newest wading pool.

Even if I sort my mail into efficient piles, based on the importance of the letter and the degree of urgency in deadlines for response, even if I tell myself to open mail at once and then put it in piles, even if I keep my mail in ever-larger plastic bins, I simply cannot keep from losing bills, never opening invitations, and generally proving myself hopelessly inept in what should be one of life's less demanding responsibilities.

Indeed, there are any number of left-branching sentences that open with qualifying phrases or just plain prepositional phrases that will produce significant degrees of suspense, as we might remember is the case with the lyrics to "My Darling Clementine," which begins "In a cavern, in a canyon, excavating for a mine." Michael Chabon's first sentence in *The Amazing Adventures of Kavalier & Clay* offers a somewhat more literary example:

In later years, holding forth to an interviewer or to an audience of aging fans at a comic book convention, Sam Clay liked to declare, apropos of his and Joe Kavalier's creation, that back when he was a boy, sealed and hog-tied inside the airtight vessel known as Brooklyn, New York, he had been haunted by dreams of Harry Houdini.

Fourth tactic: An extended subject produces similar results, initially offering an infinitive or relative clause, bringing the sentence into focus only when it becomes clear that what at first may have looked like a complete sentence is actually no more than the subject of a much longer sentence.

Herbert Read includes in his chapter on "The Sentence" in his study *English Prose Style* a suspensive sentence of this kind from William Wordsworth's *Convention of Cintra* that opens with "The history of all ages" and then seems to proceed to inventory all historical phenomena for some 280 words before completing a base clause that finally reads "... the history of all ages demonstrate incontestably that the passions of men do immeasurably transcend their objects." I know that description doesn't give you a very clear sense of the sentence, but, believe me, you should thank me for not making you listen to what a 280-word subject sounds like. And that from a poet!

But I will remind you of the much longer sentence I made by taking Nick Carraway's wonderfully suspended description of the East as having a quality of distortion and simply making Nick's sentence the subject of my sentence, with my last word coming full circle and also emphasizing "distortion," just as did Fitzgerald's original sentence. I suspect Aristotle had something like this in mind when he claimed that the periodic sentence was characterized by some form of "turning about."

Somewhat similarly, starting a sentence with an infinitive as a subject will always produce some degree of suspense, as Hamlet reminds us with his "To be or not to be, that is the question." Carl Klaus gives us a slightly less weighty example:

> To come all this way, to arrive after dark, to find the village completely abandoned, Tarzan nowhere in sight, and the banana trees stripped bare left Cheetah feeling completely nonplussed.

As does Jim Villas, who uses a second one-word sentence in place of the colon we have previously noted as an intensifying device at the end of the sentence: "To know about fried chicken you have to have been weaned and reared on it in the South. Period."

Fifth tactic: A possible fifth category of suspensive sentence must be recognized: the sentence whose message is interrupted by a colon or a semicolon but inexorably deflating, inverting, or otherwise recasting that message by the one that follows the colon or semicolon, often waiting until the very last word of the second clause to spring the sentence's rhetorical trap. This is the classical form of the balanced sentence. "The inherent vice of capitalism is the unequal sharing of blessings; the inherent virtue of socialism is the equal sharing of miseries." Intoned Churchill, pausing, no doubt, to let that final word sink in. We will consider balanced sentences and balanced form more in the next lecture.

This fifth and final strategy, with its specification of the importance of the semicolon and the colon, brings us face to face with a subject I've so far neglected: punctuation, more specifically the confusion, complexity, and anxiety surrounding the use of colons and semicolons.

Unless you have specifically researched the topic, unless you have Googled "punctuation" from every imaginable angle, unless you have wandered through the stacks of a large university library, noting title after title offering definitive guidance for correct usage, you have absolutely no idea how many books have been published on the subject of punctuation. Just a few of the currently available books on punctuation are Lynne Truss's best-selling *Eats, Shoots & Leaves*; Bill Walsh's *Lapsing into a Comma*; and Karen Elizabeth Gordon's *The New Well-Tempered Sentence: A Punctuation Handbook for the Innocent, the Eager, and the Doomed.*

These books specifically devoted to punctuation are joined by a whole raft of books devoted to English usage in general but that also contain sections on punctuation. Representative of this category would be Theodore M. Bernstein's *Miss Thistlebottom's Hobgoblins: The Careful Writer's Guide to the Taboos, Bugbears and Outmoded Rules of English Usage*; Bernstein's more sober *The Careful Writer: A Modern Guide to English Usage*; Bill Walsh's *The Elephants of Style: A Trunkload of Tips on the Big Issues and Gray Areas of Contemporary American English*; Constance Hale's *Sin and Syntax: How to Craft Wickedly Effective Prose*; Karen Elizabeth Gordon's *other* popular writing guide, *The Deluxe Transitive Vampire: A Handbook of Grammar for the Innocent, the Eager, and the Doomed*; and Patricia T. O'Conner's *Woe Is I: The Grammarphobe's Guide to Better English*. Tips and comments on punctuation can even be found in such unexpected places as Lewis Thomas's *The Medusa and the Snail: More Notes of a Biology Watcher*, which contains a brief essay entitled, "Notes on Punctuation."

Punctuation may not exactly be big business, but it apparently is a large enough source of anxiety for enough of us to support a cottage industry of punctuation guides.

OK, you may be thinking, all that may be so, but why are we being asked to think about punctuation now? The answer is pretty simple. While the cumulative sentence makes crucial use of commas, commas are pretty easy to use and pretty hard to misuse. Suspensive sentences, particularly long suspensive sentences, also make extensive use of commas, but the great majority of longer suspensive sentences would be impossible to parse without relying heavily on the semicolon and the colon. And semicolons and colons are *not* pretty easy to use and are distressingly easy to misuse.

So a short digression: I think Lynne Truss has it exactly right in her *Eats, Shoots & Leaves* when she says:

> Using the comma well announces that you have an ear for sense and rhythm, confidence in your style and a proper respect for your reader, but it does not mark you out as a master of your craft. But colons and semicolons—well, they are in a different league, my dear!

First the semicolon: My favorite description of the semicolon comes from Bill Walsh, copy desk chief at the *Washington Post*, who simply says: "The semicolon is an ugly bastard, and thus I tend to avoid it," possibly echoing novelist Donald Barthelme's feeling that the semicolon is "ugly, ugly as a tick on a dog's belly." I'm not quite sure what Walsh and Barthelme find ugly about the semicolon, but those of us who aspire to write lengthy suspensive sentences or balanced sentences of any length don't have the luxury of avoiding semicolons. Remember the long suspensive sentence I used in the last lecture from Richard Hooker on faith, hope, and charity? It used five semicolons, in great part to separate clauses that contained a total of 12 commas. We realize that this is one of the easiest-to-understand uses of the semicolon: It helps avoid confusion in sentences that contain numerous commas. And remember that Hemingway suspensive sentence about Navarra? It contained 17 semicolons.

In direct opposition to Walsh and Barthelme, celebrated biologist Lewis Thomas, author of the bestselling and highly respected *The Lives of a Cell*, explains his appreciation for the semicolon in his sequel collection of essays, *The Medusa and the Snail*:

I have grown fond of semicolons in recent years. The semicolon tells you that there is still some question about the preceding full sentence; something needs to be added ... It is almost always a greater pleasure to come across a semicolon than a period. The period tells you that that is that; if you didn't get all the meaning you wanted or expected, anyway you got all the writer intended to parcel out and now you have to move along. But with a semicolon there you get a pleasant little feeling of expectancy; there is more to come; to read on; it will get clearer.

Basically, a semicolon signals that some connection exists between what precedes it and what follows it and pretty much leaves it to the reader to figure out the exact nature of that relationship. Generally, when used between clauses in a compound sentence, a semicolon suggests a more complicated relationship than do conjunctions such as "and." A semicolon signals the kind of conceptual reversal that follows adversative conjunctions such as "however" or "nonetheless." And a semicolon also signals degree of relationship indicated by conjunctions such as "moreover" or "similarly."

For our purposes in writing suspensive sentences, the semicolon serves to mark divisions in the sentence among syntactic units within which commas are used. As Karen Elizabeth Gordon sums things up in her *The New Well-Tempered Sentence*:

> A semicolon comes between closely related independent clauses that are not linked by a coordinating conjunction. Extended clauses that contain commas certainly need a semicolon if a period is not wanted, but brief independent clauses might also be most appropriately separated with the soft pause this symbol holds.

And for our purpose in writing the specific type of suspensive sentence that is the formally balanced sentence, the semicolon is the hinge in the middle of the sentence, a kind of mirror that reverses some important part of what comes before: "Ask not what your country can do for you; ask what you can do for your country." "To err is human; to forgive, divine."

Now the colon: Colons may have gotten a bad reputation as almost required components in the titles of academic publications—a phenomenon sometimes disparagingly referred to as "the post-colonic surge," but the colon is a surprisingly emotional mark of punctuation. Lewis Thomas doesn't like colons because he finds them bossy, pointing your nose "in a direction you might not be inclined to take if left to yourself," or condescending, suggesting you need help to keep track of the writer's points. We've already seen how the colon can add emphasis to the final word in a suspensive sentence, as in "What worried me most was this: dying." We also know that the colon signals that some sort of explanation or enumeration is coming, that what follows the colon will break down or inventory something announced before the colon. "They brought strange gifts: spice from the East, gold from the New World, and a thirst for revenge from the depths of their savage hearts."

As Fowler puts it in *Modern English Usage*—his own prose and punctuation paralleling his explanation—the colon "has acquired a special function: that of delivering the goods that have been invoiced in the preceding words." Karen Elizabeth Gordon devotes more thought to the affective promise of the colon, observing "There's something assertively expectant about a colon: setting up both the reader and the sentence, it would be heartless and unfaithful to let either one down." It goes on to say:

> This is what I mean: what follows the colon further explains, illustrates, or restates, with precise, embellished, or loquacious variation, the words leading up to the colon. This is so often the case that if the goods are not delivered, you deserve to feel betrayed: *forthcoming* is the colon's middle name.

Also describing the colon in starkly emotional terms, Lynne Truss suggests that the colon "rather theatrically announces what is to come." She adds: "Like a well-trained magician's assistant, it pauses slightly to give you time to get a bit worried, and then efficiently whisks away the cloth and reveals the trick complete."

For now I simply wanted to note that suspensive or periodic sentences make heavy use of semicolons and colons and, as is the case with syntax in general, they deserve and reward so much more serious thought than most of us have ever given them.

Prefab Patterns for Suspense
Lecture 17

One of the most persistent themes in Postmodern fiction is that the media have so saturated our consciousness that we find ourselves speaking, writing, and thinking in terms of language and formulas so ubiquitous in the media, that we find ourselves more and more describing our own situations in terms of situations depicted over and over in the media— in effect "scripting our lives" to follow the scripts made so familiar in news, film, and television.

As opposed to the formal strategies described in the previous lecture, suspensive sentences can by generated simply be starting sentences with certain words. This lecture will consider prompts that force us to think in suspensive terms. For instance, if the first word of a sentence is *if* or *even* or *when* or *because* or *since* or any number of other words or phrases that posit a condition before specifying an action or result, that sentence will exploit suspensive syntax, but this is only one of a number of syntactical or conceptual patterns that will automatically delay completion of the sentence's message or purpose until near its end or until its very last word. This lecture will both review the prompts for this syntax and consider some of the reasons for making suspensiveness a significant strategy in our writing.

Twenty-first-century readers may have very different expectations and values than did their counterparts in earlier centuries. Cultural factors and the dominant cultural atmosphere are just as important today for the shaping of prose style as were attitudes toward science in the Renaissance or attitudes toward reason in the Enlightenment. Computers are almost certainly in the process of changing the way we experience and think about prose style. More specifically, the Internet has accustomed us to the hypertext link, where any word or phrase in a sentence can be hotlinked to a back text that can add detail or examples or can just allow us to explore loose associations with material in the front text we are reading on a Web page. E-mail, the Web, the blogosphere, and computer presentation programs such as the ubiquitous PowerPoint encourage us to embellish our prose with graphics and to animate it.

I wanted to raise the topic of electronic textuality here as part of a reminder that the prose we write and read, and the sentences we craft, reflect larger cultural changes that may at first seem far removed from nuts-and-bolts writing concerns. For instance, the sentences we write and read today have been shaped at least in part by their participation in or resistance to the cultural dominants of first modernism and then postmodernism. While few of us aspire to write like Gertrude Stein, her experiments with language, along with those of her fellow Modernists, have radically changed our expectations for literary narrative, right down to the level of the sentence.

Postmodernism has also had an impact on language use. Postmodernism has been shaped in great part by developments in technology, particularly media technologies such as film, television, and computers. Unlike modernism or Romanticism, postmodernism is an era or a set of prevailing cultural values and assumptions, rather than being an organized movement. I define postmodernism as the culture of the easy edit, suggesting the extent to which advances in science and technology make it seem as if anything can be almost effortlessly edited, reshaped, and recombined. In literature, postmodernism has been associated with a heightened sense of self-reflexivity—with literature turning back on itself to explore the vagaries of language and fiction as much or more as human experience.

I'm mentioning the broad idea of Postmodern scripting to provide a larger context for the sentence-level mini-scripting, yet another way to lengthen our sentences to give them a greater degree of suspensiveness. In addition to the formal and largely conceptual strategies described in the previous lecture, suspensive sentences can be generated simply by starting sentences with certain words. This lecture will review those initial prompts that force us to think in suspensive terms, and it will also consider a number of other generally overlooked and certainly unremarked phrase patterns that will automatically delay completion of the sentence's message or purpose until near its end or until its very last word. This new category of suspensive structures consists largely of phatic expressions whose functions are more social than discursive.

I want to briefly review the conditional words and phrases that generate suspensiveness whenever they open a sentence. If a sentence opens by positing some condition that must be met or avoided before something else can occur, then that sentence will create some degree of suspense. If the initial if clause is then followed by one or more other "if" clauses, if the number of preconditions grows, and if the completion of the sentence is delayed more and more by a cascade of if clauses, the degree of suspensiveness can become quite pronounced. Since there can be a veritable list of these initial conditions, and since even a single *if* clause can be stretched out to considerable length by increasing the detail of its specification, the degree of suspense or the degree of delay in sentences introduced by opening conditionals indicated by words such as "if," "since," "because," and "although" can be extended to and past the point where a reader's curiosity begins to turn to impatience. Writers who understand the appeal and emphasis of suspensive syntax may deliberately extend the conditional just to make the sentence unmistakably suspensive. Conditional opening constructions serve much more important functions than just delaying the end of the sentence, as they specify the conditional relationships that govern much of our experience of the world. Suspensive sentences that result from other prefab structures, such as initial infinitives used as subjects or any form of extended noun phrase subject, serve important logical functions quite apart from creating degrees of suspensiveness.

In literature, postmodernism has been associated with a heightened sense of self-reflexivity.

But now I want to move from the quite meaningful suspensive structures built by conditionals to consider a very different set of prefab structures that frequently add little or no propositional meaning to the sentences they extend. These are the structures of mini-scripting. These are prefab words and phrases that go bump in our sentences, serving as syntactic speed bumps to slow our sentences down, inevitably making them a bit longer, inevitably making them a bit more suspensive. Some of these phrases have very little serious propositional content, some take on what meaning they have from the context of the sentence in which they appear, and some are virtually nonsensical. For instance, we may plop down at the outset of a sentence the phrase: "It goes without saying."

We get the concept of a phatic utterance from pioneering anthropologist and ethnographer Bronislaw Malinowski, who advanced his description of "phatic communion" in his "The Problem of Meaning in Primitive Languages." While Malinowski's essay refers to "primitive languages" and his research focused on natives in the Trobriand Islands in New Guinea, he specifies at several points in his discussion of phatic utterances that they function in essentially the same way whether in savage or highly civilized cultures. What savage and civilized cultures have in common are traditions of phatic communion, which Malinowski describes as "a type of speech in which ties of union are created by a mere exchange of words." Instead of serving the purpose of reflection, these phatic utterances constitute a mode of action just in their being voiced: "Each utterance is an act serving the direct aim of binding hearer to speaker by a tie of some social sentiment or other." If we extend Malinowski's discussion of phatic speech to writing, we can see written phatic utterances as nearly content-free examples of the kind of processing I've championed in earlier lectures—a way of reminding readers they are in contact with a mind, a person, a personality rather than with some mindlessly objective recording or reporting of data. Phatic phrases can both raise and lower the dramatic emphasis of a sentence's propositional content, interrupting the flow of the sentence either to highlight what follows the intensifying phrase or to tone down or qualify following information. We will revisit this concept of prefab phatic phrases in a future lecture, when we will consider the many duple rhythm phrases we drop into our speaking and writing, paired words such as willy-nilly, hocus-pocus, wishy-washy, flip-flop, ticky-tacky, doom and gloom, rough and tumble, and so on. ∎

Questions to Consider

1. Find up to five scripted phrases from television, newspapers, radio, advertising, popular music, or movies (from any era) that have made their way into commonplace speech.

2. Do you have any favorite phatic phrases that you are in the habit of using, in speech or writing?

Prefab Patterns for Suspense
Lecture 17—Transcript

In a previous lecture, I made the largely unsupported but quite confident claim that most prose examples in most guidebooks devoted to grammar, writing, or prose style come from writers who lived before the 20th century—in many cases, long before the 20th century. There's nothing wrong with that, since those examples generally do offer very useful models of classic sentence patterns. However, there is every reason for us to remember that 21st-century readers may have very different expectations and values than did their counterparts in earlier centuries. Cultural factors and the dominant cultural atmosphere are just as important today for the shaping of prose style as were attitudes toward science in the Renaissance or attitudes toward reason in the Enlightenment. While it may still be too early to say with any confidence how prose style has changed in the late 20th and early 21st centuries, make no mistake: it has changed. Most obviously, we need to note the 800-pound digital gorilla that now sits in those 19th-century drawing rooms where readers engaged the prose of their day. I am of course referring to the fact that computers in general and computer-enabled—if not computer-driven—writing protocols are almost certainly in the process of changing the way we experience and think about prose style.

More specifically, the World Wide Web has accustomed us to the hypertext link, where any word or phrase in a sentence can be hotlinked to a "back text" that can add detail or examples to or even just explore loose associations with material in the "front text" we are reading on a webpage. And, of course, e-mail, the web, "the blogosphere," and computer presentation programs such as the ubiquitous PowerPoint encourage us to embellish our prose with graphics and to "animate it," making our pages and even our sentences appear and disappear on the screen, employing all the transitional effects of cinema—jump cuts, fades, dissolves, etc. Indeed, digital artist Eric Loyer, in Flash-driven online works such as "Chroma," "Lair of the Marrow Monkey," and most strikingly in his "Hollowbound Book," has literally animated language itself, giving sentences a kinetic dimension as the words on the screen display numerous kinds of motion.

I'm going to reserve extended consideration of the effect of computers on prose style for a future lecture, but I wanted to raise the topic of electronic textuality here as part of a reminder that the prose we write and read, the sentences we craft, reflect larger cultural changes that may at first seem far removed from nuts-and-bolts writing concerns. For instance, the sentences we write and read today have been shaped at least in part by their participation in or resistance to the cultural dominants of first modernism and then postmodernism. I opened this course with a reference to Gertrude Stein, and while few of us aspire to write like Gertrude Stein, her experiments with language—along with those of her fellow Modernists such as James Joyce, D. H. Lawrence, Virginia Woolf, Ernest Hemingway, William Faulkner, F. Scott Fitzgerald, and many, many other Modernist pioneers—have radically changed our expectations for literary narrative, right down to the level of the sentence, where Hemingway and Faulkner give us striking examples.

And now we are 80 to 100 years past the heroic days of modernism and possibly even past postmodernism. Postmodernism would be a subject for a lecture series in its own right, so I mention it only briefly and in passing here, but I want to suggest that this cultural dominant has also had an impact on language use. Postmodernism has been shaped in great part by developments in technology, particularly media technologies such as film and television and computers. Unlike modernism or Romanticism, postmodernism is an era or a set of prevailing cultural values and assumptions, rather than being an organized movement. In fact, its not even a monolithic set of beliefs or attitudes but a combination of trends in a broad range of areas, including art, literature, architecture, popular culture, and many other endeavors that reflect the time in which they unfold.

I define postmodernism as the culture of the easy edit, suggesting the extent to which advances in science and technology make it seem as if anything can be almost effortlessly edited, reshaped, recombined—from the prose we write on computers to the mixes and mashups of popular music to wildly eclectic combinations of architectural styles to the human body itself, now subject to genetic modification. In literature, postmodernism has been associated with a heightened sense of self-reflexivity—with literature turning back on itself to explore the vagaries of language and fiction as much or more as human experience: a self-conscious recognition, if not celebration, of the ways in which language constructs reality, our words more and more doing our thinking for us, as opposed to being tools with which we express our thought.

One of the most persistent themes in Postmodern fiction is that the media have so saturated our consciousness that we find ourselves speaking, writing, and thinking in terms of language and formulas so ubiquitous in the media, that we find ourselves more and more describing our own situations in terms of situations depicted over and over in the media—in effect "scripting our lives" to follow the scripts made so familiar in news, film, and television. Fiction writers who have explored this idea would include John Barth, Robert Coover, Thomas Pynchon, Stephen Wright, Mark Leyner, Douglas Coupland—to mention just a few.

Just think for a moment how many situations we negotiate with language that is not our own but that has become ubiquitous from repeated use on television. Consider just a few prefabricated phrases that will probably sound familiar to most of us and would certainly be part of the vocabularies of our children: "How's that working out for you?" "Not so much." (I have even seen that phrase in print in a New York Times editorial!) "Good to go." "That went well." "I get that a lot." "That's going to leave a mark." "True dat." "That's what I'm saying." "Git 'er done." "Keep it real." "Sounds like a plan." And so on. This is certainly not a new phenomenon, as earlier phrases such as "23 skidoo," "Don't take any wooden nickels," or the more polemical "Don't trust anyone over 30" or "Turn on, tune in, drop out" of the 60s, or John Dean's "at that point in time" during Watergate remind us how easily we appropriate prefab or formulaic phrases for our own use. But the fact that we increasingly live in a mediated world in which the language of others cascades around us 24/7 (to borrow another of those prefab terms) means that more and more of us use these expressions without being conscious of how much of our thinking and speaking and writing we are "outsourcing" to Hollywood writers, political speechwriters, and popular celebrities. I mention this not to rail against it, but merely to suggest one of the fairly obvious and fairly harmless examples of "scripting." Of much greater concern of course is the danger of scripting our lives in terms of mediascape narratives, thinking that our human relationships follow the patterns we see on reality shows, on sitcoms, on videos and videogames and hear in popular music. But that's also a topic for another course.

Here I'm mentioning the broad idea of Postmodern "scripting" to provide a larger context for and to move us closer to the sentence-level phenomenon I want to explore in this lecture, a phenomenon we might think of as "mini-scripting," yet another way in which we lengthen our sentences to give them a greater degree of suspensiveness.

In the last lecture I detailed a range of sentence openers that promote, to greater or lesser extent, degrees of suspensiveness in a sentence. Primarily these were conditional constructions, such as those opening a sentence with words such as "if," "since," "because," "although," "when," "even," and numerous combinations of those words to posit conditions that must be met before something can happen—combinations such as "even when" and "even if." Likewise, time markers such as "until" or "before" or "after" or "during," when used to specify a temporal or chronological condition, will introduce phrases that ensure some degree of suspensiveness in a sentence. Here's an example:

> Before I enter another tennis tournament, before I risk another embarrassing first-round defeat, and before I add to the mounting evidence that my athletic days are over, I need to develop a dependable topspin backhand.

In addition to the formal and largely conceptual strategies described in the previous lecture, suspensive sentences can be generated simply by starting sentences with certain words. This lecture will review those initial prompts that force us to think in suspensive terms, and it will also consider a number of other generally overlooked and certainly unremarked phrase patterns that will automatically delay completion of the sentence's message or purpose until near its end or until its very last word. This new category of suspensive structures consists largely of "phatic" expressions whose functions are more social than discursive. I'll explain what I mean by that in just a moment.

First, however, I want to briefly review the conditional words and phrases that generate suspensiveness whenever they open a sentence. If a sentence opens by positing some condition that must be met or avoided before something else can occur, then that sentence will create some degree of suspense. If the initial "if" clause is then followed by one or more other "if" clauses, if the number of preconditions grows, and if the completion of the sentence is delayed more and more by a cascade of "if" clauses, the degree of suspensiveness can become quite pronounced.

Since there can be a veritable list of these initial conditions—one conditional clause leading to another and then another—and since even a single "if" clause can be stretched out to considerable length by increasing the detail of its specification, the degree of suspense or the degree of delay in sentences introduced by opening conditionals—indicated by words such as "if," "since," "because," or "although"—can be extended to and past the point where a reader's curiosity begins to turn to impatience.

Because a sentence that begins with a conditional always kicks a bit further down the road the can of the sentence's completion, writers who understand the appeal and emphasis of suspensive syntax may deliberately extend the conditional just to make the sentence unmistakably suspensive.

You get the picture, and I'll spare you suspensive examples starting with "although" and "even" clauses, but here's one starting with "when" used as a conditional that is simply too good for me not to share it. This from Winston Churchill in his prescient 1935 assessment of Adolf Hitler:

> When the terrible German armies, which had held half Europe in their grip, recoiled on every front, and sought armistice from those upon whose lands even then they still stood as invaders; when the pride and will-power of the Prussian race broke into surrender and revolution behind the fighting lines; when then that Imperial Government which had been for more than fifty fearful months the terror of almost all nations, collapsed ignominiously, leaving its loyal faithful subjects defenseless and disarmed before the wrath of the sorely wounded, victorious Allies, then it was that one corporal, a former Austrian house-painter, set out to regain all.

As Churchill's deliciously suspended sentence reminds us, conditional opening constructions serve much more important functions than just delaying the end of the sentence, as they specify the conditional relationships that govern much of our experience of the world. Boiled down to its propositional core, Churchill's sentence specifies, "When these conditions prevailed, an Adolf Hitler became possible."

In similar fashion, suspensive sentences that result from other prefab structures such as initial infinitives used as subjects ("To be or not to be, that is the question"; "To know him is to love him") or any form of extended noun phrase subject serve important logical functions quite apart from creating degrees of suspensiveness, as we can see in this sentence from Macaulay's essay "The Puritans," in which he strives to give "the most remarkable body of men, perhaps, which the world has ever produced" their rightful due, whatever "the odious and ridiculous parts of their character":

> Those who roused the people to resistance, who directed their measures through a long series of eventful years, who formed, out of the most unpromising materials, the finest army that Europe had ever seen, who trampled down King, Church, and Aristocracy, who, in the short intervals of domestic sedition and rebellion, made the name of England terrible to every nation on the face of the earth, were no vulgar fanatics.

But now I want to move from the quite meaningful suspensive structures built by conditionals and illustrated by Churchill and Macaulay to consider a very different set of prefab structures that frequently adds little or no propositional meaning to the sentences they extend. These are the structures of "mini-scripting." They can be found almost anywhere within a sentence but are most frequently used to open sentences or to interrupt their flow. These are the prefab words and phrases we drop into our sentences like Styrofoam packing peanuts, not so much to protect something fragile as to discourage readers from handling the goods. These are prefab words and phrases that go *bump* in our sentences, serving as syntactic speed bumps to slow our sentences down, inevitably making them a bit longer, inevitably making them a bit more suspensive.

As unlikely as it may seem, these are words and phrases that amazingly enough add no discursive meaning to the sentence, in a way just marking time and taking up space, as we can see in this sentence with its gratuitous use of "as unlikely as it may seem," "amazingly enough," "in a way," and "as we can see." Some of these phrases have very little serious propositional content, some take on what meaning they have from the context of the sentence in which they appear, and some are virtually nonsensical. For instance, we may plop down at the outset of a sentence the phrase "it goes without saying":

> It goes without saying that Kinky Friedman, semi-serious detective novelist, sometime idiosyncratic country western singer, and full-time cornpone pundit, was not a particularly viable political candidate.

Or:

> Kinky Friedman, semi-serious detective novelist, sometime idiosyncratic country western singer, and full-time cornpone pundit, it goes without saying, was not a particularly viable political candidate.

No matter where it appears in the sentence, "it goes without saying" could be removed from the sentence with no loss of propositional content but suggesting, as it does, that what is being said did not really need to be said, a somewhat paradoxical acknowledgment that just perhaps it did need to be said after all. Clearly this phrase adds emphasis to the end of the sentence when placed just before its predicate ("was not a particularly viable candidate"), and clearly it prepares us for some impending truth when placed at the beginning of the sentence, and clearly in both positions it delays the completion of the sentence by four words, thus adding slightly to the sentence's suspensiveness when used at its beginning and serving as a more distinct speed bump when used near its end. But, in the final analysis, after all is said and done, if truth be known, this phrase, much like "in the final analysis," "after all is said and done," and "if truth be known," adds little or no meaning to the sentence. It is, in fact, a primarily phatic utterance—a step the sentence takes that marches in place rather than going anywhere.

We get the concept of a phatic utterance from pioneering anthropologist and ethnographer Bronislaw Malinowski, who advanced his description of "phatic communion" in his essay "The Problem of Meaning in Primitive Languages," published in 1923 in Ogden's and Richard's groundbreaking book *The Meaning of Meaning.* While Malinowski's essay refers to "primitive languages" and his research focused on natives in the Trobriand Islands in New Guinea, he specifies at several points in his discussion of phatic utterances that they function in essentially the same way whether in savage or highly civilized cultures. As he explains, "Though the examples discussed were taken from savage life, we could find among ourselves exact parallels to every type of linguistic use so far discussed."

What savage and civilized cultures have in common are traditions of phatic communion, which Malinowski describes as "a type of speech in which ties of union are created by a mere exchange of words." This is language used "in free, aimless, social intercourse ... deprived of any context of situation." Phatic utterances, such as formulas of greeting—"Hi!" "How Are You?" "How's it Going?"—are not intended to inform, not intended to connect people in action, not intended to express a thought but, as Malinowski says, "serve to establish a common sentiment, an atmosphere of sociability." Phatic utterances frequently affirm "some supremely obvious state of things"— "Nice day, isn't it?"—and begin to serve a social function just by breaking silence, since, as Malinowski explains, "the communion of words is the first act to establish links of fellowship."

However, phatic utterances proceed beyond just breaking silence or invoking formulas of greeting to sustain the flow of language with "purposeless expressions of preference or aversion, accounts of irrelevant happenings, comments on what is perfectly obvious." These phatic utterances may be nearly devoid of meaning: "They fulfill a social function and that is their principle aim, but they are neither the result of intellectual reflection, nor do they necessarily arouse reflection in the listener." Instead of serving the purpose of reflection, these phatic utterances constitute a mode of action just in their being voiced. "Each utterance," Malinowski states, "is an act serving the direct aim of binding hearer to speaker by a tie of some social sentiment or other." Or as we might illustrate this phenomenon in Iowa City, "How 'bout those Hawkeyes!" In short, a phatic utterance communicates not ideas but attitude, the speaker's presence, and the speaker's intention of being sociable.

If we extend Malinowski's discussion of phatic speech to writing, we can see written phatic utterances as nearly content-free examples of the kind of processing I've championed in earlier lectures—a way of reminding readers they are in contact with a mind, a person, a personality rather than with some mindlessly objective recording or reporting of data. If classical rhetoric discusses tropes that serve this exact function, I'm not aware of it, but it strikes me as a significant rhetorical and/or stylistic phenomenon that certainly deserves our attention.

I've been trying to list examples of this phatic phenomenon, and my list just keeps growing. Some of the phrases it currently identifies are:

as it happens	to my way of thinking	it goes without saying
it turns out	it is important to note	almost inevitably
in point of fact	it is important to remember	fittingly enough
when all is said and done	to everyone's surprise	curiously enough
my Lord	I might add	amazingly enough
for God's sake	I am reminded	that is to say
for that matter	we should remember	I suppose
in the final analysis	and I agree that it is	as unlikely as it may seem
and whatnot	and I believe that it is	one might ask
believe it or not	in my mind	as we can see
if you know what I mean	to my way of thinking	as I've pointed out
of course	after all	in a way
for some reason	in spite of everything	in a sense
just between us	it seems to me	not to mention
just between you and me	I can't help but wonder	to some extent
you know	let's face it	to a certain extent
to no one's surprise	if truth be known	as is widely known
as I believe is the case	if you must know	as everybody knows
it occurs to me	if conditions are favorable	you know what
I suppose	if time permits	let me tell you
to my dismay	after a fashion	make no mistake
to my relief		

(In a jingoistic moment, I titled my list "Things That Go Bump in the Sentence: Syntactic Speed Bumps—Spacers and Pacers and Intensity Makers.")

I believe that in much the same way that phatic utterances function in oral discourse, phatic words and phrases in written discourse serve to strengthen the connection between writer and reader. While these phatic phrases can function differently in different contexts, they all seem to imply a closer relationship between writer and reader than would be the case were they not there.

Most obviously, what we might call phatic connectors promote a confidential tone that suggests the writer is letting the reader in on information that is private or privileged or that the writer is trying to affect an ingratiating honesty:

to be honest	let's face it
just between us	if truth be known
if you must know	if you get right down to it
if I may call it that	I can't help but wonder
to my way of thinking	it seems to me
shall we say	

Phatic phrases can both raise or lower the dramatic emphasis of a sentence's propositional content, interrupting the flow of the sentence either to highlight what follows the intensifying phrase or to tone down or qualify following information. Intensifiers would be interjections such as "my Lord," "for God's Sake," "for goodness sake," "amazingly enough," and that perennial favorite: "of course." Qualifiers would include phrases such as "for that matter," "for some reason," "I suppose," "after all," "after a fashion," "in a way," "in a sense," and "to some extent."

In a sequence of sentences remarkable for their suspensiveness, Thomas Berger illustrates the use of a couple of different phatic intensifiers in this description of Candy Darling, the transvestite hero/heroine of several Andy Warhol films:

A vulnerable maiden being brutalized by a sadistic male. This may be why the scene is actually very moving, in more ways than one, *naturlich-mein Herr*—but to put kinkiness aside for a moment, if that can be done when talking about, my God, a man who is girlier than many contemporary women, what one feels most here is the old moral shock of seeing an imposter, in whatever realm, unmasked.

Phatic phrases can be used as sentence openers—"as it happens," "it turns out," "it occurs to me," "at any rate"—or these phrases can be used later in the sentence as interrupters. Phatic phrases can be used to signpost important information or claims—"in point of fact," "in fact," "it is important to note"—and they can be used to clinch a conclusion—"in the final analysis," "when all is said and done." They can be used to certify content or to undermine or decertify it. Certifying phrases might include "and I agree that it is," "to no one's surprise," "it goes without saying," and "as everybody knows." Undermining phrases might include "believe it or not," "to everyone's surprise," "curiously enough," "one might ask," or "as unlikely as it may seem."

These and countless similar examples of what I'm calling mini-scripting might be thought of as functioning in much the same way as the ever-more-ubiquitous emoticons do on the Web and in text messaging. While these phatic phrases may not really carry any content, they help signal to the reader both the writer's individuality and the writer's attitude toward the information delivered by the sentence. They also, inevitably, slow the sentence down and delay its completion, increasing at least to some extent its degree of suspensiveness. Of course, to some extent, you know you'll have some degree of suspensiveness in any sentence you open with or interrupt with "to some extent."

I don't call attention to these usually overlooked phatic phrases with the same conviction that William James and his student Gertrude Stein tried to call attention to usually overlooked words, but these mini-scripted phatic phrases are so prevalent in our writing that it makes no sense to ignore them. And we will revisit this concept of prefab phatic phrases in a future lecture when we will also consider the many, many duple rhythm phrases we drop into our speaking and writing, paired words such as "willy-nilly," "hocus pocus," "wishy-washy," "flip-flop" "ticky-tacky," doom and gloom," "rough and tumble," and so on. I'm not quite sure what to call these itsy-bitsy balances, but they are near and dear to my heart!

Balanced Sentences and Balanced Forms
Lecture 18

Most writing texts today focus on parallelism, balance having apparently fallen out of favor as too arbitrary or too artificial a writing trope.

A balanced sentence hinges in the middle, usually split by a semicolon, the second half of the sentence paralleling the first half, but changing one or two key words or altering word order. In this sense, the second half of the sentence can be thought of as a kind of mirror image of the first half, the reflection reversing the original image. Balanced sentences really call attention to themselves and stick in the mind, drawing their power from the tension set up between repetition and variation. Because the real power of the balanced sentence comes only at its end, it can be thought of as another form of periodic/suspensive sentence—perhaps the most intense form. In an odd way, the balanced sentence also works generatively or heuristically, as does the cumulative, since you can set the balance in motion without really knowing where you want the sentence to go. Apart from its aphoristic nature, the balanced sentence offers an obvious advantage to any writer who must compare two subjects.

Recently, I asked the students in my Prose Style class to think of memorable first sentences from novels. The one opening line everyone in the class remembered was "It was the best of times, it was the worst of times," the supremely balanced first words of *A Tale of Two Cities*. Dickens made that opening so memorable by exploiting in just a few words almost all of the strategies of syntactic balance. What my students did not remember is that "It was the best of times, it was the worst of times" is not the first sentence of *A Tale of Two Cities* but is instead only the first of a string of balanced clauses and conceptual balances that combine to form a first sentence that keeps going for 118 words. What makes this famous opening of Dickens's novel so memorable is variously referred to as its balanced form or its extended parallelism.

These two concepts exist in a kind of chicken-and-egg relationship: Either balance is the heart of parallelism, or parallelism is the heart of balance. A balanced sentence hinges in the middle, usually split by a semicolon, the second half of the sentence paralleling the first half, but changing one or two key words or altering word order. Dickens's first sentence in *A Tale of Two Cities* doesn't exactly fit the bill for a formally balanced sentence, but each of its seven initial paired clauses could, reminding us that sometimes a comma does the work of a semicolon in these constructions.

Edward Everett Hale, Jr., descendant of American patriot Nathan Hale, and son of the famous orator and author of the short story, "The Man Without a Country," drew this distinction between balance and parallelism in his *Constructive Rhetoric*, published in 1896. Hale explained that "parallel construction usually arranges several clauses as if side by side, connected by the punctuation, while a balance, as it were, hangs to clauses one on each side of a conjunction or its equivalent." Writing specifically about Samuel Johnson, W. K. Wimsatt Jr. offers a further distinction between balance and parallelism. Wimsatt refers to Johnson's parallelism of meaning as opposed to his parallelism of sound, suggesting that critics who refer to Johnson's balance are actually more aware of the latter kind of parallelism than of the former. He adds that references to cadence and to rhythm generally have more to do with balance than with parallelism.

While some discussions treat parallelism and balance as the same thing, others insist that these terms refer to distinct phenomena. Most writing texts today focus on parallelism. I tell my students that parallelism is the foundation that underlies both the double beats of balance and the three-part rhythms of serial construction. Double and triple rhythms are really the only rhythms the writer of prose can consistently employ to any significant effect, so I see parallelism as the building block from which we construct both crucial rhythms. Parallelism largely accounts for the ebb and flow rhythm of

> **These two concepts exist in a kind of chicken-and-egg relationship: Either balance is the heart of parallelism, or parallelism is the heart of balance.**

the cumulative sentence. Some coordinate cumulative sentences foreground parallelism. Parallelism contributes to the power of the cumulative syntax even when the parallels are less obvious, as when the final word or phrase of a base clause is matched by starting the next modifying level with a similar kind of word, adjective leading to adjective, adverb to adverb, or noun to noun. Parallelism is made unavoidably obvious if the final word of the base clause is simply repeated as the first word of the cumulative modifying phrase. Modest examples of parallelism in cumulative syntax can be heightened and extended to produce sentences with elaborately parallel phrases. Parallelism also figures prominently in a number of the patterns that produce suspensive sentences. It seems clear that parallelism, like suspensiveness, is always a matter of degree, ranging from the minutest parallels of syllable count and sound, through parallels of length and parts of speech to conceptual parallels so broad or abstract as to initially escape our notice.

Parallelism is the starting point for both powerful and playful prose, but most writing texts present parallelism in terms of rules of correctness as opposed to something we should celebrate. For example, Professor Strunk informed his writing students that they should "express coordinate ideas in similar form," explaining that the principle of parallel construction "requires that expressions similar in content and function be outwardly similar." (*Elements of Style*, p. 26) In similar fashion, *The Little, Brown Essential Handbook* (5th ed.) offers this restrained definition: "Parallelism matches the form of your sentence to its meaning: When your ideas are equally important or parallel, you express them in similar, or parallel grammatical form."

The *Harbrace College Handbook* does go on to say that to create parallel structure the writer should "balance a word with a word, a phrase with a phrase, a clause with a clause, a sentence with a sentence," followed by examples of awkward failures of parallelism and their improved parallel versions, once again placing more emphasis on error avoidance than on the rhetorical benefits of parallelism. Parallelism still has an effective champion in Virginia Tufte, who devotes a chapter to it in her *Artful Sentences: Syntax as Style*. "Parallelism," Tufte quite reasonably explains, "is saying like things in like ways. It is accomplished by repetition of words and syntactic structures in planned symmetrical arrangements and, if not overdone, has a place in day-to-day writing." (Tufte, p. 217) Tufte acknowledges that deliberately faulty parallelism, the frustration of our expectation that a structure will be repeated, can sometimes be seen as a syntactic strength. She notes that the repetition called for to achieve parallelism can sometimes be understood through ellipsis. She presents balance as a subset of parallelism and offers an extended discussion of strategies that produce balance.

Earlier, I wondered when parallelism and balance fell on hard times in the teaching of writing, and, while I can't pinpoint a date for that, I think I can offer an explanation tied to and possibly stuck in history. The problem is that the great majority of examples of sustained parallelism and extended balance in almost every writing guidebook are taken from Samuel Johnson and John Lyly. I'll turn to a discussion of the strengths and weaknesses of Dr. Johnson in my next lecture, and for now will close my brief discussion of balance and parallelism with a few words about Lyly. So patterned and mannered, paralleled and balanced was the prose in Lyly's *Euphues* that it has given us the rhetorical term *euphuism*, terming euphuism "the rhetorical prose style par excellence." Richard Lanham explains that it "emphasizes the figures of words that create balance, and makes frequent use of antithesis, paradox, repetitive patterns with single words, sound-plays of various sorts, amplification of every kind, sententiae and especially the unnatural natural history or simile from traditional natural history." The extreme limit Lyly's prose represents does not have to discourage us from occasional excursions along the continuum of parallelism. ■

Question to Consider

1. Write a good, long paragraph in which you tackle what is popularly dismissed as the toughest comparison task of all: comparing apples and oranges. Your comparison should contain a veritable three-ring circus of balanced sentences and balanced forms—like Dr. Johnson in his comparison of Dryden and Pope.

Balanced Sentences and Balanced Forms
Lecture 18—Transcript

Recently, I asked the students in my Prose Style class to think of memorable first sentences from novels. The results were actually a little disappointing, as almost everyone in the class came up with the same two or three first sentences, but only a couple of students could think of more than that. Of course, "Call me Ishmael" made almost everyone's list. "This is the saddest story I have ever heard," the very revealing sentence with which John Dowell opens Ford Maddox Ford's *The Good Soldier* popped up on several lists. "As Gregor Samsa awoke one morning from uneasy dreams he found himself transformed into a giant insect" was mentioned by a student who was also taking my Modern Fiction class, in which we were then studying *The Metamorphosis*. Another student remembered most of the words to Tolstoy's "Happy families are all alike; every unhappy family is unhappy in its own way." That was pretty much it. To my surprise, no one mentioned "Last night I dreamt I went to Manderly again," no one mentioned "It was a bright cold day in April, and the clocks were striking thirteen," no one mentioned "I am an invisible man," no one remembered the telling first line of *Slaughterhouse Five*, "All this happened, more or less," and no one mentioned the tone-setting, cyberpunk-launching first sentence from William Gibson's *Neuromancer*, "The sky above the port was the color of television, tuned to a dead channel."

Not surprisingly, the one opening line everyone in the class remembered was "It was the best of times, it was the worst of times," that supremely balanced sentence that begins *A Tale of Two Cities*. Dickens made that opening so memorable by exploiting in just a few words almost all the strategies of syntactic balance: "It was the" before the comma is mirrored by "it was the" after the comma, and the fact that each clause starts with the same words exploits the classical rhetorical trope of anaphora. The first clause ends with "times," as does the second clause, exploiting the classical rhetorical trope of epistrophe, and that both first and last words of these two clauses are the same makes it an example of yet another rhetorical trope, symploce. The only difference between the first clause and the second clause is that the word *best* before the comma is changed to *worst* after the comma, creating a simple but effective antithesis. It's hard to imagine a more perfectly balanced sentence!

What my students did not remember is that "It was the best of times, it was the worst of times" is *not* the first sentence of *A Tale of Two Cities* but is instead only the first of a string of balanced clauses and conceptual balances that combine to form a first sentence that keeps on going for 118 words:

> It was the best of times, it was the worst of times, it was the age of wisdom, it was the age of foolishness, it was the epoch of belief, it was the epoch of incredulity, it was the season of Light, it was the season of Darkness, it was the spring of hope, it was the winter of despair, we had everything before us, we had nothing before us, we were all going direct to Heaven, we were all going direct the other way—in short, the period was so far like the present period, that some of its noisiest authorities insisted on its being received, for good or for evil, in the superlative degree of comparison only.

And Dickens doesn't stop there, following this superbly balanced long sentence with even more balances:

> There were a king with a large jaw and a queen with a plain face, on the throne of England; there were a king with a large jaw and a queen with a fair face, on the throne of France. In both countries it was clearer than crystal to the lords of the State preserves of loaves and fishes, that things in general were settled for ever.

Dickens balances the English king with a large jaw against the French king with a large jaw, the English queen with a plain face against the French queen with a fair face, the throne of England against the throne of France. Then in the next sentence, he exploits the duple rhythm of *clearer than crystal* and the pairing of *loaves and fishes* and creates a subtle parallel between the three-word phrase *things in genera"* and the three-word phrase *settled for ever*.

One can almost imagine Dickens performing these sentences, emphasizing their on the one hand/on the other hand structure with the regularity of a metronome: this/that, this/that, this/that.

What makes this famous opening of Dickens's novel so memorable is variously referred to as its balanced form, or its extended parallelism. These two concepts exist in a kind of chicken-and-egg relationship: either balance is the heart of parallelism or parallelism is the heart of balance. It is easy to specify what makes a formally balanced sentence: A balanced sentence hinges in the middle, usually split by a semicolon, the second half of the sentence paralleling the first half, but changing one or two key words or altering word order. Dickens's first sentence in *A Tale of Two Cities* doesn't exactly fit the bill for a formally balanced sentence, but each of its seven initial paired clauses could, reminding us that sometimes a comma does the work of a semicolon in these constructions. But, while this sentence strings together a sequence of parallel balances, there are so many of them that we become more focused on the sentence's parallels than on each of its binary oppositions.

Edward Everett Hale Jr., descendant of American patriot Nathan Hale and son of the famous orator and author of short story "The Man Without a Country," drew this distinction between balance and parallelism in his *Constructive Rhetoric*, published in 1896. Offering as an example of balance the sentence "His ambition impelled him in one direction, but his diffidence dragged him in the other," Hale explained:

> In its arrangement of clauses balance resembles parallel construction, but parallel construction usually arranges several clauses as if side by side, connected by the punctuation, while a balance, as it were, hangs to clauses one on each side of a conjunction or its equivalent.

His enthusiasm for balance obviously waning, Hale continues:

> The reason why the balanced sentence was selected from a great number of typical sentence structures was, I take it, that it had been a favorite with the writers of the eighteenth century, and that it was used with excellent effect by Macaulay. In itself the balanced sentence has its advantages, but in spite of them all it is not much used at the present.

Hale's view, however, may have been more accurate in 1896 than it would be today, since the intervening years have seen Winston Churchill, John F. Kennedy, and even Barry Goldwater reintroduce balance to public discourse, to considerable effect. Few of us will ever forget JFK's "Ask not what your country can do for you" line in his inaugural address, and while it did not lead to his inauguration, Barry Goldwater's "Extremism in the defense of liberty is no vice. Moderation in the pursuit of justice is no virtue" is also well-remembered, if somewhat balefully.

Writing specifically about Samuel Johnson, W. K. Wimsatt Jr. offers a further distinction between balance and parallelism. Wimsatt refers to Johnson's *parallelism of meaning* as opposed to his *parallelism of sound*, suggesting that critics who refer to Johnson's balance are actually more aware of the latter kind of parallelism than of the former. He adds that references to cadence and to rhythm generally have more to do with balance than with parallelism, and concludes that, "We may begin to form an opinion of Johnson's parallelism when we consider that of sound as auxiliary to, and made significant by, that of meaning." I mention these distinctions only to establish that while some discussions treat parallelism and balance as the same thing, others insist that these terms refer to distinct phenomena.

Most writing texts today focus on parallelism, balance having apparently fallen out of favor as too arbitrary or too artificial a writing trope, its masters John Lyly and Samuel Johnson having also fallen a bit out of favor for prose styles that forced all experience into neatly ordered binary structures. We get a pretty good idea of this technique in Dr. Johnson's celebrated pronouncement in *The Rambler*:

We are all prompted by the same motives, all deceived by the same fallacies, all animated by hope, obstructed by danger, entangled by desire, and seduced by pleasure.

I'll talk more about both Lyly and Dr. Johnson in a moment, but first I want to sketch out the way I present these two important syntaxes or rhythms in my writing classes, where I tell my students that parallelism is the foundation that underlies both the double beats of balance and the three-part rhythms of serial construction. The writing structures that present the world in terms of dividing it into twos and threes fascinate me, since double and triple rhythms are really the only rhythms the writer of prose can consistently employ to any significant effect, so I see parallelism as the building block from which we construct both crucial rhythms.

Parallelism has already been prominently featured in this series of lectures, even if I have not specifically called attention to it. Parallelism largely accounts for the ebb-and-flow rhythm of the cumulative sentence. Some coordinate cumulative sentences foreground parallelism, as we can see in a sentence such as:

> The movie was a terrible disappointment, its plot ridiculous, its dialogue insulting, its acting amateurish, and even its cinematography substandard.

Or:

> This was the moment he had been so eagerly awaiting, the moment when he could step out from under the shadow of his more famous brother, the moment when he could finally show the world his own talent, the moment when all of his planning and preparation would finally pay off.

Or:

> In *Ulysses*, James Joyce may have written the first novel with a soundtrack, song lyrics continuously running through the thoughts of Leopold Bloom, actual songs frequently being heard by Bloom as he makes it through the day, the musical form of the fugue actually accounting for the odd structure of the Sirens chapter.

Indeed, parallelism contributes to the power of the cumulative syntax even when the parallels are less obvious, as when the final word or phrase of a base clause is matched by starting the next modifying level with a similar kind of word, adjective leading to adjective, adverb to adverb, noun to noun:

> His coat was tattered, frayed from daily wear.

Or:

> I returned to my studies with new dedication, concentration replacing my previous carelessness.

Or:

> She wanted to be loved, to be respected.

Of course the parallelism somewhat camouflaged in these examples is made unavoidably obvious if the final word of the base clause is simply repeated as the first word of the cumulative modifying phrase:

> His coat was tattered, tattered beyond all hope of repair.

> I returned to my studies with new dedication, dedication that was eventually to result in my graduating with highest honors.

> She wanted to be loved, loved for all reasons that were so clear to her.

But these quite modest examples of parallelism in cumulative syntax can be heightened and extended to produce sentences with phrases as elaborately parallel as:

(1) Thomas Berger is an American novelist whose career defies easy description,

> (2) his 23 novels arguably representing 23 different novel forms,

> (2) his subjects ranging from the Old West to Arthurian England to a robotic artificial woman,

> (2) his highly praised Reinhart series featuring a single protagonist but following that protagonist's misadventures in four novels of distinctly different styles,

(2) his reputation well-established as one of our best known and most celebrated "neglected" authors.

Or even more so, as in:

(1) The concepts of metempsychosis and parallax account for almost all of the structure and style of Joyce's *Ulysses*,

    (2) metempsychosis, best described as reincarnation, providing both the tie to earlier narratives such as the Odyssey and the rationale for the way words and themes are continuously "reborn" in the text,

        (3) popping up again and again,

    (2) parallax, best described as the alternation of point of view, providing both the explanation of Leopold Bloom's dominant characteristic and the rationale for the way Joyce's great novel shifts prose style from chapter to chapter,

        (3) challenging us again and again to learn a new way to read.

Parallelism also figures prominently in a number of the patterns that produce suspensive sentences. Any sentence that opens with a cascade of conditionals, whether *if* phrases, *because* phrases, *even* or *when* phrases, or which open with a string of infinitive phrases serving as an extended subject will possibly display as much parallelism as suspensiveness. While I'm not exactly sure what the analytical payoff for such an observation might be, it seems clear that parallelism, like suspensiveness, is always a matter of degree, ranging from the most minute parallels of syllable count and sound, through parallels of length and parts of speech, to conceptual parallels so broad or abstract as to initially escape our notice.

To me, parallelism is the starting point for both powerful and playful prose, but most writing texts present parallelism in terms of rules of correctness—as something we must get right or certainly should never get wrong—as opposed to something we should celebrate. For example, Professor Strunk informed his writing students that they should "express coordinate ideas in similar form," explaining that the principle of parallel construction "requires that expressions similar in content and function be outwardly similar." While Strunk cites the Beatitudes ("Blessed are the poor in spirit: for theirs is the kingdom of heaven. Blessed are they that mourn: for they shall be comforted. Blessed are the meek: for they shall inherit the earth") as an illustration of the "virtue of parallel construction," he is actually more interested in having his students avoid the vice of failing to maintain parallelism. Even then, he seems reluctant to overpraise the form. When he notes that the sentence "Formerly, science was taught by the textbook method, while now the laboratory method is employed" fails to maintain the parallelism reflected in the sentence "Formerly, science was taught by the textbook method; now it is taught by the laboratory method," he only makes the somewhat tepid claim that in the latter version "the writer has at least made a choice and abided by it." The majority of his discussion of parallelism is devoted to suggesting how to avoid failures of parallelism in the use of prepositions and correlatives such as both/and, not only/but also, and so on. One can only wonder whether Professor Strunk's little-remembered earlier edition of *Macaulay's and Carlyle's Essays on Samuel Johnson* had given him a fatal overdose of parallel and balanced constructions.

In similar fashion, *The Little, Brown Essential Handbook* (5th ed.) offers this restrained and somewhat redundant definition: "Parallelism matches the form of your sentence to its meaning: when your ideas are equally important or parallel, you express them in similar, or parallel grammatical form," and it offers the understated example "The air is dirtied by factories belching smoke and vehicles spewing exhaust." The only advantage for parallelism cited in *The Little, Brown Handbook* is that "it can work like glue to link the sentences of a paragraph as well as the parts of a sentence," and it devotes equal attention to warning that computer grammar and style checkers "cannot recognize faulty parallelism" because they "cannot recognize the relations among ideas."

My trusty old *Harbrace College Handbook* (7th ed.) is slightly more enthusiastic about parallelism, citing linguist Simeon Potter's view that "balanced sentences" [note that interchangeability of terms I previously mentioned] satisfy "a profound human desire for equipoise and symmetry." The *Handbook* follows that provocative claim with only the pedestrian advice:

"Use parallel form, especially with coordinating conjunctions, in order to express your ideas simply and logically." *The Harbrace Handbook* does go on to instruct that to create parallel structure, the writer should "balance a word with a word, a phrase with a phrase, a clause with a clause, a sentence with a sentence," followed by examples of awkward failures of parallelism and their improved parallel versions, once again placing more emphasis on error avoidance than on the rhetorical benefits of parallelism.

Washington Post Copy Desk Chief Bill Walsh continues this practice in his book *Lapsing Into a Comma: A Curmudgeon's Guide to the Many Things That Can Go Wrong in Print—and How to Avoid Them*, where—true to his title—he offers the sentence, "There are reports that the boy was beaten, molested and is now a drug addict" as "a classic non-parallel construction" because its first verb "was beaten" is not parallel with its second verb "is now a drug addict," with "molested" ambiguously hanging between the two. Walsh only prescribes fixing this error either by placing the conjunction *and* before *molested* ("The boy was beaten and molested") or repeating *was* before *molested* ("The boy was beaten, was molested, and is now a drug addict"), with absolutely no consideration to reasons why parallelism might add value to prose style as well as correct mistakes.

The general tenor of these constructions of parallelism as something not to be gotten wrong is perfectly captured in W. K. Wimsatt's highly ironic praise: "The resourcefulness of student writers in obscuring and avoiding parallels is boundless." I call attention to these discussions of parallelism because they are so restrained, while parallelism is so cool! At what point, I wonder, did this most memorable of rhetorical strategies fall on hard times? And if the broad concept of parallelism is now viewed in such restrained, if not cautionary terms, what of the more intense rhetorical protocols of balance?

I'm glad to report that parallelism still has at least one effective champion in Virginia Tufte, who devotes a chapter to it in her *Artful Sentences: Syntax as Style*. Tufte prefaces her chapter on parallelism with a cheering quotation from Richard D. Altick:

> The matching of phrase against phrase, clause against clause, lends an unmistakable eloquence to prose. That, indeed, is one of the

principal glories of the King James Bible ... And, to some extent in reminiscence and imitation of the Bible, English prose all the way down to our time has tended toward balanced structure for the sake of contrast or antithesis or climax...

"Parallelism," Tufte quite reasonably explains, "is saying like things in like ways. It is accomplished by repetition of words and syntactic structures in planned symmetrical arrangements and, if not overdone, has a place in day-to-day writing." Tufte acknowledges what most writing guidebooks fail to say: that deliberately faulty parallelism, the frustration of our expectation that a structure will be repeated, can sometimes be seen as a syntactic strength, rather than a weakness or an error, offering as an example a sentence from Steinbeck's *Sweet Thursday*: "Here was himself, young, good-looking, snappy dresser, and making dough," and she notes that the repetition called for to achieve parallelism can sometimes be understood through ellipsis, as in a sentence from Bradford Smith: "For love is stronger than hate, and peace than war."

She presents balance as a subset of parallelism and offers an extended discussion of strategies which produce balance, a number of which I'll return to in the next lecture. For now, I simply want to applaud Virginia Tufte for her celebration of parallelism and balance, a celebration that has grown far too rare in contemporary considerations of writing style.

Earlier, I wondered when parallelism and balance fell on hard times in the teaching of writing, and while I can't pinpoint a date for that, I think I can offer an explanation tied to and possibly stuck in history. The problem is that the great majority of examples of sustained parallelism and extended balance are taken in almost every writing guidebook from Samuel Johnson and John Lyly. Lyly was a Renaissance writer, very successful in his time, who lived during the last 50 years of the 16th century and is best known for his *Euphues, The Anatomy of Wit* (1578) and *Euphues and His England* (1580). Samuel Johnson, who has achieved celebrity single-name status as Dr. Johnson, lived in and wrote across much of the 18th century, and while he authored a prodigious number of works, is perhaps best known for his *A Dictionary of the English Language* (1755) and his three-volume *Lives of the Most Eminent Poets* (1781). I'll turn to a discussion of the strengths and weaknesses of Dr.

Johnson in my next lecture. For now, I'll close my brief discussion of balance and parallelism with a few words about Lyly.

A little Lyly goes a long way. Here's a brief excerpt from his dedication of *Euphues* to his patron, Sir William West. Lyly is making the case for the essential honesty of his depiction of the youth Euphues:

> Whereby I gather that in all perfect works as well the fault as the face is to be shown. The fairest leopard is set down with his spots, the sweetest rose with his prickles, the finest velvet with his brack. Seeing then that in every counterfeit as well the blemish as the beauty is coloured I hope I shall not incur the displeasure of the wise in that in the discourse of Euphues I have as well touched the vanities of his love as the virtue of his life.
>
> If then the first sight of Euphues shall seem too light to be read of the wise or too foolish to be regarded of the learned, they ought not to impute it to the iniquity of the author but to the necessity of the history.

In a selection from the novel itself that is even a bit more true to Lyly's wording and spelling:

> True it is Philautus that he which toucheth the nettle tenderly, is soonest stung, that the fly which playeth with the fire is singed in the flame, that he that dallieth with women is drawn to his woe. And as the adamant draweth the heavy iron, the harp the fleet dolphin, so beauty allureth the chaste mind to live, & the wisest wit to lust: The example whereof I would it were no less profitable than the experience to me is like to be perilous. The vine watered with wine is soon withered, the blossom in the fattest ground is quickly blasted, the goat the fatter she is the less fertile she is; yea, man the more witty he is the less happy he is.

So patterned and so mannered, paralleled and balanced was the prose in Lyly's *Euphues* that it has given us the rhetorical term *euphuism*. Terming euphusism "the rhetorical prose style par excellence," Richard Lanham explains in his *A Handlist of Rhetorical Terms* that it "emphasizes the figures of words that create balance, and makes frequent use of antithesis, paradox, repetitive patterns with single words, sound-plays of various sorts, amplification of every kind, sententiae and especially the 'unnatural natural history' or simile from traditional natural history." Somewhat discouragingly, Lanham adds:

"Lyly's style has been studied largely to be deplored." Yet, as Lanham also notes, Lyly's reputation has been to some extent rehabilitated in recent years by scholars who credit him with making some significant contributions to English prose.

I call attention to what I freely admit is the excessive balance and parallelism in Lyly's writing only to remind us that the extreme limit his prose represents does not have to discourage us from occasional excursions along the continuum of parallelism as long as we remember to stop short of the degrees of parallelism crafted by Lyly. The problem is that we have been discouraged by writing text after writing text from playing with balance and parallelism, and there are few contemporary and effective examples of these forms for us to follow. In the next lecture, however, I'll provide such an example in the wonderfully balanced prose of philosopher, essayist, and novelist William Gass, one of our most exciting and rewarding masters of prose style.

The Rhythm of Twos
Lecture 19

One of the best-known examples of the balanced sentence comes from John F. Kennedy's Inaugural Address: "Ask not what your country can do for you; ask what you can do for your country."

The double beat or duple rhythm of balanced form may derive its almost visceral power from the basic lub-dub beat of the human heart; the doubled words and forms of the balanced sentence derive their power and ability to stick in the mind from a mirroring effect that asks not what we can do with balanced form but what balanced forms do to us. Or, it may be related to the human tendency to create binary oppositions—good/bad, right/left, up/down, in/out, hot/cold, etc. Balanced syntax and forms of balance within elements of the sentence do more than just create a two-beat rhythm, however. It imparts to your writing a sense of certainty, the sound of confidence, the effect of finality. Indeed, it is no surprise that balanced form (sometimes called the *two-part series*) is frequently found in religious writing. Balanced form can rise from any use of parallel phrases, words, letters, sounds, ideas, images—two of anything, and the more extensive the balances the greater the impact of the writing, as is suggested by a sentence from its great master, Samuel Johnson: "Dryden's page is a natural field, rising into inequalities, and diversified by the varied exuberance of abundant vegetation; Pope's is a velvet lawn, shaven by the scythe, and leveled by the roller."

Balance and parallelism are often discussed as if they were interchangeable terms and, in a sense, they are. I want to discuss balance first as a formal sentence syntax and then as a form or rhythm that can appear within or among sentences whenever there is some pairing of sound, word, phrase, or concept, or any use of language that foregrounds two of anything. Balanced form can range from the obvious syntactic pairing of chiasmus to more subtle oppositional pairing. A balanced sentence hinges in the middle, usually split by a semicolon, the second half of the sentence paralleling the first half, but changing one or two key words or altering word order.

Balanced sentences really call attention to themselves and stick in the mind, drawing their power from the tension set up between repetition and variation. Since the real power of the balanced sentence comes only at its end, it can be thought of as another form of periodic sentence. In an odd way, the balanced sentence also works generatively or heuristically, as does the cumulative, since you can set the balance in motion without really knowing where you want the sentence to go. This fill-in-the-blank phenomenon suggests that the form of the balanced sentence may be more memorable than the meaning conveyed by and through that form.

Balance is the specific syntactic tool ready-made for comparisons. Samuel Johnson is probably the greatest master of the balanced form. Johnson's comparison of Pope and Dryden displays a second kind or degree of balance, that of smaller forms within the sentence and of those forms between and among sentences. Any time that a sentence, part of a sentence, or groups of sentences make us aware of pairs of things—whether objects, sounds, words, syntactic structures—that reveals some degree of balanced form. This kind of balance can take almost any shape or form and can appear at almost any time. It may come from the insinuating insistence of alliteration, assonance, or consonance, or from the pronounced parallelism of phrases and modifiers, metaphors, and the larger syntax of the sentence. Balance may even come from a conceptual dualism—a thought that focuses our thinking, inexorably, on two subjects, entities, ideas, or images. Dr. Johnson's comparison of the two poets contains almost all of these forms of balance. The question we aspiring students of the sentence must answer for ourselves before we decide whether in-your-face balance will be a feature in our syntactic arsenal is simply this: Does Dr. Johnson's prose strike us as impressive or obsessive, well-crafted to positive effect, or overdone to the point of putting readers off?

> **The problem with balance, as is the problem with any syntax pushed too hard, is that it levels reality, forcing everything into binary agreement or opposition.**

The problem with balance, as is the problem with any syntax pushed too hard, is that it levels reality, forcing everything into binary agreement or opposition. In an essay of Johnson's parallelism, W. K. Wimsatt Jr. has outlined the case against balance. Wimsatt observes that Johnson runs the risk of "preferring the meaning of parallel to a more relevant meaning of variety." Hazlitt advances much the same critique of pronounced balanced form, using Edmund Burke as his target. In his review of "Boswell's Life of Johnson," (1831), Thomas Babington Macaulay, who, it should be remembered was himself known for his use of balanced form, accused Johnson of writing in "Johnsonese," a style that he called "systematically vicious." George Saintsbury disagreed, terming Macaulay's description of Johnson's style "one of the worst parts of his essay."

What's missing so far in these discussions of balance is the fact that they are so much fun for the writer to construct and for the reader to recognize. Matthew Clark touches on this underreported aspect in his book, *A Matter of Style: On Writing and Technique*, where he recognizes that "there is a great vigor and pleasure" in the writing of sustained parallelism and balance. In the writing of William Gass, we find an even more effective brief for the use of balance, as Gass goes for balances at every opportunity. America has no more innovative a prose stylist than Gass, and it is his example, not Dr. Johnson's, that I follow when I champion the use of balanced forms in effective writing. ■

Question to Consider

1. Write five aphoristic sentences, about the most ordinary occurrences in life (such as relationships, or being placed on hold, or walking the dog) that make the maximum use of balanced forms. This is one to have fun with and go overboard.

The Rhythm of Twos
Lecture 19—Transcript

"Science fiction in the cinema often turns out to be, turns round to be, the fictional or fictive science of the cinema itself, the future feats it may achieve scanned in line with the technical feat that conceives them right now and before our eyes." I love this sentence from my colleague Garrett Stewart, who also happens to be one of the most superb prose stylists I know. This is not so surprising when we learn that a much younger Garrett Stewart collaborated with Virginia Tufte on her first two books, *Grammar as Style* and *Grammar as Style: Exercises in Creativity*. Indeed, many of the sentence examples I have drawn from Tufte's third book, *Artful Sentences: Syntax as Style*, were originally brought to her attention by Garrett Stewart.

Garrett's often-cited sentence about science fiction film appears in his essay "The Videology of Science Fiction," and it would not be inaccurate to say that this single sentence was the inspiration for an entire book I wrote about science fiction film. I love the sentence because it succinctly captures a crucial truth about the relationship of the subject matter of SF film to the production technologies that make that subject matter come alive on the screen, the amazing technologies that allow us to make science fiction films every bit as interesting, if not more so, than the stories about technology those films tell. I also love the sentence, and couldn't get it out of my mind once I read it, because of its masterful exploitation of balanced form. With that somewhat gratuitous but marvelous sounding "turns round to be" that follows the initial "turns out to be," Garrett signals the reader that this sentence will do more than present propositional content. Indeed, it paves the way for a cascade of balances: "Science fiction in the cinema" is soon balanced against the "fictional or fictive science of the cinema itself," and that pairing of "fictional or fictive" intensifies even further the sentence's commitment to balance; "future feats" that the cinema may depict are balanced by "the technical feat that conceives them," and the time, "right now," is balanced by the place, "before our eyes." While this sentence gives voice to a stunning critical insight, that insight is made more powerful, indeed unforgettable, by a voice that insistently draws authority from the duple rhythms of balanced form. Garrett's sentence may lack some of the dramatic force of Conrad's "She was savage and superb, wild-eyed and magnificent, there was something ominous and stately in her deliberate progress," but my great appreciation for that wonderfully balanced sentence from Conrad owes more than a little to another of Garrett's brilliant essays, this one on the significance of Marlow's lie in Conrad's masterpiece. It is tellingly titled with balanced brio "Lying as Dying in *Heart of Darkness*."

I'll defer the brief for a Garrett Stewart fan club until another day. Now, I want to get back to the consideration of balance I started in the last lecture.

As I've noted, balance and parallelism are often discussed as if they were interchangeable terms, and in a sense they are. However, I'm going to reserve parallelism to describe similarities that are maintained in prose beyond the duple sound and sense of balance, which focuses our eyes and our ears on pairs of things. My reasons for trying to maintain this distinction will, I hope, become more evident in a future lecture when I consider serial constructions, generally identified by their division of the world into threes, but sometimes extending parallel constructions to catalogs of four or even more terms. For now, I want to discuss balance first as a formal sentence syntax and then as a form or rhythm that can appear within or among sentences whenever there is some pairing, whether of sound, of vowels and consonants, of words of the same length or syllable count, phrases of the same construction, words or phrases linked by conjunctions, concepts that are similar or antithetical, or any use of language that foregrounds two of anything. Balanced form can range from the obvious syntactic pairing of chiasmus ("When the going gets tough, the tough get going") to more subtle oppositional pairing ("Against the iceberg of her smile I sailed the Titanic of my hopes").

As I've previously specified, a balanced sentence hinges in the middle, usually split by a semicolon, the second half of the sentence paralleling the first half, but changing one or two key words or altering word order. In this sense, the second half of the sentence can be thought of as a kind of mirror image of the first half, the reflection reversing the original image. One of the best-known examples of the balanced sentence comes from John F. Kennedy's Inaugural Address: "Ask not what your country can do for you; ask what you can do for your country." Kennedy, or his speechwriters, had an ear for parallelism as well as for balance, as we can see in another less memorable, but equally well-crafted excerpt from his Inaugural Address:

All this will not be finished in the first one hundred days. Nor will it be finished in the first one thousand days nor in the life of this administration, nor even perhaps in our lifetime on this planet. But let us begin.

Winston Churchill would certainly have to be acknowledged a modern master of balance. I've previously mentioned his classically balanced dismissal of socialism—"The inherent vice of capitalism is the unequal sharing of blessings; the inherent virtue of socialism is the equal sharing of miseries." A more effective way of stressing his point is hard to imagine, since his balanced sentence also gains emphasis from the fact that it is highly suspensive, delaying completion of his message until the final word of the sentence.

Churchill was also fond of smaller balanced forms, particularly when speaking of language: "Short words are best and the old words when short are best of all," he said. He liked to pair words: "Writing a long and substantial book is like having a friend and companion at your side, to whom you can always turn for comfort and amusement, and whose society becomes more attractive as a new and widening field of interest is lighted in the mind." And his speeches are peppered with prefab balanced pairings such as black and blue, brass and bluff, facts and figures, forgive and forget, hemmed and hawed, by hook or crook, life and limb, live and learn, rough and ready, part and parcel, thick and thin, wear and tear and so on.

Balanced sentences really call attention to themselves and stick in the mind, drawing their power from the tension set up between repetition and variation. Since the real power of the balanced sentence comes only at its end, it can be thought of as another form of periodic sentence, perhaps the most intense form. In an odd way, the balanced sentence also works generatively or heuristically, as does the cumulative, since you can set the balance in motion without really knowing where you want the sentence to go. For instance, given an informal definition—"those who talk when you wish them to listen are bores"—you can insert a semicolon, switch terms—"those who listen when you wish them to talk are_____"—and you can choose almost any word to fill in that final blank. Indeed, this fill-in-the-blank phenomenon suggests that the form of the balanced sentence may be more memorable than the meaning conveyed by and through that form—like having a humongous stretch limo drive up and deliver a perfectly nondescript rider. I can only remember the balance of Barry Goldwater's famous/infamous battle cry of 1964: "Extremism in the defense of liberty is no vice; moderation in the pursuit of justice is no virtue." I can always remember the balance between extremism and moderation and between vice and virtue, but for the life of me I never can remember that this sentence balanced liberty against justice, two terms usually paired, as in "with liberty and justice for all."

While the most rhetorically polished balanced sentences do tend to be divided by a semicolon, the balanced sentence does not demand a semicolon, as is the case with the chiasmic "When the going gets tough, the tough get going." Another example of balance without the semicolon would be Fitzgerald's "There are only the pursued, the pursuing, the busy and the tired."

Apart from its aphoristic nature—and anyone who wants to start a bumper sticker business had better know how to construct balances!—the balanced sentence offers an obvious advantage to any writer who must compare two subjects. Such a comparison can be made by treating first one subject and then the other, through splitting the comparison into two halves, each half focusing on one of the subjects; or by alternating paragraphs, each paragraph focusing on one of the subjects; or it can be made sentence-by-sentence, with each balanced sentence matching the two subjects on a point-by-point basis. This kind of comparison or contrast can really profit from the use of balanced sentences: Balance is the specific syntactic tool ready-made for comparisons.

Dr. Samuel Johnson is probably the greatest master of the balanced form, as we can see in his comparison of Dryden with Pope:

> Pope had perhaps the judgment of Dryden; but Dryden certainly wanted the diligence of Pope. In acquired knowledge the superiority must be allowed to Dryden, whose education was more scholastick, and who before he became an author had been allowed more time for study, with better means of information. His mind has a larger range, and he collects his images and illustrations from a more extensive circumference of science. Dryden knew more of man in his general

nature, and Pope in his local manners. ... There is more dignity in the knowledge of Dryden, and more certainty in that of Pope.

The style of Dryden is capricious and varied, that of Pope is cautious and uniform; Dryden obeys the motions of his own mind, Pope constrains his mind to his own rules of composition. Dryden is sometimes vehement and rapid; Pope is always smooth, uniform, and gentle. Dryden's page is a natural field, rising into inequalities, and diversified by the varied exuberance of abundant vegetation; Pope's is a velvet lawn, shaven by the scythe, and levelled by the roller.

Of genius, that power which constitutes a poet; that quality without which judgement is cold and knowledge is inert; that energy which collects, combines, amplifies, and animates—the superiority must, with some hesitation, be allowed to Dryden. ... Dryden's performances were always hasty, either excited by some external occasion, or extorted by domestick necessity; he composed without consideration, and published without correction. What his mind could supply at call, or gather in one excursion, was all that he sought, and all that he gave. The dilatory caution of Pope enabled him to condense his sentiments, to multiply his images, and to accumulate all that study might produce, or chance might supply. If the flights of Dryden therefore are higher, Pope continues longer on the wing. If of Dryden's fire the blaze is brighter, of Pope's the heat is more regular and constant. Dryden often surpasses expectation, and Pope never falls below it. Dryden is read with frequent astonishment, and Pope with perpetual delight.

Even if you read the above passage so quickly that you don't get much of its meaning, you'll notice that it has a distinct rhythm or cadence—it sounds balanced, alternating between similar sounds or beats as well as between Pope and Dryden. (Remember that a balanced view of things is a comment on fairness and even-handedness, a mental trait to be desired and valorized as well as a form or syntax.) Johnson's comparison, then, displays a second kind or degree of balance, that of smaller forms within the sentence, and of those forms between and among sentences. Any time that a sentence, part of a sentence, or groups of sentences make us aware of pairs of things—whether objects, sounds, words, syntactic structures—that reveals some degree of balanced form. This kind of balance can take almost any shape or form, can appear at almost any time. It may come from the insinuating insistence of alliteration, assonance, or consonance, or from the pronounced parallelism of phrases and modifiers, metaphors, and the larger syntax of the sentence. Balance may even come from a conceptual dualism—a thought that focuses our thinking, inexorably, on two subjects, entities, ideas, images—as in "She starved so that he could eat," or in Shelley's aphorism, "Imagination means individuation." Dr. Johnson's comparison of the two poets contains almost all of these forms of balance.

Here, with Dr. Johnson, is the second place, John Lyly's example being the first, where balance fell at least a bit into disrepute. Before we consider some of Johnson's detractors, however, let's look at a few more examples of the prose style with which he is so closely associated:

This is from his Preface to *A Dictionary of the English Language*:

> Among these unhappy mortals is the writer of dictionaries; whom mankind have considered, not as the pupil, but the slave of science, the pionier of literature, doomed only to remove rubbish and clear obstructions from the paths of Learning and Genius, who press forward to conquest and glory, without bestowing a smile on the humble drudge that facilitates their progress. Every other author may aspire to praise; the lexicographer can only hope to escape reproach, and even this negative recompense has been yet granted to very few.

> When I took the first survey of my undertaking, I found our speech copious without order, and energetick without rules: wherever I turned my view, there was perplexity to be disentangled, and confusion to be regulated; choice was to be made out of boundless variety, without any established principle of selection; adulterations were to be detected, without a settled test of purity; and modes of expression to be rejected or received, without the suffrages of any writers of classical reputation or acknowledged authority.

The question we aspiring students of the sentence must answer for ourselves before we decide whether in-your-face balance will be a feature in our own syntactic arsenal is simply this: Does Dr. Johnson's prose strike us as impressive or obsessive, well-crafted to positive affect, or overdone to the point of putting readers off? What we're really doing here is trying to decide what we feel about balance rather than about Dr. Johnson. The problem with balance, as is the problem with any syntax pushed too hard, is that it levels reality, forcing everything into binary agreement or opposition. In an essay on Johnson's parallelism, W. K. Wimsatt Jr. has outlined the case against balance. Citing Hazlitt's criticism of Johnson's style—"All his periods are cast in the same mould, are of the same size and shape, and consequently have little fitness to the variety of things he professes to treat of"—Wimsatt observes that Johnson runs the risk of "preferring the meaning of parallel to a more relevant meaning of variety." He explains in his characteristically abstract—but balanced—fashion:

> A writer may insist, by explicit or implicit means, on the equality or on the opposite, the difference of the members within their frame of equality or on the opposite, the difference of the members within their frame of equality or parallel. He may exploit one kind of meaning or the other. ... If he recurrently gives to his multiplied phrases or clauses a turn toward equality, then the relations of member to member, of premise to premise and to conclusion, will be strengthened and plain; the whole sequence of meaning will have a high degree of coherence and regularity—but this will be at the expense of modulation, of individuality of premise, of variety.

Hazlitt advances much the same critique of pronounced balanced form, using Edmund Burke as his target:

> The words are not fitted to the things, but the things to the words. Everything is seen through a false medium. It is putting a mask on the face of nature, which may indeed hide some specks and blemishes, but takes away all beauty, delicacy, and variety.

If you think that sounds like a serious indictment, wait until you hear Macaulay's critique of Dr. Johnson! In his review of "Boswell's Life of Johnson" (1831), Thomas Babington Macaulay, who, it should be remembered, was himself known for his use of balanced form, accused Johnson of writing in "Johnsonese," a style that he called "systematically vicious" and famously opined:

> His constant practice of padding out a sentence with useless epithets, till it became as stiff as the bust of an exquisite; his antithetical forms of expression, constantly employed even where there is no opposition in the ideas expressed; his big words wasted on little things; his harsh inversions, so widely different from those graceful and easy inversions which give variety, spirit, and sweetness to the expression of our great old writers—all these peculiarities have been imitated by his admirers, and parodied by his assailants, till the public has become sick of the subject.

Not so fast! rebutted George Saintsbury in 1916, who termed Macaulay's description of Johnson's style "one of the worst parts of his essay" and then used the term *tessellation* to describe Johnson's rhetorical strategy in which clauses and sentences were balanced against each other, and built up into larger sentences and paragraphs on a system of almost mathematical or military exactitude, file being drawn up against file, and squadron against squadron, while both the constituent clause members and *their* constituents of substantive, adjective, and verb were balanced or 'dressed' against each other in pairs, triplets, even quaternions of strictest equilibrium in rhythm and thought."

While Saintsbury acknowledges that this "Palladian architecture of style is no doubt more imposing than delectable," he insists it is "by no means omnipresent" nor is it "ever very conspicuous" in Johnson's "really best passages." Maybe that's not a rousing defense, but it is a much more accurate description of what Johnson does than Macaulay offers in his condemnation. I suspect that today we might be tempted to describe Johnson's style as fractal, rather than as tessellated, but both terms suggest the way that his balances contain balances which contain balances, giving his writing a balanced texture that is unmatched.

What's missing so far in these discussions of balance is the fact that they are so much fun for the writer to construct and for the reader to recognize. Mathew Clark touches on this underreported aspect in his book, *A Matter of Style: On Writing and Technique* where he recognizes that "for modern tastes," the example of sustained balance and parallelism "may be excessive," but notes that "there is a great vigor and pleasure in the writing." He adds:

> This passage must have been fun to compose, and for the reader in the right frame of mind, it's still a lot of fun to read. In this sort of style, the figure doesn't merely serve the idea; it becomes an end in itself, and ideas are sought to provide an occasion for the figure.

Clark offers an excerpt from George Bernard Shaw's *Man and Superman* as further evidence of the ludic potential of balanced form. Shaw's Don Juan is replying to the Devil's charge that he has been uncivil with a delicious blowout of balance:

> Pooh! Why should I be civil to them or to you? In this Palace of Lies a truth or two will not hurt you. Your friends are all the dullest dogs I know. They are not beautiful: they are only decorated. They are not clean: they are only shaved and starched. They are not dignified: they are only fashionably dressed ... They are not moral: they are only conventional. They are not virtuous: they are only cowardly ... They are not loyal, they are only servile; not dutiful, only sheepish; not public spirited, only patriotic; not courageous, only quarrelsome; not determined, only obstinate; not masterful, only domineering; not self-controlled, only obtuse; not self-respecting, only vain; not kind, only sentimental; not social, only gregarious; not considerate, only polite; not intelligent, only opinionated; not progressive, only factious; not imaginative, only superstitious; not just, only vindictive ... and not truthfull at all: liars every one of them, to the very backbone of their souls.

In the writing of William Gass, we find an even more effective brief for the use of balance, as Gass goes for balances at every opportunity, seemingly delighting in the rhythm. America has no more innovative a prose stylist than Gass and it is his example, not Dr. Johnson's, that I follow when I champion the use of balanced forms in effective writing. In his novels such as *The Tunnel, Omensetter's Luck*, and *Willie Master's Lonesome Wife,* in his short fiction collected in *In the Heart of the Heart of the Country*, but particularly in his collections of essays—"On Being Blue," "The World Within the Word," "Fiction and the Figures of Life," "The Habitations of the Word," and "A Temple of Texts"—Gass does more breathtaking things with sentences, gets more energy and excitement from his prose than does any other living American writer. Even wrenched from the contexts that give them so much added impact, his sentences stand as monuments to his mastery of language—and to his fascination with balance. Here are just a few examples.

This from an essay on suicide:

> Poetry is cathartic only for the unserious, for in front of the rush of expressive need stands the barrier of form, and when the hurdler's scissored legs and outstretched arms carry him over the bars, the limp in his life, the headache in his heart, the emptiness he's full of, are as absent as his street shoes, which will pinch and scrape his feet in all the old leathery ways once the race is over and he has to walk through the front door of his future like a brushman with some feckless patter and a chintzy plastic prize.

This about Malcolm Lowry's *Under the Volcano*:

> There is a cantina at every corner of the Consul's world. Sin and innocence, guilt and salvation, shape Lowry's private square of opposition, and if sanctuary and special knowledge are its gifts in one guise, and gaiety and relaxation its gifts in another, catercorner from church and gym are brothel and prison.

This on Samuel Beckett:

> He writes equally well in two languages: Nitty and Gritty. He is a minimalist because he compresses, and puts everything in by leaving most of it out. Joyce wished to rescue the world by getting it back into his book: Beckett wishes to save our souls by purging us—impossibly—of matter.

This on Borges:

> Borges is a fine poet, too, but he revolutionized our conception of both the story and the essay by blending and bewildering them. He will not be forgiven or forgotten for that.

This about *The Tale of One Thousand and One Nights*:

> In its nearly thousand-and-one-year journey to our time, these Arabian contes drew additions, endured omissions, submitted to revisions, suffered expurgations, were betrayed by translations, fussed over by annotations, and stuffed into editions aimed at special interests, while experiencing normal negligence and the customary incompetence of sellers, scribes, scholars, and consumers: the tattering dispersal, and destruction of copies, the corruption of the text, the misunderstanding of its meaning, the exploitation of its exotic scenes and settings, as well as the decline of its importance into what, so ironic for the *Nights*, we call bedtime stories.

In a fitting close to our consideration of balance, here's Gass on Dr. Johnson in the company of other noteworthy preface writers:

In the preface to his *Dictionary*, Dr. Johnson whines (another persistent feature of the genre)—"It is the fate of those who toil at the lower employments of life, to be rather driven by the fear of evil, than attracted by the prospect of good: to be exposed to censure, without hope of praise; to be disgraced by miscarriage, or punished for neglect, where success would have been without applause, and diligence without reward"—a whine, yes, but how perfectly composed.

The Rhythm of Threes
Lecture 20

Winston Weathers, in a pioneering essay on "The Rhetoric of the Series," notes that the writer can "write the two-part series and create an aura of certainty, confidence, didacticism, and dogmatism," or "can write the three-part series and create the effect of the normal, the reasonable, the believable, and the logical," or "can write the four-or-more-part series and suggest the human, emotional, diffuse, and inexplicable."

Just as Dr. Johnson is the master of balance, Bacon is the master of parallel three-part series. Balance is the rhythm of twos, series is the rhythm of threes, and parallel serial constructions echo, invoke, and build upon our penchant for measuring, describing, and constructing reality in units of threes. Three phrases of parallel construction, three-part predicates, three attempts to say exactly the right thing all invoke serial form. A series, however, is more than just a list with three or more items in it: At the heart of this form is some kind of unity, some kind of progression, some kind of intensification. What distinguishes the series is that its elements build on each other, add to each other's impact, restate and refine each other's information. The series may mark a temporal progression, establish a chronology, or outline a process.

In a way, the series is a kind of balance that has been extended since the more parallel the elements of the series—whether elements of syntax, diction, sound, or concept—the more pronounced the serial construction. *Veni, vidi, vici.* (I came, I saw, I conquered.)

The most pronounced serial construction has three parts, although a series can be extended beyond three elements.

The most pronounced serial construction has three parts, although a series can be extended beyond three elements (or reduced to two). The ties among kinds of serial constructions are quite complex; one three-part series balances quite effectively against another, a three-part series may be composed of three two-part balances, and a four-part series can easily be shaped to lend its catalog to either two- or three-part rhythm. Furthermore, serial constructions invite asyndeton (the omitting of conjunctions) or polysyndeton (the foregrounded/excessive use of conjunctions). Another rhetorical device invited by serial construction is anaphora—beginning each element in the series with the same word or words. Of course, the opposite of anaphora is epistrophe—ending each item in a series with the same word or words. Combine anaphora and epistrophe and you get—symploce.

Three-part serials can be overdone. Of course, this is true of all syntactical patterns we've been working with and, for that matter, it's true of just about everything in general. Modern readers probably have a much greater tolerance for pronounced serial constructions than they have for pronounced balance, and the three-part series does not seem as tied to the rhetoric of earlier centuries as does balance. In a word, it sounds more reasonable. Just as Dr. Johnson is the exemplum par excellence of balance, Francis Bacon is the triple-crown winner of three-part serial form, with his "Of Studies" possibly the most intense example we have of sustained serial construction.

We can consider examples by Carl Klaus, my colleague at Iowa and, along with novelist Thomas Berger, one of my two great mentors in matters having to do with prose style. From Carl Klaus we can learn that the basic patterns for serial construction can be categorized in three ways: the phasal series, the clausal series, and rhetorical schemes and tropes like the following:

- Schemes of Omission, such as asyndeton and ellipses.

- Schemes of Repetition, such as alliteration, anaphora, anadiplosis, assonance, chiasmus, epanalepsis, epistrophe, isocolon, polyptoton, polysyndeton, symploce, and tricolon.

These are but a few of the rhetorical schemes and tropes that can create and intensify parallelism in general and three-part serials in particular. There is some disagreement about the difference between a trope and a scheme, but generally tropes have primarily to do with meaning, either of a word whose meaning is changed or extended, while schemes have to do with the ordering of words and sounds. Accordingly, we might think of a metaphor as a trope, while repetition or alliteration would be a scheme. Let's just call both rhetorical moves. Richard Lanham specifies 34 different rhetorical moves associated with the creation of balance or antithesis and 36 associated with parallelism of letters, syllables, sounds, words, clauses, phrases, sentences, and ideas, so this small sampling only begins to suggest the care with which ancient orators and writers constructed their discourse. To be effective writers we certainly don't need to command all of the relatively few forms I've just mentioned, but just knowing that these forms exist increases the likelihood that we will find some occasion in which it makes sense to tap some of their power. ■

Question to Consider

1. Using only serial sentences and/or sentences brimming with parallel serial constructions of all kinds, write a short essay on the subject of being stuck in traffic. To make this assignment interesting, treat it as a chance to play in the most extravagant way with the serial and parallel constructions, that is, to go overboard in finding a creative approach to the subject and in indulging in all the resonances of these forms.

The Rhythm of Threes
Lecture 20—Transcript

Balance is the rhythm of twos, series is the rhythm of threes, and parallel serial constructions echo, invoke, and build upon our penchant for measuring, describing, and constructing reality in units of threes. In the next lecture, I'm going to return to explore further the idea that balance and three-part serials are much more than just syntactic patterns and are deeply imbricated in our understanding of the world. For now, I just want to call attention to the three-part series as the obvious counterpart and complement to the two-part rhythms and constructions of balance.

Three phrases of parallel construction, three-part predicates, three attempts to say exactly the right thing all invoke serial form. A series, however, is more than just a list with three or more items in it: at the heart of this form is some kind of unity, some kind of progression, some kind of intensification. What distinguishes the series is that its elements build on each other, add to each other's impact, restate and refine each other's information. For example, can we imagine a more effective explanation than Nabokov's three-part series reasons for granting interviews only in writing: "I think like a genius. I write like a distinguished author. I speak like a child." Or, the series may mark a temporal progression, establish a chronology, outline a process. In a way, the series is a kind of balance that has been extended since the more parallel the elements of the series—whether elements of syntax, diction, sound, or concept—the more pronounced the serial construction. As Caesar put it in perhaps the most famous three-part series we have: *Veni, vidi, vici.* (I came, I saw, I conquered.)

The most pronounced serial construction has three parts, although a series can be extended beyond three elements (or reduced to two). Winston Weathers, in a pioneering essay on "The Rhetoric of the Series," notes that the writer can "write the two-part series and create an aura of certainty, confidence, didacticism, and dogmatism," or "can write the three-part series and create the effect of the normal, the reasonable, the believable, and the logical," or "can write the four-or-more-part series and suggest the human, emotional, diffuse, and inexplicable." Weathers sees the choice a writer makes between creating the two-beat rhythm of balance or the three-beat rhythm of three-part parallel series as a choice between the almost "authoritarian" implications of balance, with its implications of "finality and totality," a sense that "there is nothing more to be said," or a sense of "massive, abrupt, and final summary" and the "aura of the true and believable sample" offered by the three-part series. Referring to the fact that the syllogism has three parts—major premise, minor premise, and conclusion—Weathers suggests that the three-part series offers a "sense of the reasonable and even the logical." To him, and I certainly agree, the series, in going one step beyond the binary oppositions of balance, achieves the rhetorical effect of "something more reasonable, ordinary, and more truly representative," and he clinches his argument with the balanced claim that the series has "the touch of the common and understandable."

Tellingly, Weathers himself employs balanced form to describe the series and three-part serial constructions to describe balance. As the example of his own prose suggests, the ties among kinds of serial constructions are quite complex, since one three-part series balances quite effectively against another. A three-part series may be composed of three two-part balances, and the four-part series can easily be shaped to lend its catalog to either two- or three-part rhythm. Furthermore, serial constructions invite *asyndeton* (the omitting of conjunctions) or *polysyndeton* (the foregrounded, excessive use of conjunctions). *I came, I saw, I conquered* could have been said *I came and I saw and I conquered*, which would be polysyndeton, or *I came, saw, conquered*, asyndeton. Sounds to me like Caesar got it right, even if he did crib the general form from the ending of Aristotle's *Rhetoric*.

Asyndeton seems to suggest simultaneity and speed (Aristotle suggested it had the added effect of seeming "to say many things at the same time"), while polysyndeton seems to suggest distinct stages or differences and deliberate intensity. "He has had his intuition, he has made his discovery, he is eager to explore it, to reveal it, to fix it down." "It was a hot day and the sky was very bright and blue and the road was white and dusty," the last example from Hemingway.

Another rhetorical device invited by serial construction is *anaphora*— beginning each element in the series with the same word or words. "The reason why I object to Dr. Johnson's style is, that there is no discrimination, no selection, no variety in it." "Art, for most Americans, is a very queer fish—it can't be reasoned with, it can't be bribed, it can't be doped out or duplicated; above all, it can't be cashed in on." Of course, the opposite of anaphora is *epistrophe*—ending each item in a series with the same word or words. "To the good American many subjects are sacred: sex is sacred, women are sacred, children are sacred, business is sacred, America is sacred, Masonic lodges and college clubs are sacred." "Raphael paints wisdom; Handel sings it, Phidias carves it, Shakespeare writes it, Wren builds it, Columbus sails it, Luther preaches it, Washington arms it, Watt mechanizes it," the last one from Emerson. Combine anaphora and epistrophe and you get *symploce*: "I was born an American; I will live an American; I shall die an American," that from Daniel Webster.

Just as was the case with balance, three-part serials can be overdone. Of course, this is true of all of the syntactical patterns we've been working with and, for that matter, it's true of just about everything in general. However, for reasons I'll try to explain shortly, modern readers probably have a much greater tolerance for pronounced serial constructions than they have for pronounced balance, and the three-part series does not seem as tied to the rhetoric of earlier centuries as does balance. In a word, it sounds more *reasonable*. Indeed its evocation of logic and reason seems to be one of the great sources of the rhetorical effectiveness of three-part serials.

Whenever I write serial constructions it's a little bit like taking a long plane flight with a couple of connections, a couple of stops that actually help me reach my destination, a couple of brief layovers during which I can rethink my itinerary, remind myself of what remains to be done, and redouble my efforts to ensure that the trip accomplishes its purpose, gets me where I need to go, or at least provides the satisfying illusion that I'm going somewhere. This analogy doesn't bear too much scrutiny, however, since my reasons for taking plane flights are almost always generated from without, required by some clear need to get to a specific destination, driven by events to which I may choose to respond or not, but which I never completely control. Writing a series, on the other hand, simply seems to come out of the blue, an opportunity that just presents itself as my sentence unfolds, generated from somewhere within my understanding of syntactic options, required by some amorphous sense that three tries are better than one, driven only by some internal metronome that is deaf to the appeal of a waltz, but that longs for the rhythm of threes in my writing—the narrative rhythm of beginning, middle, and end; the progressive rhythm of going, going, gone; the conceptual rhythm of a world that conforms itself to the debater's confidently raised three fingers, the syllogism's three parts, the three elements themselves: earth, fire, and water.

When I begin to write, I rarely have a destination in mind for each sentence, much less a plan for marching the steps of the sentence according to some specific cadence, but somewhere after my first word it must occur to me that I haven't said exactly what I wanted to say, haven't gotten the words quite right, haven't painted the picture for my reader that I see so clearly—or, as I suspect is more often the case, haven't clearly painted the picture that still remains stubbornly fuzzy to my straining imagination. In these cases, I usually try again, but something about two efforts at getting the words right often feels incomplete, unsatisfying, awkward, so I run through my options, searching for the third word, third phrase, third sound that will release me from the apparent need to sound more reasonable, ordinary, and understandable, that will free me from the compulsion to offer a reasonable sample, and that will let me start a new sentence in which, against all odds, I just might say exactly what I want to say, might get the words precisely right, might paint the masterpiece of my dreams, or, failing that, might content myself with the belligerence of the balance, the sprawl of the catalog, or any prose rhythm that startles the eye and ear, some rude reggae in place of the waltz.

Here's another example of my own attempts to tap the power of serial construction:

> Each of us has experienced moments in which for some unfathomable reason we have done exactly the inappropriate thing, made the perfectly inane remark, responded to a person, statement, or event with no sense of proportion whatsoever, no sense of self-awareness, no sense of how fatal our lack of judgment will immediately seem. In such moments of incredible awkwardness time stops, we see puzzled or shocked expressions creep across the faces of those around us, the sudden silence crashes in our ears, and we desperately want the fatal word or action back, want a second take in the movie of life, pray for a second chance. We cannot believe what we have done, cannot escape our burning embarrassment, and, finally, we

can only face the bleak prospect of trying to gloss over or undo the damage, knowing full well we have no chance. These are moments of rarest paranoia and despair, moments frozen in humiliation, a time when if life itself does not seem hopelessly absurd, we certainly do. Usually, these moments of acute, ego-shattering embarrassment come from nowhere, randomly, exploding into miserable being when a maverick thought eludes our normally vigilant censoring codes of conduct and social survival—moments when our carefully constructed defensive shields drop for the briefest moment, when for a horrifying instant we shock and dismay ourselves with a totally honest, uncalculated, and wildly free reaction to the world around us.

Just as Dr. Johnson is the exemplum *par excellence* of balance, Francis Bacon is the triple-crown winner of three-part serial form, with his "Of Studies" possibly the most intense example we have of sustained serial construction:

Studies serve for delight, for ornament, and for ability. Their chief use for delight is in privateness and retiring; for ornament, is in discourse; and for ability, is in the judgment and disposition of business. For expert men can execute, and perhaps judge of particulars, one by one; but the general counsels, and the plots and marshalling of affairs, come best from those that are learned. To spend too much time in studies is sloth; to use them too much for ornament, is affectation; to make judgment wholly by their rules, is the humor of a scholar. They perfect nature, and are perfected by experience... Crafty men contemn studies, simple men admire them, and wise men use them; for they teach not their own use; but that is a wisdom without them, and above them, won by observation. Read not to contradict and confute; nor to believe and take for granted; nor to find talk and discourse; but to weigh and consider. Some books are to be tasted, others to be swallowed, and some few to be chewed and digested ... . Reading maketh a full man; conference a ready man; and writing an exact man.

Consider the following triple-treat paragraph by Carl Klaus, my colleague at Iowa and, along with novelist Thomas Berger, one of my two great mentors in matters having to do with prose style:

I am fascinated by parallel series, I spend hours probing their mysteries, I worship their ideal form. I look for them in my reading, I strive for them in my writing, I contrive them even when I am talking. So obsessed am I by them that my thoughts are forever upon them, whether I am brushing my teeth, washing my car, hoeing my garden, eating my dinner, tying my shoes, grooming my dog, myself, or my fly line. So Bacon is my master, my idol, my bane. I study him, I imitate him, I envy him. I require my students to read him, to analyze him, to emulate him. I ask no more of them than of myself, no less of them than they are capable, as much of them as they can produce and the language will bear. I wonder how this obsession will end—in mastery, in mockery, or in madness. I cannot predict, but I know I cannot continue as I am at present—working to create, laboring to contrive, struggling to perfect the Baconian style. Doing so has led me to defy my master, to mar his masterpieces, to mend his mastery. Thus, I am committed to a single form, one style, the syntax of a perfect series, hoping to excel him and so to be free of him forever.

I should take just a moment here to recommend to you the remarkable range of nonfiction essays and contemplations of Carl Klaus. Carl has written and edited prolifically in the fields of writing and stylistic theory, and his work on composition and prose style has shaped much of my thinking and that of writing teachers across the nation. Of particular value are his *Elements of Writing*, coauthored with Robert Scholes, his *Style in English Prose*, his award-winning *Courses for Change in Writing*, coauthored with Nancy Jones, and his *In Depth: Essayists For Our Time*, coauthored with Chris Anderson and Rebecca Faery.

Carl's greatest appeal to those of us trying to improve the effectiveness of our own writing is in his own justly celebrated creative nonfiction. He is the author of *My Vegetable Love: A Journal of a Growing Season*, a memoir that celebrates Carl's love of gardening, and all of the things that touch upon his gardening, including reflections on everything from the weather to his wife, with grandchildren, academe, and dogs, cats, and neighbors in between. This book and what might be considered its sequel, *Weathering Winter: A Gardner's Daybook*, remind us that elegant prose exploiting all of the syntactic devices in the history of the English language not only need not sound artificial or strained, but can make the most natural of subjects come alive. Carl's *Taking Retirement: A Beginner's Diary* contemplates the losses and the gains of retiring from a lifetime of passionate teaching and is a book I am certain I will reread again and again as I approach my own retirement. His *Letters to Kate: Life After Life* is Carl's moving, at time heartbreaking, and always insightful exploration of loss and grief, following the sudden death in 2002 of his wife.

No, this unabashed plug for Carl Klaus's writing is not a new low in product placement, nor do I own stock in Carl's literary enterprises. What I do find and want to celebrate in his work is writing reminiscent of the wisdom we find in E. B. White, but with more joy in and crafting of language than we normally encounter in White's wonderful letters and essays. Besides, you already knew about E. B. White—it's my pleasure to introduce you to the syntactic mastery and delicious sentences of Carl Klaus. Not incidentally, Carl is also the visionary founder of Iowa's MFA in Nonfiction Program and, both directly and indirectly, his influence on several generations of award-winning nonfiction writers has been huge.

More to the point of this lecture, from Carl Klaus we can learn that the basic patterns for serial construction can be categorized in terms of those for the following.

Phrasal series:

> The lake is crystal clear, dead calm, and freezing cold.

> Aerobic exercise helps one lose weight safely, improve muscle tone, and reduce stress.

> Rain drips through the trees, in no hurry to meet the earth, trickles down the trunk, seeps into the ground, percolates down, and reaches its goal to merge with the aquifer.

Those for the clausal or elliptical series:

> Hearing their parents' car drive up, one teen hid the Jack Daniels, another turned off the X-rated movie, and a third shooed their friends out the back door.

> Traditional classrooms can foster boredom; televised classes, isolation; correspondence classes, guilt.

> Assume nothing, appropriate nothing, assign, ascribe, associate nothing, repeat not a word until you ascertain the truth of it for yourself.

And then those rhetorical tropes, several of which we have already noted, *Schemes of Omission.*

Asyndeton: to omit the conjunctions that usually link the final items in a series of coordinate words, phrases, or clauses—"I came, I saw, I conquered." "He was ten inches long, thin as a curve, a muscled ribbon, brown as fruitwood, soft-furred, alert," that from Annie Dillard. Aristotle ends his *Rhetoric* with the confident asyndeton: "I have done. You have heard me. The facts are before you. I ask for your judgement."

Ellipsis: to omit one or more words that are obviously necessary but must be inferred to make a construction grammatically complete—as we saw in Bacon's "Reading maketh a full man, conference a ready man, and writing an exact man," or we can see in Nabokov's "I prefer the specific detail to the generalization, images to ideas, obscure facts to clear symbols, and the discovered wild fruit to the synthetic jam."

Then there are *Schemes of Repetition.*

Alliteration: to repeat the initial consonants in neighboring or in grammatically corresponding words—Spiro Agnew's description of the press as "nattering nabobs of negatism" gives us an example of this serial technique used as a bludgeon.

Anaphora: to repeat a word or phrase at the beginning of successive sentences, clauses, or phrases—"I should have gone for the throat. I should have lunged for that streak of white under the weasel's chin and held on, held on through mud and into the wild rose, held on for a dearer life," that from Annie Dillard's "Living like a Weasel." Eldridge Cleaver revealed his control of both anaphora and ellipsis in his striking declaration in *Soul on Ice:* "I'm perfectly aware that I'm in prison, that I'm a Negro, that I've been a rapist, and that I have a Higher Uneducation."

Anadiplosis: to repeat a word that ends one phrase, clause, or sentence at the beginning of the next—"Learn as though you would live forever, live as though you would die tomorrow."

Assonance: to repeat similar vowel sounds in neighboring or in grammatically corresponding words—"His journal is tracks in clay, a spray of feathers, mouse blood and bone; uncollected, unconnected, loose-leaf, and blown," that also from Annie Dillard.

Chiasmus: to repeat a grammatical structure and the words it contains, but to reverse the order of the key words in the second phrase, clause, or sentence. We've seen the bumper-sticker example of chiasmus—"When the going gets tough, the tough get going" and I'm particularly fond of Hunter Thompson's variation, "When the going gets weird, the weird turn pro." But chiasmus can be a very effective and memorable persuasive device: "The press is so powerful in its image-making role that it can make a criminal look like he's the victim and make the victim look like he's the criminal," that also from Eldridge Cleaver.

Epanalepsis: to repeat the same word or phrase at the beginning and end of a clause or sentence—"Tribe follows tribe, and nation follows nation, like the waves of the sea," that from Chief Seattle.

Epistrophe: to repeat the same word or phrase at the end of successive phrases, clauses, or sentences—"They loved football, they ate football, they slept football." Of course, probably the most familiar examples we have of epistrophe are "the truth, the whole truth, and nothing but the truth," and "government of the people, by the people, and for the people."

Isocolon: a form of parallelism that stresses corresponding words, phrases, causes, and sentences of equal length and similar structure. Churchill's famous "Never in the history of mankind have so many owed so much to so few" illustrates the form, and his "He is asked to stand, he wants to sit, and he is expected to lie" reveals some of its potential for pointed humor.

Polyptoton: to repeat words with the same root but different forms or endings—"Poverty and isolation produce impoverished and isolated minds" is an example of polyptoton at the start of a much longer sentence in William Gass's *On Being Blue*. Matthew Clark points to Nabokov's fondness for polyptoton in *Ada*, where he refers to "a specular, and hence speculatory phenomenon," "divinities and divines," and the "collected works of uncollected authors." *Polysyndeton:* to repeat conjunctions between coordinate words, phrases, or clauses in a series—Joan Didion frequently relies on polysyndeton in her writing, as she does in "Some Dreamers of the Golden Dream" that opens with the almost polysyndeton of "This is a story about love and death in the golden land, and begins with the country," then quickly gets down to the real thing: "It is the season of suicide and divorce and prickly dread, whenever the wind blows." Yeats gives us a wonderful example of the calming, slowing effect of polysyndeton in the opening lines of his poem "When You Are Old": "When you are old and gray and full of sleep" and I bet more than a few of us can supply the next phrase, "And nodding by the fire."

Symploce: this is a "twofer" scheme in which the combination in a sequence of phrases, clauses, or sentences of *anaphora* (repeating the first word) and *epistrophe* (repeating the final word) creates symploce, as William Blake employed this scheme in his "Proverbs of Hell":

> The pride of the peacock is the glory of God.
> The lust of the goat is the bounty of God.
> The wrath of the lion is the wisdom of God.
> The nakedness of woman is the work of God.

Tricolon: Matthew Clark, reminding us of the human tendency to compose groups of three, specifies that a tripling of phrases, clauses, or sentences is called tricolon, and adds "if the phrases are arranged so that they progressively increase in length, the figure is called tricolon crescendo," offering Nabokov's reference in *Ada* to a character's "long, too long, never too long life" as an example. Obviously, most if not all of our examples of three-part parallel series display some form of tricolon.

These are but a few of the rhetorical schemes and tropes that can create and intensify parallelism in general and three-part serials in particular. There is some disagreement about the difference between a trope and a scheme, but generally tropes have primarily to do with meaning, either of a word whose meaning is changed or extended, while schemes have to do with the ordering of words and sounds. Accordingly, we might think of a metaphor as a trope, while repetition or alliteration would be a scheme. Let's just call both *rhetorical moves*. Richard Lanham specifies 34 different rhetorical moves associated with the creation of balance or antithesis, and 36 associated with parallelism of letters, syllables, sounds, words, clauses, phrases, sentences, and ideas, so this small sampling only begins to suggest the care with which ancient orators and writers constructed their discourse. To be effective writers we certainly don't need to command even all of the relatively few forms I've just mentioned, but just knowing that these forms exist increases the likelihood that we will find some occasion in which it makes sense to tap some of their power.

Balanced Series and Serial Balances
Lecture 21

Against binaries such as past and present, the three-part series reminds us to expand our view to consider the future. When we consider the age-old dichotomy of mind and body, the three-part serial reminds us to add soul, and so on.

Balance one three-part series against another or construct a three-part series of balanced forms and the sentence can become a pinball machine of sounds, rhythms, images, and ideas. I can't think of any modern writer who does a better job of constructing verbal pinball machines than William Gass. Gass is the David May Distinguished University Professor Emeritus in the Humanities at Washington University in St. Louis, where for many years he taught philosophy and English. More important, he is one of America's most celebrated writers and critics. Among prose stylists who have thought long and hard about prose, he has no equal. Examples from Gass's writing remind us that sentences do things, are alive, are closely tied to the body's basic rhythms, and, when in the hands of a masterful writer, can be taught steps that dance across the lips and across the page. Through his writing, Gass suggests the uncharted power a writer can tap when combining duple and triple rhythms.

In the last lecture, I gave a brief overview of the attempt by Winston Weathers to theorize the rhetorical effect and impact of two- and three-part serial constructions. Weathers suggested that the two-part series, which we have been calling balance or balanced form, has connotations of authority and expertise, if not of authoritarianism. In contrast, the three-part series, according to Weathers has connotations of the reasonable, the believable, and even the logical. I did not mention what Weathers had to say about serial constructions of four or more parts because, while these longer constructions clearly invoke the affective power or parallelism, I'm not sure readers can really process in any meaningful way four or more sound patterns or conceptual units without simply thinking of them as a list.

Before we consider the possible sources and implications of the patterns of balance and three-part serial constructions, however, let's get a better structured sense of how these rhythms can be put together, and to what effect. We can find numerous examples of the interplay of two- and three-beat rhythms in the lush style associated with Lyly and other euphuistic writers of the 16th century. The curt or pointed style of Francis Bacon, so well known for its three-part serials, also contains a striking number of balances, as we have seen in the selection from his "Of Studies." On the other hand, the fabled balances of Dr. Johnson and, as we shall soon see, of Macaulay, regularly employ three-part serials. While my own examples of the interplay of balance and series are relatively crude, they illustrate the basic options for balancing one series against another.

Gass *always* sees language as a subject every bit as interesting and important as is the referential world his language points to, invokes, or stands for.

We've seen how Gass weaves these rhythms together in patterns that are unexpected, but we should remember that they have much more frequently been combined in patterns that were almost diagrammatic. Macaulay denounced Dr. Johnson for the artificiality of his over-designed prose, but Macaulay is himself regarded as a master of balanced form, and his balances frequently employ or are employed by three-part serial constructions. The difference between Gass and Macaulay is much greater than the difference between a carefully controlled manipulation of prose rhythms and an exuberant gush; it is the difference between what we might call a classical view of rhetoric and what we might call a postmodern view. Macaulay saw his control of tropes, schemes, syntax, and other structures as a supporting adjunct to his arguments, moves that clarified and emphasized the propositional and logical content of his claims. Gass also presents his celebrations of sound and syntax in support of claims about the subject matter of his sentences but, for Gass, his sentences themselves are always part of the point of his writing, if not the main point.

In keeping with his place in the forefront of postmodern writers, Gass *always* sees language as a subject every bit as interesting and important as is the referential world his language points to, invokes, or stands for. For Gass, the instance of his discourse is always center stage, his writing always about writing just as surely as it is about the people, the prose, or whatever phenomena it seems to put forward as his subjects. I mention this aspect of Gass's prose here only to suggest that his use of sound and syntax, even when it seems to parallel or echo that of classical rhetoricians such as Macaulay, is significantly different. And we write in the context of that difference. Like it or not, our prose style takes its place in a world that has been reconfigured by the aesthetics and assumptions of postmodernism just as surely as postmodernism has been configured and constituted by the progress of technology, particularly media technology.

In this and previous lectures we've seen numerous examples of balance, three-part serials, and ways in which these two basic rhythms can be made to work together, each intensifying the other. Now it's time to consider for a few moments why these rhythms are so prominent in English prose. I have previously discussed prefab phatic phrases that act as syntactic speed bumps in sentences, slowing them down and drawing them out. Now I want to mention a very different kind of phatic prefab construction that, if anything, may serve to speed a sentence up. These prefab phrases so intensely invoke balanced rhythm that they accentuate any other balances that may have been constructed within or between sentences. Now, these minibalances can themselves be used to create the collision of two- and three-beat rhythms we've been looking at and listening to in this lecture. But such a sentence has a certain unfortunate, dare I say it, singsong quality.

My purpose in calling attention to these phrases—apart from the fact that they are really fun to read aloud—is to suggest, as they do, that balance is no artificially constructed or carefully architected rhetorical phenomenon, but speaks to something far more basic and vigorous in our lives. Binary oppositions such as up/down, in/out, good/bad, and sweet/salty, regularly divide the world of our experience into twos, and we build from these basic binaries ever larger balanced explanations of the way things are. It seems likely to me that our binging on balance has a visceral antecedent in the bilateral symmetry of our bodies, the inhalation and exhalation of our life breath, the lub-dub rhythm of the human heart. Such as rhythms connate certainty and authority because balance has to do with the very rhythms that keep us going. Against binaries such as past and present, the three-part series reminds us to expand our view to consider the future; when we consider the age-old dichotomy of mind and body, the three-part serial reminds us to add soul, and so on.

A syllogism consists of three parts: major premise, minor premise, and conclusion; and for the rhetorician the three appeals are to pathos, ethos, and logos; the color wheel suggests that all colors come from the basic trio of red, yellow, and blue; matter divides into solid, liquid, and gas; that basic building block of matter, the atom, is made up of electron, neutron, and proton. Three dimensions, a calendar divided into days, months, and years; a school system divided into elementary, middle, and high schools; our food divided into carbohydrates, proteins, and fats—all these are the three-part constructions we have chosen to make sense of our world. So, is the appeal of three-part serial constructions really much of a mystery? These artificial rhythms of rhetoric, the balance of duple rhythm, and the three-beat form of serial constructions are not artificial at all, but merely extend the central organizing constructs of human consciousness into language.

Of all the wisdom I find in Gass's electric prose, what impresses me most is that his syntactical showing off, the unexpected metaphors and sometimes silly similes, and the obvious attention he lavishes on every word—all of which remind us that words matter, that sentences matter, that there is nothing artificial in artifice. ■

Question to Consider

1. Look in magazines that pay attention to writing (*The Atlantic*, *Harper's*, *The New Yorker*, *The New York Review of Books* are a few) and find five sentences that you like. Note whether they use some of the syntactic strategies we've discussed in this course so far.

Balanced Series and Serial Balances
Lecture 21—Transcript

Balance one three-part series against another or construct a three-part series of balanced forms and the sentence can become a pinball machine of sounds, rhythms, images, and ideas, twos bouncing off threes, threes combining balances, balances containing serial constructions, and so on. I can't think of any modern writer who does a better job of constructing verbal pinball machines than William Gass. Gass is the David May Distinguished University Professor Emeritus in the Humanities at Washington University in St. Louis, where for many years he taught philosophy and English. More important, he is one of America's most celebrated writers and critics, and among prose stylists who have thought long and hard about prose, he has no equal. Just a few of his works that have shaped my understanding of language, writing, and the glories of the sentence are *Fiction and the Figures of Life* (1970), *On Being Blue: A Philosophical Inquiry* (1975), *The World Within The Word* (1978), *Finding a Form* (1996), and *A Temple of Texts* (2006).

Among several other honors, his collections of essays have twice won National Book Critics Circle awards, and he was the first winner of the PEN/ Nabokov Award "for celebrating the accomplishments of an author whose body of work represents achievement in a variety of literary genres, and is of enduring originality and consummate craftsmanship." His novels are *Omensetter's Luck* (1966), *Willie Masters' Lonesome Wife* (1968), and *The Tunnel* (1995), and he has published two collections of short stories, *In the Heart of the Heart of the Country and Other Stories* (1968), and *Cartesian Sonata* (1998). If you have never read William Gass, it's high time you start, and you are in for nothing less than a "take the top off your head" treat. If you have read Gass, revisit him—the treat is still there.

There is no other writer in America who combines Gass's stylistic verve and panache with his philosophical rigor. Nor is there any writer in America who has devoted more serious thought to language, to writing, and, most important for our purposes, to the sentence. Gass has famously claimed that "Gertrude Stein did more with sentences, and understood them better, than any writer ever has." But this is one of the only areas I can think of where William Gass is flat out wrong, since his contemplation of the sentence builds on and easily surpasses Stein's. Indeed, his essay "The Ontology of the Sentence, or How to Make a World of Words," is the most wise and the most useful contemplation of the sentence that we have. Here's a sample of Gass as he's just getting warmed up to his subject in an essay on "The Music of Prose":

> For prose has a pace; it is dotted with stops and pauses, frequent rests; inflections rise and fall like a low range of hills; certain tones are prolonged; there are patterns of stress and harmonious measures; there is a proper method of pronunciation, even if it is rarely observed; alliteration will trouble the tongue, consonance ease its sounds out, so that any mouth making that music will feel its performance even to the back of the teeth and to the glottal's stop; mellifluousness is not impossible, and harshness is easy; drum roll and clangor can be confidently called for—lisp, slur, and growl; so there will be a syllabic beat in imitation of the heart, while rhyme will recall a word we passed perhaps too indifferently; vowels will open and consonants close like blooming plants; repetitive schemes will act as refrains, and there will be phrases—little motifs—to return to, like the tonic; clauses will be balanced by other clauses the way a waiter carries trays; parallel lines will nevertheless meet in their common subject; clots of concepts will dissolve and then recombine, so we shall find endless variations on the same theme; a central idea, along with its many modifications, like soloist and chorus, will take their turns until, suddenly, all sing at once the same sound.

Of course, that's one marvelous single sentence.

Here is Gass's exultant reminder from *On Being Blue* that sentences *do things*, they are alive, are closely tied to the body's basic rhythms, and, when in the hands of a masterful writer, can be taught steps that dance across the lips and across the page:

> So sentences are copied, constructed, or created; they are uttered, mentioned, or used; each says, means, implies, reveals, connects; each titillates, invites, conceals, suggests; and each is eventually either consumed or conserved; nevertheless, the lines in Stevens

or the sentences of Joyce and James, pressed by one another into being as though the words before and the words after were those reverent hands both Rilke and Rodin have celebrated, clay calling to clay like mating birds, concept responding to concept the way passionate flesh congests, every note a nipple on the breast, at once a triumphant pinnacle and perfect conclusion, like pelted water, I think I said, yet at the same time only another anonymous cell, and selfless in its service to the shaping skin as lost forgotten matter is in all walls; these lines, these sentences, are not quite uttered, not quite mentioned, peculiarly employed, strangely listed, oddly used, as though a shadow were the leaves, limbs, trunk of a new tree, and the shade itself were thrust like a dark torch into the grassy air in the same slow and forceful way as its own roots, entering the earth, roughen the darkness there till all its freshly shattered facets shine against themselves as teeth do in the clenched jaw; for Rabelais was wrong, blue is the color of the mind in borrow of the body; it is the color consciousness becomes when caressed; it is the dark inside of sentences, sentences which follow their own turnings inward out of sight like the whorls of a shell, and which we follow warily, as Alice after that rabbit, nervous and white, till suddenly—there! climbing down clauses and passing through 'a-n-d' as it opens— there—there—we're here!...in time for tea and tantrums; such are the sentences we should like to love—the ones which love us and themselves as well—incestuous sentences—sentences which make an imaginary speaker speak the imagination loudly to the reading eye; that have a kind of orality transmogrified; not the tongue touching the genital tip, but the idea of the tongue, the thought of the tongue, word-wet to part-wet, public mouth to private, seed to speech, and speech...ah! After exclamations, groans, with order gone, disorder on the way, we subside, through sentences like these, the risk of senselessness like this, to float like leaves on the restful surface of that world of words to come, and there, in peace, patiently to dream of the sensuous, imagined, and mindful Sublime.

Whew! That's the most exciting and the most excited sentence I know of, its counter pointed rhythms, rhymes, and alliterations rising to a climax that is sensual, if not sexual, its very being a refutation to the prose prudes who claim that overly designed and structured sentences are artificial and unnatural, its orgasmic progression a celebration of language that lives, that is as organic and natural as nature itself. For the moment, that's the last contemporary example, at least from William Gass, that I'll offer to suggest the uncharted power a writer can tap when combining duple and triple rhythms, the sounds and sense of two- and three-part serials. But I wanted you to experience the unpredictable energies of Gass's prose before offering more traditional and less lively examples.

In the last lecture, I gave a brief overview of the attempt by Winston Weathers to theorize the rhetorical affect and impact of two- and three-part serial constructions. You'll remember that, in a nutshell, Weathers suggested that the two-part series, which we have been calling balance or balanced form, has connotations of authority and expertise, if not of authoritarianism. In contrast, the three-part series, according to Weathers, has connotations of the reasonable, the believable, and even the logical. I did not mention what Weathers had to say about serial constructions of four or more parts, which he saw as suggesting "the human, emotional, diffuse, and inexplicable," because while these longer constructions clearly invoke the affective power of parallelism, I'm not sure readers can really process in any meaningful way four or more sound patterns or conceptual units without simply thinking of them as a list. A test example might be James Baldwin's sentence from *Notes of a Native Son*, in which he describes the aftermath of throwing a glass at a waitress in an all-white restaurant:

> And, with that sound, my frozen blood abruptly thawed, I returned from wherever I had been, I saw, for the first time, the restaurant, the people with their mouths open, already, as it seemed to me, rising as one man, and I realized what I had done, and where I was, and I was frightened.

And the samples I just read from William Gass may also, in their extended serials that seem to inventory reality, evoke an impression of "the human, emotional, diffuse, and inexplicable" impact of the four- (or more) part series. However, as Weathers suggests with his own prose, which both employs the authority of balance to discuss the reasonability of the three-part series and the reasonability of the three-part series to bolster his account of balance, the ties among kinds of serial constructions are quite complex.

Weathers published his "Rhetoric of the Series" essay in *College Composition and Communication* in 1966, offering it as a prolegomenon to the rigorous study of serial constructions. While this essay has been subsequently reprinted in stylistic studies such as Glen Love's and Michael Payne's important *Contemporary Essays on Style: Rhetoric, Linguistics, and Criticism* (1969)—and you have to be fond of an anthology you can refer to as the "love and pain" anthology—I'm not aware of any critical efforts to accept the challenge of the Weathers prolegomenon and to extend his study of the series. That's a shame, because I think two- and three-beat constructions may reveal something quite important about the relationship between our writing syntax and our understanding of the world, and even if I'm wrong about that, it's a shame because the interplay of two- and three-part beats and constructions in writing is so prominent that no serious writer can afford not to give these patterns some serious thought.

Before we consider the possible sources and implications of the patterns of balance and three-part serial constructions, however, let's get a better-structured sense of how these rhythms can be put together and to what effect. We can find numerous examples of the interplay of two- and three-beat rhythms in the lush style associated with Lyly and other euphuistic writers of the 16th century, such as Robert Greene, whose prose in the following passage suggests that use of balance and serial form can indeed reach a point of diminishing returns:

> But let their love be never so slight, and their fancy never so fickle, yet they will be counted as constant if vows may cloak their vanity or tears be taken for truth: if prayers, protestations, and pilgrimages might be performances of promises, then the maid should have mountains that hath but molehills; treasure that hath but trash; faith that hath but flattery; truth that hath but trifles; yea, she should enjoy a trusty lover, that is glad of a trothless lechour.

The curt or pointed style of Francis Bacon, so well-known for its three-part serials, also contains a striking number of balances, as we have seen in the selections from his "Of Studies," where the drum-like beat of three-part serial constructions is counter pointed and possibly foregrounded even more by balances. Between Bacon's opening claim that "Studies serve for delight, for ornament, and for ability" and his summing up that "Reading maketh a full man; conference a ready man; and writing an exact man," we find "expert men" balanced against "those that are learned," the chiasmic claim that studies "perfect nature, and are perfected by experience," and two-beat pairs such as "execute and perhaps judge," "without them and above them," "contradict and confute," "believe and take for granted," "weigh and consider," and "chewed and digested." On the other hand, the fabled balances of Dr. Johnson and, as we shall soon see, of Macaulay, regularly employ three-part serials.

While my own examples of the interplay of balance and series are relatively crude, they illustrate the basic options for balancing one series against another. Here are the basic patterns:

> Bruised, bleeding, and exhausted, the boxer stumbled back to his corner at the end of the fifth round, desperately in need of attention to the cut over his left eye, desperately in need of the encouragement of his trainer, and desperately in need of the unlikely arrival of a miracle.

Here's a way of creating three-part serials from balances:

> As excited as I was nervous, as hopeful as I was hapless, as thankful for the opportunity as I was aware of the odds against me, I walked into the interview.

Here's a way of just weaving together balance and series without a clear blueprint for what we're doing:

> The more imaginative and inspired the instructor, the more inspiring and effective will be her instruction, the longer lasting her impact and the more grateful her students.

Or a pattern even for playing with more complicated schemes such as polyptoton, the use of a second word derived from the same root as the first:

> A walking, talking caricature of the inept politician, the silver-haired and silky-voiced senator was a functionary whose legislative proposals were rarely functional, a would-be backroom operator whose attempts at being effective usually turned out to be spectacularly ineffectual, a cut-rate visionary whose initiatives consistently failed to initiate significant change.

We've seen how Gass weaves these rhythms together in patterns that are unexpected, but we should remember that they have much more frequently been combined in patterns that were almost diagrammatic. Macaulay denounced Dr. Johnson for the artificiality of his over-designed prose, but Macaulay is himself regarded as a master of balanced form, and his balances frequently employ or are employed by three-part serial constructions.

Consider these examples from his literary criticism, which was itself balanced between critiquing books about prominent historical and literary figures and reassessments of those figures themselves—and in many cases drew the further distinction between the writing and the personal lives of those figures. Here's Macaulay on Machiavelli:

> The terms in which he is commonly described would seem to import that he was the Tempter, the Evil Principle, the discoverer of ambition and revenge, the original inventor of perjury, and that, before the publication of his fatal Prince, there had never been a hypocrite, a tyrant, or a traitor, a simulated virtue, or a convenient crime.

Another take on Machiavelli:

> The whole man seems to be an enigma, a grotesque assemblage of incongruous qualities, selfishness and generosity, cruelty and benevolence, craft and simplicity, abject villainy and romantic heroism.

This from Macaulay's review of Boswell's *Life of Johnson*. First of all, he didn't much like the edition; he said, "This edition is ill compiled, ill arranged, ill written, and ill printed." Here are his comments on Boswell:

> All the caprices of his [Boswell's] temper, all the illusions of his vanity, all his hypochondriac whimsics, all his castles in the air, he displayed with a cool self-complacency, a perfect unconsciousness that he was making a fool of himself, to which it is impossible to find a parallel in the whole history of mankind. He has used many people ill; but assuredly he has used nobody so ill as himself.

And another knock:

> He had, indeed, a quick observation and a retentive memory. These qualities, if he had been a man of sense and virtue, would scarcely have sufficed to make him conspicuous; but because he was a dunce, a parasite, and a coxcomb, they have made him immortal.

Here's Macaulay's take on Bacon:

> His faults were—we write it with pain—coldness of heart, and meanness of spirit. He seems to have been incapable of feeling strong affection, of facing great dangers, of making great sacrifices.

The difference between Gass and Macaulay is much greater than the difference between a carefully controlled manipulation of prose rhythms and an exuberant gush; it is the difference between what we might call a classical view of rhetoric and what we might call a Postmodern view. Macaulay, much like rhetoricians for a couple of thousand years before him, saw his control of tropes and schemes, syntax, and other structures as a supporting adjunct to his arguments, moves that clarified and emphasized the propositional and logical content of his claims. Gass also presents his celebrations of sound and syntax in support of claims about the subject matter of his sentences; but, for Gass, as for Gertrude Stein before him, his sentences themselves are always part of the point of his writing, if not the main point.

In keeping with his place in the forefront of Postmodern writers, Gass *always* sees language as a subject every bit as interesting and important as is the referential world his language points to, invokes, or stands for. For Gass, the instance of his discourse is always center stage, his writing always about writing just as surely as it is about the people, the prose, or whatever phenomena it seems to put forward as his subjects. As I've previously noted, postmodernism would itself be the subject of a lecture series in its own right, so I mention this aspect of Gass's prose here only to suggest that his use of sound and syntax, even when it seems to parallel or echo that of classical rhetoricians such as Macaulay, is significantly different. And we write in the context of that difference, whether or not it concerns us in the propositional sense it concerns Gass. Like it or not, our writing, our prose style takes its place in a world that has been reconfigured by the aesthetics and assumptions of postmodernism just as surely as postmodernism has been configured and constituted by the progress of technology, particularly media technology.

In this and previous lectures, we've now seen numerous examples of balance, three-part serials, and ways in which these two basic rhythms can be made to work together, each intensifying the other. Now it's time to consider for a few moments just why these rhythms are so prominent in English prose.

I have previously discussed prefab phatic phrases such as *after all* or *in a way* or *of course* that act as syntactic speed bumps in sentences, slowing them down and drawing them out. Now I want to mention a very different kind of phatic prefab construction that, if anything, may serve to speed a sentence up. Moreover, these prefab phrases so intensely invoke balanced rhythm that they accentuate any other balances that may have been constructed within or between sentences. I'm thinking of an amazing number of phrases that remind us just how prevalent balanced rhythm is in our speech and in our writing. Just a small sample of these phrases would include:

namby-pamby	helter-skelter	wishy-washy
flip-flop	moldy-oldie	flim-flam
meet and greet	hip-hop	town and gown
surf and turf	herky-jerky	topsy-turvy
hurly-burly	razzle-dazzle	itsy-bitsy
teenie-weenie	hotsy-totsy	doom and gloom

wear and tear	rough and tough	tit for tat
thrills and chills	rough and tumble	rough and ready
lean and mean	wild and woolly	ticky-tacky
shilly-shally	bump and grind	ebb and flow
rise and fall	boom and bust	near and dear
topsy-turvy	whipper-snapper	harum-scarum
slippy-slidey	splish-splash	super-duper
eager-beaver	super-saver	pooper-scooper
fixer-upper	daily-double	hour of power
oopsy-daisy	wheeler-dealer	rinky-dink
dipsy-doodle		

And, to represent the end of the alphabet—zigzag.

Believe me, I could go on and on—we have a million zillion of these prefab minibalances, and once you start thinking of them, it's hard to stop. These minibalances can themselves be used to create the collision of two- and three-beat rhythms we've been looking at and listening to in this lecture, as in the sentence "Tall and tan, lean and mean, rested and ready, the mercenaries restlessly awaited their next mission, fit and itching for a fight, feared for their ferocity, armored by their amorality"—but such a sentence has a certain unfortunate, dare I say it, singsong quality.

My purpose in calling attention to these phrases—apart from the fact that are really fun to read aloud—is to suggest, as they do, that balance is no artificially constructed or carefully architected rhetorical phenomenon, but that balance speaks to something far more basic and vigorous in our lives. Binary oppositions such as up/down, in/out, good/bad, day/night, hot/cold, happy/sad, young/old, rich/poor, sweet/salty, regularly divide the world of our experience into twos, and we build from these basic binaries ever larger balanced explanations of the way things are—"it's not the heat, it's the humidity," "what goes around comes around," "what's sauce for the goose is sauce for the gander," until we find ourselves more and more assenting to philosophies reduced to balanced forms: "if you can't walk the walk, don't talk the talk," "no taxation without representation." Indeed, it seems likely to me that our binging on balance has a visceral antecedent in the bilateral symmetry of our bodies, the inhalation and exhalation of our life breath, the lub-dub rhythm of the human heart. Connotations of certainty and authority—you bet, because balance has to do with the very rhythms that keep us going.

Then what of the power of three? How do we account for the almost irresistible impulse to make our tales about not one, not two, but three little pigs, three blind mice? Why must the genie grant us three wishes, must the argument rest on three contentions, why do we get three strikes before we're out? Against binaries such as past and present, the three-part series reminds us to expand our view to consider the future. When we consider the age-old dichotomy of mind and body, the three-part serial reminds us to add soul, and so on. A syllogism consists of three parts: major premise, minor premise, and conclusion, and for the rhetorician the three appeals are to pathos, ethos, and logos; the color wheel suggests that all colors come from the basic trio of red, yellow, and blue; matter divides into solid, liquid, and gas; that basic building block of matter, the atom, is made up of electron, neutron, and proton. Three dimensions, a calendar divided into days, months, and years; a school system divided into elementary, middle, and high schools; our food divided into carbohydrates, proteins, and fats—all these are the three-part constructions we have chosen to make sense of our world. So is the appeal of three-part serial constructions really much of a mystery?

My point is simply that these artificial rhythms of rhetoric, the balance of duple rhythm and the three-beat form of serial construction, are not artificial at all, but merely extend the central organizing constructs of human consciousness into language. Whitman knew what he was talking about when he claimed of his poetry that it was singing the body electric. We should do no less in our prose. I think William Gass is on to something very important in his wild celebrations of balance and serials and of all the other rhetorical schemes and tropes he can stuff in the suitcase of his writing, sometime needing to sit on that overstuffed bag to snap it closed, but always traveling with everything he needs.

Of all the wisdom I find in Gass's electric prose, what impresses me most is that his syntactical showing off, the unexpected metaphors and sometime silly similes, the obvious attention he lavishes on every word—all always remind us that words matter, that sentences matter, that there is nothing artificial in artifice. As he observes in his essay "Gertrude Stein and the Geography of the Sentence":

> Words are therefore weapons like the jaws of the crocodile or the claws of the cat. We use them to hold our thought as we hold a bone; we use them to communicate with the pack, dupe our enemies, manipulate our friends; we use them to club the living into food.

Master Sentences
Lecture 22

Master sentences exist at the opposite end of the syntactical continuum from kernel sentences. They tend to be much longer than readers normally expect, although length is not in itself a sign of either a master sentence or of a writer's mastery.

This lecture will examine self-conscious sentences that practically scream for our attention by virtue of their excessiveness. Very long sentences or sentences that function in remarkable ways might be called master sentences—a nod at once to their originality and to their control. However, an effective one can only be constructed by combining a number of the syntactic moves that have been the subject of this course. I've already admitted that I don't know how to teach anyone to write really short sentences. They must rise from the writer's situation and present themselves, unexpectedly, as syntactic and rhetorical opportunities.

We can prepare ourselves for the possibility that a sentence we are writing will take on a life of its own and insist on its own development far past the normal limits of our composition. In some ways, we have already begun this preparation with our work on suspensive sentences. In other ways, we have already begun to prepare for it simply by looking at striking sentences written by a wide range of writers who obviously believed the sentence itself is worthy of careful design.

In her essay "Inviting the Muses," poet, essayist, and writing teacher Marguerite Young describes one of the first exercises she assigns in her writing classes, a requirement that her students compose a sentence at least three pages long, grammatically logical, pleasingly rhythmical, and closely documented. Noting that these requirements compel the writer to put into the sentence exactly the things that are usually absent in short sentences, Young terms the result a dragnet sentence. She observed, "Anyone who can master the architectonics of a long sentence learns what its validities and uses are—and can master a short sentence thereafter."

Master sentences are by nature loners—when they form a crowd, they lose most of their impact and can actually reach a point of diminished returns, where they signal a writer's weakness rather than strength. A master sentence that works will always be a form of a suspensive sentence: If it manages to hold the reader's interest to the end of a sentence that clearly is invested in extending itself, there must bc some sense that the sentence still has something important to disclose or that there is some good reason for it to keep going. The end point of a master sentence may not be a surprise in the classic sense of coming down to the very last word before the sense or purpose of the sentence is clear, but there is usually some sense of discovery inherent in the fact that the sentence extended itself to such a degree.

We can prepare ourselves for the possibility that a sentence we are writing will take on a life of its own.

Any attempt to classify or categorize master sentences is doomed to failure. Still, there are some functions or patterns we can observe and keep in the backs of our minds for situations in our own writing where those functions or patterns may be useful. Some master sentences simply seem to meander, almost marking time, waiting for something else to occur to the writer or to happen in the prose. Some master sentences seem to twist and turn like a snake, going through syntactical moves that we might call serpentine. Some master sentences display an almost dogged sense of honing in on a final piece of information or a conclusion with radar-guided precision. Martin Luther King was a master of this technique. Master sentences do not have to be long or particularly intricate. Some master sentences clearly build to a climax, using various delaying tactics to increase the suspensive power of what the sentence finally reveals. Some master sentences simply seem reluctant, hesitant, and/or unsure of where they will finally go, or unwilling to get there, as if delaying bad news. Some master sentences simply invoke or mirror some kind of remarkable excess associated with their ostensible subject or focus; they're almost inventories. ■

1. Choose a base clause. Modify it with base clauses following the ten patterns for adding second-level modifying phrases.

Master Sentences

Lecture 22—Transcript

In the summer of 1978, my wife and I were driving through the British countryside in Wiltshire when we topped a small hill and suddenly, there before us in all its enigmatic glory, under what I rightly or wrongly remember as a brooding sky, was Stonehenge. I've read accounts that acknowledge that no one is completely certain of the original purpose this massive architectural wonder served. However, one sight of the circular design of those giant stone slabs and most of us would instantly agree with the understated comment on one British history website that "Only something very important to the ancients would have been worth the effort and investment that it took to construct Stonehenge."

I feel much the same way about the massive, monumental, and enigmatic super sentences I sometimes unexpectedly come across in my reading, their construction probably not quite the equal of the engineering feat that produced Stonehenge but in its own way, always incredibly striking.

This lecture will examine self-conscious sentences that practically scream for our attention by virtue of their excessiveness. Very long sentences or sentences that function in remarkable ways might be called master sentences, a nod at once to their originality and to their control. I call these linguistic and syntactic Stonehenges *master sentences*, and they call attention to their mastery in more different ways than I or anyone else could enumerate, much less prescribe. However, while no formula can anticipate the context and purpose that call forth a master sentence, an effective one can only be constructed by combining a number of the syntactic moves that have so far been the subject of this course.

I've already admitted that I don't know how to teach anyone to write really short sentences. Those one- and two-word kernels must rise from the writer's situation and present themselves unexpectedly as syntactic and rhetorical opportunities that could not have been predicted, could not have been prepared for, could not have been part of the writer's strategy even moments before they appear on the page.

And yet...

And yet. Ah, there we have one tiny exception to this general principle: There are a very few one-, two-, and three-word sentences we all have filed away in our memories of striking prose, prefab wonders designed by others before us, but that just might fit our needs as perfectly as a prefabricated door unit, in which the door is already hung in a modular frame, may fit our carpentry needs better than anything we could hammer out ourselves. *And yet* is one of those sentences. *So it goes* is another, and *I think not* still another. Any exclamation such as *indeed,* or *absolutely,* or *thank goodness* or even *okay* may offer us the dramatic punch of the very short sentence, and we all have an informal and uninventoried arsenal of these expressions we may trot out at appropriate moments in our writing.

Maybe there is just a little we can do to prepare for writing very short kernel sentences, but so varied are the forms in which master sentences suddenly appear that I can't think about any way to teach this phenomenon as a sentence form. And yet (that kernel once again), and yet we can prepare ourselves for the possibility that a sentence we are writing will take on a life of its own and insist on its own development far past the normal limits of our composition. In some ways, we have already begun this preparation with our work on suspensive sentences. In other ways, we have already begun to prepare for it simply by looking at striking sentences written by a wide range of writers who obviously believed the sentence itself is worthy of careful design and rewarding when thought of as a thing in itself rather than as just another brick in a wall of words, just another item in a long list of sentences.

In her essay "Inviting the Muses," poet, essayist, and noted writing teacher Marguerite Young describes one of the first exercises she assigns in her writing classes, a requirement that her students compose a sentence of at least three pages long. She further specifies that this monster sentence should not be monstrous, since it should also be grammatically logical, pleasingly rhythmical, and closely documented, by which I believe she means precise. Noting that these requirements compel the writer to put into the sentence exactly the things that are usually absent in short sentences, Young terms the result a *dragnet sentence,* since it hauls into the sentence everything the writer's net catches and she explains its value this way:

Surely, also, anyone who can master the architectonics of a long sentence learns what its validities and uses are—and can master a short sentence thereafter—has learned also the beauties of variation—has learned something of the oceanic swells, pearly combers breaking upon the shores of consciousness—his own and the reader's—ripplings, ebbings, whispers of ghostly surf, reverberations which should go on in many consciousnesses forever afterward and in the unconscious life of man. For literature is that which is memorable.

Notwithstanding the lyric exuberance of Marguerite Young's celebration of the long sentence, I'm reluctant to adopt her terminology: As richly descriptive as is her metaphor of the dragnet, recent years have made us more and more aware that fishermen's nets also bring in more than a few dolphins and endangered sea turtles, unintended victims of an undiscriminating process. I'd prefer to call very long sentences or sentences that function in remarkable ways master sentences, a nod at once to their originality and then again to their control. Master sentences call attention to their mastery, whether its mastery of length, precision, syntactical moves, prose rhythms, or cognitive or dramatic effect. They stick out. They demand attention. They slow readers down and urge them to consider the writer's purpose and skill.

Master sentences exist at the opposite end of the syntactical continuum from kernel sentences. They tend to be much longer than readers normally expect, although length is not in itself a sign of either a master sentence or of a writer's mastery. Once more, I'll invoke that old cigarette ad: "It's not how long you make it, it's how you make it long." Master sentence are by nature loners—when they form a crowd, they lose most of their impact and can actually reach a point of diminished returns, where they signal a writer's weakness rather than strength. In this sense, a master sentence that works will always be a form of a suspensive sentence: If it manages to hold the reader's interest to the end of a sentence that clearly is invested in extending itself, there must be some sense that the sentence still has something important to disclose or that there is some good reason for it simply to keep going.

The end point of a master sentence may not be a surprise in the classic sense of coming down to the very last word before the sense or purpose of the sentence is clear, but there is usually some sense of discovery inherent in the fact that the sentence extended itself to such a degree—whether to suggest a process that involved twists and turns, reversals and new directions, or to parallel or suggest the duration of a process that itself did not easily end, or to suggest a situation involving complexities that could not easily be boiled down to a clear sense of the relationships among underlying propositions.

Consider this master sentence from Loren Eiseley we've previously discussed for its cumulative structure:

> It is with the coming of man that a vast hole seems to open in nature, a vast black whirlpool spinning faster and faster, consuming flesh, stones, soil, minerals, sucking down the lightning, wrenching power from the atom, until the ancient sounds of nature are drowned out in the cacophony of something which is no longer nature, something instead which is loose and knocking at the world's heart, something demonic and no longer planned—escaped it may be—spewed out of nature, contending in a final giant's game against its master.

The 91 words of this sentence narrate a process in which man, a part of nature, wrestles with the natural order, unleashing the atom, another part of nature, to act in a way possibly never anticipated, a way that ultimately may mean the end of nature itself. This process is characterized by the metaphor of a whirlpool, sucking down everything it touches, spiraling toward some apocalyptic endpoint, the spiral itself invoked by and embodied in the cumulative phrases that spin this sentence through six levels of generality to a dramatic final image of conflict between nature and atomic power set free by man.

Or consider this master sentence by Thomas Berger, one of many in his distinctive novels, but noteworthy for its vernacular tone, a reminder that the American colloquial style frequently produces sentences that are stories in themselves. In this sentence from *The Return of Little Big Man*, Jack Crabb has just been reunited with his faithful dog, Pard, that he has not seen for several years and feared dead:

Now if you know only the kind of pets ladies keep indoors, or even sporting hounds, and so on, you might expect old Pard to make a greater display than he done when he seen me for the first time in more than three years, having tracked me over hundreds of miles, but just as he weren't the type to bear a grudge, thank goodness, he had lived the sort of life in which the interests of survival tended to hold down emotional demonstrations, in which he reminded me of myself, so we never hugged or anything, but I was real glad to see him, a feeling which alternated with amazement at his feat, which exceeded anything I had heard of at the time, though in the many years since, now and again dogs have somehow followed their families at greater distances on foot while the humans used the motorcar, so when I tell about Pard it might be easier to believe than the experiences I relate concerning historical personages, though all are equally true.

I've previously suggested that a sentence functions like a hand. A master sentence is like the very remarkable hand of a skilled surgeon or painter or magician, a hand capable of performing extraordinary tasks, capable of forming itself into shapes dictated by the need of the moment, distinguished by what it does. A hand can point, grasp, stroke, make a fist. It can wave, pinch, scratch, its functioning determined by the occasion, by what needs to be done that a hand can do. Unlike a normal unskilled hand, however, the master sentence is always doing more than needs to be done. Apart from the contextual purpose it serves, conveying information as it creates an affective impact, a master sentence is also always a reminder to readers that they are in the hands of a skilled writer, someone who wants their attention to matters of language and style as well as to information; someone who wants their recognition that they are in the hands of a writer, not just someone who is disseminating information.

So, any attempt to classify or categorize master sentences is doomed to failure. Still, there are some functions or patterns we can observe and keep in the backs of our minds for situations in our own writing where those functions or patterns may be useful.

Some master sentences simply seem to meander, almost marking time, waiting for something else to occur to the writer or to happen in the prose:

> To the great delight of Sid Liftoff, who's known her since their days as regulars at Musso and Frank's, and a senior gaffer who'd worked with Hub, Sasha had come wheeling into the valet parking at the Vineland Palace in a Cadillac the size of a Winnebago and painted some vivid fingernail polish color, alighting and sweeping into the lobby a step and a half ahead of her companion, Derek, considerably younger and paler, with a buzz cut that nearly matched the car, an English accent, and a guitar case he was never seen to open, picked up on the highway between here and the Grand Canyon, where she'd parted from her current romantic interest, Tex Wiener, after an epic screaming exchange right at the edge, and on impulse decided to attend that year's Traverse-Becker get-together up in Vineland, leaving Tex on foot among the still-bouncing echoes of their encounter, which had brought tourist helicopters nudging in for a closer look, distracted ordinarily surefooted mules on the trail below into quick shuffle-ball-changes along the rim of Eternity, proceeded through a sunset that was the closest we get to seeing God's own jaundiced and bloodshot eyeball, looking back at us without much enthusiasm, then on into the night arena of a parking lot so dangerously tilted that even with your hand brake set and your wheels chocked, your short could still end up a mile straight down, its trade-in value seriously diminished.

That, of course, from Thomas Pynchon's *Vineland.*

Some master sentences seem to twist and turn like a snake, going through syntactical moves that we might call serpentine. Here are two more sentences from Thomas Berger, this time from his first novel, *Crazy in Berlin*, also the first novel in his celebrated Reinhart series:

> The ride on the new car Reinhart forgot even as it was in progress, for he had now reached that secondary state of inebriation in which the mind is one vast sweep of summer sky and there is no limit to the altitude a kite may go, the condition in which one can repair

intricate mechanisms at other times mysterious, solve equations, craft epigrams, make otherwise invulnerable women, and bluff formidable men, when people say, "Why Reinhart!" and rivals wax bitter.

Only a few pages later Reinhart, after a drunken fight in defense of one of his army buddies, encounters the first German girl he meets after being stationed in a Berlin devastated by the recently ended war:

> She extended her hand in the genuine enthusiasm displayed by all Europeans, not just the French, upon arrivals and departures, as if for all their hatreds they love one another, or do for the moment at making and breaking contact, and at this first touch in ten minutes not motivated by hostility, Reinhart suddenly felt drunken again and feared that he might weep—for the sore opponent vanished alone in the night, for his friend who did not understand fighting fair, for the girl now under his compulsion, and for the material things in waste all about them, all the poor, weak, assaulted and assaulting people and things, and of course for himself, isolated by a power he didn't want.

Some master sentences display an almost dogged sense of honing in on a final piece of information or a conclusion with radar-guided precision. Martin Luther King was a master of this technique, as we can see in this powerful excerpt from his "Letter from Birmingham Jail." After three brief sentences that set the stage, Dr. King delivers a massive suspensive sentence few readers will ever be able to forget:

> But when you have seen vicious mobs lynch your mothers and fathers at will and drown your sisters and brothers at whim; when you have seen hate-filled policemen curse, kick and even kill your black brothers and sisters; when you see the vast majority of your twenty million Negro brothers smothering in an airtight cage of poverty in the midst of an affluent society; when you suddenly find your tongue twisted and your speech stammering as you seek to explain to your six-year-old-daughter why she can't go to the public amusement park that has just been advertised on television, and

see tears welling up in her eyes when she is told that Funtown is closed to colored children, and see ominous clouds of inferiority beginning to form in her little mental sky, and see her beginning to distort her personality by developing an unconscious bitterness toward white people; when you have to concoct an answer for a five-year-old son who is asking: "Daddy, why do white people treat colored people so mean?"; when you take a cross-county drive and find it necessary to sleep night after night in the uncomfortable corners of your automobile because no motel will accept you; when you are humiliated day in and day out by nagging signs reading "white" and "colored"; when your first name becomes "nigger," your middle name becomes "boy" (however old you are) and your last name becomes "John," and your wife and mother are never given the respected title "Mrs."; when you are harried by day and haunted by night by the fact that you are a Negro, living constantly at tiptoe stance, never quite knowing what to expect next, and are plagued with inner fears and outer resentments; when you are forever fighting a degenerating sense of "nobodiness"—then you will understand why we find it difficult to wait.

And while I have not yet read the celebrated novels of Chilean writer Roberto Bolaño, this sentence following the deadly attack of a raptor named Ta Gueule isolated in a review of his *By Night in Chile* gives me more than enough reason to start reading:

> … Ta Gueule appeared again like a lightning bolt, or the abstract idea of a lightning bolt, and stooped on the huge flocks of starlings coming out of the west like swarms of flies, darkening the sky with their erratic fluttering, and after a few minutes the fluttering of the starlings was bloodied, scattered and bloodied, and afternoon on the outskirts of Avignon took on a deep red hue, like the color of sunsets seen from an airplane, or the color of dawns, when the passenger is woken gently by the engines whistling in his ears and lifts up the little blind and sees the horizon marked with a red line, like the planet's femoral artery, or the planet's aorta, gradually swelling, and I saw that swelling blood vessel in the sky over Avignon, the

blood-stained flight of the starlings, Ta Gueule splashing color like an Abstract Expressionist painter.

Nor do master sentences have to be long or particularly intricate, as we can see in Frank Deford's 1983 description of Howard Cosell:

> He is not the one with the golden locks or the golden tan, but the one, shaking, sallow, and hunched, with a chin whose purpose is not to exist as a chin but only to fade so that his face may, as the bow of a ship, break the waves and not get in the way of that voice.

Or this from Joan Didion:

> This is my attempt to make sense of the period that followed, weeks and then months that cut loose any fixed idea I had ever had about death, about illness, about probability and luck, about good fortune and bad, about marriage and children and memory, about grief, about the ways in which people do and do not deal with the fact that life ends, about the shallowness of sanity, about life itself.

Some master sentences clearly build to a climax, using various delaying tactics to increase the suspensive power of what the sentence finally reveals, as we have previously seen in this almost paradigmatic master sentence from Joan Didion:

> They set out to find it in accountants' ledgers and double-indemnity clauses and motel registers, set out to determine what might move a woman who believed in all the promises of the middle class—a woman who had been chairman of the Heart Fund and who always knew a reasonable little dressmaker and who had come out of the bleak wild of prairie fundamentalism to find what she imagined to be the good life—what should drive such a woman to sit on a street called Bella Vista and look out her new picture window into the empty California sun and calculate how to burn her husband alive in a Volkswagen.

Or as we can see in the celebrated climactic two-sentence sequence from Hemingway's "Short Happy Life of Francis Macomber":

> "He's dead in there," Wilson said. "Good work," and he turned to grip Macomber's hand and as they shook hands, grinning at each other, the gun-bearer shouted wildly and they saw him coming out of the brush sideways, fast as a crab, and the bull coming, nose out, mouth tight closed, blood dripping, massive head straight out, coming in a charge, his little pig eyes bloodshot as he looked at them. Wilson, who was ahead, was kneeling shooting, and Macomber, as he fired, unhearing his shot in the roaring of Wilson's gun, saw fragments like slate burst from the huge boss of the horns, and the head jerked, he shot again at the wide nostrils and saw the horns jolt again and fragments fly, and he did not see Wilson now and, aiming carefully, shot again with the buffalo's huge bulk almost on him and his rifle almost level with the on-coming head, nose out, and he could see the little wicked eyes and the head started to lower and he felt a sudden white-hot blinding flash explode inside his head and that was all he ever felt.

Some master sentences simply seem reluctant, hesitant, unsure of where they will finally go, or unwilling to get there, as if delaying bad news. This from Joan Didion:

> Nine months and five days ago, at approximately nine o'clock on the evening of December 30, 2003, my husband, John Gregory Dunne, appeared to (or did) experience, at the table where he and I had just sat down to dinner in the living room of our apartment in New York, a sudden massive coronary event that caused his death.

Or, in another sentence we have previously seen from Leonard Woolf's autobiography:

> Looking back at the age of eighty-eight over the fifty-seven years of my political work in England, knowing what I aimed at and the results, meditating on the history of Britain and the world since 1914, I see clearly that I achieved practically nothing.

Some master sentences simply invoke or mirror some kind of remarkable excess associated with their ostensible subject or focus. They seem almost inventories. Here's an example from John Leonard:

> To what other literary figure in our time would it occur to go to Thailand, Colombia, Yemen, China, Vietnam, Japan, Russia, Burma, Afghanistan, Pakistan, India, Hungary, the Philippines, Ireland, England, Serbia, Congo, Syria, Kenya, Bosnia, Mexico, and Kazakhstan to chat up and even sometimes to subsidize beggars, cleaning women, campesinos, prostitutes, tuna fishermen, the homeless, and the feckless?

And here's one from John McPhee:

> Then on came the Cretaceous, with its flying reptiles, its rudistid clams, its titanosaurs, dromaeosaurs, elasmosaurs, duck-billed and ostrich dinosaurs, and introductory flowering plants, not to mention Triceratops, Tyrannosaurus rex, and all the marine invertebrates that disappeared in the Cretaceous Extinction, sixty-five million years ago, a date better known to modern schoolchildren than 1492.

And there is Dylan Thomas's lyrical inventory of aspects of his birthplace, found in his "Reminiscences of Childhood" in *Under Milk Wood.* I don't have time to quote the entire magnificent, rambling sentence, but it famously begins with Thomas describing:

> ... an ugly, lovely town (or so it was and is to me), crawling, sprawling by a long and splendid curving shore where truant boys and sandfield boys and old men from nowhere, beachcombed, idled and paddled, watched the dock-bound ships or the ships steaming away into wonder and India, magic and China, countries bright with oranges and loud with lions ...

And the sentence ends with Thomas's memory of listening to religious speakers on Sunday afternoons whose excited anger seemed to accuse the very sea "as though it were wicked and wrong to roll in and out like that, white-horsed and full of fishes." A master sentence indeed.

Sentences in Sequence
Lecture 23

Most of what we think of as the definition of and rules for the paragraph we owe to one brilliant but eccentric Scottish polymath, Alexander Bain, who in his 1866 book *English Composition and Rhetoric* made up the rules for the paragraph we now generally treat as if Moses had brought them down from the mountain.

Occasions for writing single sentences with no surrounding context are exceedingly rare. Most writing situations call for more than one sentence. Many, if not most of the sentences we write have trouble standing alone since they contain—and sometimes their effective functioning depends upon—cohesive links to surrounding sentences. Examples of this cohesion phenomenon are too numerous to mention, but my use of this cohesion phenomenon in this sentence would be a start on such an inventory of context-related, if not context-dependent aspects of sentences.

M. A. K. Halliday and Ruqaiya Hasan had pretty much both the first and the last word to say about the ways in which sentences Velcro® together in their groundbreaking and massively authoritative 1976 study, *Cohesion in English*. Halliday and Hasan identified five major categories of cohesive ties among sentences, 19 subcategories, and even a number of sub-subcategories. *Cohesion in English* remains the foundational work on the way sentences stick together, though other interesting texts address the topic as well.

The number of considerations that shape our writing multiply dramatically when we move beyond the sentence to larger units of discourse. However, some of the syntactic features we have been working with at the level of the sentence also transcend the individual sentence to work in similar fashion in sequences of sentences. Sentences in sequence can function in paragraphs much as cumulative modifying phrases function in the individual sentence. The paragraph is a unit of discourse we don't actually know that much about—or at least don't much agree on what it is we do know. There is an important visual component we should acknowledge when we write sentences in sequence. We don't speak in paragraphs; we write in paragraphs.

We know the boundaries of a paragraph not by any prescriptive standards based on logic or syntax or sound, but by the simple fact that paragraphs are those sequences of sentences we see on the page as being set off by indentations. We need to remember that writing is first and foremost and always itself a technological phenomenon, whether the inscribing technology is the end of a burned stick or a pointed rock used to scratch symbols on the wall of a cave or the most advanced computer and authoring software. The paragraph as a form is every bit as artificial, every bit as unnatural, as are the most extreme examples of euphuistic balance and serial construction.

The paragraph as a form is every bit as artificial, every bit as unnatural, as are the most extreme examples of euphuistic balance and serial construction.

Most of what we think of as the definition of and rules for the paragraph we owe to one brilliant but eccentric Scottish polymath, Alexander Bain, who, in his 1866 book *English Composition and Rhetoric* made up the rules for the paragraph we now generally treat as law. According to Bain, the paragraph is the "division of discourse next higher than the sentence," and it is "a collection of sentences with unity of purpose," each paragraph handling and exhausting a distinct topic. He then offers six "certain principles that govern the structure of the paragraph, for all kinds of composition."

Compare Bain's specifications with those offered by the *Harbrace College Handbook,* 7th ed., some 106 years later, and you will notice remarkable similarity. In the *Harbrace Handbook* and in almost every other writing with a chapter or section devoted to the paragraph, Bain's six principles have been boiled down to three—unity, coherence, and emphasis. But his starting assumption, that the paragraph was just the sentence writ large, its sentences the equivalent of phrases and subordinate clauses in the sentence, remains one of the central assumptions underlying most contemporary theories of the paragraph. Bain's belief that the paragraph developed the idea initially posited by what he called the opening sentence and what is known today as the topic sentence remains one of the, if not the, most dearly held assumptions about paragraphs.

Bain got a lot of this wrong, however, and his errors have been mechanically, if not mindlessly passed down to us as the received truths of paragraph theory. Let's start with his faith in the topic sentence as the indispensable sentence that presents the subject of paragraph. In 1974, pioneering writing teacher and theorist Richard Braddock decided to put two of Bain's assumptions to the test. Braddock put together a representative selection of essays from major magazines and set about looking for topic sentences in the paragraphs in his selection. He immediately ran into trouble. When he was able to identify a topic sentence by stretching Bain's idea to cover a number of variations, he still could only find some semblance of a topic sentence in fewer than half the paragraphs he examined. In only 13 percent of the paragraphs did the topic sentence appear where promised, at the start of the paragraph. Braddock concluded both "that the notion of what a topic sentence is, is not at all clear" and that the evidence simply "did not support the claims of textbook writers about the frequency and location of topic sentences."

Possibly even more damaging to Bain's pronouncements about paragraphs are reports by Arthur A. Stern and Edgar H. Schuster of experiments they conducted in which they had respondents try to figure out how pieces of writing had been originally divided into paragraphs. Stern's paragraphing exercise asked the teachers to decide how many paragraphs a 500-word block of prose should be divided into and where the paragraph breaks should be. Stern got responses suggesting the block should be divided into either two, three, four, or five paragraphs, with only 5 out of 100 respondents paragraphing the piece as the authors had. This result led Stern to ask, "If, as the handbooks declare, a paragraph represents a 'distinct unit of thought,' why is it that we can't recognize a unit of thought when we see one? If every paragraph contains an identifiable topic sentence, then why don't all of us identify the same topic sentence?"

Edgar H. Schuster conducted a similar experiment, handing out at a teacher's convention an unparagraphed United States Supreme Court order consisting of 38 sentences. Each one of those 38 sentences was selected by at least one respondent as the appropriate beginning of a new paragraph. No one replicated the original paragraphing by the Supreme Court. What's more, when Schuster later tried the exercise himself, for a second time, he found that his paragraphing choice did not agree with the first choices he had made, leading him to exclaim, "I disagreed with myself." Schuster went on to emphasize that, regardless of its paragraph organization, the document would still be "the same piece of work."

Most contemporary instruction concerning paragraphing is almost ridiculously normative and arbitrary rather than reflective of the myriad ways in which we actually write our paragraphs. However, I should mention one variation on the Bain paragraph you may want to add to the options open to you when you build paragraphs. Francis Christensen, for example, openly takes Bain as his guide, particularly insofar as Bain saw the paragraph as a scaled-up analogue of the sentence, each paragraph organized by a topic sentence. Christensen adds the claim that "There is a precise structural analogy, not with just any sentence, but with the cumulative sentence." He argues, "The topic sentence of a paragraph is analogous to the base clause of such a sentence, and the supporting sentences of a paragraph are analogous to the added levels of the sentence."

I'm warming up to the pitch I'll make in the next lecture for a maverick philosophy of composition. This pitch has been made a number of times before, both in writing scholarship and the compelling examples offered by writers we regularly celebrate. Its most famous articulation is Winston Weathers's argument for a Grammar B. For now, I introduce the idea of Grammar B only to leapfrog over it for a moment to suggest that we may now need to turn our attention to the possibility of a Grammar C, with that C specifically invoking the new looks and capabilities of prose made possible by computers. Winston Weathers's idea of Grammar B presciently anticipates the new world of sentences on the screen, in its identification of new shorter and more striking blocks of prose and in its discussion of double-voice as a forerunner of the kind of metacommentary available to contemporary writers and readers through the hypertext hotlink.

Jay David Bolter and Richard Lanham have considered what happens to language when it moves from page to screen. Bolter's *Writing Space* theorizes hypertext at the level of the book rather than the level of the sentence or paragraph, but a number of his speculations would be obvious starting points for our thinking of what a Grammar C might mean. In his book, *The Electronic Word: Democracy, Technology, and the Arts*, Richard Lanham views electronic textuality largely in terms of what he sees in it as a convergence of rhetorical values with the visual syntaxes of contemporary art. ∎

Question to Consider

1. Have the Internet, e-mail, and rapid electronic communications had an effect on the way you write, or on the style of the material you read in these media?

Sentences in Sequence
Lecture 23—Transcript

While I really want to maintain the focus of this course on the sentence, since that is the basic unit of writing we can most easily control and improve, I suppose it's time to openly acknowledge what has already been evident for some time in the examples I've used in previous lectures: Occasions for writing single sentences, with no surrounding context, are exceedingly rare. Single sentences may be in great demand if you're in the business of writing copy for a bumper sticker company, but most writing situations call for more than a sentence. Indeed, many if not most of the sentences we write have trouble standing alone, since they contain, and sometimes their effective functioning depends upon, cohesive links to surrounding sentences. These links can range from pronouns whose referents appear in other sentences, to extension and elaboration of similes and metaphors that appeared in earlier sentences, to offering numerical or chronological references that make sense only in the context of a larger numbering system or history. Examples of this cohesion phenomenon are too numerous to mention, but my use of *this cohesion phenomenon* in this sentence would be a start on such an inventory of context-related, if not context-dependent aspects of sentences. And of course, there are logical cohesive cues, such as *on the other hand* or *finally* or *along these lines* that remind us that sentences, while important and sometimes magnificent in stand-alone isolation, are usually team players, getting help from and lending help to surrounding sentences.

M. A. K. Halliday and Ruqaiya Hasan had pretty much both the first and the last word to say about the ways in which sentences Velcro together in their groundbreaking and massively authoritative 1976 study *Cohesion in English*. Including, but also above and beyond the crude kinds of cohesion I've just mentioned, Halliday and Hasan identified five major categories of cohesive ties among sentences, 19 subcategories, and even a number of sub-subcategories. Their five primary categories for cohesion are reference, substitution, ellipsis, conjunction, and lexical reiteration and collocation. I won't try to give more than a brief indication of each, but substitution, for example, might include my own use of *each* to refer to any one of the five categories I mentioned in the previous sentence, reference includes pronouns, conjunction covers situations such as starting a sentence with *and* or *however*, and lexical reiteration and collocation refers to using words that are closely associated due to their sharing reference to a common subject, as we might see in words all having something to do with fires, flames, or burning. *Cohesion in English* remains the foundational work on the ways sentences stick together, and it certainly rewards reading, but if you find yourself interested—but not quite that interested—in this phenomenon, you might find Stephen P. Witte's and Lester Faigley's essay "Coherence, Cohesion, and Writing Quality," published in *College Composition and Communication* in May 1981 a more than adequate but mercifully much shorter overview of the subject.

The complexities identified in *Cohesion in English* remind us why our primary concern in this course has been with single sentences, as the number of considerations that shape our writing multiply so dramatically when we move beyond the sentence to larger units of discourse that any suggestion of how to develop a sequence of sentences would be arbitrarily prescriptive, mechanical, and ultimately pretty much useless. It would be impossible to anticipate more than a tiny fraction of the situations and purposes which would shape any sequence of sentences we might write. Nevertheless, it is the case that some of the syntactic features we have been working with at the level of the sentence also transcend the individual sentence to work in similar fashion in sequences of sentences. Sentences in sequence can function in paragraphs much as cumulative modifying phrases function in the individual sentence. And sentence rhythms, particularly those associated with cumulative and balanced syntax, seem to generate clumps or clusters of sentences all displaying those rhythms.

Accordingly, this lecture will consider from several angles sentences in sequence, in clumps and clusters. Some of these clumps and clusters we call paragraphs, and that's where we will start. But the paragraph is a unit of discourse we don't actually know that much about—or at least don't much agree on what it is we do know. Furthermore, as the *graph* part of *paragraph* reminds us, there is an important visual component we should acknowledge when we write sentences in sequence. We don't speak in paragraphs; we write in paragraphs. And we know the boundaries of a paragraph not by any prescriptive standards based on logic or syntax or sound, but by the simple fact that paragraphs are those sequences of sentences we see on the page as being set off by indentations. What we see between two indentations from the left-hand margin of the page—that's a paragraph, and we have no better definition of a paragraph that will stand up under rigorous scrutiny. And in much the same way that the *graph* in *paragraph* alerts us to the visual aspect of this writing form, we need to remember that writing is first and foremost and always itself a technological phenomenon, whether the inscribing technology is the end of a burned stick or a pointed rock used to scratch symbols on the wall of a cave, or the most advanced computer and authoring software. We don't have time to do more than very briefly consider the likely impact of technology on our sentences, whether alone or in sequence, but this lecture will conclude with a few remarks about what is now being called *electronic textuality* or *multimedia writing*.

But now, back to the concept of the paragraph, the unit of organization most of us see as the next structure our sentences combine to build on their way to becoming much larger units of discourse such as reports, proposals, essays, memoirs, novels, and all of the other forms our writing can take.

Here's what may come as a surprise: The paragraph as a form is every bit as artificial, every bit as unnatural, as are the most extreme examples of euphuistic balance and serial construction. The sentence has been an object of critical interrogation for a couple of thousand years, but the paragraph as a codified unit of discourse is a concept probably first introduced as late as 1795 by Lindley Murray in his *English Grammar*, a textbook that was hugely influential in the 19th century, going through some 65 editions in England and America. But most of what we think of as the definition of and rules for the paragraph we owe to one brilliant but eccentric Scottish polymath, Alexander Bain, who in his 1866 book *English Composition and Rhetoric* made up the rules for the paragraph we now generally treat as if Moses had brought them down from the mountain, engraved in a second set of stone tablets, only slightly less authoritative than the Ten Commandments. I'll have more to say about Alexander Bain shortly; for now let me just list his prescriptions for a proper paragraph. According to Bain, the paragraph is the "division of discourse next higher than the sentence" and it is "a collection of sentences with unity of purpose," each paragraph handling and exhausting a distinct topic. He then offers six "certain principles that govern the structure of the paragraph, for all kinds of composition."

1. The first requisite of the paragraph is, that the bearing of each sentence upon what precedes shall be explicit and unmistakable.

2. When several consecutive sentences iterate or illustrate the same idea, they should, as far as possible, be formed alike. This may be called the rule of Parallel Construction.

3. The opening sentence, unless so constructed as to be obviously preparatory, is expected to indicate with prominence the subject of the paragraph.

4. A paragraph should be consecutive, or free from Dislocation.

5. The paragraph is understood to possess unity; which implies a definite purpose, and forbids digressions and irrelevant matter.

6. As in the sentence, so in the paragraph, a due proportion should obtain between principal and subordinate statements.

(Alexander Bain. *English Composition and Rhetoric: A Manual.* Appleton & Co., 1871, pp. 142–152)

Compare Bain's specifications with those offered by the *Harbrace Handbook,* 7th ed., some 106 years later, and you will notice a remarkable similarity. The *Harbrace Handbook* defines a paragraph as a "distinct unit of thought—usually a group of related sentences, though occasionally no more than one sentence—in a written or a printed composition." Noting that the form of the paragraph distinctively signals itself with a first line that is indented, the *Handbook* continues:

The content of a unified paragraph deals with one central idea. Each sentence fits into a logical pattern of organization and is therefore carefully related to other sentences in the paragraph.

So, the *Harbrace* prescription for the paragraph is that it should be "unified, coherent, adequately developed."

A paragraph is said to have unity when each sentence contributes to the central thought. Any sentence that violates the unity of the paragraph should be deleted.

In expository writing, the main idea of a paragraph is most often stated in the first sentence. However, the statement of the controlling idea (often called the *topic sentence*) may appear anywhere in the paragraph—for example, after an introductory transitional sentence or at the end of the paragraph.

A paragraph is said to have coherence when the relationship between sentences is clear and when the transition from one sentence to the next is easy and natural.

And adequate development results in part from the arrangement of sentences in the paragraph according to "time order, space order, order of climax," or according to their movement from particular to general, general to the particular, or from the familiar to the unfamiliar.

What has happened here and in almost every other writing text with a chapter or section devoted to the paragraph is that Alexander Bain's six principles have been boiled down to three—unity, coherence, and emphasis—but his starting assumption, that the paragraph was just the sentence writ large, its sentences the equivalent of phrases and subordinate clauses in the sentence, remains one of the central assumptions underlying most contemporary theories of the paragraph. And Bain's belief that the paragraph developed the idea initially posited by what he called "the opening sentence." and what is known today as the topic sentence remains one of the, if not the, most dearly held assumptions about paragraphs.

Only Bain got a lot of this wrong, and his errors have been mechanically if not mindlessly passed down to us as the received truths of paragraph theory. Let's start with his faith in the topic sentence as the indispensable sentence that presents the subject of the paragraph. In 1974 pioneering writing teacher and theorist Richard Braddock, after whom the Conference on College Composition and Communication has named one of its most important annual awards, decided to put two of Bain's assumptions to the test. Braddock put together a representative selection of essays from major magazines such as *The Atlantic, Harper's, Saturday Review,* and the *The New Yorker* and set about looking for topic sentences in the paragraphs in his selection. He immediately ran into trouble. In the first place, when he was able to identify a topic sentence by stretching Bain's idea to cover a number of variations, including the idea of a topic distributed over two sentences or one implied by parts of several sentences, or one that could be inferred but was not actually present in the sentence, he still could only find some semblance of a topic sentence in fewer than half the paragraphs he examined, and in only 13 percent of the paragraphs did the topic sentence appear where promised, at the start of the paragraph. Publishing his findings in a frequently cited article in the Winter 1974 *Research in the Teaching of English,* Braddock concluded both "the notion of what a topic sentence is, is not at all clear," and he concluded that the evidence simply "did not support the claims of textbook writers about the frequency and location of topic sentences."

Possibly even more damaging to Bain's largely deductive pronouncements about paragraphs are reports by Arthur A. Stern of Teacher's College at Columbia and Edgar H. Schuster, a writing teacher who taught for 40 years in venues ranging from secondary schools to the Graduate School of Education at Harvard, of experiments they conducted in which they had respondents try to figure out how pieces of writing had been originally divided into paragraphs. Stern conducted his experiments in the mid 1970s by asking English teachers to paragraph a 500-word passage, with no paragraph indentation, taken from Cleanth Brook's and Robert Penn Warren's *Fundamentals of Good Writing.* This paragraphing exercise asked the teachers to decide how many paragraphs that 500-word block of prose should be divided into and where the paragraph breaks should be. Stern got responses suggesting the block should be divided into either two, three, four, or five paragraphs, with only 5 out of 100 respondents paragraphing the piece as had Brooks and Warren. Reasonably enough, this result led Stern to ask

> If, as the handbooks declare, a paragraph represents a "distinct unit of thought," why is it that we can't recognize a unit of thought when we see one? If every paragraph contains an identifiable topic sentence, then why don't all of us identify the same topic sentence?

Much earlier, Herbert Read reached much the same conclusion about the cherished but apparently mistaken notion that some form of logical unity binds the sentences of a paragraph. In his *English Prose Style,* as revised for the 1952 edition, he notes

> It is nearer the truth to say that a writer seizes upon some particular aspect of his subject and holds that aspect in his mind until he has seen it in all profitable lights. This process may take two or it may take twenty paragraphs: there is no rule, and whatever unity may govern the paragraph, it is not the unity of the development of a single idea.

Edgar H. Schuster has conducted a similar experiment, handing out at a teachers convention an unparagraphed United States Supreme Court order, consisting of 38 sentences. He reports his findings in his wonderfully transgressive 2003 textbook, *Breaking the Rules: Liberating Writers Through Innovative Grammar Instruction.* Tellingly, each one of those 38 sentences was selected by at least one respondent as the appropriate beginning of a new paragraph. No one in his sample replicated the original paragraphing by the Supreme Court. What's more, when Schuster later tried the exercise himself for a second time, he found that his paragraphing choice did not agree with the first choices he had made, leading him to exclaim, "I disagreed with myself." The point Schuster makes about the outcome of his experiment, however, is much more important than its clear support of the idea that paragraphing is a subjective rather than logical process, as Schuster asks us to think what those results really mean.

> That Supreme Court order said what it said and said it cohesively or incohesively, logically or illogically, *regardless* of whether it contained three, six, ten, or even no paragraphs. Since emphasis would be affected, it's likely that a five-paragraph version would be easier to read and would be preferred by most readers, but apart from emphases, it would be *the same piece of work.*

My point is that most contemporary instruction concerning paragraphing is almost ridiculously normative and arbitrary rather than reflective of the myriad ways in which we actually write our paragraphs. Sure, follow the advice offered by Bain in 1866 or the echoes of his advice that persist in most writing guidebooks today, and you may well get a unified, coherent, and well-developed paragraph, and there's nothing wrong with that—other than the fact that it will be an artificial structure that forces your writing, your style into a box made long ago by one self-trained rhetorician at the University of Aberdeen in Scotland. And, if you go looking for examples that will fit this prescriptive model, you're almost certain to find them, since this model has been forced on writing students for nearly 150 years, but the odds are you won't find paragraphs by celebrated or even by just your favorite writers that fit this mold.

However, having said that I should mention one variation on the Bain paragraph you may want to add to the options open to you when you build your own paragraphs. Francis Christensen, whose theories of the cumulative sentence I champion so unreservedly, has also advanced "A Generative Rhetoric of the Paragraph," about which I have more than a few reservations. Basically, Christensen openly takes Bain as his guide, particularly insofar as Bain saw the paragraph as a scaled-up analogue of the sentence, each paragraph organized by a topic sentence, but Christensen adds the claim that "there is a precise structural analogy, not with just any sentence, but with the cumulative sentence." He argues, "The topic sentence of a paragraph is analogous to the base clause of such a sentence, and the supporting sentences of a paragraph are analogous to the added levels of the sentence."

Christensen then claims that the four principles that guide his theory of the cumulative sentence—addition, direction and modification, levels of generality, and texture—apply equally well to constructing paragraphs, and can be equally generative for the writer who needs guidance in developing an idea through sentences in a paragraph. While Christensen finds a number of paragraphs that do indeed seem to reflect the coordinate, subordinate, and mixed patterns of cumulative sentences, and while it is possible to write paragraphs by thinking of each of its sentences as analogous to either the base clause or modifying phrases of the cumulative sentence, this model is, like Bain's original prescription for the sentence, quite arbitrary and limiting.

In focusing on the ways in which many writing texts offer subjective, inaccurate, and ultimately misleading norms for writing paragraphs, just as

I've previously suggested ways in which conventional received truths about writing sentences so often miss the mark, and in celebrating the maverick stylistic theories of scholars such as Richard Lanham or the marvelously maverick prose of a writer and scholar such as William Gass, I'm warming up to the pitch I'll make in the next lecture for a maverick philosophy of composition. Actually, it's not my pitch, but has been made a number of times before both in writing scholarship and in the compelling examples offered by writers we regularly celebrate while somehow failing to notice that we celebrate their writing precisely for the kinds of things we have again and again been warned not to do in our own. The most famous articulation of such a maverick philosophy of composition was made back in 1976 by Winston Weathers in his essay "Grammars of Style: New Options in Composition," his famous argument for what he termed a Grammar B to complement the traditional hegemonic, highly regulated, and largely subjective Grammar A offered in most writing classes and peddled as indisputable norm in most writing texts.

The idea of Grammar B deserves a lecture in its own right, and it is an idea to which I'll return. For now, I introduce the idea of Grammar B only to leapfrog over it for a moment to suggest that we may now need to be turning our attention to the possibility, if not the emerging certainty, of a Grammar C, with that "C" specifically invoking the new looks and capabilities of prose made possible by computers.

Most of our writing textbooks, discussions of prose style, and celebrations of the sentence assume that we are talking about words on a printed page, while more and more of our engagement with language is actually an increasingly interactive interface with pixilated words on a computer screen. In this way, the materiality of writing is undergoing far-reaching changes, just as it has previously been changed by the invention of the printing press and then of the typewriter. In some ways that I will discuss in the next lecture, Winston Weathers's idea of Grammar B presciently anticipates the new world of sentences on the screen, in its identification of new shorter and more-striking blocks of prose which Weathers, after a suggestion made by Tom Wolfe, calls the *crot*, and in its discussion of Double-Voice as a forerunner of the kind of metacommentary available to contemporary writers and readers through the simple device of the hypertext hotlink.

More to the specific issue of what computers mean for contemporary prose style, building on Walter J. Ong's study of the move from oral to literary to secondary oral culture, Jay David Bolter and Richard Lanham have considered what happens to language when it moves from page to screen.

It was Father Ong who persuasively argued in his famous study *Orality and Literacy: The Technologizing of the Word* that writing was a technology, and that "Technologies are not mere exterior aids but also interior transformations of consciousness, and never more than when they affect the word." Moreover, as Ong traced the human development from oral to literary culture, from speaking to writing, he also argued that human consciousness evolved and that writing in general and specific writing technologies in particular played crucial roles in consciousness-raising. While Ong devoted little attention specifically to computers, he dismissed or defused some of the common criticisms lodged against the effects computers might have on consciousness, and included them in the broad array of technologies that he saw as promoting a resurgence of many of the positive aspects of oral culture in what he saw as an age of "secondary orality." Bolter and Lanham then picked up on Ong's theorizing of writing as a technology and applied it more directly to computers and computer writing.

Jay Bolter brought unique credentials to his highly influential 1991 study *Writing Space: The Computer, Hypertext and the History of Writing*, as he was a Classics professor who also had a degree in computer science. Almost all subsequent studies of hypertext, hypermedia, and multimedia writing build on Bolter's pioneering work with hypertext theory and with hypertext technology, as he was also one of the authors of *Storyspace*, a hypertext-authoring program that preceded the widespread development of HTML as the authoring language that underlay the features of the World Wide Web. Bolter's *Writing Space* largely theorizes hypertext—the ability to link any word in a foreground text so that it will take the reader to a background text—at the level of the book or of literature, rather than at the level of the sentence or paragraph, but a number of his speculations would seem to be obvious starting points for our thinking about what a Grammar C might mean even at the most basic levels of composition. Noting that electronic writing, such as we now take for granted on the Web, develops networks rather than the linear progression of book pages, that computer screens favor the use of short, self-contained units of discourse, and that the fact that electronic networks would almost certainly be navigated differently by different readers—calling for a radically new understanding of what we mean when we refer to the "unity" of a text—Bolter also suggested that electronic writing resisted traditional forms of closure, since there were always further hypertext links that could be established, expanding connections without limit. "Electronic writing will probably be aphoristic rather than periodic," he mused.

Richard Lanham, whose authority as a rhetorician I've already repeatedly invoked, also brought an interesting background to his book *The Electronic Word: Democracy, Technology, and the Arts*, since he was a recognized authority on classical rhetoric who welcomes the new technologies of electronic writing. Lanham views electronic textuality largely in terms of what he sees in it as a convergence of rhetorical values (rather than with the logical values usually associated with computers) with the visual syntaxes of contemporary art. He sees print as a philosophic medium, while the electronic text is a deeply rhetorical one, and this new rhetoric makes use both of the graphic and typographic versatility and innovation offered by the computer, shifting Bolter's focus on hypertext to a focus on multimedia writing. Print, he suggests, asks us to look *through* the words on the page to the ideas and objects they represent, while electronic text invites us to toggle back and forth between looking through the words on the screen and looking at those words in all the ways they can be made more interesting by the computer. As he puts it, the computer screen "makes text into a painting, frames it in a new way, asks for a new act of attention—and smiles at the seriousness that the text calls forth from us."

Sentences and Prose Style
Lecture 24

In these lectures I have consistently advocated rule breaking, but I'm no grammatical or syntactical or rhetorical anarchist. While I believe there are many rules we should break, there are also many rules we should not break.

Prose style is determined by an almost infinite number of variables, some a matter of choices and decisions made by the writer, many more beyond the writer's control. Prose style manifests itself at an almost infinite number of levels in our use of language, making it difficult to use one term to describe phenomena associated with subjects as different as the sentence, the essay, the novel, the writer, the period, and the culture in which the writer writes, and so on. We can speak of style at the level of the word, at the level of the sentence, at the level of larger prose units such as the paragraph, at the level of the completed piece of prose, at the level of a particular writer, at the level of a particular movement embraced by writers, at the level of a particular genre or form of writing, at the level of a century, at the level of a particular nation, etc.

But some of the basic building blocks of prose style can be examined closely and described precisely—particularly as those building blocks or moves appear at the level of the sentence. This lecture will provide a reminder of the aspects of prose style covered during this course, aspects that are subject to the writer's choice, within the writer's control. These aspects play an important role in helping us develop what is sometimes called the gift of style. Unlike the gifted athlete, the gifted writer counts more on learned stylistic strategies than on natural talent. In the most important sense, style is a gift that can be passed from writer to writer, age to age. Accordingly, "the gift of style" is a phrase that rewards our taking it quite seriously, thinking not of style so much as the result of a skill or gift possessed by the writer as we think of it as a gift received and passed on in our prose, a process of gifting so brilliantly explored by Lewis Hyde in *The Gift: Creativity and the Artist in the Modern World.*

The late Robert J. Connors, an influential expert in the area of rhetoric and composition, wrote an essay, starkly titled "The Erasure of the Sentence," in which he argues that sentence- or syntax-based approaches to writing have been driven underground by larger theoretical currents in composition theory. Connors divides writing instruction based on the sentence into three broad categories, starting with Christensen's advocacy of the benefits of the cumulative sentence. The next category Connors identifies consists of writing approaches that have at their center the rather precise imitation of sentence patterns, forms, schemes. The third category Connors describes consists of pedagogical approaches to writing centered on strategies for sentence combining. While it was never my conscious attempt, I've introduced you in this course to the three primary categories of sentence-based writing instruction that are the subject of Connors's essay.

Connors cites a number of empirical studies that seem to validate the assumption that sentence-based writing pedagogies do indeed improve writing—and do so rather dramatically. These pedagogies have fallen out of fashion, in part because of a larger suspicion in English studies of empirical studies as antihumanist and a suspicion that these successful teaching techniques stifle creativity, are not located in larger theories of discourse, and might actually be demeaning to students. Connors concludes, "It really does seem that the current perception that somehow sentence rhetorics 'don't work' exists as a massive piece of wish fulfillment."

I should explain that while I have a pretty solid foundation in writing pedagogy, I am a trained writing teacher, but not a composition theorist or formal rhetorician. I go with what works for me in the writing classroom, aware of but not overly concerned with the broad cultural and sociological implications of my approach to writing sentences. These lectures are investigations, interrogations, explorations, and celebrations of the sentence and of prose style. They are not meant as a verbal textbook that sets forth yet another set of guidelines or rules for good writing. While I believe there are many rules we should break, there are many rules we should not break. As Schuster suggests, we should choose a favorite writer, preferably a modern writer, and preferably a nonfiction writer, then check to see whether a certain rule is followed by that writer.

What final words do I have to offer about style? Prose style is determined by an almost infinite number of variables, some a matter of choices and decisions made by the writer, many more beyond the writer's control. Prose style manifests itself at an almost infinite number of levels in our use of language, making it difficult to use one term to describe phenomena associated with subjects as different as the sentence, the essay, the novel, the writer, the period, and the culture in which the writer writes, and so on. This course has been built on the assumption that some of the basic building blocks of prose style can be examined closely and described precisely—particularly as those building blocks or moves appear at the level of the sentence. The best attempt I know of to consider all the factors that determine prose style is that of my colleague and mentor in most things stylistic, Carl Klaus. He concludes that the most profound reason for studying prose style is that "when we recognize that it can ultimately shape our beliefs ... we assume the responsibility of mastering style lest we be mastered by it."

"The gift of style" is a phrase that rewards our taking it quite seriously.

If from Carl Klaus we get our best explanation of the importance of prose style, it is from Richard Lanham that we get the strongest argument that our characteristic approach to the importance of style is horribly wrongheaded. Lanham charges that not only is our inattention to prose style in most writing classrooms a shame, but that our valorization in writing instruction of clarity at the expense of style is nothing less than a disaster. Lanham proposes "an alternative goal: not clarity, but a self-conscious pleasure in words."

A perfect companion to Lanham's *Style: An Anti-Textbook* is Winston Weathers's *An Alternate Style: Options in Composition*, published in 1980. This book expands and provides numerous examples for the idea of Grammar B that Weathers first set forth in his "Grammars of Style: New Options in Composition." Urging us to be alert to emerging options and to "participate in creating options that do not yet exist but which would be beneficial if they did," he called for writing instruction that identified or created more stylistic options "in all areas."

Three characteristics of Grammar B are of particular relevance to us. From Tom Wolfe's introduction of and then codifications of the techniques of New Journalism, Grammar B borrowed the notion of the *crot*, a short, somewhat paragraph-like chunk of prose that functioned more like a stanza in poetry. A second intriguing feature of Grammar B is what Weathers terms "The Labyrinthine Sentence and the Sentence Fragment." The third feature of Grammar B I want to mention, Double-Voice, is a self-reflexive and metacritical commentary on the text.

In these lectures, I hope I've introduced both a number of practical approaches to crafting more effective—and more enjoyable—sentences. I hope I've also been able to touch on some of the fascinating issues involved in understanding how our sentences fit into the larger concerns of prose style. Now I'd like to offer a very, very brief gloss on the construction of style as a gift. In "A Primer for Teaching Style," published in the May 1974 *College Composition and Communication*, Richard Graves describes style as "a way of finding and explaining what is true." I love that description and I completely agree.

Looking at style as Graves does is an important first step toward thinking of style not as a gift that some writers have, something they can show off, but a gift that they can give away, by passing the truth of their style and the expression of their selves along to readers. In this important sense, style is indeed a gift that can and must be passed along. That is the sense in which I offer this course to you, and if you have found in it anything of value, I hope you will pass it along to others through your writing. ■

Question to Consider

1. Write a smooth-sounding cumulative sentence that uses no less than 100 words. Your sentence should sound as smooth and natural as possible. It may also be compound, with modifying levels for each of two or more base clauses joined by conjunctions. It's more fun, though, to see if you can construct your 100-word sentence around a single base clause.

Sentences and Prose Style
Lecture 24—Transcript

I've been rereading a fascinating article that has everything to do with this course and that has reminded me of something I really need to do before I complete my lectures for a course with "Building Great Sentences" in its title. The article, by the late Robert J. Connors, a professor of English at the University of New Hampshire and an influential expert in the area of rhetoric and composition, is starkly titled "The Erasure of the Sentence," and it was published in the September 2000 issue of *College Composition and Communication*. The bio note, which I assume was written by Professor Connors himself, ends with the tongue-in-cheek description of the author "Now in his dotage, he strives vainly for crumbs of dignity as he watches everything he holds dear swept into the dustbin of history." Tongue-in-cheek, yes, but I suspect there's more than a rueful grain or two of passive-aggressive truth in that sentiment, as Professor Connors has been detailing in his article the somewhat hard-to-explain disappearances of courses such as this one I'm offering that focus primarily on the syntax of the sentence. Early on in his essay, Connors offers this beautifully balanced sentence summarizing developments in composition theory since the 1980s: "Some elements of the older field of composition teaching became approved and burgeoned, while others were tacitly declared dead ends: lore-based and therefore uninteresting, scientistic and therefore suspect, mechanistic and therefore destructive." From that moment on, I knew I was in good hands, respecting as I do writing that shows care in its own composition—particularly when that writing is in an essay on the ways in which we care about writing.

The gist of this article is that sentence- or syntax-based approaches to writing, a famous example of which would be Christensen's theory of the cumulative sentence, have pretty much died out or been driven underground, despite their proven effectiveness, by larger theoretical currents in composition theory and by theory-centered developments in the broader field of English studies. Since another anything-but-famous example of a sentence- or syntax-based approach to writing instruction would be the course I am teaching at this moment, I have more than a passing interest—as should you—in what Connors has to say.

Sentence-based pedagogies were much the rage when I was a graduate student in the 1970s, and Connors does a great job of describing both their rise and their subsequent fall. He divides writing instruction based on the sentence into three broad categories, starting with Christensen's advocacy of the benefits of the cumulative sentence, making Christensen a category unto himself. Significant portions of this course have been devoted to Christensen's rhetoric of the cumulative sentence, so you are already familiar with its contours. The next category Connors identifies consists of writing approaches that have at their center the rather precise imitation of sentence patterns, forms, schemes, and mentions Edward P. J. Corbett's 1965 textbook, *Classical Rhetoric for the Modern Student*, as a flagship text for this approach, with two books by Winston Weathers and Otis Winchester, their 1967 *The New Strategy of Style* and their 1969 *Copy and Compose*, as also adopting an approach to writing based largely on imitating identified forms. He also includes Weathers's 1980 book *An Alternate Style: Options in Composition*, the book where Weathers developed his notion of Grammar B, as a work recommending the value of imitation. In earlier lectures, I've repeatedly drawn from *The New Strategy of Style*, and later in this lecture I'll have more to say about the Weathers notion of a somewhat transgressive Grammar B. The third category Connors describes consists of pedagogical approaches to writing centered on strategies for sentence combining. While my course has not specifically drawn from any codified theories of sentence-combining, my discussion of the surface of the sentence as the tip of an iceberg of underlying propositions shares many of the assumptions of sentence combining, and my invocation of that "Invisible God created the visible world" sentence to show how propositions get combined in sentences is right out of the sentence-combining playbook. Likewise, my enthusiasm for the Josephine Miles notion of the sentence as a progression of syntactic steps, taken by strategies of conjunction, subordination, or adjectival modification, owes much to sentence-combining theory. So while it was never my conscious attempt, I've introduced you in this course to the three primary categories of sentence-based writing instruction that are the subject of Connors's essay.

And what Connors reports has a bit of the feel of a good news/bad news joke. The good news is that he cites a number of empirical studies that seem to validate the assumption that sentence-based writing pedagogies do indeed improve writing—and do so rather dramatically. The bad news is that they have fallen out of fashion, precisely in part because of a larger suspicion in English studies of empirical studies as antihumanist and a suspicion that these successful teaching techniques stifle creativity, are not themselves located in larger theories of discourse, and might actually be demeaning to students, with exercises far removed from actual writing situations that boiled down to as "mere servile copying." More bad news is that by the mid-80s "The result of all these lines of criticism of syntactic methods was that they were stopped almost dead in their tracks as a research program and ceased being a popular teaching project just a little later." The good news, however, is that Connors concludes that "It really does seem that the current perception that somehow sentence rhetorics 'don't work' exists as a massive piece of wish fulfillment." As Connors explains (more good news!) in a sentence that is as carefully suspensive as his earlier sentence was balanced: "In other words, if people believe that research has shown that sentence rhetorics don't work, their belief exists not because the record bears it out but because it is what people want to believe."

Wow! That's a relief!

I should explain that while I have a pretty solid foundation in writing pedagogy, I am a trained writing teacher, but not a composition theorist or formal rhetorician. I go with what works for me in the writing classroom, aware of but not overly concerned with the broad cultural and sociological implications of my approach to writing sentences. Indeed, if I'm so bold as to refer to my theory of writing, it should probably be described as magpie eclectic, since like that curious bird, if I come across a bright or shiny theory or writing exercise, I bring it back to the nest of my classroom. I was in graduate school during the heady days in the 1970s when sentence-centered approaches to writing and more holistic approaches—such as those advanced by Peter Elbow and Ken Macrorie, high priests of *free-writing*, and Donald Murray, who extended our focus in composition to the revision process—seemed like they could not only coexist in the same classroom, but might even complement each other. I was in graduate school during the days when rhetorical theory even in its most formalistic articulations seemed compatible with the much broader concerns of discourse theory as proposed by James Moffett and James Kinneavy; indeed, one of my teachers at the University of Texas was Dr. Kinneavy, a noted discourse theorist, who was also well-trained in rhetorical traditions, and above all else a man who loved to teach. To this day Kinneavy's influential 1971 work, *A Theory of Discourse*, provides the broader context in which I think of all of my work with sentences.

I mention all of this as a background for my heartfelt reminder that these lectures are investigations, interrogations, explorations, and celebrations of the sentence and of prose style. They are not meant as a verbal textbook that sets forth yet another set of guidelines or rules for good writing. So much that is wrong with writing instruction is wrong because a single person's beliefs have somehow been elevated to ex cathedra pronouncements and passed along from teacher to teacher and from teacher to student through generation after generation, without ever being challenged, without ever being tested against experience, without ever really being thought about. In these lectures, I have tried to do some serious thinking about the received truths that have so largely guided our efforts to teach writing.

All of which is just to say that in these lectures I have consistently advocated rule breaking, but I'm no grammatical or syntactical or rhetorical anarchist. While I believe there are many rules we should break, there are also many rules we should not break. The distinction can get tricky, but Edgar H. Schuster makes it much easier for us to tell which is which in his deliciously naughty book, *Breaking the Rules: Liberating Writers Through Innovative Grammar Instruction*. Schuster gives us a revealing history of how a very few men and a very few books have gained so much unwarranted influence and authority in the discourse of writing. He is particularly good at identifying what he calls mythrules: "rules that rule no one—other than perhaps a handful of pop-grammarians and hardened purists who look for their authority somewhere in the sky rather than here on earth." He then proposes a simple test for deciding whether a rule deserves its authority. Here's a test: Choose a favorite writer, preferably a modern writer, and preferably a nonfiction writer, then check to see whether the rule being tested, whether it has to do with grammar, usage, or punctuation, is followed by that writer. If it isn't, it's almost certainly a mythrule.

So much for my focus on the sentence; now, what final words do I have to offer about style?

Prose style is determined by an almost infinite number of variables, some a matter of choices and decisions made by the writer, many more beyond the writer's control. Prose style manifests itself at an almost infinite number of levels in our use of language, making it very difficult to use one term to describe phenomena associated with subjects as different as the sentence, the essay, the novel, the writer, the period and culture in which the writer writes, and so on. We can speak of style at the level of the word, at the level of the sentence, at the level of larger prose units such as the paragraph, at the level of the completed piece of prose, at the level of a particular writer, at the level of a particular movement embraced by writers, at the level of a particular genre or form of writing, at the level of a century, at the level of a particular nation, and so on. This course has been built on the assumption that some of the basic building blocks of prose style can be examined closely and described precisely—particularly as those building blocks or moves appear at the level of the sentence.

The best attempt I know of to consider all the factors that determine prose style is that of my colleague and mentor in most things stylistic, Carl Klaus. In his well-known essay "Reflections on Prose Style," which serves to introduce his *Style in English Prose* and has been reprinted in several major collections of essays on style, including (and I never get tired of saying this) the Love and Payne anthology, *Contemporary Essays on Style*, Klaus considers the factors that complicate our thinking about style, most obviously the fact that we use this one term to refer to many different aspects of language use, and he works his way through the different approaches to style offered by commentators such as Puttenham, author of the famous aphorism "Style is the man"; Chesterfield, Hazlitt, Thoreau, Franklin, Ascham, Burton, Bunyan, and Orwell, whose "Politics and the English Language" is quite possibly the most important essay on the subject we have or could ever have. As Klaus contemplates the nature of style, he both complicates and confirms Puttenham's claim that "Style is the man," noting that "if style is the man, it is only so in a fairly complicated sense. ... And it may well be that style is always to some extent an invention of the writer, a fiction that conceals the man as surely as it reveals him." I should note that Puttenham's gender-limiting use of *man* is itself a reminder of the way style continuously evolves, and Klaus's continuing references to the writer always as a man both reflects the date of his writing, pre-1968, and his need to maintain parallelism with

Puttenham's famous aphorism. Of course, as Klaus points out, "Style may also describe the deliberate use of language, the self-conscious process of composing, to achieve specific purposes and calculated effects," and, "having chosen a purpose the writer has also chosen a style, or has had a style chosen for him." He explains: "Style is formative, then; it determines the man as much as he determines it." Most important, Klaus insists on the "influential nature of our stylistic heritage, for language is the basis of thought, and it follows from this truth that inherited forms of expression will inevitably perpetuate the forms of thought associated with them." Thus, he concludes, the most profound reason for studying prose style is that "when we recognize that it can ultimately shape our beliefs ... we assume the responsibility of mastering style lest we be mastered by it."

If from Carl Klaus we get our best explanation of the importance of prose style, it is from Richard Lanham that we get the strongest argument that our characteristic approach to the importance of style is horribly wrongheaded. In one of the most radical, most enjoyable, and most compelling educational polemics I have ever read, Lanham charges in his 1974 *Style: An Anti-Textbook* that not only is our inattention to prose style in most writing classrooms a shame, but our valorization in writing instruction of clarity at the expense of style is nothing less than a disaster. Boiled down to its simplest form, Lanham's eloquent argument is that contemporary writing instruction with its hyper-emphasis on clarity drains all the pleasure out of writing. "We pare away all the sense of verbal play, of self-satisfying joy in language, then wonder why American students have a motivation problem and don't want to write." As he also argues, "Prose written without joy can only be read in the same spirit." The pervasive emphasis on clarity—on the simple and direct—in American writing instruction Lanham calls the "Fallacy of Normative Prose":

> All prose style (as taught in most classrooms) cherishes a single goal and that goal is to disappear. The aim is the same for all: clarity, denotation, conceptual fidelity. The imperative of imperatives in The Books [his term for most writing texts] is "Be clear." The best style is the never-noticed. Ideally, prose style should, like the state under Marxism, wither away, leaving the plain facts shining unto themselves.

As Lanham sums things up, The Books "do not teach style, they abolish it."

To rectify this dismal state of stylistic affairs, Lanham proposes "an alternative goal: not clarity, but a self-conscious pleasure in words," arguing that "Such self-consciousness is the only stylistic attitude likely to last beyond the classroom." Style, Lanham insists, "must be taught for and as what it is—a pleasure, a grace, a joy, a delight."

Lanham makes some provocative suggestions for how we can bring this self-conscious pleasure in words into our writing practice. In what remains one of his most surprising turns in a book full of surprises is a chapter in defense of jargon, which he calls "The Fun of a Special Language." Whether we agree or disagree with Lanham's radical and controversial stance and, as you might guess, I love it, every serious student of writing should know this contrarian masterpiece.

A perfect companion to Lanham's *Style: An Anti-Textbook* is Winston Weathers's *An Alternate Style: Options in Composition*, published in 1980. This book expands and provides numerous examples for the idea of Grammar B that Weathers first set forth in his *Freshman English News* article, "Grammars of Style: New Options in Composition." Writing almost as if in direct response to Lanham's critique of joyless writing instruction, Weathers, in the persona of a Professor X, complains:

> I write for many reasons, to communicate many things. And yet much of what I wish to communicate does not seem to be expressible within the ordinary conventions of composition as I have learned them and mastered them in the long years of my education.

> What I've been taught to construct is the well-made box. I have been taught to put "what I have to say" into a container that is always remarkably the same, that—in spite of varying decorations—keeps to a basically conventional form: a solid bottom, four upright sides, a fine-fitting lid. Indeed, I may be free to put "what I have to say" in the plain box or in the ornate box, in the large box or in the small box, in the fragile box or in the sturdy box. But always the box—squarish or rectangular. And I begin to wonder if there isn't

somewhere a round box or oval box or tubular box. If somewhere there isn't some sort of container (1) that will allow me to package "what I have to say" without trimming my "content" to fit into a particular compositional mode, (2) that will actually encourage me to discover new "things to say" because of the very opportunity a newly-shaped container gives me, (3) that will be more suitable perhaps to my own mental processes, and (4) that will provide me with a greater rhetorical flexibility, allowing me to package what I have to say in more ways than one and thus reach more audiences than one.

Urging us to be alert to emerging options and to participate in creating options that do not yet exist but which would be beneficial if they did, Professor X calls for writing instruction that identifies or creates more stylistic options "in all areas—in vocabulary, usage, sentence forms, dictional levels, paragraph types, ways of organizing material into whole compositions: options in all that we mean by style." Professor X suggests that these new options would constitute an entirely new "grammar of style," many of the features of which are already in use in not only experimental writing, but also in our own more mundane efforts, but are usually not recognized and almost never approved of by conventional writing instruction.

Against the established rules petrified in what Lanham referred to as The Books, rules that Professor X dubs Grammar A, he proposes that we recognize and, when appropriate, embrace an alternate Grammar B, whose "characteristics of variegation, synchronicity, discontinuity, ambiguity, and the like [would be] an alternate grammar, no longer an experiment, but a mature grammar used by competent writers and offering students of writing a well tested 'set of options' that, added to the traditional grammar of style, will give them a much more flexible voice, a much greater communication capacity, a much greater opportunity to put into effective language all the things they have to say."

The idea of a Grammar B emerged coterminously with the innovations of the New Journalism and with some of the experiments of metafiction. I don't have time to describe all of the major characteristics of Grammar B, but three are of particular relevance to us. From Tom Wolfe's introduction of and then codifications of the techniques of New Journalism, Grammar B borrowed the notion of the crot, a short, somewhat paragraph-like chunk of prose that functioned more like a stanza in poetry. The crot, as described by Professor X, can range from one to 20 or 30 sentences and is a new unit of prose organization:

> ... fundamentally an autonomous unit, characterized by the absence of any transitional devices that might relate it to preceding or subsequent crots and because of this independent and discrete nature of crots, they create a general effect of metastasis [in rhetoric the quick dismissal or passing over an issue] used in this context to suggest rapid transition from one point of view to another.

As Tom Wolfe explained the crot, "In the hands of a writer who really understands the device, it will have you making crazy leaps of logic, leaps you never dreamed of before." Both Wolfe's and Professor X's explanations of the crot, although made some 20 years before the Internet, strike me as nearly perfect descriptions of the units of prose we have already become used to on webpages, a reminder that a Grammar C for electronic text may already be developing beyond Grammar B.

A second intriguing feature of Grammar B is what Professor X terms the *labyrinthine sentence* and the *sentence fragment*. We've already discussed labyrinthine sentences, which I called master sentences, and sentence fragments need no further description.

Professor X uses an example given from John Barth to help illustrate the third feature of Grammar B I want to mention, double-voice. The example from Barth's *Lost in the Funhouse* is a self-reflexive and metacritical commentary on the text, which interrupts the description of a character's thoughts, represented by italics, with a brief tutorial on manuscript preparation. And Weathers lists several other techniques for achieving this double-voice effect. Not only has metacommentary of this form become a norm in postmodern fiction and nonfiction alike, but also—once again—can easily be achieved and regularly is by now-familiar webpage devices such as the hotlink or mouseover animation of selected pieces of text.

Other primary characteristics of Grammar B such as Repetition/Repetends/ Refrains, The List, Collage/Montage, and Synchronicity would also seem to have obvious analogues in electronic textuality, and indeed, Grammar B did a marvelous job of anticipating many of the features we now take for granted when we surf the Web or when we suffer through interminable PowerPoint presentations.

Having come out from behind the persona of Professor X, Weathers ends his initial description of Grammar B with a passionate plea:

> Even if we believe our commitment to the traditional grammar is so strong that we must give our full time to teaching it, we should at least acknowledge the alternate grammar. Say something about it. Point out its existence. Even if we exclude it from our daily work in the classroom. Even if we say to the student, "We can't deal with such matters here ..." and tell him he must wait ... before he can try such things, we will at least have been honest with him and not left him with the impression that traditional grammar is all there is. We can at least avoid, in our profession, the conspiracy of silence that is tantamount to restriction and suppression.

In these lectures I hope I've introduced both a number of practical approaches to crafting more effective—and more enjoyable—sentences. I hope I've also been able to touch on some of the fascinating issues involved in understanding how our sentences fit into the larger concerns of prose style. Oddly enough, both formal and informal references to prose style frequently form an implicit balance, some approaching style as a problem, some approaching style as a gift. We've seen how Richard Lanham responds to the construction of prose style as a problem; now I'd like to offer a very, very brief gloss on the construction of style as a gift.

In "A Primer for Teaching Style," published in the May 1974 *College Composition and Communication,* Richard Graves, now professor emeritus of Curriculum and Teaching at Auburn, describes style as "a way of finding and explaining what is true." I love that description and I completely agree with Graves when he adds that the purpose of style "is not to impress but to express." Looking at style as Graves does is an important first step toward thinking of style not as a gift that some writers have, something they can show off, but as a gift that they can give away, by passing the truth of their style and the expression of their selves along to readers. In this sense, style is itself the gift, passed from writer to writer, from writer to reader, age to age. As Lewis Hyde has so brilliantly explained the process of gifting in his *The Gift*, most indigenous peoples believe that the essence of gift-giving is that the gift must remain in motion—that it must keep moving as it is given again and again, passed from hand to hand. In this important sense, style is indeed a gift that keeps on giving just as it is a gift that can and must be passed along. That is the sense in which I offer this course to you, and if you have found in it anything of value, I hope you will pass it along to others through your writing.

Glossary

action verb: A verb that expresses an action.

base clause: The subject-verb core of a cumulative sentence that could stand alone as a sentence.

bound modifier: A modifier that is *bound* to what it modifies by a relative pronoun such as *that*, *which*, or *who*.

clause: A subject-verb combination that can stand alone in a sentence because the verb is inflected in relation to person and time.

comma splice: Two clauses joined by a comma.

connective: A strategy for building sentences by using conjunctions to add information.

coordinate: A cumulative sentence in which there is more than one second-level modifying phrase, all pointing back to the base clause and free to move.

cumulative sentence: A sentence made up of a base clause to which free modifiers have been added.

cumulative syntax: The syntax that adds information to a base clause by adding free modifiers.

dangling modifier: A modifier that appears in a sentence without anything in the sentence that it modifies.

dominantly subordinate: A mix of coordinate and subordinate cumulative modifying phrases in which there is more subordination than coordination.

ethos: The appeal of a piece of writing that is based on the character of the writer.

figurative language: Language that uses metaphors and similes.

final: Placement of a modifying phrase at the end of a sentence.

finite verb: A verb that occurs in a base clause and is inflected in relation to person and tense.

free modifier: A modifier that can be placed in any syntactic position relative to the base clause.

gerund phrase: A phrase that begins with a gerund (a verb that has been turned into a noun with an -ing ending).

heuristic: Having the characteristic of readily suggesting or generating a solution to a problem.

initial: Placement of a modifying phrase at the start of a sentence.

intransitive verb: A verb that does not require a direct object.

kernel sentence: The initial sentence to which more information is to be added in the form of modifiers.

left-branching sentence: A sentence in which the modifying phrase or phrases are placed to the left of the base clause.

linking verb: A verb that expresses a state of being.

logos: The appeal of a piece of writing that is based on reason and logic.

loose syntax: Syntax in which the modifying phrases are more free to move around.

medial: Placement of a modifying phrase in the middle of a sentence.

metaphor: A description of one thing in terms used to describe another.

misplaced modifier: A modifying phrase that, because of its placement, is unclear about what it modifies.

mixed syntax: A cumulative syntax in which there is a mix of both coordinate and subordinate modification.

noun phrase: A phrase that can act in a sentence as if it is a noun.

paradigmatic: Related to the choice of words or phrases in a sentence and their level of abstraction.

parallelism: In a sentence, a balance of two or more words, phrases, or clauses.

participial phrase: A phrase that begins with a present participle (a verb that ends in -ing) or a past participle (a verb that ends in -d, -ed, -en, -t, or -n).

pathos: The appeal of a piece of writing that is based on emotion.

periodic sentence: A sentence that delays or suspends the completion of its subject-verb clause until the very end (see also **suspensive sentence**).

phrase: A combination of words that functions as a single syntactical unit in a sentence but does not contain a finite verb and therefore cannot stand alone.

predicate: The part of a sentence that consists of what is said about the subject of the sentence.

prepositional phrase: A phrase that begins with a preposition and contains the object of the preposition and any modifiers of the object.

proposition: A statement in which the subject is affirmed or denied by the predicate.

pure subordinate: A sequence of modifiers, each modifying the phrase that immediately precedes it.

relative clause: A clause that begins with a relative pronoun such as *that*, *which*, or *who*.

right-branching sentence: A sentence in which the modifying phrase or phrases are placed to the right of the base clause.

simile: A description of one thing in terms of its similarity to another.

speculative phrase: A modifying phrase in a cumulative sentence that begins with a speculative expression such as *perhaps* or *as if.*

subordinate: In a cumulative sentence, a sequence of modifying phrases in which each phrase modifies the phrase that precedes it, moving the sentence toward more levels of specificity.

suspension: The deferring of the completion of a base clause to the very end of the sentence.

suspensive sentence: A sentence that saves the completion of the base clause till the very end (see also **periodic sentence**).

syntagmatic: Related to the order in which words or phrases are placed in a sentence.

transitive verb: A verb that requires a direct object.

vers libre: Verse that is not written in a regular metrical pattern.

Biographical Notes

Chris Anderson: Professor of English and noted writing teacher at Oregon State University, author of *Free/Style: A Direct Approach to Writing.*

Alexander Bain: Scottish rhetorician and University of Aberdeen professor whose 1866 *English Composition and Rhetoric* has greatly influenced contemporary theories of the paragraph.

Jacques Barzun: Professor of History and longtime dean at Columbia University. Author of dozens of books, including *Simple and Direct: A Rhetoric for Writers* (1975).

Thomas Berger: Celebrated American novelist best known as the author of *Little Big Man* and the four novels in the Reinhart Series: *Crazy in Berlin, Reinhart in Love, Vital Parts*, and *Reinhart's Women*. Other noteworthy novels include *Arthur Rex, Neighbors, The Feud*, and *Meeting Evil*. His 23 novels uniquely span a range of years and novel forms, and offer a mastery of prose style unmatched in contemporary American literature.

Jay David Bolter: Wesley Chair in New Media and a codirector of the Wesley Center for New Media Research and Education at Georgia Institute of Technology, and director of the Writing Program in the School of Literature, Communication, and Culture at Georgia Tech. One of the pioneers of hypertext theory, Bolter is the author of *Writing Space: The Computer, Hypertext and the History of Writing* and coauthor (with Richard Grusin) of *Remediation: Understanding New Media.*

Richard Braddock: Former professor of English at the University of Iowa and a leader in composition research. He coauthored with R. Lloyd-Jones and L. Schoer the influential *Research in Written Composition* (1963). His "The Frequency and Placement of Topic Sentences in Expository Prose," *Research in the Teaching of English* 8 (Winter, 1974) was one of the earliest critiques of Alexander Bain's pronouncements concerning topic sentences in the paragraph.

Noam Chomsky: MIT professor of Linguistics, father of transformational grammar.

Francis Christensen: USC rhetorician and writing teacher who theorized the cumulative sentence. Author of *Notes Toward a New Rhetoric: Six Essays for Teachers.*

Matthew Clark: Teaches ancient Greek culture and literature at York University. He is the author of *A Matter of Style.*

Robert J. Connors: Late Rhetoric and Composition scholar at the University of New Hampshire, author of "The Erasure of the Sentence," *College Composition and Communication* 52:1 (2000).

Don DeLillo: Noted American novelist whose 15 books include *White Noise, Libra, Mao II, Underworld, The Body Artist, Cosmopolis*, and *Falling Man.*

Joan Didion: Celebrated American novelist and essayist, whose works include *Slouching Towards Bethlehem* and *The Year of Magical Thinking.*

William Faulkner: Nobel Prize-winning American novelist.

H. W. Fowler: Author of *A Dictionary of Modern English Usage*. The authoritative book on English usage which has been subsequently revised, first by Sir Ernest Gowers in 1965, and then by R. W. Burchfield in 2004.

William H. Gass: Celebrated and award-winning fiction writer, essayist, and philosopher. Gass is David May Distinguished University Professor Emeritus in the Humanities at Washington University in St. Louis, where for many years he taught philosophy and English. Just a few of his works that explore language, literature, and the glories of the sentence are *Fiction and the Figures of Life* (1971); *On Being Blue: A Philosophical Inquiry* (1976); *The World Within The World* (1978); *Finding a Form* (1996), and *A Temple of Texts* (2006).

Walker Gibson: Former professor of English, University of Massachusetts. Author of several influential books on writing, including *Tough, Sweet, & Stuffy: An Essay on Modern American Prose Styles.*

Richard L. Graves: Professor Emeritus of curriculum and teaching at Auburn University, author of several works devoted to prose style, including "A Primer for Teaching Style," *College Composition and Communication* 25:2 (May, 1974).

M. A. K. Halliday: Coauthor of *Cohesion in English.*

Ruqaiya Hasan: Coauthor of *Cohesion in English.*

S. I. Hayakawa: Former English professor, college president, and influential general semanticist, author of the well-known textbook *Language in Thought and Action* (1949).

Ernest Hemingway: Nobel Prize-winning American novelist.

Lewis Hyde: Richard L. Thomas Professor of Creative Writing at Kenyon College. Author of *The Gift: Imagination and the Erotic Life of Property* (1983), which in a new edition has been retitled *The Gift: Creativity and the Artist in the Modern World.*

James L. Kinneavy: Late English professor and professor of Curriculum and Instruction in the Division of Rhetoric and Composition at the University of Texas at Austin. Kinneavy was highly influential in shaping the field of rhetoric and composition; his *A Theory of Discourse* (1971) is a foundational work of discourse theory.

Martha Kolln: Former English professor at Pennsylvania State University and an authority on composition, grammar, and rhetoric. Author of several books on grammar and writing, including *Rhetorical Grammar: Grammatical Choices, Rhetorical Effects.*

Carl H. Klaus: Professor Emeritus, English Department, University of Iowa, where he was instrumental in founding the MFA Program in Nonfiction Writing. An expert on prose style and on the essay and a noted stylist himself, Klaus is the author of four works of creative nonfiction: *Letters to Kate: Life After Life*; *My Vegetable Love: A Journal of a Growing Season*; *Taking Retirement: A Beginner's Diary*; and *Weathering Winter: A Gardner's Daybook*. He is the editor or coeditor of *Style in English Prose; In Depth: Essayists for Our Time*; and *Courses for Change in Writing*.

George P. Landow: Professor of English and the History of Art at Brown University and one of the pioneering scholars of electronic textuality. His books on hypertext and multimedia writing include the coedited *Hypermedia and Literary Studies* (MIT, 1991), and *The Digital Word* (1993), and he is the author of *Hypertext: The Convergence of Contemporary Critical Theory and Technology* (Hopkins, 1992) and *Hypertext 2.0* (1997). He has also edited *Hyper/Text/Theory* (Hopkins, 1994).

Richard A. Lanham: Professor Emeritus of English at UCLA, where he earned an impressive reputation as a rhetorician and prose style scholar. His books include *Handlist of Rhetorical Terms* (1991) (the standard reference in the field); *Analyzing Prose* (2nd ed., 2003); *Style: An Anti-Textbook*; *Literacy and the Survival of Humanism* (1974); and *The Electronic Word: Democracy, Technology, and the Arts* (1993). He is also the author of *Revising Prose* (1979), and *Revising Business Prose* (1981), both now in their 4th editions).

Ursula K. Le Guin: One of the most acclaimed American writers of science fiction and fantasy, Le Guin is also the author of a writing guidebook, *Steering the Craft: Exercises and Discussions on Story Writing for the Lone Navigator or the Mutinous Crew.*

Glen A. Love: Professor Emeritus of English at the University of Oregon and a pioneering ecocritic. Coeditor with Michael Payne of the influential collection of stylistic theory, *Contemporary Essays on Style: Rhetoric, Linguistics, and Criticism.*

Bronislaw Malinowski: Pioneering Polish anthropologist and ethnographer and Yale professor whose works include the essay that first theorized phatic communication: "The Problem of Meaning in Primitive Languages," in C. K. Ogden's and I. A. Richard's *The Meaning of Meaning: A Study of the Influence of Language Upon Thought and of the Science of Symbolism.*

Josephine Miles: Poet and critic, the first woman to be tenured in the Berkeley English Department. Author of *Style and Proportion: The Language of Prose and Poetry*, a rigorous attempt to theorize period style through quantitative means.

Walter J. Ong: Late professor of English at St. Louis University, Jesuit priest, and noted literary critic and cultural commentator. Of his many publications, I have drawn most heavily from *Orality and Literacy: The Technologizing of the Word.*

William Morrison Patterson: Professor of English at Columbia in the early years of the 20th century. Author of *The Rhythm of Prose: An Experimental Investigation of Individual Difference in the Sense of Rhythm* (1916).

Michael Payne: Coeditor with Glen A. Love of the influential collection of stylistic theory, *Contemporary Essays on Style: Rhetoric, Linguistics, and Criticism.*

Thomas Pynchon: Reclusive American novelist, generally considered one of the leading postmodern writers, author of *Gravity's Rainbow, Vineland, Against the Day*, and numerous other major novels.

Herbert Read: English poet, literary and art critic, author of *English Prose Style.*

George Saintsbury: Professor of Rhetoric and English at the University of Edinburgh in the early 20th century, author of the influential *A History of English Prosody.*

Edgar H. Schuster: Writing teacher and author of *Breaking the Rules: Liberating Writers Through Innovative Grammar Instruction.*

Gertrude Stein: Famed modernist writer, author of more than 600 experimental works in almost every imaginable literary genre.

John Steinbeck: Nobel Prize-winning American novelist and author of the nonfiction *The Log from the Sea of Cortez* and *Travels with Charley*.

Arthur A. Stern: Professor Emeritus, Teacher's College, Columbia University.

William Strunk Jr.: Longtime English professor at Cornell University whose "little book," a writing guide for his students, forms the core of *The Elements of Style*.

Lewis Thomas: Noted educator and physician known for his superb science writing; author of *The Lives of a Cell: Notes of a Biology Watcher* and *Medusa and the Snail: More Notes of a Biology Watcher.*

Virginia Tufte: English Professor Emeritus at USC and author of several books on prose style, including *Artful Sentences: Syntax as Style*, generally recognized as the best study of sentence style.

John R. Trimble: English professor and Advanced Expository Writing pioneer at the University of Texas. His *Writing with Style* is one of the most influential writing texts in the United States.

Winston Weathers: Influential writing teacher, coauthor with Otis Winchester of *The New Strategy of Style, Copy and Compose*, and other texts. In his *An Alternate Style: Options in Composition*, Weathers made the famous case for Grammar B, an innovative and unfettered writing style to complement the traditional and limiting standards of most writing instruction.

E. B. White: Famed essayist and *New Yorker* author, revised and added to a writing handbook created by Professor Will Strunk for his students at Cornell, resulting in *The Elements of Style*, probably the best known writing guidebook in the United States.

Otis Winchester: Influential writing teacher, coauthor with Winston Weathers of *The New Strategy of Style, Copy and Compose*, and other texts.

Tom Wolfe: Novelist and journalist, one of the leading proponents and practitioners of the New Journalism.

Virginia Woolf: Novelist and essayist known as one of the most important literary modernists.

Marguerite Young: American writer, social critic, and writing teacher, author of *Inviting the Muses: Stories, Essays, Reviews.*

William Zinsser: Noted journalist and writing teacher, and author of the influential and widely used *On Writing Well.*

Bibliography

Primary texts:

Almost everything. Seriously. The study of English prose style in general and of sentences in particular profits from nothing so much as from wide reading—of all sorts and kinds, fiction and nonfiction, from all periods and all writers who write in or whose work has been translated into English. Just a few of the writers who have most guided my thinking about prose style, primarily because they pay so much attention to the crafting of their own sentences are, in no particular order: Thomas Berger, Jonathan Lethem, John Updike, Marilynne Robinson, Joan Didion, Nicholson Baker, Virginia Woolf, William Faulkner, Ernest Hemingway, F. Scott Fitzgerald, Gabriel García Márquez, James Joyce, Don DeLillo, Octavia Butler, Carl Klaus, Joyce Carol Oates, Flannery O'Connor, James Alan McPherson, Thomas Pynchon, William Gibson, Karen Joy Fowler, Ursula K. Le Guin, William Gass, James Hynes, Cormac McCarthy, Tom Wolfe, Mark Leyner, Gertrude Stein, Kathy Acker, Margaret Atwood, Toni Morrison, Robert Coover, Susan Sontag. Any list such as this one is always a travesty, and I'm sure I'll regret leaving out other writers whose works have influenced me: Read everything!

Collections of Creative Essays and Stylistic Samples:

D'Agata, John, ed. *The Next American Essay*. Saint Paul, MN: Graywolf Press, 2003. Not your father's essays!

Editors of *Esquire* (compiled by). *Mom, The Flag, & Apple Pie: Great American Writers on Great American Things*. New York: Doubleday, 1976.

Klaus, Carl H., ed. *Style in English Prose*. New York: Macmillan, 1968. I drew many of my examples from this collection, and Klaus's introductory essay, "Reflections on Prose Style," is indispensable for any serious student of style.

Klaus, Carl H., Chris Anderson, Rebecca Faery. *In Depth: Essayists For Our Time*. San Diego: Harcourt Brace Jovanovich, 1990.

Levin, David, and Howard E. Hugo, eds. *Varieties of English and American Prose*. Englewood Cliffs, NJ: Prentice-Hall, 1962.

Miles, Josephine, ed. *Classic Essays in English*. 2nd ed. Boston: Little, Brown & Co., 1965.

Milic, Louis T. *Stylists on Style: A Handbook with Selections for Analysis*. New York: Scribner's, 1969. A very useful collection of examples of period/author styles and of writers who comment on style.

Smart, William. *Eight Modern Essayists*. 3rd ed. New York: St. Martin's Press, 1980.

Writing Guidebooks:

These range from the very practical to the very atmospheric. Few, if any, pay much attention to the sentence, but they do offer writing strategies that may be of help with larger writing projects. And, of course, they are themselves well-written!

Anderson, Chris. *Free/Style: A Direct Approach to Writing*. Boston: Houghton Mifflin, 1992. A fine guide from a teacher who admires the cumulative sentence.

Goldberg, Natalie. *Writing Down the Bones: Freeing the Writer Within*. Boston: Shambhala, 2005. Zen and the art of writing.

Hale, Constance. *Sin and Syntax: How to Craft Wickedly Effective Prose*. New York: Broadway Books, 1999. The first serious style guide for writing in the late age of print? Hale, a former editor at *Wired*, writes for those whose writing may appear online.

Hodges, John C., and Mary E. Whitten, eds. *Harbrace College Handbook.* 7th ed. New York: Harcourt Brace Jovanovich, 1972. This happens to be the edition I used when I first started teaching; subsequent editions are probably preferable.

Johnston, Bret Anthony, ed. *Naming the World: and Other Exercises for the Creative Writer.* New York: Random House, 2007. Lots of short exercises and bits of advice from a host of savvy creative writing teachers.

King, Stephen. *On Writing: A Memoir of the Craft.* New York: Pocket Books, 2000. It works for him!

Le Guin, Ursula K. *Steering the Craft: Exercises and Discussions on Story Writing for the Lone Navigator or the Mutinous Crew.* Portland, Oregon: Eighth Mountain Press, 1998. A beautiful little book from a wonderful writer!

Scholes, Robert, and Carl H. Klaus. *Elements of Writing.* New York: Oxford UP, 1972. A fascinating step-by-step exploration of writing that is more contemplation than a guidebook.

Schuster, Edgar H. *Breaking the Rules: Liberating Writers Through Innovative Grammar Instruction.* Portsmouth, NH: Heinemann, 2003. More fun than a barrel of monkeys—and about how many books on writing can that be said!

Strunk Jr., William, and E. B. White. *The Elements of Style.* 4th ed., with a foreword by Roger Angell. New York: Longman, 2000. Conservative, a bit limiting, and still indispensable.

Thiel, Diane. *Writing Your Rhythm: Using Nature, Culture, Form and Myth.* Ashland, Oregon: Story Line Press, 2001.

Trimble, John R. *Writing With Style: Conversations on the Art of Writing.* Englewood Cliffs, NJ: Prentice Hall, 1975. A personal favorite—the book I gave my children when they got serious about their writing.

Weathers, Winston. *An Alternate Style: Options in Composition.* Rochelle Park, NJ: Hayden Book Company, 1980.

Weathers, Winston, and Otis Winchester. *The Strategy of Style.* New York: McGraw Hill, 1967.

Williams, Joseph M. *Style: Ten Lessons in Clarity & Grace.* Glenview, IL: Scott, Foresman & Co., 1981.

Zinsser, William. *On Writing Well: An Informal Guide to Writing Nonfiction.* New York: Harper & Row, 1976. Solid, no frills, good advice.

Essay Collections on Style and Stylistic Theory:

Bennett, James R. *Prose Style: A Historical Approach Through Studies.* San Francisco: Chandler Publishing, 1971. A wide-ranging historical survey containing both examples of and studies of distinctive stylists and distinctive patterns in prose style.

Chatman, Seymour, ed. *Literary Style: A Symposium.* Oxford: Oxford UP, 1971.

Graves, Richard L. *Rhetoric and Composition: A Sourcebook for Teachers and Writers.* Upper Montclair, NJ: Boynton/Cook, 1984.

Love, Glen A., and Michael Payne. *Contemporary Essays on Style: Rhetoric, Linguistics, and Criticism.* Glenview, IL: Scott, Foresman, 1969. The most useful introduction to stylistic considerations and stylistic theory. I drew heavily from essays in this collection by Christensen, Klaus, Ohmann, Miles, Gibson, Milic, et al. An indispensable anthology for the serious student of prose style.

National Council of Teachers of English. *The Sentence and the Paragraph: Articles on Rhetorical Analysis from College Composition and Communication and College English.* Champaign, IL: NCTE, 1966.

Sebeok, Thomas A., ed. *Style in Language.* Cambridge, MA: MIT University Press, 1960.

Tate, Gary, ed. *Teaching Composition: 10 Bibliographical Essays.* Forth Worth, TX: Texas Christian Universe Press, 1976.

Wermuth, Paul C., ed. *Modern Essays on Writing and Style.* New York: Holt, Rinehart and Winston, 1964.

Wolfe, Tom. *The New Journalism.* New York: Harper & Row, 1973. Wolfe's introduction to this influential collection of pieces from writers who wrote "the New Journalism" into being details some of the major features of this writing. The New Journalism developed a number of features that seem similar to those Winston Weathers suggested might form an alternative Grammar B for writers.

Creative and Critical Work by Individual Authors:

Aristotle. *On Poetry and Style.* Translated, with an introduction by G. M. A. Grube. Indianapolis: Bobbs Merrill, 1958.

Bain, Alexander. *English Composition and Rhetoric (1871). A Facsimile Reproduction with an Introduction by Charlotte Downey.* Delmar, New York: Scholar's Facsimiles & Reprints, 1996. Most of what we know—or think we know—about the paragraph dates from this smart, but largely deductive and very prescriptive textbook by Alexander Bain. He got a lot right, but he also got a lot wrong.

Barzun, Jacques. *Simple & Direct: A Rhetoric for Writers.* Revised Edition. Chicago: University of Chicago Press, 1994.

Bernstein, Theodore M. *The Careful Writer: A Modern Guide to English Usage.* New York: The Free Press, 1998.

————. *Miss Thistlebottom's Hobgoblins: The Careful Writer's Guide to the Taboos, Bugbears and Outmoded Rules of English Usage.* With an Introduction by Mark Singer. New York: Noonday Press, 1991.

Bolter, Jay David. *Writing Space: The Computer, Hypertext and the History of Writing.* Hillsdale, NJ: Lawrence Erlbaum Associates, 1991. A pioneering consideration of the implications of computer technology for writing. When it is finally codified, the rhetoric of electronic textuality will honor this book as a foundational study.

Braddock, Richard. "The Frequency and Placement of Topic Sentences in Expository Prose," *Research in the Teaching of English* 8 (Winter, 1974). Braddock was the researcher who demonstrated that Bain's pronouncements concerning topic sentences in the paragraph did not hold up under rigorous testing.

Burchfield, R. W. *Fowler's Modern English Usage.* Revised 3rd ed. of Fowler's Modern English Usage. Oxford: Oxford University Press, 2004.

Chomsky, Noam. *Cartesian Linguistics: A Chapter in the History of Rationalist Thought.* New York: Harper & Row, 1966.

Christensen, Francis. *Notes Toward a New Rhetoric: 6 Essays for Teachers.* New York: Harper & Row, 1967. Contains Christensen's brilliant "A Generative Rhetoric of the Sentence," and his less persuasive "A Generative Rhetoric of the Paragraph."

Clark, Albert C. *Prose Rhythm in English: A Lecture Delivered on June 6, 1913.* Oxford: Clarendon Press, 1913.

Clark, Matthew. *A Matter of Style.* Oxford: Oxford University Press, 2002. A contemporary look at style that still retains much of the feel of older approaches. An interesting book.

Coles Jr., William E. *Teaching Composing.* Rochelle Park, New Jersey: Hayden Book Company, 1974.

Connors, Robert J. "The Erasure of the Sentence," *College Composition and Communication*, 52:1 (2000): 96–128. A masterfully researched, reasoned, and written overview of the reasons why sentence-based pedagogies lost purchase both in writing scholarship and in the writing classroom even though empirical research seemed to support claims that they were quite effective in improving writing.

D'Agata, John. *Halls of Fame.* Saint Paul, MN: Graywolf Press, 2001. D'Agata represents a wave of contemporary essayists who experiment with the form of the essay. He is particularly known for his work with the lyric essay, which the editors of the *Seneca Review*, who devoted its 30th anniversary issue to this newly named form, described as an essay that "partakes of the poem in its density and shapeliness, its distillation of ideas and musicality of language. It partakes of the essay in its weight, in its overt desire to engage with facts, melding its allegiance to the actual with its passion for imaginative forms." D'Agata teaches in the Nonfiction Writing Program at the University of Iowa.

Didion, Joan. *Slouching Towards Bethlehem.* New York: Delta, 1968. One of the most impressive examples of the New Journalism, this collection of essays represents Didion's mastery of prose rhythms and the haunting insight of her vision. It has been taught in writing classes steadily since its publication.

———. *The Year of Magical Thinking.* New York: Knopf, 2006.

Fowler, H. W. *A Dictionary of Modern English Usage.* Oxford: Clarendon Press, 1926. There are many books on English usage, but Fowler's remains the giant in the field. It is also a delight to read.

———. *Fowler's Modern English Usage.* 2nd ed. Revised and edited by Sir Ernest Gowers. Oxford: Oxford UP, 1965. Updates Fowler in important ways.

Gass, William H. *Fiction and the Figures of Life*. Boston: Nonpareil Books, 1971. We have no contemporary writer who matches Gass's unique combination of philosophical training and prose mastery. No other contemporary writer puts as much thought into or squeezes as much excitement out of language.

―――. *Finding a Form*. New York: Knopf, 1997.

―――. *The Habitations of the Word*. New York: Simon & Schuster, 1985.

―――. *On Being Blue*: *A Philosophical Inquiry*. Boston: David R. Godine, 1976.

―――. *A Temple of Texts*. New York: Knopf, 2006.

―――. *The World Within the Word*. New York: Basic Books, 1979.

Gibson, Walker. *Tough, Sweet, & Stuffy: An Essay on Modern American Prose Styles*. Bloomington: Indiana University Press, 1975.

Gordon, Karen Elizabeth. *The Deluxe Transitive Vampire: The Ultimate Handbook of Grammar for the Innocent, the Eager, and the Doomed*. New York: Pantheon, 1993.

―――. *The New Well-Tempered Sentence: A Punctuation Handbook for the Innocent, the Eager, and the Doomed*. Revised and Expanded. Boston: Houghton Mifflin, 1993.

Graves, Richard. "A Primer for Teaching Style," *College Composition and Communication*. 25:2 (May, 1974), 186–190. With his observation that style "is a way of finding and expressing what is true" and is meant not to impress, but to express, Graves establishes himself as one of our most wise commentators on prose style.

Hale Jr., Edward Everett. *Constructive Rhetoric*. New York: Holt, 1896.

Halliday, M. A. K., and Ruqaiya Hasan. *Cohesion in English*. London: Longman, 1976.

Hayakawa, S. I. *Language in Thought and Action*. 3rd ed. New York: Harcourt Brace Jovanovich, 1972.

Hayles, N. Katherine. *Writing Machines*. Cambridge, MA: MIT Press, 2002. One of our leading authorities on electronic textuality, Hayles uses this uniquely designed and printed book to argue for the importance of the materiality of writing.

Hyde, Lewis. *The Gift: Creativity and the Artist in the Modern World*. New York: Vintage, 1983. A brilliant and moving study of gifting cultures, Hyde's book suggests to me the need for a new perspective on what has long been called the gift of style.

Johnson, Samuel. *Lives of the English Poets*. G. B. Hill, ed. Georg Olms. (Reprografischer Nachdruck der Ausg.) Oxford: Clarendon Press, 1905. A 1968 facsimile edition.

Kinneavy, James. *A Theory of Discourse: The Aims of Discourse*. New York: W. W. Norton, 1971.

Klaus, Carl. *Letters to Kate: Life After Life*. Iowa City: University of Iowa Press, 2006.

———. *My Vegetable Love: A Journal of a Growing Season*. Iowa City: University of Iowa Press, 1996.

———. *Taking Retirement: A Beginner's Diary*. Boston: Beacon Press, 1999.

———. *Weathering Winter: A Gardner's Daybook*. Iowa City, IA: University of Iowa Press, 1997.

Kolln, Martha. *Rhetorical Grammar: Grammatical Choices, Rhetorical Effects*. 3rd ed. Boston: Allyn and Bacon, 1999.

Landow, George P. *Hypertext 2.0: The Convergence of Contemporary Critical Theory and Technology.* Baltimore: The Johns Hopkins University Press, 1997.

———, ed. *Hyper/Text/Theory.* Baltimore: Johns Hopkins University Press, 1994.

Lanham, Richard A. *Analyzing Prose.* 2nd ed. London: Continuum, 2003. The best-sustained consideration of this topic we have.

———. *The Electronic Word: Democracy, Technology, and the Arts.* Chicago: University of Chicago Press, 1993. A classical rhetorician considers and welcomes the new world of electronic textuality.

———. *A Handlist of Classical Rhetorical Terms.* 2nd ed. Berkeley: University of California Press, 1991.

———. *Revising Prose.* New York: Scribner's, 1979.

———. *Style: An Anti-Textbook.* New Haven: Yale University Press, 1974. A must read for anyone interested in prose style, in the teaching of writing, or just in the writing in the world around us. This is Lanham's argument that the stress on clarity in American writing instruction has largely worked to banish pleasure from writing.

Malinowski, Bronislaw. "The Problem of Meaning in Primitive Languages," in C. K. Ogden's and I. A. Richard's *The Meaning of Meaning: A Study of Language Upon Thought and of The Science of Symbolism.* Oxford: Oxford University Press, 1923. Malinowski was the first to study the social rituals of phatic utterances.

Miles, Josephine. *Style and Proportion: The Language of Prose and Poetry.* Boston: Little, Brown & Co., 1967. Possibly the most systematic attempt to establish the metric for describing the prose style of a historical period.

Nabokov, Vladimir. *Strong Opinions.* New York: McGraw-Hill, 1973.

O'Conner, Patricia T. *Woe Is I: The Grammarphobe's Guide to Better English.* New York: Riverhead Books, 2003. New and expanded.

Ong, Walter J. *Orality and Literacy: The Technologizing of the Word.* London: Routledge, 1982.

Partridge, Eric. *Usage and Abusage: A Guide to Good English.* New ed., edited by Janet Whitcut. New York: W. W. Norton, 1973.

Patterson, William Morrison. *The Rhythm of Prose: An Experimental Investigation of Individual Difference in the Sense of Rhythm.* New York: Columbia University Press, 1916.

Read, Herbert. *English Prose Style.* 1952 ed. Boston: Beacon Press, 1966.

Saintsbury, George. *History of English Prose Rhythm.* Bloomington: Indiana University Press, 1965. Originally published between 1906 and 1910 with major republished editions in 1923 and 1961.

Steinbeck, John. *The Log from the Sea of Cortez: The Narrative Portion of the Book Sea of Cortez.* (1941), by John Steinbeck and E. F. Ricketts. Introduction by Richard Astro. New York: Penguin, 1995. *The Log* presents both an epistemology and a phenomenology of observation; it is one of Steinbeck's most interesting works.

Stern, Arthur A. "When Is a Paragraph?" *College Composition and Communication,* 27:3 (Oct 1976): 253–257.

Thomas, Lewis. *The Medusa and the Snail: More Notes of a Biology Watcher.* Toronto: Bantam Books, 1979. Apart from containing more of the superb writing about science we expect from the author of *The Lives of the Cell,* this book contains a chapter on punctuation.

Truss, Lynne. *Eats, Shoots & Leaves: The Zero Tolerance Approach to Punctuation.* New York: Gotham Books, 2003.

Tufte, Virginia. *Artful Sentences: Syntax as Style*. Cheshire, Connecticut: Graphics Press, 2006.

————, with the assistance of Garrett Stewart. *Grammar As Style*. New York: Holt, Rinehart, & Winston, 1971.

Tufte, Virginia, and Garrett Stewart. *Grammar As Style: Exercises in Creativity*. New York: Holt, Rinehart, & Winston, 1971.

Walsh, Bill. *The Elephants of Style: A Trunkload of Tips on the Big Issues and Gray Areas of Contemporary American English*. New York: McGraw Hill, 2004.

————. *Lapsing into a Comma: A Curmudgeon's Guide to the Many Things That Can Go Wrong in Print—and How to Avoid Them*. Chicago: Contemporary Books, 2000.

Weathers, Winston. "Grammars of Style: New Options in Composition," *Freshman English News*. 4:3 (Winter 1976): 1–4, 12–18. Republished in Weathers, *An Alternate Style*, and in slightly abridged form in Graves, *Rhetoric and Composition: A Sourcebook for Teachers and Writers*.

————. "The Rhetoric of the Series," *College Composition and Communication*, 17:5 (December 1966): 217–222. Republished in Love and Payne, *Contemporary Essays on Style*.

White, E. B. *Essays of E. B. White*. New York: Harper & Row, 1977.

Witte, Stephen P., and Lester Faigley. "Coherence, Cohesion, and Writing Quality," *College Composition and Communication*, 32:2 (May 1981): 189–204. Offers a succinct overview of Halliday's and Hasan's landmark (and long) *Cohesion in English*.

Young, Marguerite. *Inviting the Muses: Stories, Essays, Reviews*. Normal, IL: Dalkey Archive Press, 1994.

Bibliography

Notes

Notes

Notes

Notes

Notes

Notes